ACCA

STUDY TEXT

Paper 3.1

Audit and Assurance Services

BPP's NEW STUDY TEXTS FOR ACCA's NEW SYLLABUS

- Targeted to the **syllabus** and **study guide**
- Quizzes and questions to check your understanding
- Clear layout and style designed to save you time
- Plenty of exam-style questions
- Chapter Roundups and summaries to help revision
- Mind Maps to integrate the key points

BPP Publishing
June 2001

First edition June 2001

ISBN 0 7517 0740 6

British Library Cataloguing-in-Publication Data
A catalogue record for this book
is available from the British Library

Published by

BPP Publishing Ltd
Aldine House, Aldine Place
London W12 8AW

www.bpp.com

Printed in Great Britain by W M Print
45 - 47 Frederick Street
Walsall, West Midlands WS2 9NE

We are grateful to the Association of Chartered Certified Accountants for permission to reproduce past examination questions and questions from the pilot paper. The answers have been prepared by BPP Publishing Limited.

BPP
PUBLISHING

THE BPP STUDY TEXT

Aims of this Study Text

To provide you with the knowledge and understanding, skills and application techniques that you need if you are to be successful in your exams

This Study Text has been written around the **Audit and Assurance Services** syllabus.

- It is **comprehensive**. It covers the syllabus content. No more, no less.
- It is written at the **right level**. Each chapter is written with the ACCA's **study guide** in mind.
- It is targeted to the **exam**. We have taken account of the **pilot paper**, questions put to the examiners at the recent ACCA conference and the assessment methodology.

To allow you to study in the way that best suits your learning style and the time you have available, by following your personal Study Plan (see page (ix))

You may be studying at home on your own until the date of the exam, or you may be attending a full-time course. You may like to (and have time to) read every word, or you may prefer to (or only have time to) skim-read and devote the remainder of your time to question practice. Wherever you fall in the spectrum, you will find the BPP Study Text meets your needs in designing and following your personal Study Plan.

To tie in with the other components of the BPP Effective Study Package to ensure you have the best possible chance of passing the exam (see page (vi))

Recommended period of use	Elements of the BPP Effective Study Package
Three to twelve months before the exam	**Study Text** Use the Study Text to acquire knowledge, understanding, skills and the ability to use application techniques.
One to six months before the exam	**Practice & Revision Kit** Attempt the tutorial questions which are provided for each topic area in the Kit. Then try the numerous examination questions, for which there are realistic suggested solutions prepared by BPP's own authors.
From three months before the exam until the last minute	**Passcards** Work through these short, memorable notes which are focused on what is most likely to come up in the exam you will be sitting.
One to six months before the exam	**Success Tapes** These cover the vital elements of your syllabus in less than 90 minutes per subject with these audio cassettes. Each tape also contains exam hints to help you fine tune your strategy.
Three to twelve months before the exam	**Breakthrough Videos** Use a Breakthrough Video to supplement your Study Text. They give you clear tuition on key exam subjects and allow you the luxury of being able to pause or repeat sections until you have fully grasped the topic.

HELP YOURSELF STUDY FOR YOUR ACCA EXAMS

Exams for professional bodies such as ACCA are very different from those you have taken at college or university. You will be under **greater time pressure before** the exam - as you may be combining your study with work as well as in the exam room. There are many different ways of learning and so the BPP Study Text offers you a number of different tools to help you through. Here are some hints and tips: they are not plucked out of the air, but **based on research and experience**. (You don't need to know that long-term memory is in the same part of the brain as emotions and feelings - but it's a fact anyway.)

The right approach

1 **The right attitude**

Believe in yourself	Yes, there is a lot to learn. Yes, it is a challenge. But thousands have succeeded before and you can too.
Remember why you're doing it	Studying might seem a grind at times, but you are doing it for a reason: to advance your career.

2 **The right focus**

Read through the Syllabus and Study guide	These tell you what you are expected to know and are supplemented by Exam Focus Points in the text.
Study the Exam Paper section	The pilot paper is likely to be a reasonable guide of what you should expect in the exam.

3 **The right method**

The big picture	You need to grasp the detail - but keeping in mind how everything fits into the big picture will help you understand better. • The **Introduction** of each chapter puts the material in context. • The **Syllabus content**, **Study guide** and **Exam focus points** show you what you need to **grasp.** • **Mind Maps** show the links and key issues in key topics.
In your own words	To absorb the information (and to practise your written communication skills), it helps **put it into your own words.** • **Take notes.** • Answer the **questions** in each chapter. As well as helping you absorb the information you will practise your written communication skills, which become increasingly important as you progress through your ACCA exams. • Draw **mind maps**. We have some examples. • Try 'teaching' to a colleague or friend.

Give yourself cues to jog your memory	The BPP Study Text uses **bold** to **highlight key points** and **icons** to identify key features, such as **Exam focus points** and **Key terms.** • Try **colour coding** with a highlighter pen. • Write **key points** on cards.

4 **The right review**

Review, review, review	It is a **fact** that regularly reviewing a topic in summary form can **fix it in your memory**. Because **review** is so important, the BPP Study Text helps you to do so in many ways. • **Chapter roundups** summarise the key points in each chapter. Use them to recap each study session. • The **Quick quiz** is another review technique to ensure that you have grasped the essentials. • Use the **Key term** as a quiz. • Go through the **Examples** in each chapter a second or third time.

Suggested study sequence

Tackle the chapters in the order you find them in the Study Text. Taking into account your individual learning style, you could follow this sequence.

Key study steps	Activity
Step 1 **Topic list**	Each numbered topic is a numbered section in the chapter.
Step 2 **Introduction**	This gives you the **big picture** in terms of the **context** of the chapter. The content is referenced to the **Study Guide**, and **Exam Guidance** shows how the topic is likely to be examined. In other words, it sets your **objectives for study**.
Step 3 **Knowledge brought forward boxes**	In these we highlight information and techniques that it is assumed you have 'brought forward' with you from your earlier studies. If there are topics which have changed recently due to legislation for example, these topics are explained in more detail.
Step 4 **Explanations**	Proceed methodically through the chapter, reading each section thoroughly and making sure you understand.
Step 5 **Key terms and Exam focus points**	• **Key terms** can often earn you *easy marks* if you state them clearly and correctly in an appropriate exam answer (and they are indexed at the back of the text). • **Exam focus points** give you a good idea of how we think the examiner intends to examine certain topics.
Step 6 **Note taking**	Take brief notes if you wish, avoiding the temptation to copy out too much.
Step 7 **Examples**	Follow each through to its solution very carefully.
Step 8 **Case examples**	Study each one, and try to add flesh to them from your own experience - they are designed to show how the topics you are studying come alive (and often come unstuck) in the real world.
Step 9 **Questions**	Make a very good attempt at each one.
Step 10 **Answers**	Check yours against ours, and make sure you understand any discrepancies.
Step 11 **Chapter roundup**	Work through it very carefully, to make sure you have grasped the major points it is highlighting.
Step 12 **Quick quiz**	When you are happy that you have covered the chapter, use the **Quick quiz** to check how much you have remembered of the topics covered.

Key study steps	Activity
Step 13 **Question(s) in the Question bank**	Either at this point, or later when you are thinking about revising, make a full attempt at the **Question(s)** suggested at the very end of the chapter. You can find these at the end of the Study Text, along with the **Answers** so you can see how you did. We highlight those that are introductory, and those which are of the standard you would expect to find in an exam.

Developing your personal Study Plan

Preparing a Study Plan (and sticking closely to it) is one of the key elements in learning success.

Step 1. How do you learn?

First you need to be aware of your style of learning. There are four typical learning styles. Consider yourself in the light of the following descriptions and work out which you fit most closely. You can then plan to follow the key study steps in the sequence suggested.

Learning styles	Characteristics	Sequence of key study steps in the BPP Study Text
Theorist	Seeks to understand principles before applying them in practice	1, 2, 3, 4, 7, 8, 5, 9/10, 11, 12, 13 (6 continuous)
Reflector	Seeks to observe phenomena, thinks about them and then chooses to act	
Activist	Prefers to deal with practical, active problems; does not have much patience with theory	1, 2, 9/10 (read through), 7, 8, 5, 11, 3, 4, 9/10 (full attempt), 12, 13 (6 continuous)
Pragmatist	Prefers to study only if a direct link to practical problems can be seen; not interested in theory for its own sake	9/10 (read through), 2, 5, 7, 8, 11, 1, 3, 4, 9/10 (full attempt), 12, 13 (6 continuous)

Step 2. How much time do you have?

Work out the time you have available per week, given the following.

- The standard you have set yourself
- The time you need to set aside later for work on the Practice & Revision Kit and Passcards
- The other exam(s) you are sitting
- Very importantly, practical matters such as work, travel, exercise, sleep and social life

		Hours
Note your time available in box A.	A	

Step 3. Allocate your time

• Take the time you have available per week for this Study Text shown in box A, multiply it by the number of weeks available and insert the result in box B.	B	
• Divide the figure in Box B by the number of chapters in this text and insert the result in box C.	C	

Step 4. Implement

Set about studying each chapter in the time shown in box C, following the key study steps in the order suggested by your particular learning style.

This is your personal **Study Plan**.

Short of time: *Skim study technique*?

You may find you simply do not have the time available to follow all the key study steps for each chapter, however you adapt them for your particular learning style. If this is the case, follow the **skim study** technique below (the icons in the Study Text will help you to do this).

- Study the chapters in the order you find them in the Study Text.
- For each chapter, follow the key study steps 1-3, and then skim-read through step 4. Jump to step 11, and then go back to step 5. Follow through steps 7 and 8, and prepare outline answers to questions (steps 9/10). Try the Quick quiz (step 12), following up any items you can't answer, then do a plan for the Question (step 13), comparing it against our answers. You should probably still follow step 6 (note-taking), although you may decide simply to rely on the BPP Passcards for this.

Moving on...

However you study, when you are ready to embark on the practice and revision phase of the BPP Effective Study Package, you should still refer back to this Study Text, both as a source of **reference** (you should find the list of key terms and the index particularly helpful for this) and as a **refresher** (the Chapter roundups and Quick quizzes help you here).

And remember to keep careful hold of this Study Text - you will find it invaluable in your work.

SYLLABUS

Aim

To ensure that candidates can exercise judgement and apply techniques in the analysis of matters relating to the provision of audit and assurance services, and can evaluate and comment on current practices and developments.

Objectives

On completion of this paper candidates should be able to:

- Demonstrate their ability to work within a professional and ethical framework
- Understand current issues and developments relating to auditing and the provision of audit-related and assurance services
- Explain and evaluate the auditor's position in relation to the acceptance and retention of professional appointments
- Evaluate and recommend quality control policies and procedures
- Identify and describe the work required to meet the objectives of audit and non-audit assignments
- Apply and evaluate the requirements of relevant Statements of Auditing Standards
- Evaluate findings and results of work performed and draft suitable reports on assignments
- Demonstrate the skills expected in Part 3

Position of the paper in the overall syllabus

Candidates need a thorough understanding of Paper 2.6 *Audit and Internal Review* and knowledge of Paper 2.5 *Financial Reporting* concerning the preparation and presentation of financial statements. Paper 3.1 may draw on aspects of information technology covered in Paper 2.1 *Information Systems* by considering its impact on assignments.

Paper 3.1 develops the knowledge gained in Paper 2.5 *Financial Reporting* by introducing the audit implications of accounting treatments.

Paper 3.1 develops the knowledge gained in Paper 2.6 *Audit and Internal* Review by:

- Extending the basic awareness of professional codes and fundamental principles to a detailed understanding of rules of professional conduct
- Introducing practice management
- Extending the application of procedures involved in planning, conducting and reporting on audit assignments to group audits, audit-related services and non-audit assignments
- Critically evaluating procedures and reports
- Introducing current issues and developments

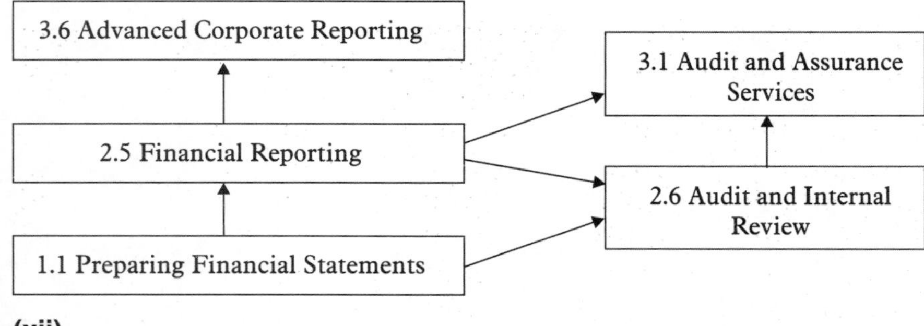

SYLLABUS

1 Professional and ethical considerations

(a) Rules of professional conduct

- (i) Integrity, objectivity and independence
- (ii) Professional duty of confidence
- (iii) Changes in professional appointments
- (iv) Books, documents and papers
- (v) Corporate financial advice
- (vi) Conflicts of interest

(b) Professional responsibility and liability

- (i) Fraud and error
- (ii) Professional liability (including negligence)
- (iii) Misconduct
- (iv) Expectation gap
- (v) Professional indemnity insurance
- (vi) Insider dealing

(c) Regulatory environment

- (i) Corporate governance
- (ii) Code of Best Practice
- (iii) Audit committees
- (iv) Internal financial control effectiveness
- (v) Laws and regulations in an audit of financial statements

2 Practice management

- (a) Quality control practices and procedures
- (b) Advertising, publicity and obtaining professional work
- (c) Fees
- (d) Tendering
- (e) Terms of engagement

3 Audit process

(a) Audit strategy including:

- (i) Risk-based auditing
- (ii) System audits
- (iii) Balance sheet approach
- (iv) Revenue, expenditure and other cycles
- (v) Directional testing
- (vi) Analytical procedures

(b) Planning including:

- (i) Materiality
- (ii) Risk assessments

(c) Evidence including:

- (i) Documentation
- (ii) Related parties
- (iii) Management representations
- (iv) Using work of others

(d) Evaluation and review including:

- (i) Opening balances and comparatives
- (ii) Other information
- (iii) Subsequent events
- (iv) Going concern

4 Assignments

(a) Audit of financial statements

(b) Group audits

(c) Audit-related services including:

- (i) Reviews
- (ii) Agreed-upon procedures
- (iii) Compilations

(d) Assurance services including:

- (i) Risk assessment
- (ii) Performance measurement
- (iii) System reliability
- (iv) Electronic commerce

(e) Prospective financial information

(f) Internal audit

(g) Outsourced finance and accounting functions

(h) Social and environmental audits

5 Reporting

(a) Auditors' reports
(b) Conclusions and reporting for agreed-upon procedures and assurance services
(c) Reports to management

6 Current issues and developments

(a) Professional ethics
(b) Corporate governance
(c) Fraud and litigation
(d) Environmental issues
(e) Information technology
(f) Multinational accountancy firms
(g) SMEs and audit exemption

Excluded topics

The following topics are specifically excluded from the syllabus:

- Stock Exchange Listing Requirements
- Financial Reporting Exposure Drafts
- Effects on a company of insolvency law and of employment and social security law (eg wrongful trading and national insurance contributions)

Key areas of the syllabus

Key topic areas are as follows:

- Rules of professional conduct
- Quality control practices and procedures
- Audit strategy
- Assignments
- Auditors' reports
- Current issues and developments

Paper 3.1(U)

Audit and Assurance Services
(United Kingdom)

Study Guide

1 RULES OF PROFESSIONAL CONDUCT I

Candidates should be able to interpret, apply and appraise specific statements of professional ethics which govern the auditors' conduct and are included in ACCA's *Rules of Professional Conduct* and IFAC's *Code of Ethics for Professional Accountants*.

Syllabus reference 1a i-ii

i Integrity, Objectivity and Independence

- Revise the purpose of a professional ethical code from Paper 2.6 (U)
- Compare and contrast the Fundamental Principles of ACCA's *Rules of Professional Conduct* and with those of IFAC's *Code of Ethics* for Professional Accountants'
- Outline the contents of ACCA's and IFAC's code of ethics
- Identify and explain common threats to independence and explain how risks may be minimised or resolved
- Discuss and evaluate the effectiveness of available safeguards
- Outline the practical implications for an audit practice in relation to quality control procedures
- Discuss the benefits of providing other services (including internal audit) to audit clients and whether the drawbacks (eg objectivity impairment) can be overcome
- Define 'specialist valuations' and discuss how the objectivity of the audit may be threatened
- explain how and why an auditor should respond to a request to provide a second opinion

ii Professional duty of confidence

- Explain the importance of the role of confidentiality to the auditor-client relationship
- Distinguish between disclosure and use of information
- Identify circumstances in which disclosure is permitted or required
- Discuss the factors which may justify disclosure in the 'public interest'
- Describe how a client's information should be protected when the auditor also acts for a competitor company

2 RULES OF PROFESSIONAL CONDUCT II

Syllabus references 1a iii-iv

iii Changes in professional appointments

- Discuss the reasons why entities change their auditors
- Explain the matters to be considered and the procedures which an audit firm/professional accountant should carry out before accepting new clients and new engagements
- Describe the procedures for agreeing the terms of an agreement
- Outline the procedures for the transfer of books, papers and information following a new appointment

iv Books, documents and papers

- Explain the general principals governing the ownership of, and rights of access to, documents and papers
- Explain the legal right of lien and describe the circumstances in which it may be exercised
- Discuss the extent to which clients and third parties may have access to documents and papers

v & vi

Corporate Financial Advice and Conflicts of interest

- Outline the role of auditors in advising clients involved in take-over bids and share issues and explain how conflicts can arise
- Distinguish conflicts between members' and clients' interests from those between the interests of different clients
- Describe how conflicts may be avoided or managed with safeguards

3 PROFESSIONAL RESPONSIBILTY AND LIABILITY

Syllabus reference 1b, 6c

i Fraud and error

- Define and distinguish between the terms 'error', irregularity', 'fraud' and 'misstatement'
- Compare and contrast the respective responsibilities of management and auditors for fraud and error
- Describe the matters to be considered and procedures to be carried out to investigate actual and/or potential misstatements
- Explain how, why, when and to whom fraud and error should be reported and the circumstances in which an auditor should withdraw from an engagement
- Discuss the current and possible future role of auditors in preventing, detecting and reporting error and fraud

ii Professional liability

- Identify the circumstances in which auditors may have legal liability
- Describe the factors to determine whether or not an auditor is negligent in given situations
- Explain the other criteria for legal liability to be recognised (including 'due professional care' and 'proximity')
- Distinguish between liability to client and liability to third parties
- Comment on precedents of case law
- Identify and evaluate the practicability and effectiveness of ways in which liability may be restricted
- Discuss how the audit and other opinions may be affected by limiting audit liability
- Discuss the advantages and disadvantages of audit liability claims being settled out of court

iii Misconduct

- Explain and illustrate what is meant by professional misconduct
- Outline the penalties and sanctions which may be imposed by disciplinary bodies

iv Expectation gap

- Identify and discuss the factors which contribute to the expectation gap (eg responsibility for fraud and error, litigation)
- Suggest ways in which the gap might be bridged

v Professional indemnity insurance

- Explain the terms professional indemnity insurance (PII) and fidelity guarantee insurance (FGI)
- Discuss arguments for and against mandatory cover

vi Insider dealing

- Explain the term 'insider dealing' and why it is damaging
- Relate the Fundamental Principles to insider dealing
- Suggest measures to reduce the exposure of partners and staff to the risks arising

4 REGULATORY ENVIRONMENT

Syllabus reference 1c, 6b

Revision of Regulatory Framework from Paper 2.6 (U)

i Corporate governance

- Explain the objective, relevance and importance of corporate governance
- Discuss the relative merits and disadvantages of voluntary codes and legislation
- Discuss current issues in corporate governance

ii Code of Best Practice

- Outline the provisions of the Code of Best Practice (based on the Cadbury Report) that are most relevant to auditors
- Outline the requirements of the Combined Code of the Committee on Corporate Governance) relating to directors' responsibilities (eg for risk management and internal control) and the reporting responsibilities of auditors
- Outline the central corporate governance statement

iii Audit committees

- Explain the structure and roles of audit committees and discuss their benefits and drawbacks
- Discuss the relative merits and disadvantages of regulation by a voluntary code of practice rather than law
- Discuss independence in respect of non-executive directors

iv Internal financial control effectiveness

- Outline the importance of internal control and risk management
- Compare the responsibilities of management and auditors (internal and external) for the design and operation of systems and controls, and the reliability of management information (financial and non-financial)

- Describe the factors to be taken into account when assessing the need for an internal audit function

v **Laws and Regulations in an Audit of Financial Statements**

- Compare and contrast the respective responsibilities of management and auditors concerning compliance with laws and regulations
- Describe the auditors considerations of compliance and audit procedures when possible non-compliance is discovered

5 PRACTICE MANAGEMENT I

Syllabus reference 2a

General

- Describe the risks to which practices are exposed and the steps which can be taken to manage them

Quality control practices and procedures

- Outline the regulatory framework for ensuring quality services
- Outline the organisation of international accountancy practices
- Specify the objectives of quality control policies
- Identify the factors which affect the nature, timing and extent of an audit firm's quality control policies and procedures
- Recommend policies and procedures which can be exercised internally at the level of the audit firm and on individual audits
- Describe review procedures including second partner reviews
- Discuss the matters particularly relevant to smaller firms relating to quality control

6 PRACTICE MANAGEMENT II

Syllabus reference 2b, 2c, 2d, 2e

Advertising, publicity, obtaining professional work and fees

- Explain the need for guidance in these areas
- Illustrate the circumstances in which advertising is acceptable
- Discuss the restrictions on practice descriptions, the use of the ACCA logo and the names of practising firms
- Discuss the extent to which fees may be referred to in promotional material
- Outline the determinants of fee-setting and describe the bases on which fees and commissions may and may not be charged for services
- Discuss the problems involved in establishing and negotiating fees, etc

d **Tendering**

- Describe the matters to be considered when a firm is invited to submit a proposal or fee quote for an audit
- Identify the information required for the proposal
- Outline the content of an engagement proposal document (for both continuing and new clients)
- Suggest the criteria which might be used to evaluate tenders received from audit firms
- Suggest reasons why audit fees may be lowered from the previous year's fees
- Describe 'lowballing' and discuss whether or not it impairs independence

e **Terms of engagement**

- Explain the key issues which underlie the agreement of the scope and terms of an audit engagement with a client

7 AUDIT PROCESS I

Syllabus reference 3a i, ii

General (approaches to auditing)

- Select and justify an appropriate approach to a given assignment
- Explain the circumstances in which a specific approach is not appropriate

i **Risk-based auditing**

- Describe the business risk approach to auditing and its relationship to the audit risk model
- Outline the reasons why it is adopted in preference to other methodologies
- Describe the consequences of such a 'top down' approach to evidence gathering procedures (eg testes of controls, analytical procedures and test of detail)

ii **Systems audits**

- Describe the components of an effective system of internal controls
- Identify the factors which contribute to a strong control environment
- Revise control objectives, control procedures, walk-through tests and tests of control ('compliance tests')

8 AUDIT PROCESS II

Syllabus references 3a iii, iv, v, vi

iii Balance sheet approach

- Explain the importance of the balance sheet as a primary statement
- Discuss why this approach may be more appropriate for the audit of small business than a business risk approach
- Discuss the limitations of this approach

iv Revenue, expenditure and other cycles

- Illustrate how accounting transactions can be analysed into 'cycles' which correspond to the line items in the balance sheet and profit and loss account
- Identify cycles relevant to a given situation (eg the conversion cycle for a manufacturing enterprise)
- Describe the approach to each cycle

v Directional testing

- Explain the concept of directional testing as a methodology
- Describe how this approach helps to detect misstatements and determines the populations from which samples are drawn
- Illustrate the use of directional testing within cycles
- Discuss the advantages and limitations of this approach

vi Analytical procedures

- Explain the nature and role of analytical procedures in the conduct of an assignment
- Recognise situations in which analytical procedures may be used extensively
- Describe the criteria for assessing the extent to which reliance can be placed on substantive analytical procedures

9 PLANNING

Syllabus references 3b

General

- Identify and illustrate the matters to be considered in planning an assignment including:
  - Logistics (eg staff and clients management, multiple locations, deadlines)
  - Use of IT in administration
  - Time budgets
  - Assignment objectives and reports required
  - Preliminary materiality
  - Financial statement or other assertions
  - Components of audit risk
  - Audit strategy

i Materiality

- Define materiality and describe how it is applied in financial reporting and auditing
- Explain the criteria which determine whether or not a matter is material
- Discuss the use and limitations of prescriptive rules in making decisions about materiality

ii Risk assessments

- Identify and distinguish between assignment (eg audit) and business risks
- Describe the factors which influence the assessment of a specific risk (eg inherent risk) for a given assignment
- Explain how and why the assessments of risks and materiality affect the nature, timing and extent of auditing procedures
- Critically appraise the audit risk model
- Recognise and assess the implications of a specified computer system (eg network) on an assignment

10, 11 EVIDENCE

Syllabus reference 3c

General

- Critically appraise the appropriateness and sufficiency of different sources of audit evidence and the procedures by which evidence may be obtained including:
  - Management representations
  - The work of others (including internal auditors and specialists)
  - Sampling techniques and selection methods
  - Direct communication
  - Audit automation tools
- Identify and illustrate suitable investigative methods (eg audit procedures such as enquiry and observation) to obtain sufficient evidence from identified sources
- Select and explain substantive analytical procedures appropriate to given financial and other data
- Identify and evaluate the audit evidence expected to be available to:

- Verify specific assets, liabilities, transactions and events
- Support financial statement assertions and accounting treatments

i Documentation

- Explain the reasons for preparing and keeping working papers and the importance of reviewing them

ii Related parties

- Explain the specific audit problems and procedures concerning related parties and related party transactions
- Recognise circumstances that may indicate the existence of unidentified related parties

iii Management representations

- Illustrate the use of written management representations as the primary source of audit evidence and as complementary audit evidence
- Discuss the implications of contradictory evidence being discovered

iv Using work of others

- Explain when it is justifiable to place reliance on the work of a specialist (eg a surveyor employed by the audit client)
- Assess the appropriateness and sufficiency of the work internal auditors

12 EVALUATION AND REVIEW I

Syllabus reference 3d i-iii

General

- Explain review procedures (including the use of analytical procedures and checklists)
- Evaluate findings quantitatively and qualitatively, eg
  - The results of audit tests and procedures
  - The effect of actual and potential misstatements

i Opening balances and comparatives

- Describe how the auditor's responsibilities for corresponding figures and comparative financial statements are discharged
- Describe the further considerations and audit procedures relevant to initial engagements

ii Other information

- Explain the auditor's responsibilities for 'other information'
- Discuss the courses of action available to an auditor if a material inconsistency exists

iii Subsequent events

- Specify the nature and timing of audit procedures designed to identify subsequent events that may require adjustment to, or disclosure in, the financial statements

13 EVALUATION AND REVIEW II

Syllabus reference 3d iv

iv Going concern

- Give examples of indicators that the going concern basis may be in doubt and recognise mitigating factors
- Evaluate the evidence which might be expected to be available and assess the appropriateness of the going concern basis in given situations
- Describe the disclosures in financial statements relating to going concern
- Understand the implications for the auditors' report where doubts about the going concern basis:
  - Have been resolved
  - Remain unresolved
- Comment on the auditors responsibilities in respect of going concern statements

14, 15 AUDIT OF FINANCIAL STATEMENTS

Syllabus reference 4a, 5a

- Explain the objectives and principal characteristics of statutory audit and discuss its value (eg in assisting management to reduce the risk and improve performance)
- Distinguish between the respective responsibilities of auditors and management in relation to the audit of financial statements
- Describe the limitations of assurance provided by a statutory audit
- Evaluate the matters (eg materiality, risk, relevant accounting standards, audit evidence) relating to:
  - Stock
  - Standard costing systems
  - Cash flow statements
  - Long-term contracts
  - Deferred taxation
  - Segmental information
  - Fair value
  - Leases
  - Revenue recognition
  - Government grants and assistance

- Borrowing costs
- Related party transactions
- Investments
- Earnings per share
- Discontinuing operations
- Impairment
- Provisions, contingent liabilities and contingent assets
- Goodwill
- Brand valuations
- Research and development
- Other intangible assets
- Distributable profits

(This list is not exhaustive, in particular, the audit of transactions, balances and other events examined in Paper 2.6 is now assumed knowledge.)

16 GROUP AUDITS

Syllabus reference 4b, 5a

- Identify the specific matters to be considered before accepting appointment as principal auditor to a group
- Explain the organisation, planning, management and administration issues specific to group and joint audits
- Identify the specific audit problems and describe audit procedures in relation to:
  - The correct classification of investment
  - Acquisitions and disposals
  - Related party transactions
  - Inter-company balances, transactions and profits
  - Goodwill on consolidation
  - Enterprises in developing countries
- Discuss support letters as audit evidence
- Describe the matters to be considered and the procedures to be performed when a principal auditor uses the work of another auditor
- Explain the implications for the auditors' report on a financial statements of an entity where the opinion on a component is qualified

17 'AUDIT-RELATED' SERVICES[1]

[1]May also be termed 'non audit' services

Syllabus reference 4c, 5b

General

- Distinguish between audit and audit-related services and the comparative levels of assurance provided by the auditor

i Reviews

- Distinguish between an attestation engagement and a direct reporting engagement
- Describe, for example:
  - A review of interim financial information
  - 'Due diligence' (when acquiring a company, business or other assets)
- Explain and illustrate the importance of inquiry and analytical procedures
- Discuss the effectiveness of the current 'negative assurance' form of reporting

ii Agreed-upon procedures

- Explain why these and compilation engagements do not (usually) meet the requirements for an assurance engagement
- Illustrate the form and content of a report of factual findings

iii Compilations

- Describe the general principles and procedures relating to a compilation engagement (eg to prepare financial statements)
- Illustrate the form and content of a compilation report

18, 19 ASSURANCE SERVICES

Syllabus reference 4d, 5b

General

- Explain the need for a range or assurance services and discuss to what extent these can be provided by auditors
- Explain the effects of assurance services being provided by the external auditor
- Describe how the level of assurance (high or moderate) provided by an engagement depends on the subject matter evaluated, the criteria used, the procedures applied and the quality and quantity of evidence obtained
- Describe the form and content of the professional accountant's report for an assurance engagement
- Discuss the situations in which it would be appropriate to express a reservation or deny a conclusion

i Risk assessment

- Distinguish between management risk assessment and auditor risk assessment
- Explain the meaning of risk and the importance of risk thresholds
- Describe and illustrate different types of risk (eg financial, operational, information/IT, environment)
- Describe ways in which risks may be identified and analysed (eg in terms of their significance, the likelihood of occurrence and how they should be managed)
- Discuss the relative advantages and disadvantages of qualitative and quantitative risk assessment methods
- Explain the different ways in which management can respond to risk (eg manage it, eliminate it, develop a recovery plan)

ii Performance management

- Describe the benefits of providing assurance on business performance measures
- Discuss the relevance of traditional financial accounting performance measures and operational measures
- Describe how the reliability of performance information systems is assessed (including benchmarking)
- Describe the elements of a value for money audit (ie economy, efficiency and effectiveness) and give examples of its use

iii Systems reliability

- Describe the need for information integrity and controls
- Discuss the demand for reliable and explain the benefits of providing assurance to management and external users
- Describing the procedures for assessing internal control effectiveness (eg in real-time systems)

iv Electronic commerce

- Describe and illustrate the ways in which organisations are using core technologies (eg EDI, email, Internet, World Wide Web)
- Explain how e-commerce affects the business of risk of an entity
- Describe the issues of privacy and security of information for transactions and communications
- Outline and illustrate the principles and criteria which underlie web assurance

20 PROSPECTIVE FINANCIAL INFORMATION

Syllabus reference 4e

- Define 'prospective financial information' and distinguish between a 'forecast' and a 'projection'
- Describe the matters to be considered before accepting an engagement to report on prospective financial information
- Discuss the level of assurance which the auditor may provide and explain the other factors to be considered in determining the nature, timing and extent of examination procedures
- Describe examination procedures to verify forecasts and projections relating to:
  - Capital expenditure
  - Profits
  - Cash flows
- Discuss the basis on which auditors should form an opinion on prospective financial information

21 INTERNAL AUDIT

Syllabus reference 4f

- Revise internal audit and:
  - Its role in corporate governance
  - Its relationship (eg with audit committees, external auditors)
  - The factors which determine the extent to which reliance can be placed on its work
- Compare the objectives and principal characteristics of internal audit with other assurance engagements
- Compare and contrast operational and compliance audits
- Describe possible approaches to multi-site operations (eg cyclical compliance audits)
- Discuss the provision of outsourced internal auditing services

22 OUTSOURCED FINANCE AND ACCOUNTING FUNCTIONS

Syllabus reference 4g

- Explaining the different approaches to 'outsourcing' and compare with 'insourcing'
- Discussing the advantages and disadvantages of outsourcing finance and accounting functions including:
  - Data (transaction) processing

- Pensions
- Information technology (IT)
- Internal auditing
- Due diligence work
- Taxes

- Explain the impact of outsourced functions on the conduct of an audit

23 SOCIAL AND ENVIRONMENTAL AUDITS

Syllabus references 4h, 6d

- Discuss the increasing importance of policies which govern the relationship of an organisation to its employees, society and the environment
- Describe the difficulties in measuring social and environmental performance and give examples of targets and sustainability indicators
- Explain the auditors' main considerations with respect to social and environmental matters and give examples of how they impact on companies and their financial statements (eg impairment of assets, provisions and contingent liabilities)
- Discuss how control over social and environmental risks may be exercised by management and evaluated by auditor
- Describe substantive procedures to detect potential misstatements in respect of socio-environmental matters
- Explain what actions may be taken by the auditor in situations of non-compliance with relevant laws and regulations (eg environmental acts and health and safety regulations)
- Discuss the form and content of an independent verification statement (eg on an environmental management system (EMS) and a report to society)

24 AUDITORS' REPORT

Syllabus reference 5a

- Explain and critically appraise the form and content of a standard qualified auditors' report
- Describe the factors to be taken into account when forming an audit opinion
- Make judgements and form audit opinions which are consistent with the results of audit procedures relating to the sufficiency of audit evidence and/or the appropriateness of accounting treatments (including the going concern basis)
- Critically evaluate a proposed audit opinion
- Discuss 'a true and fair view'
- Discuss and illustrate special purpose auditors' report (eg on summarised financial statements)

2 REPORTS TO MANAGEMENT

Syllabus reference 5c

- Identify and report system weaknesses and their potential effects and make appropriate recommendations to management (eg accounting procedures and financial records)
- Describe the criteria for evaluating the effectiveness of a management letter
- Outline the content of a report to an audit committee
- Explain the need for timely communication, clearance, feedback and follow up
- Discuss communication methods

26 CURRENT ISSUES AND DEVELOPMENTS I

Candidates will be expected to demonstrate the ability to discuss the relative merits and the consequences of different standpoints taken in current debates and express opinions supported by reasoned arguments.

Syllabus references 6a, 6e

Professional ethics

- Discuss the relative advantages of an ethical framework and a rulebook
- Comment on the adequacy of existing ways in which objectivity may be safeguarded and suggest additional measures to improve independence
- Suggest advantages and identify the problems and safeguards associated with, for example, audit staff leaving to join an audit client

Information technology

- Describe recent trends in IT and their current and potential impact on auditors (eg identify and discuss the audit implications of financial reporting on the Internet)
- Explain how IT may be used to assist auditors and discuss the problems which may be encountered in automating the audit process

27 CURRENT ISSUES AND DEVELOPMENTS II

Syllabus references 6f, 6g

Multinational accountancy firms

- Describe the different ways in which the auditing profession and audit markets are regulated
- Discuss the advantages and disadvantages of partnerships and incorporation of audit firms
- Describe current developments in the limitations of auditors' liability and the practical ways in which the risk of litigation can be reduced
- Distinguish between the 'Big Five' firms, 'non-Big Five' firms and second-tier firms
- Discuss the impact of globalisation on audit firms and their clients
- Explain the advantages and problems of current trends (eg to merge, to divest consultancy services)

SMEs and audit exemption

- State the case for and against audit exemption for small businesses
- Discuss how the potential problems associated with the audit of small enterprises may be overcome

28 REVISION

OXFORD BROOKES BSc (Hons) IN APPLIED ACCOUNTING

The standard required of candidates completing Part 2 is that required in the final year of a UK degree. Students completing Parts 1 and 2 will have satisfied the examination requirement for an honours degree in Applied Accounting, awarded by Oxford Brookes University.

To achieve the degree, you must also submit two pieces of work based on a **Research and Analysis Project**

- A 5,000 word **Report** on your chosen topic, which demonstrates that you have acquired the necessary research, analytical and IT skills.
- A 1,500 word **Key Skills Statement,** indicating how you have developed your interpersonal and communication skills.

BPP was selected by the ACCA to produce the official text *Success in your Research and Analysis Project* to support students in this task. The book pays particular attention to key skills not covered in the professional examinations.

AN ORDER FORM FOR THE NEW SYLLABUS MATERIAL, INCLUDING THE OXFORD BROOKES PROJECT TEXT, CAN BE FOUND AT THE END OF THIS STUDY TEXT.

THE EXAM PAPER

The examination is a three hour paper constructed in two sections. Questions in both sections will be almost entirely discussive. However, candidates will be expected, for example, to be able to see materiality and calculate relevant ratios where applicable.

Section A will be based on 'case study' type scenarios. That is not to say that they will be particularly long, rather that they will provide a setting within which a range of topics, issues and requirements can be addressed. Different types of question will be encountered in Section B and will tend to be more focused on specific topics, for example 'auditors' reports', 'quality control and topics of SASs which are not examinable in Paper 2.6 *Audit and Internal Review*. (This does not preclude these topics from featuring in Section A.) These questions will have less scenario than in Section A and one will be a discussion question.

		Number of Marks
Section A:	3 compulsory questions	70
Section B:	Choice of 2 from 3 questions (15 marks each)	30
		100

Additional information

Candidates need to be aware that questions involving knowledge of new examinable regulations will not be set until at least six months after the last day of the month in which the regulations was issued.

The Study Guide provides more detailed guidance on the syllabus. Examinable documents are listed in the 'Exam Notes' section of ACCA's *Student Accountant.*

Analysis of pilot paper

Section A

1 Review of financial information, group planning issues
2 Planning, business risk, strategy, control procedures
3 Accounting issues, evidence

Section B

4 Comparatives, audit report
5 Confidentiality, independence issues
6 Environmental issues

Part A

Audit framework

Chapter 1

RULES OF PROFESSIONAL CONDUCT

Topic list		Syllabus reference
1	Fundamental principles and professional guidance	1(a)
2	Independence	1(a)
3	Threats to independence	1(a)
4	Safeguards	1(a)
5	Areas of controversy: independence	1(a)
6	Confidentiality	1(a)
7	Areas of controversy: confidentiality	1(a)

Introduction

You have learnt about rules of professional conduct for auditors previously in Paper 2.6 *Audit and Internal Review* (old paper 6). In Paper 3.1 we will examine the issues in more detail and consider some of the complex ethical issues that auditors may face.

Knowledge brought forward from 2.6

The nature of audit

Regulations governing qualification as an auditor

ACCA's fundamental principles and ethical guidance

Throughout this chapter we refer to the ethical guidance of the International Federation of Accountants and contrast it to that of the ACCA.

Much of this chapter is likely to be revision, but that does not mean you should ignore it. Professional issues are a key syllabus area. Complex ethical issues are introduced in this chapter, particularly in Sections 5 and 7.

Study guide

Section 1

Integrity, Objectivity and Independence

- Revise the purpose of a professional ethical code from Paper 2.6(U)
- Compare and contrast the Fundamental Principles of ACCA's 'Rules of Professional Conduct' and with those of the IFAC's 'Code of Ethics for Professional Accountants'
- Outline the contents of ACCA's and IFAC's codes of ethics
- Identify and explain common threats to independence and explain how the risks may be minimised or resolved
- Discuss and evaluate the effectiveness of available safeguards
- Outline the practical implications for an audit practice in relation to quality control procedures

- Discuss the benefits of providing other services (including internal audit) to audit clients and whether the drawbacks (eg objectivity impairment) can be overcome
- Define 'specialist valuations' and discuss how the objectivity of the audit may be threatened
- Explain how and why an auditor should respond to a request to provide a second opinion

Professional duty of confidence

- Explain the importance of the role of confidentiality to the auditor-client relationship
- Distinguish between disclosure and use of information
- Identify circumstances in which disclosure is permitted or required
- Discuss the factors which may justify disclosure in the 'public interest'
- Describe how a client's information should be protected when the auditor also acts for a competitor company

Section 2

Corporate financial advice and conflicts

- Outline the role of auditors in advising clients involved in take-over bids and share issues and explain how conflicts can arise
- Distinguish conflicts between members' and clients' interests from those between the interests of different clients
- Describe how conflicts may be avoided or managed with safeguards.

Section 3

Insider dealing

- Explain the term 'insider dealing' and why it is damaging
- Relate the Fundamental Principles to insider dealing
- Suggest measures to reduce the exposure of partners and staff to the risks arising

Section 26

- Discuss the relative advantages of an ethical framework and a rulebook
- Comment on the adequacy of existing ways in which objectivity may be safeguarded and suggest additional measures to improve independence
- Suggest advantages and identify the problems and safeguards associated with, for example, audit staff leaving to join an audit client

Exam guide

This is a key topic area. You should expect a question on ethics to come up in the exam. You are likely to have to apply your knowledge of the rules and guidance to a particular scenario. Remember always to use your (educated!) common sense.

1 FUNDAMENTAL PRINCIPLES AND PROFESSIONAL GUIDANCE

1.1 The reasons why accountancy bodies produce ethical guidance are summed up in IFAC's *Code of Ethics*.

> The Code recognises that the objectives of the accounting profession are to work to the highest standards of professionalism, to attain the highest levels of performance and generally meet the public interest requirement. These objectives require four basic needs to be met.

(a) **Credibility**

In the whole of society, there is a need for credibility in information and information systems.

(b) **Professionalism**

There is a need for individuals who can clearly be identified by clients, employers and other interested parties as professional people in the accountancy field.

(c) **Quality of services**

There is a need for assurance that all services obtained from a professional accountant are carried out to the highest standards of performance.

(d) **Confidence**

Users of the services of professional accountants should be able to feel confident that there exists a framework of professional ethics which governs the provision of those services.

1.2 The code refers to the public interest requirement. The **key reason** that **accountants need** to have an **ethical code** is that **people rely on them.**

1.3 Accountants deal with a range of issues on behalf of clients. They often have access to confidential and sensitive information. Auditors claim to give an independent view. It is therefore critical that accountants, and particularly auditors, are, and are seen to be, independent.

Rules of professional conduct

1.4 As the auditor is required to be, and seen to be, ethical in his dealings with clients, ACCA publishes guidance for its members, the *Rules of Professional Conduct.* This guidance is given in the form of fundamental principles, specific guidance and explanatory notes.

1.5 IFAC also lays down fundamental principles in its *Code of Professional Ethics,* mentioned above. The fundamental principles of the two associations are extremely similar. They are given in the table below for comparison.

The fundamental principles

ACCA	IFAC
All members should	The fundamental principles are:
• Behave with **integrity** in all professional, business and personal financial relationships. Integrity implies not merely **honesty,** but **fair dealing** and **truthfulness.**	• **Integrity.** A professional accountant should be **straightforward** and **honest** in performing professional services.
• Strive for **objectivity** in all professional and business judgements. Objectivity is the **state of mind which has regard to all considerations relevant to the task in hand but no other.** It presupposes intellectual honesty.	• **Objectivity.** A professional accountant should be **fair** and **should not allow prejudice or bias, conflict of interest or influence of others** to override objectivity.

ACCA	IFAC
• Not accept or perform work which they are not **competent** to undertake unless they obtain such assistance as will enable them competently to carry out the work. • Carry out their professional work with due skill, care, diligence and expedition and with proper regard for the technical and professional standards expected of them.	• **Professional Competence and Due Care**. A professional accountant should perform professional services with **due care, competence and diligence** and has a continuing duty to maintain professional knowledge and skill at a level required to ensure that a client or employer received the advantage of competent professional service based on up to date developments in practice, legislation and techniques.
	• **Confidentiality**. A professional accountant should respect the confidentiality of information acquired during the course of performing professional services **and should not use or disclose** any such information **unless there is a legal duty or professional right or duty to disclose**.
• Behave with **courtesy** and **consideration** towards all with whom they come into contact during the course of performing their work.	• **Professional Behaviour**. A professional accountant should **act in a manner consistent with the good reputation of the profession** and refrain from any behaviour which might bring discredit to the profession. The obligation to refrain from any conduct which might bring discredit to the profession requires IFAC member bodies to consider, when developing ethical requirements, the responsibilities of a professional accountant to clients, third parties, other members of the accountancy profession, staff, employers and the general public.

1.6 The only real difference between the two statements of fundamental principles is that the IFAC explicitly mention **confidentiality.**

1.7 However, the fact that confidentiality is not mentioned explicitly in ACCA's professional rules does not mean that that ACCA believe that accountants can be indiscreet. ACCA give detailed guidance on the area of confidentiality in their **Statement 2.** This will be considered in more detail later in the chapter.

Ethical framework

1.8 The ethical guidance discussed above is in the form of a framework. It contains some rules, for example, ACCA prohibits making loans to clients, but in the main it is flexible guidance. It can be seen as being a **framework rather than a set of rules**.

1.9 There are a number of advantages of a framework over a system of ethical rules. These are outlined in the table below.

Advantages of an ethical framework over a rules based system
A framework of guidance places the onus on the auditor to **actively consider** independence for every given situation, rather than just agreeing a checklist of forbidden items. It also requires him to **demonstrate** that a responsible conclusion has been reached about ethical issues.
The framework **prevents auditors interpreting legalistic requirements narrowly** to get around the ethical requirements. There is an element to which rules engender deception, whereas principles encourage compliance.
A framework **allows for** the variations that are found in every **individual situation**. Each situation is likely to be different.
A framework can accommodate a **rapidly changing environment**, such as the one that auditors are constantly in.
However, a **framework can contain prohibitions** (as noted above) where these are necessary as safeguards are not feasible.

IFAC Independence Exposure Draft

1.10 IFAC issued an exposure draft on the issue of independence in April 2001. It is a re-issue of an exposure draft which now covers assurance engagements, in the light the guidance given in ISAE 100, Assurance Engagements.

1.11 It states that three types of safeguard exist:

- Safeguards created by the **profession, by legal requirement and by regulation**
- Safeguards within the **client**
- Safeguards within the **firm** giving the assurance

1.12 You have studied extensively the types of safeguard included in the first bullet point. These include strict entry requirements into the profession and all guidance issued by ACCA and IFAC.

1.13 A key example of a safeguard within a client is an audit committee. We will discuss these in this chapter and they are discussed further in Chapter 5.

1.14 Lastly, the third safeguard is policies within the client firm. We will discuss these briefly in terms of quality control and review procedures in the firm in this chapter. We shall consider them at more length in Chapter 4 when we look at aspects of practice management.

Auditors in the EC

1.15 The European Commission issued a consultative paper on auditor independence on 18 December 2000. It seeks to address the issue of independence in the EC. Currently, under the provisions of the EC's 8th Directive, national practice surrounding auditor independence varies significantly.

1.16 It discusses a number of threats and safeguards to independence, which will largely be discussed in this chapter as part of ACCA and IFAC guidance. However, it is a thorough critique of the issues surrounding auditor independence, and you might like to read it as part of considering the issues surrounding auditors' independence. It can be found at www.europa.eu.int/comm/internal_market/en/company/audit/news/.

2 INDEPENDENCE

2.1 ACCA gives specific guidance relating to independence in their *Statement 1: Integrity, Objectivity and Independence.*

ACCA statement

'A member's objectivity must be beyond question if he is to report as an auditor. That objectivity can only be assured if the member is, and is seen to be, independent.'

'The threat to independence may be reduced by the nature and extent of the precautions taken by the practice to guard against loss of objectivity.'

2.2 IFAC make further general points about integrity and objectivity in their Code.

IFAC Code

- Professional accountants are exposed to situations which involve the possibility of **pressures** being exerted on them. These pressures may impair their objectivity.
- It is impracticable to define and prescribe all such situations where these possible pressures exist.
- **Relationships** should be **avoided** which allow **prejudice, bias or influence of others to override objectivity.**
- Professional accountants have an obligation to ensure that personnel engaged in professional services adhere to the principle of **objectivity**.

Threats to independence

2.3 Threats to independence and objectivity could arise for many reasons. As shown above, IFAC believes that it is impracticable to define and prescribe all such situations where these possible pressures exist. The following general reasons can be given, however.

- The auditors' own **personal interests**, for example, fear of losing fees.
- The independent audit being **a review of the work carried out by the auditors**, for example, auditing accounts that they have prepared.
- Issues arising from any **disputes** the auditors might have concerning their clients, where it may appear that his objectivity is threatened.
- The auditors being **intimidated** by a dominant or aggressive atmosphere.

Auditors' response to threats

2.4 In the face of these threats, the simplest answer is for the auditors to **withdraw from the engagement** where they are faced with the threats. However, this rigid approach brings disadvantages to clients.

- They lose auditors who know their business.
- They are denied the freedom to be advised by accountants of their choice.

2.5 There is a better three-step approach to responding to a threat to objectivity.

Step 1. **Consider whether** the **auditors' own objectivity** and the **safeguards** operated in the professional environment are sufficient to **offset the threat.**

Step 2. **Consider** whether **safeguards over and above** the general safeguards **are required,** for example, specified partners or staff not working on this assignment.

Step 3. **Withdrawal** from an engagement or refusal to act. (This is always the fallback option).

2.6 Much of the rest of ACCA and IFAC guidance is taken up with discussions of specific threats and recommendations of safeguards concerning **specific areas of risk.** This is summarised below.

3 THREATS TO INDEPENDENCE

3.1 The area of threats to independence should not be new to you. You should be aware of many of the threats to independence from you studies at *2.6 Audit and Internal Review* (old paper 6).

3.2 To refresh your memory about independence issues, try the following two questions.

Question 1

From your knowledge brought forward from Paper 2.6 (old paper 6), and any practical experience of auditing you may have, write down as many potential ethical risk areas as you can in the areas below. (Some issues may be relevant in more than one column.)

Personal interests	Review of your own work	Disputes	Intimidation

Answer

Personal interests	Review of your own work	Disputes	Intimidation
Undue dependence on an audit client due to fee levels Overdue fees becoming similar to a loan An actual loan being made to a client Contingency fees being offered Accepting commissions from clients Provision of lucrative other services to clients Relationships with persons in associated practices Relationships with the client Long association with clients Beneficial interest in shares or other investments Hospitality	Auditor prepares the accounts Auditor participates in management decisions Provision of any other services to the client	Actual litigation with a client Threatened litigation with a client Client refuses to pay fees and they become long overdue	Any threat of litigation by the client Personal relationships with the client Hospitality Threat of other services provided to the client being put out to tender Threat of any services being put out to tender

Question 2

In your earlier auditing studies, you learnt about the ACCA's statements regarding independence. List as many of the statements and rules as you can, explaining what the rule is and what it aims to achieve.

Answer

Area	ACCA statement/rule	Objective of the rule
Fees	'Objectivity may be threatened or appear to be threatened by undue dependence on any audit client or group of connected clients.' Fees from one client should not exceed 15% of practice income (10% in the case of listed companies).	This rule is about level of fee income that is acceptable from one client is designed to prevent the auditor losing independence due to his over-dependence on the fees of that client and therefore a fear of losing that client
	'The existence of significant overdue fees from an audit client or group of associated clients can be a threat or appear to be a threat to objectivity akin to that of a loan.' 'Objectivity may be threatened or many appear to be threatened by a loan to or from an audit client.'	If a client owes the firm a substantial amount of money, the firm's own financial situation becomes more closely connected to that of the client, which may affect the firm's independence, if the client seems to be unable to pay or if they try to make payment conditional on actions of the auditors.
Other services	'There are occasions when objectivity may be threatened or may appear to be threatened by the provision to an audit client of services other than the audit.'	An auditor should not make management decisions or undertake any kind of management function on behalf of the client because he is later to audit that client and independence will be affected. This can be a grey area.

Area	ACCA statement/rule	Objective of the rule
Litigation	'A firm's objectivity may be threatened or appear to be threatened when it is involved in, or even threatened with litigation in relation to a client.'	Disputes arising with clients will affect objectivity, due to breakdown in the relationship between client and auditor.
Outside influences	'A firm's objectivity may be threatened or appear to be threatened as a result of pressures arising from associated practices or organisations, or from other external sources, such as bankers, solicitors, government or those introducing business.'	The auditor's objectivity may be affected if any of these groups of people have a vested interest in the firm retaining the client.
Family	'A member's objectivity may be threatened or appear to be threatened as a consequence of a family or other close personal or business relationship.'	The auditor should avoid the threat to independence raised by having close personal relationships with people involved in the business being audited. He might otherwise have a vested interest in the audit.
Beneficial interests	'A members objectivity may be threatened or appear to be threatened where he (or she) holds a beneficial interest in the shares or other forms of investment in a company upon which the practice reports.' 'The objectivity of a practice may be threatened or appear to be threatened where a partner or a person closely connected with the partner has a beneficial interest in a trust having a shareholding in an audit client company. 'A member's objectivity may be threatened or appear to be threatened by trustee shareholding and other trustee investments	Auditors should not have a shareholding in the client as this, again, could give them a vested interest in the opinion given in the auditor's report.
	'Where a partner of staff member holds shares in any capacity in a company which is an audit client of the practice they should not be voted at any general meeting of the company in relation to the appointment, removal or remuneration of auditors'.	If the auditor takes decisions traditionally in the realm of management then he is not independent when he comes to do the audit.
Hospitality	'Objectivity may be threatened or appear to be threatened by acceptance of goods, services or hospitality from an audit client ... Acceptance on normal commercial terms, or with only a modest benefit is acceptable.'	Again, accepting benefit from a client might appear to others to be accepting some form of bribe and might result in a situation where the auditor felt beholden to the client in some way, which would prevent him from being independent.

Exam focus point

How did you do on question 2? If you did not identify many of the areas of ACCA guidance given in the answer, or do not understand the objectives behind them, you should go back to your 2.6 (old paper 6) text and revise this area as it is assumed knowledge at Paper 3.1.

Guidance provided by IFAC

Contingency fees

> **IFAC Code of Ethics**
>
> Professional services should not be offered or rendered to a client under an arrangement whereby no fee will be charged unless a specified finding or result is obtained or when the fee is otherwise **contingent** upon the findings or the results of such services.

3.3 Offering services on a contingency fee basis poses a threat to objectivity because a situation might arise where the accountant gave the answer which resulted in him being paid rather than the correct answer.

3.4 In this situation the accountant would not have 'a state of mind which has regard to all considerations relevant to the task in hand but no other', as required by the ACCA's fundamental principles.

Commissions

> **IFAC Code of Ethics**
>
> A professional accountant in public practice should not pay a commission to obtain a client nor should a commission be accepted for referral of a third party.

3.5 Commission can impair objectivity because it means that an accountant stands to make a gain from dealing with a client not related to a fee for services. That fact reduces his objectivity in relation to the client.

Influences outside the practice

> **IFAC Code of Ethics**
>
> Where outside shareholders are involved with firms of accountants, capital may be owned by people other than the accountants if the majority of both capital ownership and voting rights are held by the professional accountants. Ideally, all the capital should be held by the accountants.

Former partners

3.6 On leaving a practice, a partner may accept a position with a continuing audit client of the practice. Safeguards are recommended so that independence and objectivity are retained in future dealings with that client.

> **IFAC Code of Ethics**
>
> (a) Payments of the amounts due to a former partner for his or her interest in the practice or for unfounded, vested retirement benefits are made in accordance with a schedule that is fixed as to both payment dates and amounts. In addition, the amounts owed should be such that they do not cause a substantial doubt about the practice's ability to continue as a going concern.

(b) The former partner does not participate or appear to participate in the practice's business of professional activities whether or not compensated. Indications of participation include the provision of office space and related amenities to the former partner by the practice.

3.7 It is not unusual for audit partners, or even lower level audit staff to move to the audit client. There are two risks inherent in such moves.

- There may be a significant connection between former and current audit staff members and this may detract from objectivity.
- The staff member's own objectivity may be affected if he works on the client audit while aware that he is going to move there.

3.8 The approach you should take to ethical questions about such staff movements between audit firm and client is to apply the basic principles of independent and objectivity. Try the following questions, bearing in mind what you know of the guidance on these basic principles.

Question 3

The fact that auditors may be perceived not to be independent is a cause for concern. For example, if auditors provide non audit services to their clients, their objectivity may be impaired by undue dependence on those clients. A further concern is the situation where audit clients hire staff who were previously employed by their auditors. In this case the objectivity of future audits may be at risk.

(a) Explain the problems that may arise if an audit client hires, as finance director, a former audit partner.

(b) What are the advantages to a client of their auditor becoming a senior executive in their company?

(c) How does current ethical guidance attempt to deal with the problems surrounding an auditor becoming a senior member of staff with one of the firm's major clients? What additional safeguards might help?

Answer

(a) The **problems** associated with an audit partner becoming the finance director of the firm's client are as follows.

(i) The ex-partner will have a **detailed knowledge** of the audit approach being applied to the company. This knowledge may give him the opportunity to **conceal certain matters** from the auditors. The audit firm will need to approach their audit with this in mind. Additionally, if there is still a significant connection between the ex partner and the audit firm, the audit firm's objectivity may be threatened. An example of this would be where the ex partner receives retirement benefits from the audit firms.

(ii) There may be a general perception by the public that the **two parties** are not **independent.** The ex partner may well have had a close working relationship with members of the audit team, making it difficult for both the ex partner and the audit team to adjust to their new roles and the new relationship between them. The ex partner may still have some influence over members of the audit team and the public may question whether the audit team can deal with such a situation without there being a threat to objectivity.

(iii) The audit personnel may feel that they can place greater reliance on representations and evidence obtained from the ex partner. However, to ensure objectivity, the audit team should not place **undue reliance** on evidence received from the ex partner and should evaluate risk as they would with any client. If any disagreement occurs between the two parties, there is a risk that any agreement reached may be seen to be a compromise.

(iv) If an audit partner who is about to become the finance director of a client firm participates in the audit of that firm, the audit firm's **objectivity may be threatened.** The audit partner is likely to have significant influence within the audit firm and will be keen to ensure that nothing adversely affects their relationship with the client. In this situation it is probable that the general public will find it hard to accept that the audit firm is independent and objective.

(b) The following **advantages** exist for a client if their auditor becomes a senior executive.

(i) The auditor should have a **good understanding of the environment** in which the client operates and its accounting systems. This should mean that it will be relatively easy for him to become integrated with the rest of the management team and familiarise himself with his new environment.

(ii) Employing an auditor will **remove the costs** involved in using a recruitment consultant and reduce the risks of the consultant recruiting an unsuitable employee. An employee of the audit firm should be well known to the client.

(iii) The auditor should be **familiar** with a number of different accounting systems and should have the ability to solve different accounting problems. In addition, it is likely that the auditor is up to date when it comes to accounting techniques and current thinking.

(iv) The relationship that normally exists between the auditor and key members of the client staff means that the client should be **aware of the quality of the auditor's work.** If the client feels that this work meets the levels required by a senior executive then they are likely to approach the auditor.

(c) The current **ACCA rules do not specifically prohibit an audit firm from continuing to act as auditors to a client if an ex partner or employee now works in a senior position for that client.**

The current rules of professional conduct state that a member's **objectivity** must be **beyond question** if he (she) is to act as an auditor. That objectivity can only be assured if the member is and is seen to be independent. More specifically, the rules state the following.

(i) A member's objectivity may be threatened or appear to be threatened as a consequence of a family or other close personal or business relationship. Where a relationship exists between an officer of a company and a partner or member of staff of the audit firm, safeguards should be set up to ensure objectivity. For example, a review should be performed to ensure that each engagement should be continued or accepted and to identify whether there is a risk to independence.

(ii) Objectivity may be threatened by undue dependence on an audit client. It is suggested that the public perception of an auditor's objectivity is likely to be impaired where the fees for audit and other recurring work for a client exceeds 15% of gross practice income.

There are no current rules relating to the appointment of a former auditor as an officer of the client, the rules simply state that a member should not take part in the audit of a company if that member has been an officer or employee of that company within the previous two years. Therefore it is currently **up to the audit firm** to determine whether there is a threat to objectivity. Improvements that could be made would be to ensure that audit partners have accepted positions with clients this fact should be disclosed in the financial statements. Alternatively rules could be introduced to prohibit such appointments.

Long association

IFAC Code of Ethics

Use of the same senior personnel on an audit engagement over a prolonged period of time may pose a threat to independence.

3.9 The risk arises that if the auditor maintains a long relationship with the client, over time, the relationship could grow more personal than is appropriate.

3.10 A safeguard against loss of objectivity from long association is the concept of **audit rotation** which is discussed below in section 4.

Financial involvement

3.11 IFAC lists various types of financial involvement which may appear to impair auditor objectivity.

IFAC Code of Ethics

- Direct financial interest in a client
- Indirect material financial interest (for example, by being a trustee or executor)
- A financial interest in a joint venture with a client or employee of a client
- A financial interest in any company with an investor/ee relationship with a client

Goods and services, hospitality

IFAC Code of Ethics

Professional accountants should neither accept nor offer gifts or entertainment which might be reasonably be believed to have a significant and improper influence on their professional judgement or those with whom they deal.

3.12 What constitutes an excessive gift or offer of entertainment varies from country to country. Professional accountants should avoid circumstances which will bring their professional standing into disrepute.

Employing non-accountants

IFAC Code of Ethics

Accountants must recognise the need for supporting non-accountants to be aware of, and respect, the ethical requirements to which the accountants are subject.

Question 4

Comment on the similarities and dissimilarities between the IFAC code and ACCA's guidance. What are the key differences?

Answer

The IFAC has similar rules to the ACCA with regard to:

- Hospitality and accepting goods and services
- Contingency fees
- Influences outside the practice
- Financial involvement with clients

However, some **key differences** are:

Commissions

The IFAC code disallows member to give or accept commissions for referring clients. ACCA's guidance on this issue is contained within its statement on obtaining professional work which is covered in Chapter 2. However, briefly, it allows members to deal in commissions, but only with people who are accountants and therefore subject to the same ethical considerations as themselves.

Former partners

The IFAC code gives some guidance on how members should behave when former partners become staff of clients. The ACCA does not give any specific guidance on this point. The firm would have to review its independence in relation to that audit assignment and exercise judgement is such a situation arose.

Long association

The ACCA do not specifically mention the dangers of long association with a client.

Employing non-accountants

The IFAC state then when employing non-accountants, the accountant should ensure that they are made aware of the importance of the accountant's ethical code. Again, ACCA make no specific reference to this point. It is not practice in the UK to employ professional people who are not accountants in an accountancy firm.

Other services

The ACCA guidance makes reference to the fact that it can be a threat to objectivity to provide services other than audit to a client. It does not give any set rules about how to deal with this situation however. The IFAC makes no mention of it in its code. Therefore the question of other services falls under the general principles of objectivity.

4 SAFEGUARDS

ACCA and IFAC rules

4.1 The guidance from ACCA and IFAC provides various safeguards against loss of independence. The most obvious of such rules is the ACCA rule relating to fees, where a percentage value is imposed on maximum fees to safeguard independence.

Question 5

List as many safeguards given in ACCA's rules as you can.

Answer

- Fees percentage
- Loans forbidden
- Officers of a company prohibited from auditing it
- Partners owning shares in an audit client are prohibited from voting on audit appointment
- Goods and services should not be accepted unless they are of modest value
- Auditors of listed companies should not prepare the accounts

4.2 However, there are other practical safeguards individual members and firms can use. These are outlined in the rest of this section.

Quality control

4.3 SAS 240 *Quality control for audit work* was revised in September 2000. It defines quality control policy and process as being

> 'Policy and processes designed to provide reasonable assurance as to the appropriateness of the auditor's report and of adherence to Auditing Standards, **ethical** and other requirements'.

4.4 Professional ethics are at the heart of the quality control processes that the auditing standards lays out. The standard will be considered in more detail later in this text, but the following table gives some examples of how the SAS enforces ethical issues.

Para no	Section title	Text of SAS
10	The importance of audit quality	If audit engagement partners believe that their objectivity or the firm's independence may be impaired by the actions of a client service partner, or others in the firm wishing to market other services, they should discuss their concerns, and agree appropriate actions…
15	Acceptance and continuance of audit engagements	Before accepting a new audit engagement firms should ensure that they: … (d) Comply with the ethical requirements of the professional accountancy bodies in relation to changes in appointment.
21	Acceptance and continuance of audit engagements	If, after accepting an engagement, firms become aware of any facts which would have caused them to decline the appointment, they should consider whether to complete the current audit or whether to resign.
69	Monitoring	The objective of monitoring reviews is to provide an independent assessment of: (a) The appropriateness of the auditor's report, and the conduct of the audit in accordance with Auditing Standards, ethical and other regulatory requirements …

4.5 A good quality control system at firm level can provide a safeguard against ethical problems arising.

4.6 SAS 240 states that monitoring the firm's behaviour and relationships is a key part of quality control. The next safeguard to consider is the monitoring procedures firms can put into place, perhaps as part of an overall quality control system.

Procedures to resolve ethical problems

Review

ACCA Statement

'Every audit firm should establish adequate review machinery, including an annual review, in order to satisfy itself that each engagement may properly be accepted or be continued having regard to the guidance given in this statement, and to identify situations where independence may be at risk and where the appropriate safeguards should be applied.

4.7 Any additional safeguards required should be assessed by an independent partner. They might include:

- Rotation of the senior engagement partner
- Rotation of the audit staff

Procedures

IFAC Code of Ethics

The organisation should have procedures to resolve problems. If not:

- Review the conflict problem with the immediate superior
- If not resolved, go to higher superior, but notify immediate superior of action
- If not resolved, go to next highest superior in the organisation

If ethical conflict still exists after exhausting all levels of the organisation, professional accountants may have to resign and submit an information memorandum.

Audit rotation

4.8 Audit rotation is when, either:

- The client changes auditors on a regular basis (say, every five years), or
- The audit engagement staff within the firm are rotated between audit engagements.

4.9 Audit rotation was discussed as a potential action to strengthen public confidence in audit in the Cadbury Report of 1992.

4.10 The key advantage of an audit rotation is that independence is **seen** to be maintained and also that is prevents a client/partner relationship becoming 'too comfortable'.

4.11 It is sometimes the case that audit staff and client staff work so closely over the years that they grow to have a **relationship which could be seen as more personal than business.** At this point, the ACCA guidance concerning personal relationships becomes relevant.

4.12 However, there are several drawbacks to audit rotation as well. These are:

- **Inconvenience** to client staff, who become accustomed to audit staff
- **High recurring costs** of the first audit if the firm changes
- **Loss of respect and trust** built up over the years

Audit committee

4.13 The Cadbury committee also recommended the presence of an audit committee at all UK listed firms. This was not to suggest that they would not be useful at other UK companies as well.

4.14 The key benefit to the external auditor of an audit committee is that they provide a link between client staff and audit staff. As they are made up of non-executive directors they are, in theory, a less biased reference point for auditors within the company than other client staff.

4.15 The audit committee can serve a purpose to a client/auditor relationship that has grown familiar over the years as mentioned above. It can act as an independent buffer.

5 AREAS OF CONTROVERSY: INDEPENDENCE

5.1 There are areas of controversy with regard to independence that have not been considered previously in your ACCA studies.

5.2 The following paragraphs highlight some topical issues that you should be able to discuss if they came up in an exam situation. They are not exhaustive, you should be able to apply ACCA and IFAC rules and guidance and your own (educated) common sense to any ethical problem.

Other services

5.3 These have been mentioned previously. The question of provision of other services is highlighted again here because it is perennially a controversial issue and can be extremely difficult to make a judgement on. The guidance given by ACCA allows 'grey areas' because it is an area where ACCA believe that auditors should make their own judgements, based on circumstances.

5.4 Many audit firms are moving away from their traditional roles as straightforward audit firms and are offering a wider variety of services to their clients. Sometimes, audit is even seen as a loss leader which leads to other, more lucrative work.

5.5 This can be because clients see the audit merely as a statutory necessity and are more prepared to pay money for work which they can see the direct benefit of. If this is the case, pressure can be put on audit firms to reduce the audit fee, sometimes possibly with the incentive that clients will pay higher fees for the other work.

5.6 This leads to two ethical problems.

- The auditor loses his objectivity with regard to the audit opinion because he fears losing the other work.
- The auditor is not perceived to be independent with regard to his audit, because he performs so much other work for the client.

5.7 Currently, UK guidance is left open ended so that auditors can judge each situation on its merits. It is argued that if the situation was legislated more, then clients would be more restricted on whom they could choose to give them business advice, and there is a synergy in the auditor also providing other services such as business advice or tax work.

5.8 However, some feel that more legislation is required on this point so that auditors are not allowed to provide other services to clients. Some would argue that **the provision of any other service necessarily detracts from the independence of the auditor.**

5.9 In the United States, the Securities and Exchange Commission revised its rules concerning auditor independence during 2000. The SEC is the regulator of the US securities markets, so these rules only apply to **listed** companies.

5.10 Their rules now state that an accountant is not independent if they provide certain non-audit services to an audit client. The relevant services are:

- Bookkeeping
- Financial information systems design and implementation
- Appraisal or valuation services or fairness opinions
- Actuarial services
- Internal audit services
- Management functions
- Human resources
- Broker-dealer services
- Legal services

5.11 The distinction between listed companies, or public limited companies, and private companies is perceived to be an important issue in the question of providing other services to clients.

5.12 In their discussion of the issue of other services in its guidance ACCA states:

> 'In the case of a listed company or public interest company audit client, a practice should not participate in the preparation of the company's accounting records save:
>
> (a) In relation to assistance of a mechanical nature. Such assistance might include, for example, work on the finalisation of statutory accounts, including consolidations and tax provisions. However, the scale and nature of such work should be regularly reviewed, or
>
> (b) In emergency situations'

KEY TERMS

Listed companies are those whose shares have been admitted to a recognised exchange, such as the Stock Exchange, or the AIM.

Public interest companies are those which for some reason (size, nature, product) are in the 'public eye'. Auditors should treat these as if they are listed companies.

Exam focus point

In exam questions, bear in mind the nature of the entity being audited. Is it a small owner-managed business where the auditor is in effect an all-round business adviser and accountant, or is it a listed company where the above rule is relevant?

Specialist valuations

5.13 For the purposes of the independence guidance, the following definition is relevant.

KEY TERM

Specialist valuations include: actuarial valuations, valuations of intellectual property and brands, other intangible assets, property and unquoted investments, but **not** valuation of shares and report produced in accordance with S 108 Companies Act 1985, before the allotment of shares of a public company otherwise than for cash. *ACCA*

5.14 The term is not supposed to cover the giving of normal advice.

> **ACCA Statement**
>
> A firm should not audit a client's financial statements which include the product of a specialist valuation carried out by it or an associated practice.

Second opinions

5.15 If a company is unhappy with the audit opinion which it receives (or may receive) from its current auditors, then it might approach other audit firms for a second opinion. (This is called opinion shopping.)

5.16 This is acceptable, but not if the current auditors are **pressurised** into accepting the (more favourable) second opinion. To avoid such a situation there should be constant communication between both firms of auditors.

5.17 The second firm of auditors has a professional duty to seek permission for an approach to the current auditors from the client. Without such communication, the second opinion may be formed negligently.

5.18 This is because the second opinion may be formed on the incorrect facts or inadequate evidence unless all the facts have been requested from the initial auditor.

6 CONFIDENTIALITY **Pilot Paper**

6.1 The ACCA give guidance relating to confidentiality in their *Statement 2: The Professional Duty of Confidence.*

6.2 A member acquiring information in the course of his professional work should not use, or appear to use, that information for his personal advantage or for the advantage of a third party.

6.3 A member must make clear to a client that he may only act for him if the client agrees to disclose in full to the member all information relevant to the engagement.

6.4 Where a member agrees to serve a client in a professional capacity both the member and the client should be aware that it is an implied term of that agreement that the member will not disclose the client's affairs to any other person save with the client's consent within the terms of certain recognised exceptions.

Recognised exceptions to the rule of confidence

> **ACCA Statement**
>
> **Obligatory disclosure.** If a member knows or suspects his client to have committed an offence of treason he is obliged to disclose all the information at his disposal to a competent authority. Local legislation may also require auditors to disclose other infringements.
>
> **Voluntary disclosure.** In certain cases voluntary disclosure may be made by the member where:
>
> - Disclosure is reasonably required to protect the member's interests

- Disclosure is required by process of law
- There is a public duty to disclose

6.5 IFAC extend this list in their guidance.

IFAC Code of Ethics

- To comply with technical standards and ethical requirements
- To comply with the quality review of a member or professional body
- To respond to an inquiry or investigation by a member body or regulatory body

Also, having decided that confidential information can be disclosed, accountants should consider:

- Whether all relevant facts are known and substantiated
- What type of communication is expected and to whom should it be addressed
- Whether the accountant will incur legal liability as a result of disclosure

6.6 If an ACCA member is requested to assist the police, the tax authorities or any other authority by providing information about a client's affairs in connection with enquiries being made he should enquire under what **statutory authority** the information is demanded

6.7 Unless he is satisfied that such statutory authority exists he should decline to give any information until he has obtained his client's authority. If the client's authority is not forthcoming and the demand for information is pressed, he should not accede unless advised to by a solicitor.

6.8 If an ACCA member knows or suspects that a client has committed a wrongful act he must give careful thought to his own position. He is under no obligation, even in a criminal matter (excluding treason and terrorist offences), to convey his information to a competent authority, but he must ensure that he has not prejudiced himself by, for example, relying on incorrect information.

6.9 However, it would be a criminal offence for a member to act positively, without lawful authority or reasonable excuse, in such a manner as to impede with intent the arrest or prosecution of a client whom he knows or believes to have committed an arrestable offence.

Disclosure in the public interest

6.10 The courts have never given a definition of 'the public interest'. This means that again, the issue is left to the judgement of the auditor. It is often therefore appropriate for the member to seek legal advice.

6.11 It is only appropriate for information to be disclosed to certain authorities, for example,

- The police
- The Financial Services Authority
- The Department of Trade and Industry

6.12 The ACCA guidance states that there are several factors that the member should take into account when deciding whether to make disclosure.

ACCA guidance

- The size of the amounts involved and the extent of likely financial damage
- Whether members of the public are likely to be affected
- The possibility or likelihood of repetition
- The reasons for the client's unwillingness to make disclosures to the authority
- The gravity of the matter
- Relevant legislation, accounting and auditing standards
- Any legal advice obtained

6.13 Under SAS 120, if auditors become aware of a suspected or actual instance of non-compliance with law and regulation which gives rise to a statutory right or duty to report, they should report it to the proper authority immediately.

7 AREAS OF CONTROVERSY: CONFIDENTIALITY

Conflict of interest

7.1 Conflicts of interest can arise when a firm has two or more audit clients, both of whom have reason to be unhappy that their auditors are also auditors to the other client.

7.2 This situation can arise when the clients are in direct competition with each other, particularly when the auditors have access to sensitive information, which is often the case.

7.3 This situation is difficult for an audit firm. Audit firms tend to claim that problems do not arise from these situations, as different teams of audit staff and engagement partners are used on the two audits. This helps to maintain independence and confidentiality with regard to the two clients.

7.4 However, clients often perceive these safeguards to be insufficient, and in such a situation, the audit firm might well face losing a substantial client.

7.5 Auditors often give their clients business advice unrelated to audit. In such a position, they may well become involved when clients are involved in issues such as:

- Share issues
- Takeovers

7.6 Neither situations is inherently wrong to an auditor to be in. The following things should be considered, however.

Share issues

7.7 Auditor firms should not underwrite an issue of shares to the public of a client they audit.

Takeovers

7.8 If the auditors are involved in the audits of both predator and target company, they must take care in a takeover situation. They should not:

- Be the principal advisors to either party
- Issue reports assessing the accounts of either party other than their audit report

7.9 If they find they possess material confidential information, they should contact the appropriate body or regulator.

Safeguards

Engagement letters

7.10 It is the duty of an auditor to ensure that he has an up to date engagement letter in place with each client, to ensure that the details of their relationship are clear to each party.

7.11 The auditor should make provision in their standard engagement letter for occasions when conflict between clients might arise, so that the issue has been raised with the client prior to any difficult circumstances arising. As mentioned below, this may avoid the firm having to rely on Chinese walls, which can be mistrusted by clients.

Chinese walls

7.12 In smaller firms, it is extremely hard to create safeguards of independence and confidentiality when there are two clients in competition with each other. Smaller firms may well have to resign themselves to losing one of their clients.

7.13 However, in larger firms, the safeguard that can be put in place is one which is referred to as 'Chinese Wall'.

7.14 This means that the audits are undertaken by different 'groups' of staff. The engagement partners would be different and all other audit staff are allowed to work on one of the audits only. This creates a theoretical wall in the firm, through which confidential information cannot penetrate.

7.15 The Chinese Wall concept often appears to be flimsy, and the case below cast doubt on the ability of accountants to rely on them.

Case example

Prince Jefri of Brunei

The facts: Prince Jefri of Brunei had been a client of KPMG and argues that its forensic department had a full knowledge of his finances. After KPMG's relationship with Prince Jefri ended, the firm were hired by the Brunei Investment Agency (BIA) to investigate the Sultanate's financial affairs. Prince Jefri argued that in effect that meant that KPMG would be investigating his affairs and that information obtained from the firm's previous dealings with himself might be given to the BIA.

Decision: Prince Jefri's claim was upheld. The House of Lords concluded that accountants were similar to solicitors in this respect, that they had a duty to ensure that the former client is not put at risk that confidential information obtained previously by the accountant could be used against him.

7.16 In this case, the Lords commented that large firms would have to introduce established organisational arrangements, including the physical separation of personnel, to protect former clients.

7.17 The judgement did however suggest that the courts might be more likely to believe that effective Chinese Walls were in place if different departments were involved with the different clients. The major problem in this case was that the forensic department was involved both times.

7.18 If consent has not been given by clients in a conflict situation, a Chinese wall may be effective providing the departments concerned are physically separated and there are strict procedures and monitoring in place. The Chinese wall needs to be part of the organisational culture.

7.19 Firms may be able to avoid the need for a Chinese wall in these circumstances by a paragraph in the engagement letter saying that information will be kept confidential expect as required by law, regulatory or ethical guidance, and the client permits the firm to take such steps as the firm thinks fit to preserve confidentiality.

Insider dealing

Knowledge brought forward

From Paper 2.2 *Corporate and Business Law* (old paper 2).

Insider dealing can be described as dealing in securities whilst in possession of insider information as an insider, the securities being price-affected by the information.

There are various anti-avoidance measures in legislation, including those relating to the disclosure of information to other parties. (Criminal Justice Act 1993).

7.20 Auditors can be seen as insiders in the context of insider dealing as they are privy to sensitive information which might price-affect the securities.

7.21 For auditors, the duty not to deal as an insider is an extension of their professional duty of confidence which they owe to clients. This duty of confidence does not just cover information passed to third parties but information used for personal gain.

7.22 Audit firms must take care that the insider dealing regulations are not breached for two reasons then, the law and their professional duties. Many firms insist that their staff sign forms each year which state that neither they nor any of their 'connected persons' have dealt in any client company shares.

Safeguard

Staff disclosure procedures

7.23 If such confirmations reveal that relationships do exist, the firm should lay down clear procedures for ensuring that the member of staff concerned is not involved in undertaking work for that client on behalf of the firm and that controls exist from preventing that member of staff from having access to the files on the client if considered prudent. Such restrictions can easily be set up in computer systems, for example.

Exam focus point

Ethics questions at this level are unlikely to require you to regurgitate all the rules. Rather, they will present scenarios in which you, as an auditor, must make an ethical judgement. Therefore you must be familiar enough with the guidelines to **apply** them to a scenario, and to **justify** your application.

Chapter roundup

- Accountants require an ethical code because they hold positions of trust, and people rely on them.
- Both ACCA and IFAC publish ethical guidelines. These are given in the format:
  - Fundamental principles
  - Detailed guidance
- You should be aware of ACCA's independence guidance from your studies for 2.6, *Audit and Internal Review.*
- The IFAC guidance is very similar to ACCA's. Major differences are:
  - Commissions
  - Former partners
  - Long association
  - Employing non-accountants
- There are various safeguards to audit independence, including:
  - Quality control policies and procedures
  - Audit rotation
  - Audit committees
- Some areas are particularly controversial with regard to auditor independence, either because the ethical guidance does not include them or because they are judgmental areas. Examples are:
  - Other services
  - Specialist valuations
  - Second opinions
- Both IFAC and ACCA recognise a duty of confidence and several exceptions to it. Exceptions include:
  - Obligatory disclosure (in suspicion of certain offences eg treason)
  - Voluntary disclosure (member's interests/process of law/public duty)
- ACCA gives further guidance on disclosure 'in the public interest'. Accountants should usually seek legal advice before making disclosures.
- Particularly controversial areas with regard to confidentiality are:
  - Conflict of interest
  - Insider dealing
- Safeguards relating to confidentiality include:
  - Engagement letters
  - Chinese walls
  - Staff disclosure policies

Quick quiz

1 List the four basic needs IFAC believe have to be met for accountants to reach the standard of performance required by the public.

(1) ________________

(2) ________________

(3) ________________

(4) ________________

2 Match the fundamental principle to the characteristic.

(a) Integrity

(b) Objectivity

(i) A professional accountant should be straightforward and honest in performing professional services.

(ii) A professional accountant should be fair and should not allow prejudice or bias, conflict or interest or influence of others to override objectivity.

3 Name four general threats to independence

(1) ________________

(2) ________________

(3) ________________

(4) ________________

4 Complete the definition.

Audit ________________ is when

- Either, the client ________________ auditors on a regular basis.
- Or, the audit engagement ________________ are ________________ between audit engagements.

5 List three drawbacks to audit rotation

(1) ________________

(2) ________________

(3) ________________

6 What is a specialist valuation?

7 Complete the following definition.

Insider dealing can be described as ________________ in ________________. Whilst in possession of ________________ ________________ as an insider, the securities being ________________ - ________________ by the information.

BPP PUBLISHING

Answers to quick quiz

1. (1) Credibility
   (2) Professionalism
   (3) Quality of service
   (4) Confidence
2. (a)(i), (b)(ii)
3. (1) Personal interests
   (2) Review of own work
   (3) Disputes
   (4) Intimidation
4. Rotation, change, staff, rotated
5. (1) Inconvenience to client staff
   (2) High recurring cost of first audit
   (3) Loss of respect and trust
6. They include:

   Actuarial valuation, valuation of intellectual property and brands, other intangible assets, property and unquoted investments
7. Dealing, securities, insider information, price-affected.

Now try the question below from the Exam Question bank

Number	Level	Marks	Time
1	Exam	15	27 mins

Chapter 2

CHANGES IN PROFESSIONAL APPOINTMENT

	Topic list	Syllabus reference
1	**Change in auditors**	**1(a)**
2	**Advertising and fees**	**2(b), (c)**
3	**Tendering**	**2(d)**
4	**Acceptance**	**1(a)**
5	**Agreeing terms**	**2(e)**
6	**Books and documents**	**1(a)**

Introduction

It is a commercial fact that companies change their auditors. The question that firms of auditors need to understand the answer to is; **why do companies change their auditors?** There could be any number of reasons. We shall examine some of the common reasons in this chapter. Some of the reasons are things the auditor can take steps to prevent, and others are out of his control.

Related to the fact that entities change their auditors is the fact that **many auditing firms advertise their services**. The ACCA have set out rules for their members who advertise their services. We shall examine these rules and the reasons behind them in Section 2.

As we will discover in section 1, the **audit fee** can be a very key item for an entity when it makes decisions about its auditors. We shall also give consideration to the audit fee in Section 3.

Determining the price to offer to potential clients can be a difficult process, but it is just one part of the whole process that is **tendering.** Audits are often put out to tender by companies. Several firms are requested to put together a presentation concerning why their firm is the best option to carry out the audit. We shall examine all the matters firms consider when tendering for an audit in Section 3.

Linked in with the tendering process is the process **of determining whether to accept the audit engagement** if it is offered. This issue will be considered at all stages of the tendering process, as more information and impressions of the potential client are obtained. The audit firm might refuse to tender in the first instance. In contrast, it might win the audit and then in the course of obtaining professional clearance discover a reason to decline the audit. This is discussed in Sections 4 and 5.

Lastly, if an audit is accepted, the questions surrounding the ownership of and access to **books and documents** arise for the outgoing and incoming auditors arise. The general issues surrounding books and documents are discussed in Section 6.

Study Guide

Section 2

Changes in professional appointments

- Discuss the reasons why entities change their auditors

- Explain the matters to be considered and the procedures which an audit firm/professional accountant should carry out before accepting new clients and new engagements
- Describe the procedures for agreeing terms of an engagement
- Outline the procedures for the transfer of books, papers and information following a new appointment

Books, documents and papers

- Explain the general principle governing the ownership of, and rights of access to, documents and papers
- Explain the legal right of lien and describe the circumstances in which is might be exercised
- Discuss the extent to which clients and third parties may have access to documents and papers

Section 6

Advertising, Publicity, Obtaining Professional Work and Fees

- Explain the need for guidance in these areas
- Illustrate the circumstances in which advertising is acceptable
- Discuss the restrictions on practice descriptions, the use of the ACCA logo and the names of practising firms
- Discuss the extent to which fees may be referred to in promotional material
- Outline the determinants of fee-setting and describe the bases on which fees and commissions may and may not be charged for services
- Discuss the problems involved in establishing and negotiating fees, etc

Tendering

- Describe the matters to be considered when a firm is invited to submit a proposal or fee quote for an audit
- Identify the information required for the proposal
- Outline the engagement proposal document (for both continuing and new clients)
- Suggest the criteria which might be used to evaluate tender received from audit firms
- Suggest reasons why audit fees may be lowered from the previous year's fees
- Describe 'lowballing' and discuss whether or not it impairs independence

Terms of engagement

- Explain the key issues which underlie the agreement of the scope and terms of an audit engagement with a client.

Exam guide

Ethics is a key topic area and many of the issues in this chapter are ethical. You could be faced with a change in appointment scenario in the exam.

1 CHANGE IN AUDITORS

1.1 It is an indisputable fact of life that companies change their auditors sometimes. Not all new clients of a firm are new businesses, some have decided to change from their previous auditors.

1.2 Obviously, it is often not in the interests of the auditor to lose his clients (although sometimes it may be). Therefore a key issue in practice management for auditors is to understand why companies change their auditors, so that, as far as they are able, they can seek to prevent it.

Why do companies change their auditors?

Question 1

Before you read the rest of this chapter, spend a minute thinking about the reasons that companies might change their auditors. You might want to shut the text and write them down and then compare them with the reasons that we give in the rest of this section.

Answer

Read through the rest of section 1 and compare your answers to ours.

1.3 The following diagram shows some of the more common reasons that companies might change their auditors.

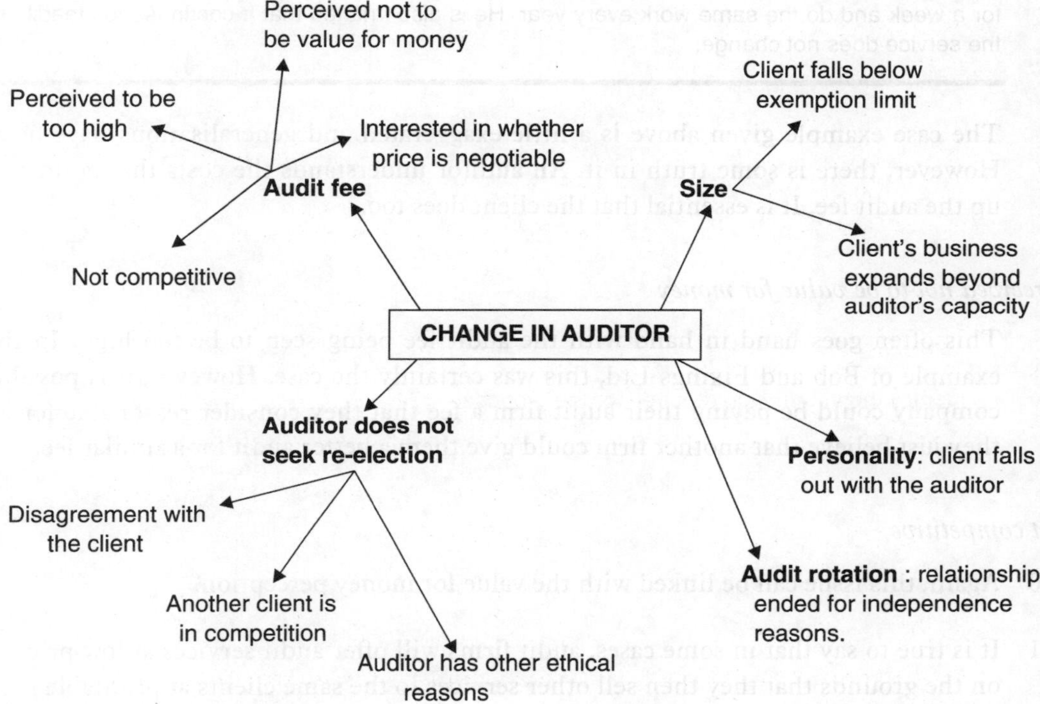

Audit fee

1.4 The audit fee can be a very **sensitive issue**. Audit is required by statute. Many people perceive that it has very little intrinsic value. However, when setting audit fees, auditors must take account of the fact that clients may hold this opinion.

1.5 Setting fees will be discussed later in the chapter. Here, we shall explore some of the fee related reasons that companies change their auditors.

Perceived to be too high

1.6 This is a common reason for auditors being changed. It is strongly linked to people's perception that audit has no intrinsic value. If directors of a company believe that audit is a necessary evil, they will seek to obtain it for as little money as they can.

1.7 Much of the 'value', in cost terms, of an audit is carried out away from a client's premises. This is because the most expensive audit staff (managers and partners) often do not carry out their audit work on site. If the client does not understand this, the following sort of situation may arise.

Case example

Bob is the owner-manager of Fixings Ltd, a small business which manufactures metal fixings. It has a turnover of £4.5 million and the auditors come in for the second week of October every year. Every year a different senior is in charge and he or she asks similar questions to the ones asked the previous year, because the business rarely changes and the audit is low risk. The partner and manager rarely attend the audit itself because it is not considered cost effective or necessary to do so.

Bob's audit fee was set at £4,500 five years ago when the business was incorporated for tax and inheritance reasons, and has gone up at three percent a year ever since. It now stands at £5,200. During that time, he has paid the same firm £1,200 a year to organise his tax return and deal with the Inland Revenue on his behalf. He considers this service far more valuable as he has no understanding of tax issues and is exceedingly nervous of an Inland Revenue inspection.

Bob cannot understand how the audit fee is four times the size of the tax fee when the auditors attend for a week and do the same work every year. He is also irritated that it continues to steadily rise while the service does not change.

1.8 The case example given above is a little exaggerated and generalisations have been made. However, there is some truth in it. An auditor understands the costs that go in to making up the audit fee. It is essential that the client does too.

Perceived not to be value for money

1.9 This often goes hand in hand with the audit fee being seen to be too high. In the above example of Bob and Fixings Ltd, this was certainly the case. However, it is possible that a company could be paying their audit firm a fee that they consider reasonable for an audit, they just believe that another firm could give them a better audit for a similar fee.

Not competitive

1.10 Again, this issue can be linked with the value for money perception.

1.11 It is true to say that in some cases, audit firms will offer audit services at low prices. This is on the grounds that they then sell other services to the same clients at profitable prices. It is through practices like this that the problem of low-balling can arise. You should remember the issue of low-balling from your 2.6 studies.

1.12 In such conditions, a well-set audit fee may not be competitive even if it is a reasonable fee for the service provided.

Interest in whether price is negotiable

1.13 This reason may be linked to all of the above fee-related issues, or it may just arise out of interest on the client's part.

1.14 It costs the client very little except some time on his part to put his audit out to tender. He might even do this with every intention of keeping the present auditor.

1.15 This would for his purposes give him more insight into how competitive the fee he is paying his auditor is, and keep his auditor 'honest', in that he will have to justify his fee and risk it being higher than competitors in the tender.

1.16 The by-product might be that he received a competitive tender which offered him far more than he receives from his current auditor and changes his auditor anyway. It could also mean that, when forced to justify his position, the current auditor reassesses his service and comes up with a far more competitive deal.

The auditor does not seek re-election

1.17 Another key reason for the auditor changing is that the auditor chooses not to stand for election for another year. You should be familiar with many of the reasons behind this:

- There could be ethical reasons behind the auditor choosing not to stand
- The auditor might have to resign for reasons of competition between clients
- The auditor might disagree with the client over accounting policies
- The auditor might not want to reduce his audit fee

Question 2

Name three ethical reasons why an auditor might not seek re-election or might resign, explaining the nature of the problem and the reasoning behind the resignation.

Answer

As you know from your studies at 2.6 *Audit and Internal Review* (old paper 6) and from studying Chapter 1, there are countless ethical issues that could have arisen. Here are some common ones. Refer to Chapter 1 if you have included one that does not appear here.

(a) **Fee level**

The audit fee which is necessary to carry out the audit at a profit may have reached a level which is inappropriate according to the ACCA's guidance on fee levels. If the audit fee constituted more than 15% of the total practice income, this would be considered to be an independence problem. This is because the audit opinion might be influenced by a fear of losing the client.

In such a situation, or if the practice had a large client below the limits but whose forecast suggested future growth, it might be necessary for the auditor to end the relationship to ensure that he did not become dependent on the client.

(b) **Integrity of management**

The auditor might feel that he has reason to doubt the integrity of management. There are many reasons why this could be the case. It could be as a result of a breakdown in relationship, or an unproven suspected fraud.

However, if the auditor does not feel that the client is trustworthy he should not continue his relationship with him. This is suggested by revised SAS 240 *Quality control for audit work*, which states that if the auditor becomes aware of issues which would have lead him not to accept appointment in the first place, he should resign.

(c) **Other services**

The auditor may offer a number of services to the client. He may be offered some lucrative consultancy work by the client which he wants to undertake, but he feels that the independence of the audit will be severely affected by the provision of the consultancy work because of the heavy involvement that means he will have in the client's business.

As the audit fee is substantially lower than the fees associated with the consultancy work and the auditor is trying to develop his business advice department, he may decide to resign from the audit to take on the consultancy.

Size of the company

1.18 This can be a major reason for a change in auditors. There are two key reasons, one of which has been touched on already.

- Client experiences rapid growth to the point where the audit is no longer practicable for the auditor
- Client retrenches or restructures in such a way that it no longer needs a statutory audit and refuses the option of an independent professional review.

1.19 In the first instance, the auditor may no longer be able to provide the audit for several reasons:

- Insufficient resources
- Staff
- Time
- Fee level issue

1.20 In the second instance, the client has chosen no longer to take advantage of the audit.

1.21 In either situation, there is little that the auditor can do to prevent losing the work.

Other reasons

1.22 These reasons may have been touched on in relation to the other reasons given above. We shall consider them briefly here.

Personality

1.23 For many small owner-managed companies, audit is almost a personal service. The relationship between such a client and auditor may be strongly based on personality, and if relationships break down, it may be necessary for the audit relationship to discontinue.

1.24 Personality may not be such an issue for bigger entities and audit firms where the audit engagement partner could be transferred if required, while the audit stayed within the firm.

Audit rotation

1.25 Audit rotation was discussed in Chapter 1 as a safeguard to audit independence. By its nature, audit rotation may sometimes mean that the audit is moved from one firm to another.

Exam focus point

From the nature of the issues raised above, it is clear that some of them will affect small firms and not larger ones and some will more pre-dominantly affect larger ones. You should bear that in mind when approaching exam questions, and as usual, apply common sense.

Question 3

(a) Of the reasons for a change in auditors given above in paragraphs 1.4 – 1.25, which do you feel that an auditor may have control over and which he can therefore guard against? Ignore the cases when the auditor does not seek re-election or resigns.

(b) What should the auditor do to guard against the issues you have identified in part (a)?

Answer

(a) **Issues auditor may have control over**

There are two key issues identified above that an auditor may have some control over:

(i) **Fees**

- Perception
- Competitiveness

(ii) **Personality**

(b) **Actions to guard against issues arising**

(i) With regard to fees, the auditor can ensure that the audit is conducted in such a way as to foster the perception that the audit is good value for the fee. This can be done by encouraging the attitude of audit staff and ensuring that a professional manner is always maintained. It also requires a constant awareness by staff of the need to add value, and to ensure that the audit provides more of a service than fulfilling a statutory requirement. This can be achieved by offering relevant advice to the client as a by-product of the audit, predominantly through the report to management, but also as an integral part of the culture of the audit.

(ii) Also with regard to fees, the auditor can ensure he is competitive in the first instance, by setting reasonable fees and in the second instance by conducting research into what his competitors charge. As companies have to file accounts and the audit fee must be disclosed, this is readily available information.

(iii) Personality is obviously not an issue that an auditor can legislate against. However, part of an auditor's professionalism is to ensure that if personality problems arise, they are handled sensitively and they arise only due to issues on the side of the client.

If serious conflict arise, firms should have a procedure for rotating audits between audit partners.

---

2 ADVERTISING AND FEES

2.1 Auditors are in business, and in business it is necessary to advertise. However, accountants are professional people and they operate in work which people rely on. It is important therefore that his advertisements do not project an image that is inconsistent with that.

2.2 ACCA give guidance about advertising in their *Statement 3: Advertising, Publicity and Obtaining Professional work*. In general, the ACCA allow members to advertise their work in any way they see fit, in other words, it is a matter of judgement for the member.

2.3 The above is subject to the following general rule:

> The medium used to advertise **should not reflect adversely** on the member, ACCA or the accountancy profession.

2.4 The guidance on the next page is also given.

Advertisements and promotional material should **not**:

- Discredit the services offered by others whether by claiming superiority for the member's or firm's own services or otherwise
- Be misleading, either directly or by implication
- Fall short of the requirements of the British Code of Advertising Practice and the IBA Code of Advertising Standards and Practices, including
  - Legality
  - Decency
  - Clarity
  - Honesty
  - Truthfulness

Fees

2.5 Three issues arise with regard to fees:

- Referring to fees in promotional material
- Commissions
- Setting fees and negotiating fees

2.6 The last two issues are inter-related and are also closely connected with tendering, which is discussed in the next section.

Advertising fees

2.7 The fact that it is difficult to explain the service represented by a single fee in the context of an advertisement and that **confusion might arise as to what a potential client might expect to receive in return for that fee** means that it is seldom appropriate to include information about fees in short advertisements.

2.8 In longer advertisements, where reference is made to fees in promotional material, the **basis** on which those fees are calculated, hourly and other charging rates etc, **should be clearly stated.**

2.9 The key issue to remember with regard to advertising fees is that the **greatest care should be taken to not mislead potential clients.**

2.10 It is appropriate to advertise free consultations to discuss fee issues. This free consultation will allow fees to be explained, thus avoiding the risk of confusion.

2.11 It is inappropriate to advertise discounts on existing fees.

Setting and negotiating fees

2.12 As this is a key part of the tendering process, this is discussed below in Section 3.

Commissions

2.13 Commissions were discussed in Chapter 1 as part of the IFAC ethical guidance.

2.14 ACCA includes guidance on commissions as part of their Statement 3. ACCA members are allowed to offer commission (and by implication receive commission) for introducing clients from the following people:

- An employee of the member
- Another public accountant

2.15 The reason given behind this is that it is **only appropriate to deal in commissions with people who are subject to similar ethical requirements** as you. This results in independence not being affected.

Use of the ACCA logo

2.16 Members of the ACCA may be either associates or fellows. In which case they are allowed to use the designatory letters ACCA or FCCA behind their name.

2.17 A firm may describe itself as a firm of 'Chartered Certified Accountants' where:

- At least half of the partners are ACCA members, and
- Those partners hold at least 51% of voting rights under the partnership agreement

2.18 A firm in which all the partners are Chartered Certified Accountants may use the description 'Members of the Association of Chartered Certified Accountants'.

2.19 A firm which holds a firm's auditing certificate from ACCA may describe themselves as Registered Auditors.

Question 4

Felicity Carr and Frank Harrison both qualified as chartered certified accountants five years ago. They have now decided to set up in practice together. Their new firm holds an auditing certificate from ACCA and they intend to undertake small audits and some tax work. They will charge themselves out at £100 per hour initially. They will operate from Frank's home. They are a little rusty on the rules concerning advertising and obtaining professional work and so have asked you to advise them.

They have decided to call their practice Harrison Carr and to advertise in the local paper. As they are launching themselves, they have decided to take out a full page advertisement one week and then run a series of smaller adverts in the future. They have also decided to advertise in a local business newspaper.

They seek your advise generally on the issue of advertising, and particularly with regard to fees. They would also like specific guidance about the adverts they are planning to run in the paper, including guidance on how they may describe the firm.

Answer

General guidance on advertising

Generally members may not advertise in a manner that reflects adversely on themselves and their profession. This means that they should consider the quality of the paper they intend to advertise in. The local paper is appropriate. They should also ensure that they do not discredit the services offered by others in their advert.

Advertising fees

The key issue of importance when advertising fees is to ensure that the reference to fees is not misleading. Generally, it is seldom appropriate to mention fees on a small advert.

Description of firm

As both partners are chartered certified accountants it is acceptable to advertise the firm as being a member of the association of chartered certified accountants. They may also describe themselves as registered auditors.

The proposed advertisements

While they are planning a larger advert followed by several smaller ones, it may still not be appropriate to mention fees. This is because while they could refer to charge out rates, it would be impossible in the paper to describe how much each service would cost without estimating the time jobs would take. It is impossible to generalise such matters and the reference to fees could therefore be misleading.

It would be more appropriate to advertise that they will give free consultations to discuss fees. They may include all the details given above, their name, the membership of the ACCA and their registered auditor status.

3 TENDERING — Pilot Paper

Approach

3.1 A firm puts together a tender if

- They have been approached by a prospective client, and
- They have decided that they are capable of doing the work for a reasonable fee.

3.2 When approached to tender, the auditor has to consider whether he wants to do the work. You should be aware of all the ethical considerations that would go into this decision. The auditor will also have to consider

- Fees
- Practical issues

Fees

3.3 Determining if the job could be done for a reasonable price will involve a substantial number of estimates. The key estimate will be how long the firm considers it will take to do the work. This will involve meeting with the prospective client to discuss their business and systems and making the estimate from there.

3.4 The first stage of setting the fee is therefore to ascertain **what the job will involve**. The job should be broken into its respective parts, for example, audit and tax, or if it is a complex and/or pure audit, what aspects of the job would be undertaken by what level staff.

3.5 The second stage is closely linked with the first, therefore. It involves **ascertaining which staff**, or which level of staff, **will be involved** and in what proportions they will be involved.

3.6 Once estimates have been made of how long the work will take and what level of expertise is needed in each area, **the firm's standard charge out rates can be applied** to that information, and a **fee estimated.**

3.7 Clearly, it is **commercially vital** that the estimates of time and costs are **reasonable**, or the audit firm will be seeking to undertake the work at a loss. However, it is also ethically important that the fee estimate is reasonable, or the result will be that the client is being misled about the sustainable fee level.

Lowballing

3.8 Problems can arise when auditing firms appear to be charging less than this, or at least less than the 'market rate' for the audit. The practice of undercutting, usually at tender for the audit of large companies, has been called **lowballing**. In other cases, the audit fee has been reduced even though the auditors have remained the same. The problem here is that, if the audit is being performed for less than it is actually worth, then the auditors' independence is called into question.

3.9 This is always going to be a topical debate, but in terms of negotiating the audit fee the following factors need to be taken into account.

(a) The audit is perceived to have a fluctuating 'market price' as any other commodity or service. In a recession, prices would be expected to fall as companies aim to cut costs everywhere, and as auditors chase less work (supply falls). Audit firms are also reducing staffing levels and their own overhead costs should be lower.

(b) Companies can **reduce external audit costs** through various legitimate measures:

- Extending the size and function of internal audit
- Reducing the number of different audit firms used world-wide
- Selling off subsidiary companies leaving a simplified group structure to audit
- The tender process itself simply makes auditors more competitive
- Exchange rate fluctuations in audit fees

(c) Auditing firms have increased productivity, partly through the use of more sophisticated information technology techniques in auditing.

3.10 The ACCA's guidance on quotations states that it is **not improper** to secure work by **quoting a lower fee** so long as the **client has not been misled** about the level of work that the fee represents.

3.11 In the event of investigations into allegations of unsatisfactory work, the level of fees would be considered with regard to member's conduct with reference to the ethical guidelines.

Practical issues

3.12 The firm will have to consider the practical points arising from the approach. Common considerations include:

- Does the proposed timetable for the work fit with the current work plan?
- Does the firm have suitable personnel available?
- Where will the work be performed and is it accessible/cost effective?
- Are (non-accounting) specialist skills necessary?
- Will staff need further training to do the work?
- If so, what is the cost of that further training?

Information required

3.13 Certain information will be required to put together a proposal document. This has already been touched on briefly, when discussing the audit fee. It is likely that audit staff would have to have a meeting with the prospective client to discuss the following issues:

- What the client requires from the audit firm, for example:
  - Audit
  - Number of visits (interim and final)
  - Tax work
- What the future plans of the entity are, for example:
  - Is it planning float in the near future
  - Do they anticipate growth, or diversification

- Whether the entity is seeking its first auditors and needs an explanation of audit
- Whether the entity is seeking to change its auditors
- If the entity is changing its auditors, why they are changing them

Content of an audit proposal

3.14 An audit proposal, or tender, does not have a set format. The prospective client will indicate the format that he wants the tender to take. This may be merely in document form, or could be a presentation by members of the audit firm.

3.15 Although each tender will be tailored to the individual circumstances, there are some matters which are likely to be covered in every one. These are set out below.

Matters to be included in audit proposal
• The fee, and how it has been calculated
• An assessment of the needs of the prospective client
• An outline of how the firm intends to meet those needs
• The assumptions made to support that proposal
• The proposed approach to the engagement
• A brief outline of the firm
• An outline of the key staff involved

3.16 If the tender is being submitted to an **existing client**, some of those details will be unnecessary. However, if it is a competitive tender, the firm should ensure they submit a comparable tender, even if some of the details are already known to the client.

3.17 This is because the tender must be **comparable** to competitors and must appear professional.

Evaluation of the tender

3.18 Each company will have its own criteria for what it wants from a firm of auditors. This means that there are no hard and fast rules about how a tender will be evaluated. However, there are some general points to bear in mind when putting together a proposal.

Evaluation factors	
Fee	The fee, as discussed earlier, **can be the most important factor** for people assessing tenders. It is possible that a reader might look at the fee and decide not to continue reading the tender, despite the rest of the content.
Professionalism	Auditors provide a **professional service** and the first impressions a prospective client may have of the firm are the staff involved with the proposal and the tender document itself. It is therefore vital that the professionalism which should mark the audit relationship is clear.
Proposed approach	An audit can cause a disruption to the ordinary course of a business, particularly in the finance department. The client might be seeking the **least disruptive approach**. This might mean they look for an audit will the shortest number of proposed days on site.

Personal service	It is important that the relationship between the auditors and the management of the entity is good and the client perceives that they are getting value for money. It is important to highlight key staff and to **foster relationships** with management from the outset of a relationship, and this means during the tender process.

4 ACCEPTANCE

4.1 There are a number of ethical procedures associated with accepting engagements which you have studied previously. The auditor will also have to consider the requirements of SAS 240 *Quality control for audit work*.

Knowledge brought forward

From paper 2.6 *Audit and Internal Review* (old paper 6)

Procedures before accepting nomination

(a) Ensure that there are **no ethical issues** which are a **barrier** to accepting nomination. This is the key requirement of SAS 240.

(b) Ensure that the auditor is **professionally qualified** to act and that there are no legal or technical barriers.

(c) Ensure that the existing **resources** are **adequate** in terms of staff, expertise and time.

(d) Obtain **references for the directors** if they are not known personally to the audit firm.

(e) **Consult the previous auditors** to ensure that there are not any reasons behind the vacancy which the new auditors ought to know. This is also a courtesy to the previous auditors.

Procedures after accepting nomination

(a) **Ensure** that the **outgoing auditors' removal** or **resignation** has been **properly conducted** in accordance with the Companies Act 1985.

The new auditors should see a valid notice of the outgoing auditors' resignation (under s 392 CA 1985), or confirm that the outgoing auditors were properly removed (under s 391 CA 1985).

(b) **Ensure** that the **new auditors' appointment is valid.** The new auditors should obtain a copy of the resolution passed at the general meeting appointing them as the company's auditors.

(c) Set up and **submit a letter of engagement** to the directors of the company (see below).

Question 4

You are a partner in Hamlyn, Jones and Co, a firm of Chartered Certified Accountants. You have just successfully tendered for the audit of Lunch Limited, a chain of sandwich shops across West London. The tender opportunity was received cold, that is, the company and its officers are not known to the firm. The company has just been incorporated and has not previously had an audit. You are about ready to accept nomination.

(a) What procedures should you carry out prior to accepting nomination?

In the course of your acceptance procedures you received a reference from a business contact of yours concerning one of the five directors of Lunch Limited, Mr V Loud. It stated that your business contact had done some personal tax work for Mr Loud ten years previously, when he had found Mr Loud to be difficult to keep in contact with, slow to provide information and he had suspected Mr Loud of being economical with the truth when it came to his tax affairs. As a result of this distrust, he had ceased to carry out work for him.

(b) What effect will do you think this reference will have on your accepting nomination for this audit?

Answer

(a) The following procedures should be carried out:

- Ensure that I and my audit team are professionally qualified to act and there are no ethical barriers to my accepting nomination.
- Ensure that there are sufficient resources to enable my firm to carry out the audit.
- Obtain references about the directors as they are not known personally by me or anyone else in my firm.

(b) The auditor must use his professional judgement when considering the responses he gets to references concerning new clients. The guidance cannot legislate for all situations so it does not. In the circumstance given above there is no correct answer therefore, in practice an auditor would have to make a justified decision.

Matters to be considered

The reference raises **three issues** for the auditor considering accepting nomination.

- The issue that the director has been difficult to maintain a relationship with in the past
- The issue that the director was slow to provide information in the past
- The suspicion of a lack of integrity in relation to his tax affairs.

The auditor must **consider** these **in the light of several factors:**

- The length of time that has passed since the events
- What references which refer to the interim time say
- The difference between accepting a role of auditing a company and personal tax work
- The director's role in the company and therefore the audit
- The amount of control exercised by the director
  - Relationships with other directors
  - Influence

At this stage he **should not be considering** how highly he **value**s the **opinion** of the referee. That should have been considered before he sent the reference. At this stage he should only be considering the implications of the reference for his current decision.

Auditing a company is different from auditing personal affairs in terms of obtaining information and contacting personnel. In this case, the **key issue** is the question over the **integrity** of the director.

As we do not have information about interim references and details of the business arrangements it is difficult to give a definite answer to this issue. However, Mr Loud is likely to only have **limited control over decisions** of the entity being one of five directors, which might lead to the auditor deciding that the reference was insufficient to prevent him accepting nomination. If Mr Loud were the **finance director**, the auditor would be more inclined not to take the nomination.

Exam focus point

You can see from the answer above that there are no easy answers to ethical questions. You might be asked questions in the exam similar to the ones above as part of a scenario highlighting several ethical issues. It is not enough just to state the rules at this level, you must **explain** what the practical issues are and try to **draw conclusions** based on the facts you know. Once qualified, you may face issues like this in your working life and will have to make judgements like this in practice. That is what the exam is trying to imitate.

Client screening

4.2 Many audit firms have their own additional procedures when considering accepting nomination as auditors. They are likely to have a client acceptance checklist to assist them

in making the decision. An example of a client acceptance checklist is given in the appendix towards the back of this text.

5 AGREEING TERMS

5.1 It is important when entering into a contract to provide services to ensure that both parties fully understand what the agreed services are.

5.2 Misunderstanding could lead to a break down in the relationship, and eventually result in legal action being undertaken.

5.3 An auditor will outline the basis for the audit agreement in his tender to provide services. However, once he has accepted nomination, it is vital that the basis of his relationship is discussed with the new client and laid out in contractual form. This is the role of the **engagement letter**, which you should be familiar with.

Matters which should be clarified in the audit agreement

- **Responsibilities** of both parties
  - Auditor responsible for reporting on the financial statements to members
  - Directors have a statutory duty to maintain records and take responsibility for the financial statements
  - Directors are responsible for the detection and prevention of fraud
- **Fees**
  - Level
  - Billing and credit terms
  - Potential increases
- **Timing**
  - Audit timing

5.4 An example of an engagement letter is given in the appendix of this text. You should already be familiar with it. You should also be familiar with SAS 140 *Engagement letters* which sets out best practice concerning engagement letters.

5.5 In practice, the auditor and the new client will meet to negotiate the terms of the audit agreement, which the auditor will later clarify in the engagement letter. The first audit should not take place until the client has returned the engagement letter with an indication that he agrees to its terms.

Question 5

Look up SAS 140. It lists a series of matters which may be referred to in an engagement letter. What are they?

Answer

The SAS includes the following matters:

- Fees and billing arrangements
- Procedures in the case of complaints arising
- Reference to arrangements concerning the use of other auditors or experts, where applicable
- Reference to the extent of the use of the work of internal audit, where applicable
- Procedures to obtain information from the previous auditors, where applicable

- Any restriction on the liability of the auditor, if applicable
- Reference to the laws governing the agreement (if not obvious)
- Any further agreements between the auditor and the client, for example, for other work
- A timetable for the audit

Exam focus point

In exam questions you might be asked to discuss matters that an auditor in a particular scenario should discuss with his potential client, in order to come to an agreement about the audit. You should therefore be aware of this list of items, as well as the points made at para 5.3, and be prepared to identify which are relevant in any given circumstance.

6 BOOKS AND DOCUMENTS

6.1 As you know, **audit working papers are owned by the auditor**. In the event of auditors taking over an audit from another firm, they are **not entitled** to take over all the audit files that that firm has put together on the client.

6.2 The ACCA rules state that in order to ensure continuity of a client's affairs, the previous auditors must provide the new auditors will all the **reasonable carry-over information** they request, and they should do this **promptly**.

6.3 The previous auditor should ensure that he transfers all the books and documents belonging to the client to the new auditors without delay.

6.4 The previous auditor is allowed to keep the books only where he is entitled to exercise a **lien**.

The right of lien

KEY TERM

A **lien** is a creditor's right to retain possession of a debtor's property until the debtor pays what is owed to the creditor.

6.5 If the previous auditor is still owed fees by the client, he may have a right to exercise a lien over some of the client's books. General liens over property can rarely be established. However, it may be possible for an auditor to have a particular lien when a debtor owes a debt specifically in respect of that property.

6.6 A right of particular lien will only exist where the following conditions are fulfilled.

- The documents must be the property of the client itself (not a closely related third party)
- The documents must have come into the member's possession by proper means
- The work must have been done and a fee note rendered in respect of it
- The fee must relate to the retained documents

Third party rights to information

6.7 As discussed in Chapter 1, the auditor owes a duty of confidentiality to the client. This means that documents containing information about the client should not be given to third parties unless:

- The client agrees to the disclosure before it is made
- Disclosure is required by statute or court order
- Disclosure is otherwise in accordance with the rules of professional conduct

6.8 These rules on disclosure are closely connected to the rules on confidentiality.

Client rights to information

6.9 **Audit working papers** are the property of the auditor and as such, the **client has no right of access to them**. The member may allow the client access to the working papers if he so chooses.

6.10 However, the position is more complicated when the work undertaken is something other than audit. For example, if the accountant puts together the **financial statements** on behalf of the client, those financial statements will belong to the client.

6.11 With tax work, documents created in carrying out **tax compliance work** will belong to the client.

Chapter roundup

- There are many reasons why companies might change their auditor. Common reasons include:
  - Audit fee
  - Auditor not seeking re-election
  - Size of company
- ACCA give guidance on obtaining professional work. The general rule is:
  - The medium used should not reflect adversely on the member, ACCA or the accountancy profession
- Care must be taken when advertising fees. It is generally inappropriate to advertise fees as it might cause misunderstandings
- ACCA only allows members to deal in commissions from fellow accountants
- When approaching a tender, the auditor must consider:
  - Fees
  - Practical issues
- They will need to obtain certain information from the company in order to make their tender relevant
- The following matters should usually be included in an audit proposal
  - Fee and its basis
  - Needs assessment/relevant plan and approach
  - Outline of form and key staff
  - Assumptions made

- You should be aware of acceptance procedure from your work at 2.6, *Audit and Internal Review* (old paper 6)
- Certain issues must be agreed when an audit is accepted, including:
  - Responsibilities of both parties
  - Fees
  - Audit timing
- This is traditionally done in an audit engagement letter
- You should be aware of who owns and his rights to the books and papers an auditor comes into contact with during the course of this work

Quick quiz

1 Name three reasons why an auditor might not seek re-election.

(1) ______________

(2) ______________

(3) ______________

2 Fill in the blanks

Advertising and promotional material should not:

- ____________________ the service offered ______ ____________________
- Be ______________, either directly or by implication
- Fall short of the requirements of the ____________ ______________ ____ ____________ ____________________

3 Why should accountants not usually advertise fees?

4 List five practical issues that an auditor should consider when approaching a tender.

(1) ______________

(2) ______________

(3) ______________

(4) ______________

(5) ______________

5 Draw a diagram showing the key stages in a tender, explaining what happens at each stage.

6 List five matters which may be referred to in an engagement letter.

(1) ______________

(2) ______________

(3) ______________

(4) ______________

(5) ______________

Answers to quick quiz

1. (1) Ethical reasons (eg fees)
   (2) Another client in competition
   (3) Disagreement over accounting policy

2. Discredit, by others, misleading, British Code of Advertising Practice

3. The advert is unlikely to be detailed, and facts given about fees could mislead potential clients

4. (1) Does the timetable fit with current work plan?
   (2) Are suitable personnel available
   (3) Where will work be performed? Is it cost effective
   (4) Are specialist skills needed?
   (5) Will staff need further training? If so, what is the cost?

5.

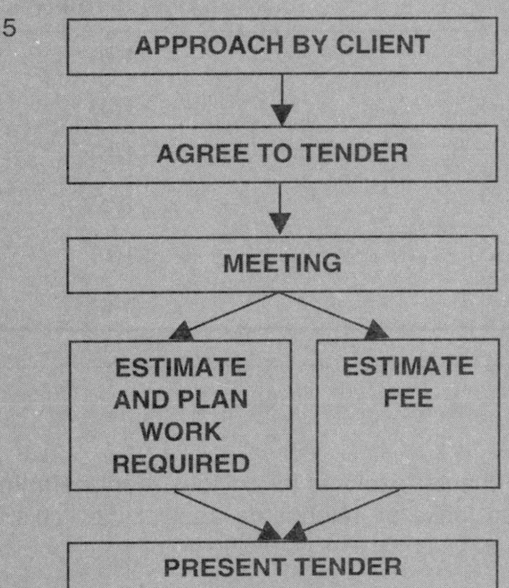

Auditor considers if it is possible to undertake work at a reasonable fee

Arrange meeting to obtain information prior to tender

Obtain knowledge of the business and the service required

Allocate potential staff to work plan and calculate fee by reference to standard charge out rates

This could be in the form of:

- Letter
- Report
- Presentation

6. See the answer to question 5 in the body of the chapter

Now try the question below from the Exam Question bank

Number	Level	Marks	Time
2	Exam	20	36 mins

Chapter 3

PROFESSIONAL RESPONSIBILITY AND LIABILITY

Introduction

Auditors have responsibilities to several parties. This chapter explores the various **responsibilities** and the **liability that can arise** out of them. It also looks at safeguards against the liabilities, particularly the issue of insurance, covered in Section 5.

Auditors have responsibilities to:

- The members to whom they report
- Some other readers of financial statements
- ACCA (in their role as accountants, not specifically auditors)
- Other members of the association

These responsibilities are explored in Sections 2, 3 and 4.

Critically, and contrary to widespread public belief, **auditors do not have a responsibility to detect and prevent fraud.** The responsibilities that auditors do have with regard to fraud and error are outlined in Section 1. Auditors are required to follow the guidance of SAS 110 *Fraud and error* in relation to this issue.

The auditors' responsibility to members and other readers of the accounts in tort and contract can give rise to **liability,** particularly in the event of **negligence.** Case law on this matter is complex and not wholly satisfactory. It results in auditors being liable to some readers and not others. However, **auditors' liability** is a dynamic issue in that it **evolves as cases are brought to court.**

There are some interesting **current developments** for auditors with regard to liability. The key issue is the introduction of **limited liability partnerships** into English law. This and other current issues pertaining to the topics covered in this chapter are outlined in section 6.

Study guide

Section 3

Fraud and Error

- Define and distinguish between the terms 'error', 'irregularity', 'fraud' and 'misstatement'
- Compare and contrast the respective responsibilities of management and auditors for fraud and error

- Explain how, why, when and to whom fraud and error should be reported and the circumstances in which the auditor should withdraw from an engagement
- Discuss the current and possible future role of auditors in preventing, detecting and reporting error and fraud

Professional liability

- Identify the circumstances in which auditors may have legal liability
- Describe the factors to determine whether or not an auditor is negligent in given situations
- Explain the other criteria for legal liability to be recognised (including 'due professional care' and 'proximity')
- Distinguish between liability to client and liability to third parties
- Comment on precedents of case law
- Identify and evaluate the practicability and effectiveness of ways in which liability may be restricted
- Discuss how the audit and other opinions may be affected by limiting audit liability
- Discuss the advantages and disadvantages of audit liability claims being settled out of court

Misconduct

- Explain and illustrate what is meant by professional misconduct
- Outline the penalties and sanctions which may be imposed by disciplinary bodies

Professional indemnity insurance

- Explain the terms professional indemnity insurance (PII) and fidelity guarantee insurance (FGI)
- Discuss arguments for and against mandatory cover.

Section 27

- Discuss the advantages and disadvantages of partnerships and incorporation of audit firms.
- Describe current developments in the limitations of auditors' liability and the practical ways in which the risk of litigation can be reduced.

Exam guide

Fraud is a key issue for auditors, particularly in the perception of the public. Remember also in the exam that for some 'other services' discussed in this paper, liability will not necessarily be the same as for **audit.** You should consider the information given in the question.

1 FRAUD AND ERROR

1.1 The incidence of financial fraud, particularly in a computer environment, is increasing and has been a central feature in a number of financial scandals in recent years.

1.2 There are some who would argue that the detection of fraud should be the auditors' principal function. This prevailing attitude clearly gives rise to a **public expectation** which is neither shared nor fulfilled by the profession.

1.3 SAS 110 *Fraud and error,* which is quite long and complicated, is covered briefly here.

Introduction

Auditors should plan and perform their audit procedures and evaluate and report the results thereof, recognising that fraud or error may materially affect the financial statements. (SAS 110.1)

The approach to be adopted by the auditors

When planning the audit the auditors should assess the risk that fraud or error may cause the financial statements to contain material misstatements. (SAS 110.2)

Based on their risk assessment, the auditors should design audit procedures so as to have a reasonable expectation of detecting misstatements arising from fraud or error which are material to the financial statements. (SAS 110.3)

Procedures when there is an indication that fraud or error may exist

When auditors become aware of information which indicates that fraud or error may exist, they should obtain an understanding of the nature of the event and the circumstances in which it has occurred, and sufficient other information to evaluate the possible effect on the financial statements. If the auditors believe that the indicated fraud or error could have a material effect on the financial statements, they should perform appropriate modified or additional procedures. (SAS 110.4)

When the auditors become aware of, or suspect that there may be, instances of error or fraudulent conduct, they should document their findings and, subject to any requirement to report them direct to a third party, discuss them with the appropriate level of management. (SAS 110.5)

The auditors should consider the implications of suspected or actual error or fraudulent conduct in relation to other aspects of the audit, particularly the reliability of management representations. (SAS 110.6)

Reporting to management

The auditors should as soon as practicable communicate their findings to the appropriate level of management, the board of directors or the audit committee if:

(a) they suspect or discover fraud, even if the potential effect on the financial statements is immaterial (save where SAS 110.12 applies); or

(b) material error is actually found to exist. (SAS 110.7)

Reporting to addressees of the auditors' report on the financial statements

Where the auditors conclude that the view given by the financial statements could be affected by a level of uncertainty concerning the consequences of a suspected or actual error or fraud which, in their opinion, is fundamental, they should include an explanatory paragraph referring to the matter in their report. (SAS 110.8)

Where the auditors conclude that a suspected or actual instance of fraud or error has a material effect on the financial statements and they disagree with the accounting treatment or with the extent, or the lack, of disclosure in the financial statements of the instance or of its consequences they should issue an adverse or qualified opinion. If the auditors are unable to determine whether fraud or error has occurred because of limitation in the scope of their work, they should issue a disclaimer or a qualified opinion. (SAS 110.9)

Reporting to third parties

Where the auditors become aware of a suspected or actual instance of fraud they should:

(a) consider whether the matter may be one that ought to be reported to a proper authority in the public interest; and where this is the case

(b) except in the circumstances covered in SAS 110.12, discuss the matter with the board of directors, including any audit committee. (SAS 110.10)

Where having considered any views expressed on behalf of the entity and in the light of any legal advice obtained, the auditors conclude that the matter ought to be reported to an appropriate authority in the public interest, they should notify the directors in writing of their view and, if the entity does not voluntarily do so itself or is unable to provide evidence that the matter has been reported, they should report it themselves. (SAS 110.11)

When a suspected or actual instance of fraud casts doubt on the integrity of the directors auditors should make a report direct to a proper authority in the public interest without delay and without informing the directors in advance. SAS 110.12)

Overseas activities

Where any of the activities of a company or group are carried on outside the United Kingdom or the Republic of Ireland, the auditors should take steps to ensure that the audit work in relation to the detection and reporting of any fraud and error is planned and carried out in accordance with the requirements of this SAS. (SAS 110.13)

KEY TERMS

Fraud comprises both the use of deception to obtain an unjust or illegal financial advantage, and intentional misrepresentation by management, employees or third parties.

Error is an unintentional mistake.

An **irregularity** is something which is contrary to a rule, standard or convention.

A **misstatement** is something stated wrongly or inaccurately.

Responsibility

1.4 The SAS emphasises that it is the **responsibility** of the **directors** to take reasonable steps to **prevent** and **detect fraud.**

Risk factors

1.5 In an appendix to the SAS there is a list of examples of conditions or events which may increase the risk of either fraud or error or both.

FRAUD AND ERROR	
Previous experience or incidents which call into question the integrity or competence of management	Management dominated by one person (or a small group) and no effective oversight board or committee Complex corporate structure where complexity does not seem to be warranted High turnover rate of key accounting and financial personnel Personnel (key or otherwise) not taking holidays Significant and prolonged under-staffing of the accounting department Frequent changes of legal advisors or auditors
Particular financial reporting pressures within an entity	Industry volatility Inadequate working capital due to declining profits or too rapid expansion Deteriorating quality of earnings, for example increased risk taking with respect to credit sales, changes in business practice or selection of accounting policy alternatives that improve income The entity needs a rising profit trend to support the market price of its shares due to a contemplated public offering, a takeover or other reason

FRAUD AND ERROR

	Significant investment in an industry or product line noted for rapid change
	Pressure on accounting personnel to complete financial statements in an unreasonably short period of time
	Dominant owner-management
	Performance-based remuneration
Weaknesses in the design and operation of the accounting and internal controls system	A weak control environment within the entity
	Systems that, in their design, are inadequate to give reasonable assurance of preventing or detecting error or fraud
	Inadequate segregation of responsibilities in relation to functions involving the handling, recording or controlling of the entity's assets
	Indications that internal financial information is unreliable
	Evidence that internal controls have been overridden by management
	Ineffective monitoring of the operation of system which allows control overrides, breakdown or weakness to continue without proper corrective action
	Continuing failure to correct major weakness in internal control where such corrections are practicable and cost effective
Unusual transactions	Unusual transactions, especially near the year end, that have a significant effect on earnings
	Complex transactions or accounting treatments
	Unusual transactions with related parties
	Payments for services (for example to lawyers, consultants or agents) that appear excessive in relation to the services provided
Problems in obtaining sufficient appropriate audit evidence	Inadequate records, for example incomplete files, excessive adjustments to accounting records, transactions not recorded in accordance with normal procedures and out-of-balance control accounts
	Inadequate documentation of transactions, such as lack of proper authorisation, supporting documents not available and alternation to documents (any of these documentation problems assume greater significance when they relate to large or unusual transactions)
	An excessive number of differences between accounting records and third party confirmations, conflicting audit evidence and unexplainable changes in operating ratios
	Evasive, delayed or unreasonable responses by management to audit inquires
	Inappropriate attitude of management to the conduct of the audit, eg time pressure, scope limitation and other constraints

Some factors unique to an information systems environment which relate to the conditions and events described above	Inability to extract information from computer files due to lack of, or non-current, documentation of record contents or programs Large numbers of program changes that are not documented, approved and tested Inadequate overall balancing of computer transactions and data bases to the financial accounts

Reporting

1.6 The SAS highlights three classes of people whom the auditor might have to report fraud and error to in particular circumstances. The table below shows the reporting requirements.

REPORTING REQUIREMENTS OF SAS 110	
Reporting to management	If the auditors suspect or detect any fraud (even if immaterial) or if a material error is discovered, as soon as they can they should tell • The appropriate level of management, or • The board of directors, or • The audit committee
Reporting to members	In terms of the audit opinion given on the financial statements, if the auditor feels that the financial statements are affected by a fraud or error, he should **qualify his report** accordingly.
Reporting to third parties	This was discussed in chapter 1 in relation to the public interest. When the auditors discover or suspect a fraud they should consider whether it is in the **public interest** to disclose it. They should **discuss** disclosing the matter to third parties with the **directors** and request that they make the appropriate disclosure. If the directors do not disclose the matter, the auditors should. When a suspected or actual instance of fraud **casts doubt on the integrity of management,** the auditors should report the matter without informing the directors. (In the latter case, the auditors would in practice seek legal advice to ensure that they were not breaching their ethical duties.)

Question 1

The judge in a US court ruling has drawn a distinction between fraud on behalf of the company (such as by management) and fraud against the company (by a single employee).

Required

(a) Discuss what responsibility auditors in the UK have to detect fraud and comment on whether you consider there is a greater expectation for him to detect 'management' fraud or 'employee' fraud.

(b) Outline how the auditors might conduct their audit in the light of this responsibility.

Answer

(a) The primary responsibility for the prevention and detection of fraud and irregularities rests with management. This responsibility may be partly discharged by the institution of an adequate system of internal control including, for example, authorisation controls and controls covering segregation of duties.

The auditors' duties do not require them specifically to search for fraud unless required by statute or the specific terms of their engagement.

However, the auditors should recognise the possibility of material irregularities or frauds which could, unless adequately disclosed, distort the results or state of affairs shown by the financial statements. SAS 110 *Fraud and error* states: 'Auditors should plan and perform their audit procedures and evaluate and report the results thereof, recognising that fraud or error may materially affect the financial statements'.

Accordingly, in obtaining sufficient appropriate audit evidence to afford a reasonable basis of support for their report, the auditors seek reasonable assurance, through the application of procedures that comply with auditing standards, that frauds or irregularities which may be material to the financial statements have not occurred or that, if they have occurred, they are either corrected or properly accounted for in the financial statements.

The auditing standards do not distinguish 'employee' and 'management' fraud; the auditors must be able to recognise the possibility of either fraud type where the effect of the fraud may be material. The characteristics of the two categories of fraud are as follows.

Employee fraud involves theft, misappropriation or embezzlement of the enterprise's funds, usually in the form of cash or other readily realisable assets such as stock or fixed assets.

Management fraud often involves the manipulation of the records and the accounts (for example by 'window dressing'), typically by the enterprise's senior officers with a view to benefiting in some indirect way.

(b) **Employee frauds**

Employee frauds are more likely to be encountered where internal controls are weak. When evaluating controls the auditors will need to place special emphasis on the following control aspects:

- Segregation of duties
- Authorisation (particularly of expense items and new ledger accounts)
- Completeness and accuracy of accounting data
- Safeguard procedures (for example, signing cheques)
- Comprehensiveness of controls (for example, including all relevant sub-systems)
- Custody arrangements (cash, portable fixed assets)

In addition, where accounting procedures are computerised, the auditors should be concerned to ensure that a lack of computer controls cannot be exploited to suppress evidence that an irregularity may exist or indeed to allow an irregularity to occur.

When carrying out their detailed audit testing they could discover circumstances that are indicative of employee fraud. Examples of such circumstances include:

- Missing vouchers or documents, inadequate accounting records
- Evidence of falsified documents
- Unsatisfactory explanations
- Figures, trends or results which do not accord with expectations
- Unexplained items on reconciliations or suspense accounts
- Evidence of disputes
- Evidence of unduly lavish life styles by employees
- Unusual investment of funds held in fiduciary capacity
- Evidence that the system of internal control is not operating as intended

The auditors' programme of work needs to be sufficiently flexible to follow up any such points arising and any irregularities or frauds detected.

Many substantive procedures normally performed by the auditors may assist in isolating employee frauds, if they are occurring. For example, tests performed on the debtors ledger may be aimed at revealing overstatement or bad debts, but the design of such tests also assists with cash understatement objectives and may reveal irregularities such as 'teeming and lading'.

Management frauds

When seeking to evaluate the possibility of management fraud the auditors will need to consider the business environment by identifying:

(i) Circumstances which may exert undue influence on management (for example the desire to retain the confidence of depositors or creditors may encourage overstatement of results)

(ii) Company performance (for example the deliberate distortion of the financial statements to meet a profit forecast, to increase profit related remuneration or to avoid the appearance of insolvency)

Some of the signs listed above, for example lavish lifestyle, unusual investment of funds and control problems (particularly management over-ride of controls) may indicate management frauds. Other signs include manipulation of evidence, or an unduly complex corporate structure.

If the auditors conclude that there is a high risk of management fraud they will concentrate on techniques such as analytical procedures, scrutiny of unusual transactions, review of post balance sheet events (including going concern evaluation), and review of the financial statements for any material distortions.

2 MISCONDUCT

KEY TERM

Misconduct includes (but is not confined to) any act or default likely to bring discredit to the member, relevant firm or registered student in question.

2.1 ACCA's bye-law 8 states that:

'A member, relevant firm or registered student shall be liable to disciplinary action if he or it, in the course of carrying out his or its professional duties or otherwise, has been guilty of misconduct.'

2.2 Bye-law 8 goes on to say that the following are **conclusive proof** of misconduct.

- Pleading or being found guilty of any offence discreditable to him, the Association or the profession before a competent court, or
- Being found to have acted fraudulently or dishonestly by a competent court.

2.3 It also states that 'any code of practice, ethical or technical, adopted by the Council' and 'any regulation affecting members, relevant firms or registered students laid down or approved by the Council' may be considered when determining whether misconduct had taken place.

Types of misconduct

2.4 The ACCA gives examples of misconduct:

- Convictions relating to personal life, for example
  - Obtaining money/goods by false pretences
  - Forgery
  - Theft
  - Other offences involving dishonesty

2.5 However, the disciplinary committee judges each case on its merits. The investigations committee **might** take a more lenient view if the conviction had arisen over a petty issue, such as a student prank, or isolated instances of disorderliness due to intoxication.

2.6 **Honesty** is considered to be a key virtue of accountants. This is because they are people in a **position of trust.** Therefore incidents involving dishonesty will be taken seriously.

Penalties

2.7 The penalties for misconduct are at the discretion of the Investigations, Disciplinary and Appeals Committees.

Summary

2.8
- Bye-law 8 governs disciplinary action, which will arise in the event of **misconduct.**
- It applies to students as well as members and personal as well as professional lives.
- A misconduct charge is likely to arise after a conviction by a UK court.
- Dishonesty is a key element of misconduct.
- Penalties are at the committees' discretion.

3 PROFESSIONAL LIABILITY

Litigation against auditors

3.1 Auditors' liability can be categorised under the following headings:

- Liability under statute, civil and criminal
- Negligence under the common law to:
  - Clients under contract law (and possibly law of tort)
  - Third parties under law of tort

Negligence and the duty of care

KEY TERM

Negligence is some act or omission which occurs because the person concerned has failed to exercise the degree of professional care and skill, appropriate to the case, which is expected of accountants or auditors.

(Professional liability of accountants and auditors, November 1983)

3.2 It would be a defence to an action for negligence to show that:

- There has been **no negligence**.
- **No duty of care** was owed to the plaintiff in the circumstances.
- **No financial loss** has been **suffered** by the plaintiff (in tort actions).

The third defence would not be available to a claim in contract, but only nominal damages would be recoverable and in those circumstances it is unlikely that such an action would be brought.

3.3 In recent years there have been a number of cases where substantial sums have been claimed as damages for negligence against accountants and auditors. In a number of cases the claims may have arisen as a result of some **misunderstanding** as to the **degree of responsibility** which the accountant was expected to assume in giving advice or expressing an opinion rather than negligence in carrying out agreed terms.

Liability under statute

Civil liability

3.4 S 212 Insolvency Act 1986 (IA 1986) provides that officers including possibly auditors of the company may be liable for financial damages in respect of the civil offences of '**misfeasance**' and '**breach of trust**'.

Criminal liability

3.5 Ss 206-211 Insolvency Act 1986 relate to criminal offences involving officers in a winding-up including possibly auditors.

3.6 S 17 Theft Act 1968 states that a person commits an offence who dishonestly, with a view to gain for himself or another or with intent to cause loss to another:

(a) Destroys, defaces, conceals or falsifies any account or any record or document made or required for any accounting purpose

(b) In furnishing information for any purpose produces or makes use of any account, or any such record or document as aforesaid, which to his knowledge is or may be misleading, false or deceptive in a material particular

3.7 Under s 19 an officer of a company will be guilty of an offence if he publishes or concurs in the publication of a written statement or account which to his knowledge is or may be misleading, false or deceptive in a material particular with intent to deceive members or creditors of the company about its affairs. A written statement may be considered false not only by what it actually states, but also by virtue of any significant matter which it may have concealed, omitted or implied.

3.8 An officer found guilty may be imprisoned for up to 7 years. Again, the term 'officer' may include an auditor for the purposes of ss 17, 18 and 19.

3.9 Under s 47(1) Financial Services Act 1986 a person who seeks to induce or is reckless as to whether someone will be induced to invest or not to invest, by:

- Making a statement, promise or forecast which he knows to be misleading, false or deceptive or dishonestly concealing any material facts
- Recklessly making (dishonestly or otherwise) a statement, promise or forecast which is misleading, false or deceptive

3.10 Guilty parties are liable to imprisonment 'for a term not exceeding seven years'. Note that **mere recklessness** is sufficient for a criminal prosecution: fraud does not have to be proven. This somewhat harsh measure reflects the long history of situations where prospectuses, inviting the public to subscribe for shares, have contained positively dishonest or wildly optimistic statements.

Liability under contract law

3.11 When auditors accept appointment, they enter into a contract which imposes certain obligations upon them. These obligations arise from the terms of the contract. Both **express** and **implied** terms of contracts impact upon auditors. Express terms are those stated explicitly in the contract.

Express terms

3.12 The express terms of the audit contract cannot over-ride the Companies Act by restricting company auditors' statutory duties or imposing restrictions upon auditors' statutory rights which are designed to assist them in discharging those duties.

3.13 Express terms will however be significant if auditors and client agree that auditor responsibilities should be extended beyond those envisaged by the Companies Act. Additionally if auditors are involved in a non-statutory audit, the express terms will only be those contained in any specific contract that may exist with the client.

3.14 In these circumstances auditors are always likely to be judged on the content of any **report** which they have issued, and so they should always ensure that their report clearly states the effect of any **limitations** that there have been upon the extent and scope of their work where such limitations exist. The auditors must take special care to ensure that their report does not in any way imply that they have in fact done more work than that required by the terms of his contract.

Implied terms

3.15 'Implied terms' are those which the parties to a contract may have left unstated because they consider them too obvious to express, but which, nevertheless, the law will impart into a contract.

3.16 The 'implied terms' which the law will impart into a contract of the type with which we are currently concerned are that the auditors have:

- A duty to exercise **reasonable care**
- A duty to carry out the work required with **reasonable expediency**
- A right to **reasonable remuneration**

3.17 Implied terms will be particularly important when there is no or an inadequate engagement letter.

Case example

Fawkes-Underwood v Hamiltons & Hereward Phillips 1997

The court held that the accountants were liable in failing to provide the client with advice relating to the appropriateness of investments in high risk Lloyds' syndicates, since they had held themselves as generally able to advise on Lloyds' syndicates. There were no relevant letters of engagement.

The auditors' duty of care

3.18 As explained above the standard of work of auditors is generally as defined by the Supply of Goods and Services Act 1982. A number of celebrated judgements show how the auditors' duty of care has been gauged at various points in time.

3.19 However nowhere in the Companies Act does it clearly state the manner in which the auditors should discharge their duty of care; neither is it likely that this would be clearly spelt out in any contract setting out the terms of an auditors' appointment.

Case example

Re Kingston Cotton Mill

When Lopes L J considered the degree of skill and care required of an auditor in he declared:

'... it is the duty of an auditor to bring to bear on the work he has to perform that skill, care and caution which a reasonably competent, careful and cautious auditor would use. What is reasonable skill, care and caution, must depend on the particular circumstances of each case.'

Lopes was careful to point out that what constitutes reasonable care depends very much upon the **facts** of a particular case. Another criteria by which the courts will determine the adequacy of the auditors' work is by assessing it in relation to the generally accepted auditing standards of the day.

Case example

The courts will be very much concerned with accepted advances in auditing techniques, demonstrated by Pennycuick J in *Re Thomas Gerrard & Son Ltd 1967* where he observed:

'... the real ground on which *Re Kingston Cotton Mill* ... is, I think, capable of being distinguished is that the standards of reasonable care and skill are, upon the expert evidence, more exacting today than those which prevailed in 1896.'

Case example

Lord Denning in the case of *Fomento (Sterling Area) Ltd v Selsdon Fountain Pen Co Ltd 1958* sought to define the auditors' proper approach to their work by saying:

'... they must come to it with an inquiring mind - not suspicious of dishonesty .... - but suspecting that someone may have made a mistake somewhere and that a check must be made to ensure that there has been none.'

3.20 As regards the auditors' responsibility to keep themselves abreast of professional developments, it is perhaps worth noting again what the APB says in relation to auditing standards and the law.

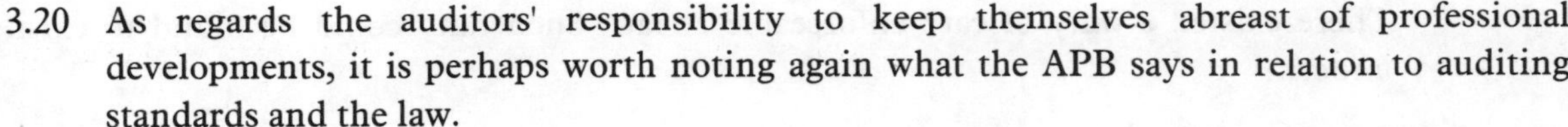

> 'All APB pronouncements and in particular Auditing Standards are likely to be taken into account when the adequacy of the work of auditors is being considered in a court of law or in other contested situations.' *(Scope and authority of APB pronouncements)*

3.21 When the auditors are exercising judgement they must act both honestly and carefully. Obviously, if auditors are to be 'careful' in forming an opinion, they must give due consideration to all relevant matters. Provided they do this and can be seen to have done so, then their opinion should be above criticism.

3.22 However if the opinion reached by the auditors is one that no reasonably competent auditor would have been likely to reach then they would still possibly be held negligent. This is because however carefully the auditors may appear to have approached their work, it clearly could not have been careful enough, if it enabled them to reach a conclusion which would be generally regarded as unacceptable.

3.23 It should be added that the auditors' duty of care extends beyond the giving of an audit opinion.

Case example

Coulthard and Others v Neville Russell 1997

Auditors were held to be in breach of their duty of care because they failed to advise directors that certain payments breached the Companies Act financial assistance rules.

The auditors' duty when put upon enquiry

3.24 If the auditors' suspicions are aroused, they must conduct further investigations until such suspicions are either confirmed or allayed. Over the years, there have been many occasions where the courts have had to consider cases in which it has been held, on the facts of those cases, that the auditors ought to have been put upon enquiry.

Actions for negligence against auditors

3.25 There are two methods by which civil proceedings may be taken against auditors for damages.

- Action for negligence
- Misfeasance summons

3.26 A client who brings a civil claim does so in order to fasten on the auditors the financial responsibility for loss occasioned to them through the failure of the auditors to perform their duty or through their negligence in the manner of performing it.

3.27 If a client is to bring a successful action against an auditors then the client, as the plaintiff, must satisfy the court in relation to three matters, all of which must be established.

(a) *Duty of care*

There existed a duty of care enforceable at law. Such duty could be found to exist, under:

- Common law
- Contract
- Statute

(b) *Negligence*

In a situation where a duty of care existed, the auditors were negligent in the performance of that duty, judged by the accepted professional standards of the day.

(c) *Damages*

The client has suffered some pecuniary loss as a direct consequence of the negligence on the part of the auditors.

Case example

A good early example of a client action for negligence is that of *Wilde & Others v Cape & Dalgleish 1897.* In this case the auditors were held to have been negligent in failing to detect defalcations, the primary reason for this being that they did not examine the bank pass books contrary to generally accepted best practice.

Excluding or restricting liability to a client

3.28 An agreement with a client designed to exclude or restrict an accountant's liability may not always be effective in law. The following are the main relevant considerations.

3.29 S 310 Companies Act 1985 made void, save in exceptional circumstances, any provision in a company's articles or any contractual arrangement purporting to exempt the auditors from, or to indemnify them against, any liability for negligence, default, breach of duty or breach of trust.

3.30 In addition the Unfair Contract Terms Act 1977 (UCTA 1977) introduced extensive restrictions upon the enforceability of exclusions of liability for negligence and breaches of contract.

Impact of restricting liability on audit opinion

3.31 A danger of restricting liability is that this would also result in the restriction of audit work done to make the audit conclusion, which could result in an audit being completed which did not meet ethical and professional standards.

Duty to clients in tort

3.32 The duty of care to a client is generally a contractual one. In addition in recent years it has been held that a professional man, such as an auditor, may owe a duty of care to his clients in tort as well as in contract. Lord Denning in the case of *Esso Petroleum v Marden 1976* said:

> '... in the case of a professional man, the duty to use reasonable care arises not only in contract, but is also imposed by the law apart from contract, and is therefore actionable in tort.'

4 PROFESSIONAL LIABILITY TO THIRD PARTIES

4.1 You should be up to date with the current legal situation of the liability of the auditor to third parties. Here is a brief summary of the position at the time of writing (June 2001).

The *Caparo* case

4.2 The **current deciding case** is still that of *Caparo Industries plc v Dickman and Others 1990*, which is described here.

Case example

The **facts as pleaded** were that in 1984 Caparo Industries purchased 100,000 Fidelity shares in the open market. On June 12 1984, the date on which the accounts (audited by Touche Ross) were published, they purchased a further 50,000 shares. Relying on information in the accounts, further shares were acquired. On September 4, Caparo made a bid for the remainder and by October had acquired control of Fidelity. Caparo alleged that the accounts on which they had relied were misleading in that an apparent pre-tax profit of some £1.3 million should in fact have been shown as a loss of over £400,000. The plaintiffs argued that Touche owed a duty of care to investors and potential investors.

The conclusion of the **House of Lords** hearing of the case in February 1990 was that the auditors of a public company's accounts owed **no duty of care** to members of the public at large who relied upon the accounts in deciding to buy shares in the company. And as a purchaser of further shares, while relying upon the auditors' report, a shareholder stood in the same position as any other investing member of the public to whom the auditor owed no duty. The purpose of the audit was simply that of fulfilling the statutory requirements of CA 1985. There was nothing in the statutory duties of company auditors to suggest that they were intended to protect the interests of investors in the market. And in particular, there was no reason why any special relationship should be held to arise simply from the fact that the affairs of the company rendered it susceptible to a takeover bid.

4.3 In its report *The Financial Aspects of Corporate Governance*, the Cadbury Committee gave an opinion on the current situation as reflected in the *Caparo* ruling. It felt that *Caparo* did not lessen auditors' duty to use skill and care because auditors are **still fully liable in negligence** to the companies they audit and their shareholders collectively. Given the number of different users of accounts, it was impossible for the House of Lords to have broadened the boundaries of the auditors' legal duty of care.

4.4 The conclusion must be that the decision in *Caparo v Dickman* has considerably **narrowed the auditors' potential liability to third parties** and that the case could have far-reaching implications for the idea of there being various classes of 'user groups' who may make use of audited accounts. The judgement would appear to imply that members of various such user groups, which could include creditors, potential investors or others, will not be able to sue the auditors for negligence by virtue of their placing reliance on audited annual accounts.

4.5 A case which pre-dates *Caparo* upholds this view.

Case example

In *Al Saudi Banque v Clarke Pixley 1989* it was held that the auditor did not owe a duty of care to a bank which lent on the basis of the accounts and audit report.

Case example

In *James McNaughton Paper Group Ltd v Hicks Anderson & Co 1990,* Lord Justice Neill set out the following position in the light of *Caparo* and earlier cases:

'(a) In England a restrictive approach was now adopted to any extension of the scope of the duty of care beyond the person directly intended by the maker of the statement to act upon it.

(b) In deciding whether a duty of care existed in any particular case it was necessary to take all the circumstances into account,

(c) Notwithstanding (b), it was possible to identify certain matters which were likely to be of importance in most cases in reaching a decision as to whether or not a duty existed.'

BBH/ADT judgement

4.6 A more recent court case has produced a **development** in the subject of audit liability. In December 1995, a High Court judge awarded electronic security group ADT £65m plus interest and costs (£40m) in damages for negligence against the former BDO Binder Hamlyn (BBH) partnership.

Case example

The firm had jointly audited the 1988/89 accounts of Britannia Security Group (BSG), which ADT acquired in 1990 for £105m, but later found to be worth only £40m. Although, under *Caparo*, auditors do not owe a duty of care in general to third parties, the judge found that BBH audit partner Martyn Bishop, who confirmed that the firm stood by BSG's accounts at a meeting with ADT in the run-up to the acquisition, had thereby **taken on a contractual relationship** with ADT. This development has occurred, apparently, because (post-*Caparo*) solicitors and bankers are advising clients intent on acquisitions to get direct assurances from the target's auditors on the truth and fairness of the accounts.

BBH appealed this decision; the liable partners, because of a shortfall in insurance cover, were left facing the prospect of coming up with £34m. An out of court settlement was reached with ADT.

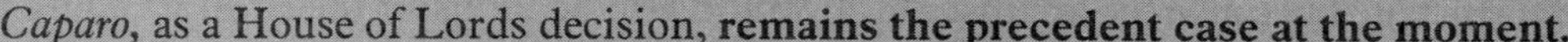

KEY TERM

Caparo, as a House of Lords decision, **remains the precedent case at the moment.**

Recent case law

Case example

In *Peach Publishing Ltd v Slater & Co 1997* the Court of Appeal ruled that accountants are not automatically liable if they give oral assurances on accounts to the purchaser of a business. The case involved management accounts, which the accountant stated the accounts were right subject to the qualification that they had not been audited. The Court held that the purpose of giving the assurance was not to take on responsibility to the purchaser for the accuracy of the accounts. The purchaser's true objective in this case was to obtain a warranty from the accountant's client, the target. Therefore the accountant was not assuming responsibility to the purchaser but giving his client information on which it could decide whether or not to give the warranty. The Court of Appeal also observed that the purchaser should not have relied on the management accounts without having them checked by its advisers.

4.7 Thus the courts will take into account the facts of the cases when deciding on accountant liability for oral assurances. However you should note that this case related to unaudited management accounts on which no written report had been made by the accountant.

Case examples

In a further case the Court of Appeal gave guidance on the effect of a disclaimer which stated that the report had been prepared for the client only and no-one else should rely on it. In *Omega Trust Co Ltd v Wright Son & Pepper 1997* (which related to surveyors but the facts of which can be applied to accountants) the court held that the surveyor was entitled to know who his client was and to whom his duty was held. He was entitled to refuse liability to an unknown lender or any known lender with whom he had not agreed.

Another case related to the responsibilities accountants undertake in a particular assignment. In *Fawkes-Underwood v Hamiltons & Hereward Philips 1997* the court held that the accountants were liable in failing to provide the client with advice relating to the appropriateness of investments in Lloyds' syndicates, since they had held themselves as generally able to advise on Lloyds' syndicates and they should have advised the client which syndicates were high risk. The case underlines the importance of letters of engagement defining specifically what accountants' responsibilities are. (In fact in the case there were no relevant letters of engagement and the judge had to rely on the narrative in the accountants' bills for an indication of the work carried out.)

The case of *Coulthard and Others v Neville Russell 1997* related to auditors' failure to advise a company's directors that certain payments breached the financial assistance rules in the Companies Act. The court held that this failure to advise breached the auditors' common law duty of care.

4.8 The recent case law has raised some **problems**. In spite of the judgement in *Caparo*, the commercial reality is that creditors and investors (especially institutional ones) do use audited accounts. S 241 CA 1985 requires a company to file accounts with the Registrar. Why is this a statutory requirement? It is surely because the public, including creditors and potential investors, have a need for a credible and independent view of the company's performance and position.

4.9 It would be unjust if auditors, who have **secondary responsibility** for financial statements being prepared negligently, bore the full responsibility for losses arising from such negligence just because the are insured. It would also be unjust if the auditors could be sued by all and sundry. While the profession has generally welcomed *Caparo*, two obvious problems are raised by decision.

- Is a restricted view of the usefulness of audited accounts in the profession's long-term interests?
- For private companies there will probably be an increase in the incidence of personal guarantees and warranties given by the directors to banks and suppliers.

APC Practice Note 4

4.10 This practice note, entitled *Reliance by banks on audited financial statements*, was produced in answer to some of the controversy surrounding the auditors' liability to third parties. The practice note contains a joint statement by the APC and the Committee of London and Scottish Bankers. The statement:

(a) Recognises that banks do place reliance on financial statements

(b) Outlines some of the inherent limitations of financial statements (historical not predictive, presence of estimates and so on

(c) Considers the conditions which may affect the extent to which a bank may rely (date of reliance compared with date of accounts, should reliance require more forward looking information and so on)

4.11 The practice note ends with the following statement.

> 'The degree of reliance that should be placed by a bank on a company's audited financial statements in connection with its assessment and monitoring of the financial condition of that company will vary according to the particular circumstances. Therefore, it is preferable for the auditor, the bank and the borrower to have a common understanding of the context in which the bank is using the company's audited financial statements.
>
> Whether this understanding of the bank's position extends to a legal duty of care by the auditor to the bank can only be determined by an examination of the facts of each individual case.'

Settlements out of court

4.12 Many liability claims are settled out of court. The advantages of doing so are claimed to be a **saving in time** and **cost**, and also perhaps a **lower settlement**. An out of court settlement also avoids a high profile court case which **potentially damages** a firm's **reputation**.

4.13 Arguments against an out-of-court settlement include the allegations that they often arise through the **unwillingness** of an auditors' **insurance company** to risk a settlement in court. An out of court settlement also **leaves** the **question** of the audit **firm's responsibility unsettled,** but nevertheless the firm's **insurance premiums** may **rise**.

Disclaimers

4.14 The cases above suggest that a duty of care to a third party may arise when an accountant does not know that his work will be relied upon by a third party, but only knows that it is work of a kind which is liable in the ordinary course of events to be relied upon by a third party.

4.15 Conversely, an accountant may sometimes be informed, before he carries out certain work, that a third party will rely upon the results. An example is a report upon the business of a client which the accountant has been instructed to prepare for the purpose of being shown to a potential purchaser or potential creditor of that business. In such a case an accountant should assume that he will be held to owe the same duty to the third party as to his client.

Case example

Omega Trust Co Ltd v Wright Son & Pepper 1997

In this case (which related to surveyors but the facts of which can be applied to accountants) the court held that the surveyor was entitled to know who his client was and to whom his duty was held. He was entitled to refuse liability to an unknown lender or any known lender with whom he had not agreed.

4.16 However there are areas of professional work (for example when acting as an auditor under the Companies Act), where it is not possible for liability to be limited or excluded. There are other areas of professional work (for example when preparing reports on a business for the purpose of being submitted to a potential purchaser) where although such a limitation or exclusion may be included, its effectiveness will depend on the view which a court may subsequently form of its reasonableness.

Litigation avoidance

4.17 The other aspect of how firms are trying to deal with litigation is what they are trying to do to avoid litigation. This strategy has various aspects.

- The **client acceptance procedures** we discussed in Chapter 2 are very important, particularly the screening of new clients and the use of engagement letters.
- **Performance of audit work**. Firms should make sure that all audits are carried out in accordance with professional standards and best practice.
- **Quality control**. This includes not just controls over individual audits but also stricter 'whole-firm' procedures. This is considered in more detail in Chapter 4.
- **Issue of appropriate disclaimers**. We discussed above the importance of these.

Exam focus point

Read the financial and accountancy press on a regular basis between now and your examination and note any new cases or developments in the question of auditor liability.

Question 2

Although auditors can incur either civil or criminal liability under various statutes it is far more likely that they will incur liability for negligence under the common law, as the majority of cases against auditors have been in this area. Auditors must be fully aware of the extent of their responsibilities, together with steps they must take to minimise the danger of professional negligence claims.

Required

(a) Discuss the extent of an auditors' responsibilities to shareholders and others during the course of their normal professional engagement.

(b) List six steps which auditors should take to minimise the danger of claims against them for negligent work.

Answer

(a) *Responsibility under statute*

An auditor of a limited company has a responsibility, imposed upon him by statute, to form and express a professional opinion on the financial statements presented by the directors to the shareholders. He must report upon the truth and fairness of such statements and the fact that they comply with the law. In so doing, the auditor owes a duty of care to the company imposed by statute. But such duty also arises under contract and may also arise under the common law (law of tort).

Responsibility under contract

The Companies Act does not state expressly the manner in which the auditor should discharge his duty of care; neither is it likely that this would be clearly spelt out in any contract setting out the terms of an auditor's appointment (eg the engagement letter). Although the articles of a company may extend the auditor's responsibilities beyond those envisaged by the Companies Act, they cannot be used so as to restrict the auditor's statutory duties, neither may they place any restriction upon the auditor's statutory rights which are designed to assist him in the discharge of those duties.

The comments of Lopes L J when considering the degree of skill and care required of an auditor in *Re Kingston Cotton Mill* are still relevant.

> '... It is the duty of an auditor to bring to bear on the work he has to perform the skill, care and caution which a reasonably competent, careful and cautious auditor would use. What is reasonable skill, care and caution must depend on the particular circumstances of each case.'

Clearly, with the advent of auditing standards, a measure of good practice is now available for the courts to take into account when considering the adequacy of the work of the auditor.

Responsibility in tort

The law of tort has established that a person owes a duty of care and skill to 'our neighbours' (common and well-known examples of this neighbour principle can be seen in the law of trespass, slander, libel and so on). In the context of the professional auditor the wider implications, however, concern the extent to which the auditor owes a duty of care and skill to third parties who rely on financial statements upon which he has reported but with whom he has no direct contractual or fiduciary relationship.

Liability to third parties

Decisions of the courts, including three important decisions of the House of Lords, expanded the classes of case in which a person professing some special skill (as an auditor does) may be liable for negligence to someone other than his own client: *Hedley Byrne & Co Ltd v Heller & Partners 1964*, *Anns v Merton London Borough Council 1978* and *Junior Books Ltd v Veitschi Co Ltd 1982*. Such liability arose whenever a professional person does work for his client in circumstances where he knows or ought to know:

(i) That his work is liable to be relied upon by a third party, and

(ii) That that third party may suffer financial loss if the work in question has been done negligently.

Liability arises when the work in question was of a kind which it was reasonable for the third party to rely on for his particular purpose.

A duty of care to a third party could arise when an auditor does not know that his work will in fact be relied upon by a third party, but only knows that it is work of a kind which is liable in the ordinary course of events to be relied upon by a third partly. For this purpose it is immaterial whether the third party be identifiable in advance or not. In *Jeb Fasteners v Marks Bloom & Co 1981* and *Twomax Ltd v Dickson McFarlane & Robinson 1983* the courts held that auditors should foresee that a person seeking to acquire a company might rely on its accounts.

However in *Caparo Industries plc v Dickman & Others 1990*, it was held that the auditors of a public company's accounts owed no duty of care to members of the general public who relied upon the accounts in deciding to buy shares in the company. And as a purchaser of more shares, a shareholder placing reliance on the auditors' report stood in the same position as any other investing member of the public to whom the auditor owed no duty. This decision appeared to radically reverse the tide of cases concerning the auditor's duty of care. The purpose of the audit was simply that of meeting the statutory requirements of the Companies Act 1985. There was nothing in the statutory duties of a company auditor to suggest that they were intended to protect the interests of investors in the market. In particular, there was no reason why any special relationship should be held to arise simply from the fact that the affairs of the company rendered it susceptible to a take-over bid.

A case between BDO Binder Hamlyn and ADT seems to have moved the argument on. In this case it was argued that proximity between a prospective investor and the auditors of a company could be created if the investor asked the auditors whether they stood by their last audit. An appeal is likely in this case as the auditors involved face a large shortfall in insurance proceeds. The precedent is still set by *Caparo.*

(b) In order to provide a means of protection for the auditor arising from the comments in (a) above, the following steps should be taken.

(i) Agreements concerning the duties of the auditor should be:

(1) Clear and precise
(2) In writing
(3) Confirmed by a level of engagement, including matters specifically excluded

(ii) Audit work should be:

(1) Relevant to the system of internal control, which must be ascertained, evaluated and tested. Controls cannot be entirely ignored: for the auditor to have any confidence in an accounting system there must be present and evident the existence of minimum controls to ensure completeness and accuracy of the records)

(2) Adequately planned before the audit commences

(3) Reviewed by a senior member of the firm to ensure qualify control of the audit and to enable a decision to be made on the form of audit report

(iii) Any queries arising during the audit should be:

(1) Recorded on the current working papers
(2) Cleared and filed

(iv) A management letter should be:

(1) Submitted to the client or the Board of Directors in writing immediately following an audit

(2) Seen to be acted upon by the client

(v) All members of an auditing firm should be familiar with:

(1) The standards expected throughout the firm

(2) The standards of the profession as a whole by means of adequate training, which should cover the implementation of the firm's audit manual and the recommendations of the professional accountancy bodies

(vi) Insurance should be taken out to cover the firm against possible claims.

5 PROFESSIONAL INDEMNITY INSURANCE

KEY TERMS

Professional indemnity insurance is insurance against civil claims made by clients and third parties arising from work undertaken by the firm.

Fidelity guarantee insurance is insurance against liability arising through any acts of fraud or dishonesty by any partner, director or employee in respect of money or goods held in trust by the firm.

5.1 It is important that accountants have insurance so that if negligence occurs, the client can be **compensated** for the error by the accountant. The appropriate compensation could be far greater than the resources of the accountancy firm.

5.2 Remember that accountants usually trade as **partnerships,** so all the partners are jointly and severally liable to claims made against individual partners.

ACCA requirements

5.3 ACCA require that firms holding practising certificates and auditing certificates have professional indemnity insurance with a reputable insurance company. If the firm has employees, it must also have fidelity guarantee insurance.

5.4 The insurance must cover 'all civil liability incurred in connection with the conduct of the firm's business by the partners, directors or employees'.

5.5 The cover must continue to exist for **6 years** after a member ceases to engage in public practice.

Advantages and disadvantages

5.6 The key **advantage** of such insurance is that it provides funds for an innocent party to be compensated in the event of a wrong having been done to them.

5.7 An **advantage** to the auditor is that it provides some protection against bankruptcy in the event of successful litigation against the firm.

5.8 This is particularly important for a partnership, as partners may be sued personally for the negligence of their fellow partners.

5.9 A key **disadvantage** is that the existence of insurance against the cost of negligence might encourage auditors to take less care than

- Would otherwise be the case
- Their professional duty requires.

5.10 Another problem associated with such insurances are that there are limits of cover (linked with the cost of buying the insurance) and any compensation arising from a claim could be higher than those limits. This could lead to partners being bankrupted despite having insurance.

5.11 A simple disadvantage associated with the above is the regular cost of the insurance to the partnership.

6 CURRENT ISSUES

Fraud

6.1 In November 1998 the Auditing Practices Board issued a consultation paper *Fraud and Audit: Choices for Society.* While this may not seem recent, it highlights the interest the APB have in the subject. Research carried out by the APB of recent major frauds suggests that:

- Most material frauds involve **management.**
- Frauds are more likely to involve **misstated financial reporting than diversion of funds** from the company.

- **Management fraud,** particularly if it involves collusion with third parties, is **unlikely** to be **discovered.**
- **Far more** is **spent** on **investigating** and **prosecuting fraud** within a **company than on its audit.**

6.2 The Auditing Practices Board's work also suggests that there is still a major gap between auditors and users' understanding of the audit.

6.3 The paper goes on to identify the following problems auditors face when trying to identify fraud:

(a) Auditors rarely have **sufficient evidence** to be certain fraud has occurred, and hence must report on the basis of suspicions and not certainty.

(b) Auditors normally have to rely on **management representations** particularly over items requiring a significant amount of judgement.

(c) Directors and managers can **override controls.**

(d) Collusion can **destroy** the **value** of **audit evidence,** and often happens when fraud occurs.

(e) Auditors' **investigatory** powers are **limited**. They have no legal right to seek evidence from third parties, for example suppliers and customers, without authorisation from the directors.

(f) The auditor seeks to **fulfil** the **legal requirement** of a **true and fair audit**. There is no requirement for the disclosure of fraud, and true and fair incorporates the concept of materiality. Initially frauds are often immaterial.

(g) **Time constraints,** especially for listed companies, discourage auditors from seeking evidence to resolve uncertainties such as suspicions of fraud.

(h) Investigating suspicions of fraud can mean **heavy costs** for auditors.

6.4 The Auditing Practices Board plans to review the SASs that have strong links to fraud. However the APB believes that additional improvements are needed to the audit to increase the detection of management fraud:

- A greater emphasis on **professional scepticism**
- Introducing **tighter rules of evidence**
- **Changing requirements** for **audit reports** so that they identify material matters which are solely supported by representations by the directors

6.5 However the report points out that these changes would have a number of costs.

- **Higher** or **more variable audit fees** due to the need for more audit time and an increase in the amount of information that management would need to provide to their auditors
- **Possible delays** in **reporting** by auditors or more qualifications in their reports
- A **more intrusive audit** which may damage audit effectiveness by damaging the open and co-operative relationship between auditors and management
- **Longer and more discursive audit reports** which would however provide valuable additional information on tax issues

6.6 The report suggests that there are a number of other ways in which auditors could do more.

- **Reporting** to **boards** and **audit committees** on the adequacy of controls to prevent and detect fraud
- Encouraging the use of **targeted forensic fraud** reviews, based on the assessment of risks of fraud inherent in a business
- Considering whether **more reporting** of suspected frauds would be beneficial. The regulatory authorities would have to give appropriate back-up for this to be effective

6.7 The report sets out a number of ways in which the law could be tightened to make it more robust against fraud.

- Placing **more emphasis** on **fraud prevention** by clarifying directors' responsibilities for establishing safeguards against fraud
- **Clarifying companies' responsibilities** for directors' fraudulent acts
- Introducing **more robust requirements** for systems of internal controls
- **Tightening duties** of **directors** to provide information to auditors
- **Improving arrangements** for **audit changeovers**, by facilitating the exchange of information between auditors

Liability

6.8 The major accountancy firms have been interested in methods of reducing personal liability for partners in the event of negligence for some time.

6.9 For example, some years ago KPMG (one of the big five of accountancy firms) incorporated its UK audit practice. This is allowed under Companies Act 1989.

6.10 The new arrangement created 'a firm within a firm'. KPMG Audit plc is a limited company wholly owned by the partnership, KPMG. The reason behind this is to protect the partners from the crushing effects of litigation.

6.11 The other side of incorporation means that KPMG Audit plc are subject to the statutory disclosure requirements of companies.

6.12 An alternative to incorporation as a company was considered by two other (at the time) big six firms, Price Waterhouse and Ernst & Young. They announced in 1997 that they intended to register as limited liability partnerships in Jersey, where the law is different to the UK.

6.13 The law concerning limited liability partnerships in the UK has recently changed, as outlined below.

Limited liability partnerships

6.14 The Limited Liability Partnership Act 2000 received Royal Assent during the summer of 2000. Its main purpose is to establish limited liability partnerships as separate legal entities. These combine the flexibility and tax status of a partnership with limited liability for members.

6.15 The effect of this is that the partnership, **but not its members**, will be liable to third parties; however the personal assets of **negligent** partners will still be at risk.

6.16 Limited liability partnerships could be formed from 6 April 2001. Ernst and Young and certain law firms have taken the opportunity to establish separate legal entity.

6.17 Limited liability partnerships are set up by similar procedures to those for incorporating a company. An incorporation document is sent to the Registrar of Companies. The Registrar will issue a certificate of incorporation to confirm that all statutory requirements have been fulfilled.

6.18 In a similar way to traditional partnerships, relations between partners will be governed by internal partner agreements, or by future statutory regulations.

6.19 Each member of the partnership will still be an agent of the partnership unless he has no authority to act and an outside party is aware of this lack of authority.

Law Commission proposals

6.20 The Law Commission has issued a consultation paper on partnership law. It proposes that unlimited partnerships should be given separate legal personality. This would mean that an unlimited partnership could hold property in its own name, and the partners would be agents of the firm and not each other.

6.21 Firms would be primarily liable; partners liability, although unlimited, would be subsidiary. This would mean that creditors could only pursue individual partners if they had first obtained a judgement against the firm.

6.22 Other recommendations included enshrining duties of good faith, skill and care in statute, providing a better mechanism for a firm's dissolution, and removing the legislative assumption that a partnership is automatically dissolved on the departure of a partner.

Question 3

(a) You are required to write an essay, in which you consider the extent to which an auditor should be responsible for detecting fraud and other irregularities when auditing the accounts of limited companies. Your essay should:

  (i) Briefly outline on the extent to which an auditor is responsible for detecting irregularities and fraud (as expressed in the auditing guidelines)

  (ii) Consider the extent to which it would be reasonable to extend the auditor's responsibilities beyond that and the practical problems of extending auditor's responsibilities

  (iii) Reach a conclusion on and provide a definition of the extent to which you consider it reasonable for an auditor to be responsible for detecting irregularities and fraud.

(b) You have been informed by one of your clients, Butler Textiles plc, that they have recently detected a fraud by a cashier at one of their branch factories. The cashier was responsible for banking the taking from the shop in the factory, which sold products to their employees. The employee responsible for the shop had given the takings to the cashier, who had delayed paying them into the bank, and misappropriated the unbanked takings (the cashier had thus carried out a teeming and lading fraud). After finding the fraud, the company had checked the takings from the shop and subsequent banking by the cashier, and had found that the fraud had been taking place for over two years. Subsequent investigation revealed that there was no supervision of the cashier's actions by management, despite the fact that the cashier had custody of the takings from the shop and was responsible for banking and recording the transaction.

  You are required to consider whether the auditor is legally negligent in his work in relation to this fraud.

  (i) Assuming the fraud, amounting to £5,000, is immaterial and your audit files reveal:

(1) You did not check any transactions in relation to the staff shop and subsequent banking of the takings, because you considered them to be immaterial;

(2) You checked the till rolls from the cash register to the cash book, but failed to check to the bank paying in slips that the takings were banked the next day.

(ii) Assuming the fraud, amounted to £50,000, is material.

Answer

(a) Before considering whether it is practical or desirable for auditors to accept a general responsibility to detect fraud and other irregularities it should be recognised that they already have a responsibility to plan the audit so that they have a reasonable expectation of detecting material misstatements in the financial statements resulting from irregularities or fraud.

It must also be acknowledged that the **primary responsibility** for preventing and detecting fraud must always **rest with the management of the enterprise.** It is they who have been given the responsibility to safeguard the assets of the enterprise while the auditor's primary responsibility is to express an opinion on the financial statements.

However, it can be seen that the shareholders', the government's and the public's expectations of the auditor are changing and they are **increasingly calling on the auditor** to **widen his responsibility.**

One of the problems that may arise is the **difficulty of defining fraud.** Associated with this is the need for the auditor to determine an **appropriate level of materiality.**

Currently the auditor assesses materiality in relation to the true and fair view shown by the financial statements. This may no longer be the correct basis if all or most frauds have to be detected.

Fraud itself can cover several types of activities at various levels within the company. Should the auditor be expected to detect a petty theft committed by a junior employee? If not, how is a line drawn between insignificant and important frauds? The guidelines defines fraud as involving the use of deception to obtain an unjust of illegal financial advantage.

The desirability of changing the auditor's responsibility has to be considered in the light of different types of organisations and different interested parties. It would seem to be reasonable for the auditor of a financial institution, where depositors' savings are at risk, to have a greater responsibility for the detection of fraud than the auditor of a small private company run by proprietors. Similarly the auditors of public companies should have a greater responsibility than those of private companies. This would reflect the public's expectations of the role of the modern auditor and legislation should react to these expectations.

Since fraud invariably has an impact on either the accounting records of the financial statements, it is generally accepted that auditors need to plan their audits so that they have a reasonable expectation of detecting material misstatements caused by fraud.

While few people would disagree that the auditor should have some responsibility for the detection of fraud, it may be that widening the auditor's role would mean that additional audit costs would be incurred by all organisations to detect fraud in a mere handful of cases.

Perhaps auditors should advise management how to prevent and detect fraud and penalties for it should be increased so that there is a greater deterrent. If organisations could prevent fraud more effectively there would not be such a need for auditors to try to detect it.

As to the practicalities of detection, fraud can be very difficult to detect where internal control systems are very weak. Some types of fraud may require special expertise to be detected. All auditors should already be detecting frauds and irregularities which give rise to material errors in financial statements. Procedures used to detect immaterial frauds would principally be an extension of the usual audit procedures but the time taken to **extend the level of testing** would be considerable.

The auditor judges the amount of work necessary on the need to obtain sufficient, reliable evidence on which to form an opinion on the view shown by the financial statements. If the auditor's objective was changed, whilst the **method would principally be the same**, the amount of **work necessary** would **increase significantly.** The auditor would not accept a greater responsibility for detecting fraud without a **substantial fee increase.** It is questionable whether this would be considered worthwhile for most organisations.

There is also the **practical difficulty** of **to whom the auditors reports a fraud.** If senior management are involved and the auditor has no real proof and there is no material effect on the financial statements, then the auditor will have to seek legal advice on what action should be taken. The auditor is bound by his **duty of confidentiality** from disclosing it to the appropriate authorities without the client's permission. However, the duty of confidence is not absolute, and the auditors may disclose matters to a proper authority either in the public interest or for other specific reasons.

An associated problem which might arise is a **deterioration in the relationship** between the auditor and the client. If he had to report directly to the authorities, the client may be reluctant to provide information which might cast suspicion over everyone.

Auditors have the skills necessary to detect most types of fraud but the **cost** of so doing **may exceed the likely benefits.** The approach I recommend is for the auditor to make recommendations to management about how they could reduce the likelihood of fraud or irregularities and increase the possibility of detection.

(b) (i) (1) The amount involved in the fraud was immaterial and management controls in the area were apparently inadequate and so at first sight, it might appear that the auditors were not negligent.

The auditors apparently carried out no audit work in relation to the staff shop because they considered this area of the company's activities to be immaterial. Since such decision on materiality could not be made without a review of the systems it would appear that the auditors could be open to some charge of negligence in so far as they had not advised management of the possible consequences of the weak controls in this relatively 'high risk' area of cash sales.

(2) In that the auditor felt it necessary to carry out some audit work in this area, it would appear that they had been negligent in not checking the bank paying-in slips as this would normally be considered necessary audit work to ensure the prompt banking of cash takings.

However, the primary responsibility for establishing an effective control system in this area rests with management and thus any damages awarded against the auditor would probably be minimal.

(ii) As the fraud is material it would appear that, in accordance with the profession's accepted view of the auditor's responsibilities in the area of fraud detection, that the auditors were negligent.

Chapter roundup

- **Fraud** is a controversial issue in relation to auditors. Auditors **do not** have a responsibility to prevent and detect fraud.
- SAS 110 outlines the approach auditors should take to fraud.
- **Misconduct** is generally an act which is likely to bring discredit to the member, firm or profession.
- ACCA's disciplinary committees have discretion over punishments for misconduct (from fines to expulsion from membership).
- Auditors can be liable under statute or negligence under the common law.
- Auditors may attempt to limit liability to clients. This may not always be effective in law.
- *Caparo* is the key case in relation to an accountant's liability to third parties. Auditors do not owe a duty of care to the public at large.
- In a negligence action, accounting firms will often like to settle out of court to avoid bad publicity, and to save time and legal costs.

- There are various methods of litigation avoidance:
  - Client acceptance procedures (screening and engagement letters)
  - Audit work in accordance with SASs
  - Quality control procedures
  - Use of disclaimers
- ACCA requires that auditors take out professional indemnity insurance.

Quick quiz

1 Define fraud

2 Draw a table showing the reporting requirements of SAS 110

3 Complete the definition

________ includes (but is not confined to) any act or ______________ likely to bring discredit to _____ _____________, relevant _____________ or registered _________ in question.

4 ACCA have set penalties for misconduct.

True ☐

False ☐

5 What three matters must a plaintiff satisfy the court in an action for negligence?

(1) _____________

(2) _____________

(3) _____________

6 Name four aspects of litigation avoidance.

(1) _____________

(2) _____________

(3) _____________

(4) _____________

7 Professional indemnity insurance is insurance against liability arising through any acts of fraud or dishonesty by partners in respect of money held in trust by the firm.

True ☐

False ☐

Answers to quick quiz

1 Fraud is the use of deception to obtain unjust or illegal financial advantage and intentional misrepresentation by management, employees or third parties.

2 **REPORTING REQUIREMENTS OF SAS 110**

Reporting to management	If the auditors suspect or detect any fraud (even if immaterial) or if a material error is discovered, as soon as they can they should tell • The appropriate level of management, or • The board of directors, or • The audit committee
Reporting to members	In terms of the audit opinion given on the financial statements, if the auditor feels that the financial statements are affected by a fraud or error, he should **qualify his report** accordingly.
Reporting to third parties	When the auditors discover or suspect a fraud they should consider whether it is in the **public interest** to disclose it. They should **discuss** disclosing the matter to third parties with the **directors** and request that they make the appropriate disclosure. If the directors do not disclose the matter, the auditors should. When a suspected or actual instance of fraud **casts doubt on the integrity of management**, the auditors should report the matter without informing the directors. (In the latter case, the auditors would in practice seek legal advice to ensure that they were not breaching their ethical duties.)

3 Misconduct, default, the member, firm, student

4 False

5 (1) A duty of care existed
(2) Negligence occurred
(3) The client suffered pecuniary loss as a result

6 (1) Client acceptance procedures
(2) Performance of audit work in line with SASs
(3) Quality control
(4) Disclaimers

7 False. That is fidelity guarantee insurance.

Now try the question below from the Exam Question Bank

Number	Level	Marks	Time
3	Exam	15	27 mins

Chapter 4

PRACTICE MANAGEMENT

Topic list		Syllabus reference
1	**Risks to which firms are exposed**	2(a)
2	**Regulatory framework**	2(a)
3	**Quality control framework**	2(a)
4	**Audit firms**	2

Introduction

Some **practice management** issues were considered in Chapter 2, for example, consideration of why clients change auditors and how an auditor should go about obtaining professional work. We continue our consideration of practice management issues in this chapter.

Two of the **key risks** to a firm have been touched on in previous chapters, namely

- The risk of **losing clients**, and consequently the business failing
- The risk of **litigation**, and consequently the business failing

We shall review these, and other risks faced by the audit firm, in Section 1.

There are a number of safeguards that a firm can put in place against these risks. We shall consider the key safeguards in sections 2 and 3. They involve having a **framework** in place **to mitigate the risks**. We shall consider the guidance issued by the APB to auditors.

Lastly in the chapter, we shall familiarise ourselves with the audit sector, and the issues facing various types of audit firms.

Study guide

Section 5

General

- Describe the risks to which practices are exposed and the steps which can be taken to manage them

Quality control practices and procedures

- Outline the regulatory framework for ensuring quality services
- Outline the organisation of international accountancy practices
- Specify the objectives of quality control policies
- Identify the factors which affect the nature, timing and extent of an audit firm's quality control policies and procedures
- Recommend policies and procedures which can be exercised internally at the level of the audit firm and on individual audits
- Describe review procedures including second partner reviews
- Discuss the matters particularly relevant to smaller firms relating to quality control

Section 27

- Describe the different ways in which the auditing profession and audit markets are regulated
- Distinguish between the 'Big Five' firms, 'non-Big Five' firms and second tier firms
- Discuss the impact of globalisation on audit firms and their clients
- Explain the advantages and problems of current trends (eg to merge, to divest consultancy services)

Exam guide

Issues of quality control and practice management are closely linked with ethics.

1 RISKS TO WHICH FIRMS ARE EXPOSED

1.1 An audit firm is a business. It faces risks as any business does, and, as with any other business, the **key risk is that the business will fail.**

1.2 In this section we will consider the risks specific to audit firms which may result in business failure. The risks are outlined in the diagram below.

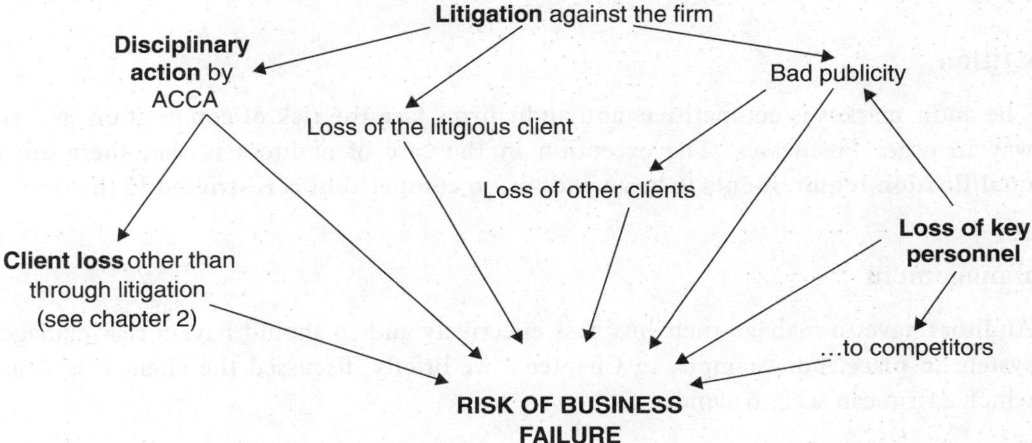

1.3 The diagram shows the links which can exist between some of the risks. These should be self explanatory links. The risks shall be considered individually below.

Litigation

1.4 In Chapter 3 we discussed the responsibilities that auditors have in tort and contract law. The auditor also has professional duties of care to his clients.

1.5 Should the auditor fail to uphold those responsibilities, the result can be litigation against the auditor. As the claim would be made under civil law, the redress to the claimant would be **compensation** should be claim be upheld.

1.6 This could result in business failure for several reasons:

- The loss of the client itself may impact so heavily on the business that it cannot continue

  (Under the ethical fee guidance, loss of the litigious client only should not cause business failure.)

- There might be bad publicity arising from the litigation which could cause
  - Loss of existing clients
  - Inability to grow or replace client base over time

Client loss

1.7 The firm might lose clients for reasons other than litigation. Possible reasons for this have been discussed already in Chapter 2.

Disciplinary action by ACCA

1.8 A situation might arise where ACCA felt it necessary to discipline the firm for **misconduct** under bye-law 8. This could result in the partners being **excluded from membership of ACCA**, which would result in them not being able to practice as auditors.

Key personnel

1.9 This is a particular risk to small firms. As with all small businesses, the risk might exist that the **firm relies** too heavily on **particular personnel**, to the extent that the firm cannot continue in existence in the absence of that person.

Competition

1.10 The audit market is competitive, and audit firms face the risk of competition in a similar way to other businesses. The exception in the case of auditors is that there are **strict qualification requirements** to be an auditor, so **competition is restricted** in that way.

Risk management

1.11 Auditors have to manage their business effectively and so should have a risk management system in place. For example, in Chapter 2 we briefly discussed the client loss situations which a firm can seek to avoid.

1.12 The firm can take steps to mitigate general business risks, for example, by taking out key man insurance, or instigating client care procedures. In the next two sections, we shall consider some accountancy-specific safeguards.

2 REGULATORY FRAMEWORK

2.1 The first of the safeguards that we shall consider is the regulatory framework.

2.2 As you know, auditors are required to follow the guidance of the Auditing Practices Board (APB).

2.3 The APB issue guidance in the form of

- Statements of Auditing Standards (SASs)
- Practice Notes (PNs)
- Bulletins

2.4 Of the above, **SASs are prescriptive** and PNs and Bulletins are persuasive.

2.5 You should be aware of the SASs from paper 2.6 *Audit and Internal Review* (old paper 6). They are listed again here, for revision purposes.

Revision from Paper 2.6, Audit and Internal Review

Statements of Auditing Standards (SASs): APB

		Issue date
Series 001/099	*Introductory matters*	
010	Scope and authority of APB pronouncements	May 93
Series 100/199	*Responsibility*	
100	Objective and general principles governing an audit of financial statements	Mar 95
110	Fraud and error	Jan 95
120	Consideration of law and regulations	Jan 95
130	The going concern basis in financial statements	Nov 94
140	Engagement letters	Mar 95
150	Subsequent events	Mar 95
160	Other information in documents containing audited financial statements	Mar 95
Series 200/299	*Planning, controlling and recording*	
200	Planning	Mar 95
210	Knowledge of the business	Mar 95
220	Materiality and the audit	Mar 95
230	Working papers	Mar 95
240	Quality control for audit work	Sept 00
Series 300/399	*Accounting systems and internal control*	
300	Accounting and internal control systems and audit risk assessments	Mar 95
Series 400/499	*Evidence*	
400	Audit evidence	Mar 95
410	Analytical procedures	Mar 95
420	Audit of accounting estimates	Mar 95
430	Audit sampling	Mar 95
440	Management representations	Mar 95
450	Opening balances and comparatives	Mar 95
460	Related parties	Nov 95
470	Overall review of financial statements	Mar 95
480	Service organisations	Jan 99
Series 500/599	*Using the work of others*	
500	Considering the work of internal audit	Mar 95
510	The relationship between principal auditors and other auditors	Mar 95
520	Using the work of an expert	Mar 95
Series 600/699	*Reporting*	
600	Auditors' report on financial statements	May 93
601	Imposed limitation of audit scope	Mar 99
610	Reports to directors or management	Mar 95
620	The auditors' right and duty to report to regulators in the financial sector	Mar 94

Notes

1 You should be aware of the nature and meaning of the audit report and should be able to discuss the contents and wording of the report. You would not be asked to reproduce the audit report in full in an exam question, but you may be requested to prepare the paragraphs for inclusion in the sections dealing with the basis of the auditor's opinion

on the financial statements for unqualified and qualified audit reports and reports on financial statements affected by uncertainty.

2 Questions will be based on the principles and good practice set out in the Statements of Auditing Standards and Guidelines.

Auditing Guidelines: APC		*Issue date*
308	Guidance for internal auditors	Jun 90
405	Attendance at stocktaking	Oct 83
407	Auditing in a computer environment (now withdrawn)	Jun 84

2.6 These SASs give a **framework** for all auditors in the UK to follow. This **ensures a level of quality and consistency** between audit firms. It means that a **client can have assurance** of that level of quality being used.

2.7 For this reason, if auditors do not follow the statements of auditing standards, they face disciplinary action, and in negligence litigation, the courts will take into account if the auditor followed the appropriate guidance when conducting the audit.

3 QUALITY CONTROL FRAMEWORK

3.1 The requirement for auditors to follow the guidance of the APB provides a general quality control framework within which audits should be conducted.

3.2 One of the SASs within this framework gives more specific guidance on quality control procedures that firms should carry out to ensure that audits are carried out to the highest professional standards.

3.3 This SAS is SAS 240 *Quality control for audit work*. It was re-issued in September 2000. The new SAS gives more general guidance about firm procedures than its predecessor, which concentrated on the quality control aspects of a single audit.

3.4 We have briefly considered the ethical implications of SAS 240 in Chapter 1, but will look at the requirements of the SAS in more detail here.

3.5 The standard states that it seeks to achieve a balance between the following drivers of quality:

- Between individual responsibilities and the collective responsibilities of the firm
- Between personal accountability and teamworking
- Between building quality into processes and monitoring the results

The standard examines quality control issues firstly in terms of the firm and secondly in terms of the engagement partner.

The firm

SAS 240.1

Firms should establish, and communicate to audit engagement partners and audit staff, and others who need to be aware of them, quality control policy and processes; this will involve the establishment of an appropriate structure within the firm, including the appointment of a senior audit partner to take responsibility for these matters.

3.6 The SAS states that it is important to have quality control policies to ensure that

- Work is carried out with due regard for audit quality
- Audit quality is never compromised due to commercial considerations

3.7 In order for them to be effective, it is vital that the policies are **communicated** to all members of the firm's staff. This will involve the policies being **documented**.

SAS 240.2

Before accepting a new audit engagement firms should ensure that they:

(a) are competent to undertake the work;

(b) consider carefully whether there are threats to their independence and objectivity and, if so, whether adequate safeguards can be established;

(c) assess the integrity of the owners, directors and management of the entity;

(d) comply with the ethical requirements of the professional accountancy bodies in relation to changes in appointment.

Firms should also ensure that the reconsider these matters, before the end of their term of office, when deciding whether they are willing to continue in office as auditor.

3.8 This refers to the ethical issues surrounding audit appointment, which were considered in Chapter 2.

3.9 The SAS reinforces the ethical requirements, even after appointment.

SAS 240.3

If, after accepting an engagement, firms become aware of any factors, which would have caused them to decline the appointment, they should consider whether to complete the current audit or whether to resign.

3.10 The SAS then turns to the resources of audit firms, concentrating on the key resource of an audit firm, its staff.

SAS 240.4

Firms should have sufficient audit engagement partners and audit staff with the competencies necessary to meet their needs.

SAS 240.5

An audit engagement partner should be appointed to each audit engagement undertaken by the firm, to take responsibility for the engagement on behalf of the firm.

SAS 240.6

Firms should assign audit staff with the competencies necessary to perform the audit work expected of them to individual audit engagements.

3.11 Consultation is an important part of audit procedure. The SAS requires that procedures for consultation are formalised, so the results of consultation can be referred back to after the event, if necessary (for example, during litigation).

SAS 240.7

Firms should establish procedures to facilitate consultation and to ensure that sufficient resources are available to enable appropriate consultation to take place in relation to difficult or contentious matters. The results of consultation that are relevant to audit conclusions should be documented.

The audit engagement partner

3.12 The second half of the SAS deals with issues more related to individual audits and, having said that all audit assignments require one, the engagement partner himself.

SAS 240.8

Audit engagement partners should, in all cases, take responsibility on behalf of the audit firm for the quality of the audit engagements to which they are assigned.

SAS 240.9

Audit engagement partners should consider whether adequate arrangements are in place to safeguard their objectivity and the firm's independence, and document their conclusions.

SAS 240.10

Audit engagement partners should ensure that audit work is directed, supervised and reviewed in a manner that provides reasonable assurance that the work has been performed competently.

3.13 This area is the area that SAS 240 historically concentrated on, so you should be aware of these issues from your previous studies.

3.14 The last areas of quality control that the SAS makes provision for are review and monitoring. Review is an important aspect of auditing, as much of the detailed audit work is carried out by someone other than the person giving the audit opinion.

3.15 Monitoring is a vital aspect of quality control. It regulates the procedures, and ensures that they are being maintained as planned.

SAS 240.11

Firms should ensure that an independent review is undertaken for all audit engagements where the audited entity is a listed company. In addition, firms should establish policies setting out the circumstances in which an independent review should be performed for other audit engagements, whether on the grounds of the public interest or audit risk.

SAS 240.12

The independent review should take place before the issue of the auditors' report in order to provide an objective, independent assessment of the quality of the audit. Firms' policies should set out in detail the manner in which this objective is to be achieved.

SAS 240.13

Firms should establish procedures for dealing with conflicting views regarding important matters between audit staff, between audit staff and the audit engagement partner, and between the audit engagement partner and the independent partner.

3.16 Guidelines should require resolution of any issues arising at an early stage. They should provide for the documentation of how disputes have been resolved.

> **SAS 240.14**
>
> Firms should appoint a senior audit partner to take responsibility for monitoring the quality of audits carried out by the firm.

3.17 This is an important role, and if at all possible it should be carried out by someone other than the partner responsible for quality control identified in SAS 240.1. The objectives of this review are to provide an **independent assessment** of whether

- The audit report is appropriate
- The audit work is in accordance with relevant external guidance
- The firm's own quality control procedures have been complied with
- Consultation has taken place over difficult issues

4 AUDIT FIRMS

4.1 The accountancy sector is divided into three generally accepted 'tiers':

(a) 'Big five' firms – the top five firm by fee incomes

(b) Medium sized firms – defined more fluidly than the big five. One description is firms with more than sixteen partners which includes around the next fifty firms by fee income.

(c) Small firms – the remainder

4.2 However, a key recent characteristic of the sector has been the tendency of firms to **merge.** So while the above situation is the current picture, it is not the picture of five years ago, and it may well not be the picture of tomorrow.

Big five

4.3 The big five audit firms are so called because there is a significant gap in fee income between audit firm 5 and audit firm 6. After that, fee income levels fall in a more even curve.

4.4 The big five became the big five in 1998, when two of what had been the big six, Coopers and Lybrand and Price Waterhouse, merged. This has created a firm at the head of the big five which has reported fee income in 1999 of 3.5 times the lowest placed big five firm.

Medium sized

4.5 As discussed above, there is no definition of medium sized. The definition given above gives a group of firms with a range in reported income from approximately £160 million to £6 million.

4.6 An alternative classification of 'medium-sized' is the next '20 or so' after the big five, but this gives a similar range of fees.

4.7 The medium tier is split into two sections, 7 or 8 of the firms with a fee income of £50 million and 'the rest'. Of the 7 or 8, three firms have income of around £100 million.

4.8 There is currently a trend for the upper end of the medium sized firms to merge in an attempt to reach up towards the big five, or at least secure supremacy in the medium tier firms. The key examples of this are Grant Thornton and BDO Stoy Hayward.

Small firms

4.9 By far the largest number of audit and accountancy firms fall into the last sector; the 'small firms'. The High Street firm with one or two partners is the most common type of accountancy firm in the UK.

Current trends

Globalisation

4.10 Globalisation is an issue which affects the larger of the medium-sized firms and the big five. There are two approaches to globalisation:

(a) **Affiliation.** This method allows an international brand name to develop and is commonly used by big five firms which have international coverage by a firm using the same name.

(b) **Co-operation.** Medium sized firms often attach themselves to an international co-operative of firms operating under a title which can be incorporated into the firm's name (for example, **HLB** Kidsons) so that a UK firm has an international network of 'sister firms'.

4.11 The key benefit of internationalisation is that many clients are companies which are international, so the audit firm can meet their needs around the world.

Mergers

4.12 One key current trend already discussed is merging. This is currently an issue in the medium firm tier as the firms seek to establish dominance over the tier and reach up towards the big five.

4.13 It is also an issue in the light of the audit exemption limit rising. Many smaller firms face loss of fees through their clients no longer requiring their services. Merging can result in a larger firm with the resources to conduct larger audits.

4.14 There are some **disadvantages of mergers,** particularly to clients. A key disadvantage is that it results in **reduced choice** of audit firm for clients.

4.15 Another disadvantage, which is specifically relevant to larger firms, is that merger can often result in the new combined firm holding the audits of two highly competitive companies, which often results in one of the audits being lost. These two disadvantages combined represents a particular problem for large, listed companies, whose audits are usually provided by big five firms.

Divesting services

4.16 Another trend is related to the other services audit firms provide. A recent big five trend has been to divest key other services, such as consultancy.

4.17 Other services are a problem for audit firms in relation to their independence ethics. The current trend towards divesting was driven by the amendment of the US Securities Exchange Commission's amendment to their rules on auditor independence.

Quality control regulations

4.18 The regulation of audit is the same for all audit firms regardless of size. However, it is logical to see that it will impact on large and small firms differently.

4.19 For example, a big five firm may have international quality control procedures. If not, it will certainly have national and regional ones. A one partner firm, in contrast, will be unable to apply all the provisions of SAS 240 *Quality control for audit work,* specifically provisions relating to multiple partners.

4.20 This does not mean that small firms should ignore the requirements of SAS 240. All the aspects relating to new clients, review of work, the importance of having and documenting procedures are still relevant.

4.21 In the absence of second partner reviews and monitoring, small firms should ensure that they remain technically up to date, that they follow the quality control procedures that they do have and they make use of the technical support facilities offered by the ACCA.

Chapter roundup

- A key risk facing audit firms is that the business will fail. Two key factors in this risk are:
  - Client loss
  - Litigation (which can lead to client loss)
- The risk can be mitigated by:
  - Client care policies
  - Quality control policies
- Auditors are required to follow the guidance on audits issued by the APB. These will help to ensure audit quality.
- SAS 240 also requires the firms design quality control frameworks.
- The audit sector is varied, but it has three key elements:
  - Big five
  - Medium firms
  - Small firms

Quick quiz

1 There is a mindmap on Page 77 showing the key risks to audit firms and links between them. Reproduce the diagram, or draw your own, showing the risk and the links.

2 Name two reasons an audit may be lost due to size.

(1) ________________

(2) ________________

3 SASs are prescriptive and Practice Notes and Bulletins are persuasive.

True ☐

False ☐

4 SAS 240 gives two reasons why audit quality policies are required. Complete them.

- Work is ________________ out with due ________________ for audit quality.
- Audit quality is never compromised due to ______________ __________________.

5 Why are the 'big five' accountancy firms so called?

Answers to quick quiz

1

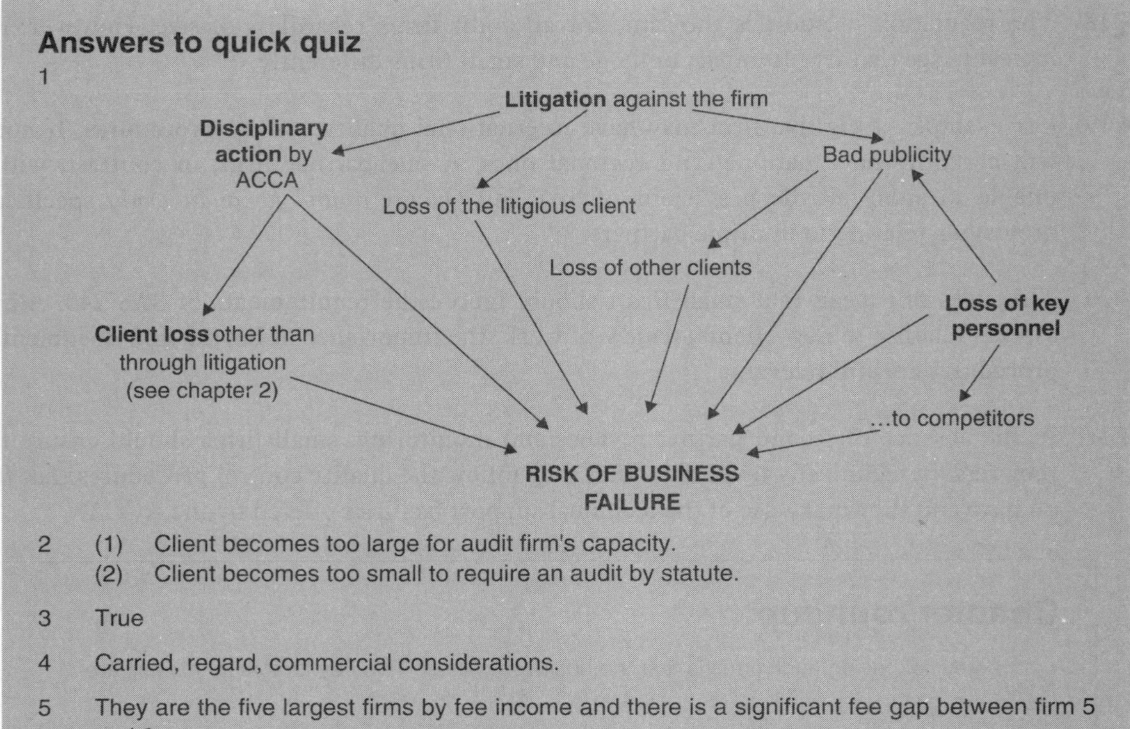

2 (1) Client becomes too large for audit firm's capacity.
(2) Client becomes too small to require an audit by statute.

3 True

4 Carried, regard, commercial considerations.

5 They are the five largest firms by fee income and there is a significant fee gap between firm 5 and 6.

Now try the question below from the Exam Question Bank

Number	Level	Marks	Time
4	Exam	20	36 mins

Chapter 5

REGULATORY ENVIRONMENT

Introduction

In Chapter 4, we looked at the frameworks that audit firms use to ensure that the services they offer are quality services. In this chapter we will look at the **frameworks that have been developed to ensure that companies deal fairly with their members**, and the auditors role in respect of that framework, given their pivotal position between the company and its members.

It is a well-known fact of company law that management and owners of companies are often not the same. In recent years, in the wake of some high profile frauds and business failure after some high profile, questionable business practices, the **importance of good corporate governance** has been highlighted. We introduce the concept of corporate governance in Section 1.

In its reviews of corporate practice, the government set up several committees to look into corporate practice. The first, and possibly the most famous of these is the **Cadbury Committee** of 1992. It issued a **code of best practice**. This has been augmented by other committees until in 1998, a **combined code** was issued, deriving key features from all the reports. The key aspects of these codes for directors and auditors are considered in Section 2.

A key feature of these codes of best practice for the auditor is the recommendation that companies use **audit committees**. The benefits to the auditor of audit committees have been discussed in Chapter 1. Section 3 outlines the role of an audit committee in a company.

Internal controls are a vital function for management to ensure that the business operates properly, does not suffer fraud and that the financial statements give a true and fair view. It has also been the subject of attention by government committees. Section 4 discusses issues for both auditors and directors relating to internal controls.

Lastly, in addition to the codes of practice, **all business operate in an environment controlled by law and regulations**. Section 5 looks briefly at this environment and discusses the role of the auditor in ensuring the company meets the requirements, looking specifically at the guidance of SAS 120 *Consideration of law and regulations.*

Study guide

Section 4

Corporate governance

- Explain the objective, relevance and importance of corporate governance
- Discuss the relative merits and disadvantages of voluntary codes and legislation
- Discuss current issues in corporate governance

Code of Best Practice

- Outline the provisions of the Code of Best Practice (based on the Cadbury Report) that are most relevant to auditors
- Outline the requirements of the Combined Code (of the Committee on Corporate Governance) relating to directors' responsibilities (eg for risk management and internal control) and the reporting responsibilities of auditors
- Outline the content of a corporate governance statement

Audit Committees

- Explain the structure and roles of audit committees and discuss their benefits and drawbacks
- Discuss the relevant merits and disadvantages of regulation by a voluntary code of practice rather than law
- Discuss independence in respect of non-executive directors

Internal financial control effectiveness

- Outline the importance of internal control and risk management
- Compare the responsibilities of management and auditors (internal and external) for the design and operation of systems and controls and the reliability of management information (financial and non-financial)
- Describe the factors to be taken into account when assessing the need for an internal audit function

Laws and Regulation in an Audit of Financial Statements

- Compare and contrast the respective responsibilities of management and auditors concerning compliance with laws and regulations
- Describe the auditors considerations of compliance and audit procedures when possible non-compliance is discovered

Exam guide

Corporate governance is an important, topical issue. It could be examined in connection with internal audit (see Chapter 16).

1 CORPORATE GOVERNANCE

KEY TERM

The Cadbury Report defines **corporate governance** as 'the system by which companies are directed and controlled'.

1.1 The roles of those concerned with the financial statements are described in the Cadbury Report.

- The **directors** are responsible for the corporate governance of the company.
- The **shareholders** are linked to the directors via the financial reporting system.
- The **auditors** provide the shareholders with an external objective check on the directors' financial statements.
- Other concerned **users**, particularly employees, are indirectly addressed by the financial statements

1.2 Before looking at the codes that have been issued to support good corporate governance, it is important to understand **why good corporate governance is considered to be important**.

Importance of good corporate governance

1.3 The ideas which are central to the importance of good corporate governance are illustrated in the two diagrams below.

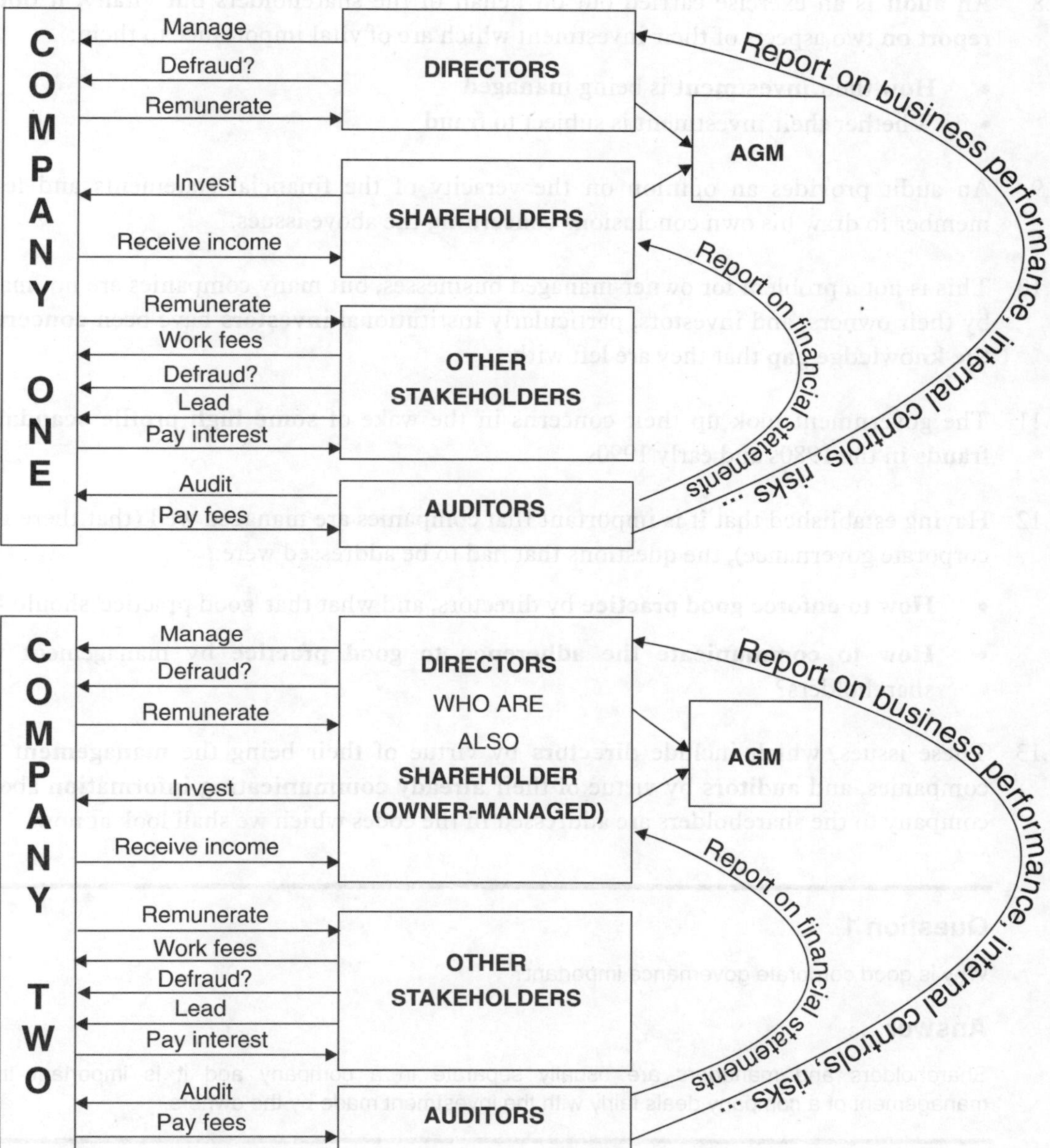

1.4 The diagrams show two companies and their relationships with the key people associated with corporate governance.

1.5 The key difference between the diagrams is that while in **company two**, the **shareholders** are **fully informed about** the **management** of the business, being directors themselves, in **company one**, the **shareholders** only have an opportunity to find out about the management of the company at the **AGM**.

1.6 The **day-to-day running of a company is the responsibility of the directors** and other management staff to whom they delegate, and although the company's results are submitted for shareholders' approval at the annual general meeting (AGM), there is often apathy and acquiescence in director's recommendations.

1.7 AGMs are often very poorly attended. For these reasons, there is the **potential** for **conflicts of interest** between management and shareholders.

1.8 An **audit** is an exercise carried out on behalf of the shareholders but vitally, it **does not report on** two aspects of their investment which are of vital importance to them:

- **How** their **investment** is being **managed**
- Whether their investment is subject to **fraud**

1.9 An audit provides an opinion on the veracity of the financial statements and leaves a member to draw his own conclusions concerning the above issues.

1.10 This is not a problem for owner-managed businesses, but many companies are not managed by their owners, and investors, particularly institutional **investors** have been **concerned at the knowledge gap** that they are left with.

1.11 The government took up their concerns in the wake of **some high profile scandals and frauds** in the 1980s and early 1990s.

1.12 Having established that it is important that companies are managed well (that there is good corporate governance), the questions that had to be addressed were:

- **How to enforce good practice** by directors, and what that 'good practice' should be?
- **How to communicate the adherence to good practice** by management to the shareholders?

1.13 These issues, which include **directors** by virtue of their being the **management** of the companies, and **auditors** by virtue of their **already communicating information** about the company to the shareholders are addressed in the codes which we shall look at now.

Question 1

Why is good corporate governance important?

Answer

Shareholders and managers are usually separate in a company and it is important that the management of a company deals fairly with the investment made by the owners.

2 CODES OF BEST PRACTICE

The Cadbury Report

2.1 Financial aspects of corporate governance in the UK have been addressed in the report of the Cadbury Committee, which was formed in 1991. The terms of reference of the committee were to consider, along with any other relevant matters, the following issues.

(a) The responsibilities of executive and non-executive directors for reviewing and reporting on performance to shareholders and other financially interested parties, and the frequency, clarity and form in which information should be provided

(b) The case for audit committees of the board, including their composition and role (this is discussed in its own right in Section 3)

(c) The principal responsibilities of auditors and the extent and value of the audit

(d) The links between shareholders, boards, and auditors

2.2 The committee aimed to set out the responsibilities of each group involved in the reporting process and to make recommendations on good practice.

2.3 The **Code of Best Practice** included in the Cadbury Report is aimed at the directors of all UK public companies, but the directors of all companies are encouraged to use the Code for guidance.

2.4 Directors should state in the annual report and accounts whether they comply with the Code and give reasons for any non-compliance. **This statement of compliance should only be published after a review by the auditors.**

Provisions of the Cadbury code	
The board of directors	The **board of directors** must meet on a regular basis, retain full control over the company and monitor the executive management. A **clearly accepted division of responsibilities is necessary** at the head of the company, so no one person has complete power, answerable to no-one. The report encourages **the separation of the posts of Chairman and Chief Executive**. Where they are not separate, a strong independent group should be present on the board, with their own leader. There should be a **formal schedule of matters which must be referred to the board** stating which decisions require a single director's signature and which require several signatures. **Procedures** should be in place to make sure the schedule is followed. The schedule should include **acquisitions and disposals of assets of the company**/subsidiaries that are material to the company and **investments, capital projects, bank borrowing** facilities, **loans** and their repayment, foreign currency transactions, all above a predetermined size.
Non-executive directors	The following points are made about **non-executive directors**, who are those directors not running the day to day operations of the company. They should bring **independent judgement** to bear on important issues, including key appointments and standards of conduct. There should be **no business, financial or other connection between the non-executive directors and the company**, apart from fees and shareholdings. **Fees should reflect the time they spend on the business** of the company, so extra duties could earn extra pay. They should **not take part in share option schemes** and their service should not be pensionable, to maintain their independent status. **Appointments should be for a specified term and reappointment should not be automatic**. The board as a whole should decide on their nomination and selection. **Procedures** should exist **whereby non-executive directors may take independent advice**, at the company's expense if necessary.

Executive directors	In relation to the **executive directors**, who run companies on a day to day basis, the main points in the Code relate to service contracts (contracts of employment) and pay. The length of such contracts should be three years at most, unless the shareholders approve a longer contract. Directors' emoluments and those of the highest paid directors should be fully disclosed and analysed between salary and performance-related pay. The basis of measuring performance should also be shown. A remuneration committee of non-executive directors should decide on the level of executive pay.
Audit	The code states that audit is a **cornerstone of corporate governance**. It is an **objective and external check** on the **stewardship** of management. There are design problems in the framework of auditing however, including: • Choices in accounting treatments • Poor links between shareholders and auditors • Price competition associated with auditing Another problem associated with the audit is the 'expectations gap' between what an audit actually achieves and what people think it achieves, This is discussed further in Chapter 19. Some of these matters are being addressed by the APB. The threat to objectivity of auditors offered other services to audit clients should be safeguarded against by **disclosing fees for audit** in the financial statements. The code also **recommends** that the auditing profession draw **up formal guidelines concerning audit rotation**. The advantages and disadvantages of audit rotation were discussed in Chapter 1. It recommends the accountancy profession being involved in setting criteria for evaluation of **internal control** (this is discussed more in Section 4.) It recommended that auditors report on **going concern**. This has now been reflected in auditing standards and is common practice. It also recommended that auditors have guidelines about how to act in the event of suspicion of **fraud.** This is dealt with in SAS 110.

Smaller companies

2.5 Many **smaller companies** have complained that the Cadbury Code is too burdensome for them, raising fears that if its requirements are not diluted then many smaller companies will simply fail to comply with them.

2.6 In response to this, a special version of the code aimed at listed companies with market capitalisation below £250 million was published in 1994 by the City Group for Smaller Companies ('Cisco'), with the endorsement of the Cadbury Committee.

2.7 Differences between the Cisco code and the Cadbury code include reduction of the number of non-executives on a company board from three to two and not requiring smaller companies to split the roles of Chief Executive and Chairman.

The combined code

2.8 The Cadbury code was issued in 1992, and the comments in the table above show that some of the points have been addressed subsequently by the APB, particularly those in relation to fraud and going concern.

2.9 Since the Cadbury report, there have been several other committees, which all produced recommendations about various issues such as directors' remuneration. In 1998, the key guidance from all the reports was re-issued in the form of the combined code.

2.10 The combined code is issued as part of the stock exchange guidance and so generally relates to listed companies. However, this does not mean that following the guidance is not good practice for other companies also.

Provisions of the combined code	
Directors' responsibilities	
The board	Should **meet regularly**, and have a **formal schedule of matters** reserved to it for its decision. There should be clear division of responsibilities between chairman and chief executive. **Non-executive directors** should comprise at least a third of the board. Directors should submit themselves for re-election every three years.
The AGM	Companies should propose **separate resolutions** at the AGM on each substantially different issue. The chairman should ensure that members of the audit, remuneration and nomination committees are available at the AGM to **answer questions**. Notice of AGMs should be sent out at least 20 days before the meeting.
Accountability and audit	The directors should **explain** their **responsibility for preparing accounts**. They should **report that the business is a going concern**, with supporting assumptions and qualifications as necessary.
Internal control	The directors should review the **effectiveness of internal control** systems, at least annually, and also **review the need for an internal audit function**.
Audit committee	The board **should establish an audit committee.**
Auditors' responsibilities	
Statement of responsibilities	The auditors **should include** in their report a statement of their reporting responsibilities.

Corporate governance statement

2.11 The stock exchange rules require that, as part of the **annual report**, a company must **include** a narrative **statement of how it has applied the principles set out in the combined code**. This statement must include an explanation which allows the shareholders to evaluate how the company have applied the principles.

2.12 The statement must also provide explanation of whether the company has **complied** with the principles of the combined code.

2.13 They must also provide a statement showing how they have applied the principles relating to directors' remuneration (not examined in detail here).

2.14 The auditors must review the corporate governance statement before it is published. Their duty to review it only extends to the following items:

- Board having a formal schedule of matters for their attention
- Procedure for board members to seek independent, professional advice
- Non-executive directors having specific terms of office
- Directors being subject to election and re-election by the shareholders
- The directors and auditors stating their respective responsibilities
- The directors conducting a review of internal control effectiveness
- The board establishing an audit committee

Benefits of a voluntary code

2.15 The combined code is a **voluntary code**. The Stock Exchange requires that disclosures be made as to whether it has been complied with, but there are **no statutory requirements to comply** with it.

2.16 The main benefit in having a voluntary code is that the code can be **applied flexibly**, where management believe that it is relevant. The **disclosure** requirements ensure that **shareholders** are **aware** of the position and they can make any points they want to about compliance with the code at the AGM.

2.17 It has been argued that making such a code obligatory would have **punitive effects** on some companies, due to their size or investor make up and that legislation would create a **burden of requirement** which **could be excessive in many cases**.

2.18 Critics of the view would argue:

- Disclosure of non-compliance is insufficient as the AGM is still not sufficient protection for shareholders.
- Having a voluntary code allows some companies not to comply freely, to the detriment of their shareholders.
- The requirement to disclose is only a Stock Exchange requirement, and there are many unlisted companies who should be encouraged to apply the codes.

2.19 The government has shown concern for this area in the past and it is believed that it **might take action in the future to regulate this area** more heavily.

2.20 However, at the moment, having a **voluntary code is a compromise** based on the points made above.

3 AUDIT COMMITTEES

3.1 A major recommendation in the Cadbury Code is that **all listed companies must establish effective audit committees** if they have not already done so.

3.2 The Code takes its example from countries such as Canada where audit committees for listed companies are compulsory.

3.3 The audit committees should have formal terms of reference dealing with their membership, authority and duties. They should meet at least three times every year and membership of the committee, which should be comprised of **non-executive directors,** should be shown in the annual report.

- The committee must have the authority, resources and means of access to investigate anything within its terms of reference.
- Review of the external auditors' management letter and the company's statement on the internal control system

3.4 The key advantage to an auditor of having an audit committee is that a committee of independent non-executive directors provides the auditor with an independent point of reference other than the executive directors of the company, in the event of disagreement arising.

3.5 Other **advantages** that are claimed to arise from the existence of an audit committee include:

(a) It will lead to **increased confidence** in the credibility and objectivity of financial reports.

(b) By specialising in the problems of financial reporting and thus, to some extent, fulfilling the directors' responsibility in this area, it will allow the **executive** directors to **devote their attention to management.**

(c) In cases where the interests of the company, the executive directors and the employees conflict, the audit committee might provide an **impartial body** for the auditors to consult.

(d) The internal auditors will be able to report to the audit committee.

3.6 Opponents of audit committees argue that:

(a) There may be **difficulty selecting** sufficient non-executive directors with the necessary competence in auditing matters for the committee to be really effective.

(b) The establishment of such a **formalised reporting procedure** may **dissuade** the **auditors** from raising matters of judgement and limit them to reporting only on matters of fact.

(c) **Costs** may be **increased.**

3.7 In an appendix to the *Cadbury Report*, the Committee expands on the role and function of the audit committee.

> 'If they operate effectively, audit committees can bring significant benefits. In particular, they have the potential to:
>
> (a) improve the quality of financial reporting, by reviewing the financial statements on behalf of the Board;
>
> (b) create a climate of discipline and control which will reduce the opportunity for fraud;
>
> (c) enable the non-executive directors to contribute an independent judgement and play a positive role;
>
> (d) help the finance director, by providing a forum in which he can raise issues of concern, and which he can use to get things done which might otherwise be difficult;
>
> (e) strengthen the position of the external auditor, by providing a channel of communication and forum for issues of concern;

(f) provide a framework within which the external auditor can assert his independence in the event of a dispute with management;

(g) strengthen the position of the internal audit function, by providing a greater degree of independence from management;

(h) increase public confidence in the credibility and objectivity of financial statements.'

3.8 In practice the main duties of the audit committee are likely to be as follows.

3.9 **Review of financial statements**. The committee should review both the half yearly and annual accounts. The committee should assess the **overall appearance** and **presentation** of the accounts, in particular the treatment of material changes from previous years, significant events and other exceptional items. The review should also cover.

3.10 **Liaison with external auditors**. The audit committee's tasks here will include:

(a) Being responsible for the **appointment** or **removal** of the **external auditors** as well as fixing their remuneration; the committee should also consider non-audit services provided by the external auditors, paying particular attention to whether there may be a conflict of interest

(b) Discussing the **scope** of the **external audit** prior to the start of the audit; this should include consideration of whether external audit's coverage of all areas of the business is fair, and how much external audit will rely on the work of internal audit

(c) Acting as a **forum** for **liaison** between the external auditors, the internal auditors and the finance director

(d) **Helping** the **external auditors** to **obtain** the **information** they require and in resolving any problems they may encounter

(e) Making themselves available to the external auditors for **consultation**, with or without the presence of the company's management

(f) Dealing with any **serious reservations** which the auditors may express either about the accounts, the information published with the accounts, the records, the control environment or the quality or views of the company's management

3.11 **Review of internal audit.** The review should cover the standards used, the scope of the function, the reporting arrangements and the results of internal audit work.

3.12 **Review of internal control.** The audit committee can play a significant role in reviewing internal control.

(a) Committee members can use their own experience to monitor continually the **adequacy** of **internal control systems**, focusing particularly on the control environment, management's attitude towards controls and overall management controls. The audit committee's review should cover legal compliance and ethics, for example listing rules, Financial Service Act requirements or environmental legislation.

(b) Each year the committee should be responsible for reviewing the company's statement on internal controls prior to its approval by the board.

(c) The committee should consider the recommendations of the auditors in the management letter and management's response. Because the committee's role is ongoing, it can also ensure that recommendations are publicised and see that actions are taken as appropriate.

3.13 **Investigations.** The committee will also be involved in implementing and reviewing the results of one-off investigations

Question 2

What are the benefits of corporate governance codes being voluntary?

Answer

- Code can be applied flexibly, as is best for the company.
- Burden of statutory requirement is not created

Question 3

Since 1978 all public companies in the United States of America have been required to have an audit committee as a condition of listing on the New York Stock Exchange.

(i) Explain what you understand by the term audit committee.
(ii) List and briefly describe the duties and responsibilities of audit committees.
(iii) Discuss their advantages and disadvantages.

Answer

(i) An **audit committee** reviews financial information and liases between the auditors and the company. It normally consists of the non-executive directors of the company, though there is no reason why other senior personnel should not also be involved.

(ii) Although no specific responsibilities and duties are laid down, they would be likely to include the following.

(1) Being responsible for **recommending the appointment or removal of the external auditor** as well as for fixing their remuneration;

(2) Helping to **ensure good relations** between the external auditors and the management as well as with the internal auditors;

(3) **Helping the external auditors to obtain the information** they require and in resolving problems they encounter;

(4) Making themselves **available to the external auditors** for consultation, with or without the presence of the company's management;

(5) **Dealing with any serious reservations** which the auditor may express either about the accounts, the records or the quality of management.

In addition to these responsibilities, any responsible audit committee is likely to want:

(1) To **ensure that the review procedures** for interim statements, rights documents and similar information are **adequate;**

(2) To **review both the management accounts** used internally and the **statutory accounts** issued to shareholders for reasonableness;

(3) To make **appropriate recommendations for improvements in management control.**

(iii) There are a number of advantages and disadvantages.

Disadvantages

(1) Since the finding of audit committees are rarely made public, it is **not** always **clear what they do** or how effective they have been in doing it.

(2) It is possible that the audit committee's **approach** may prove somewhat **pedestrian,** resolving little of consequence but acting as a drag on the drive and entrepreneurial flair of the company's senior executives.

(3) Unless the requirement for such a body were made compulsory, as in the US, it is likely that those **firms most in need** of an audit committee would nevertheless **choose not to have**

one. (Note that the Cadbury report now requires listed companies to have an audit committee.)

Advantages

(1) By its very existence, the audit committee should make the **executive directors more aware of their duties and responsibilities.**

(2) It could act as a **deterrent to the commission of illegal acts** by the executive directors and may discourage them from behaving in ways which could be prejudicial to the interests of the shareholders

(3) Where **illegal or prejudicial acts** have been carried out by the executive directors, the **audit committee** provides an **independent body** to which the auditor can turn. In this way, the problem may be resolved without the auditor having to reveal the matter to the shareholders, either in his report or at the AGM.

4 INTERNAL CONTROL EFFECTIVENESS

Importance of internal control and risk management

4.1 Internal controls are essential to management, as they contribute to

- Safeguarding the company's assets
- Helping to prevent and detect fraud
- Therefore, safeguarding the shareholders' investment

4.2 Good internal control helps the business to run efficiently. It helps to ensure reliability of reporting, and compliance with laws.

Directors' responsibilities

4.3 The **ultimate responsibility** for a company's system of internal controls lies with the board of directors. It should set procedures of internal control and regularly monitor that the system operates as it should.

4.4 Part of setting up an internal control system will involve **assessing the risks** facing the business, so that the **system** can be **designed** to ensure those **risks are avoided**.

4.5 As you know from your studies at 2.6, *Audit and Internal Review* (old paper 6), the system of internal control in a company will reflect the **control environment**, which includes the attitude of the directors towards risk, and their awareness of it.

4.6 Internal control systems will always have **inherent limitations**, the most important being that a system of internal control cannot eliminate the possibility of human error, or the chance that staff will collude in fraud.

4.7 Once the directors have set up a system of internal control, they are responsible for **reviewing** it regularly, to ensure that it **still meets its objectives**.

4.8 The board may decide that in order to carry out their review function properly they have to employ an **internal audit function** to undertake this task. The role of internal audit is discussed in more detail in Chapter 16, but this is potentially part of its function.

4.9 If the board does not see the need for an internal audit function, the combined code suggests that it revisits this decision on an annual basis, so that the **need for internal audit is regularly reviewed**.

4.10 The combined code recommends that the board of directors **report** on their review of internal controls as part of their annual report.

4.11 The statement should be based on an annual assessment of internal control which should confirm that the board has considered **all significant aspects** of internal control. In particular the assessment should cover:

(a) The **changes** since the last **assessment** in **risks** faced, and the company's **ability** to **respond** to **changes** in its business environment

(b) The **scope** and **quality** of management's monitoring of risk and internal control, and of the work of internal audit, or consideration of the need for an internal audit function if the company does not have one

(c) The **extent** and **frequency** of reports to the board

(d) **Significant controls, failings** and **weaknesses** which have or might have material impacts upon the accounts

(e) The effectiveness of the public reporting processes

Auditors' responsibilities

4.12 The Auditing Practice Board's Bulletin 1999/5 *The Combined Code: Requirements of Auditors Under the Listing Rules of the London Stock Exchange* considered what auditors should do in response to a statement on internal controls by directors.

4.13 The guidance states that the auditors should concentrate on the review carried out by the board. The objectives of the auditors' work is to assess whether the company's summary of the process that the board has adopted in reviewing the effectiveness of the system of internal control is supported by the documentation prepared by the directors and reflects that process.

4.14 The auditors should make appropriate enquiries and review the statement made by the board in the accounts and the supporting documentation.

4.15 Auditors will have gained some understanding of controls due to their work on the accounts; however what they are required to do by auditing standards is narrower in scope than the review performed by the directors.

4.16 Auditors therefore are not expected to assess whether the directors' review covers all risks and controls, and whether the risks are satisfactorily addressed by the internal controls. To avoid misunderstanding on the scope of the auditors' role, the Bulletin recommends that the following wording be used in the audit report.

> 'We are not required to consider whether the board's statements on internal control cover all risks and controls, or form an opinion on the effectiveness of the company's corporate governance procedures or its risk and control procedures.'

4.17 The Bulletin also points out that it is particularly important for auditors to communicate quickly to the directors any material weaknesses they find, because of the requirements for the directors to make a statement on internal control.

4.18 The directors are required to consider the material internal control aspects of any significant problems disclosed in the accounts. Auditors work on this is the same as on other aspects of the statement; the auditors are not required to consider whether the internal control processes will remedy the problem.

4.19 The auditors may report by exception if problems arise such as:

(a) The **board's summary** of the process of review of internal control effectiveness does **not reflect** the **auditors' understanding** of that process.

(b) The **processes** that **deal with** material internal control aspects of **significant problems** do **not reflect** the **auditors' understanding** of those processes.

(c) The board has **not made** an **appropriate disclosure** if it has **failed** to **conduct** an **annual review**, or the disclosure made is not consistent with the auditors' understanding.

4.20 The report should be included in a separate paragraph below the opinion paragraph. The Bulletin gives the following example.

Other matter

> We have reviewed the board's description of its process for reviewing the effectiveness of internal control set out on page x of the annual report. In our opinion the boards comments concerning ... do not appropriately reflect our understanding of the process undertaken by the board because...

4.21 Critics of recent developments have argued that listed company directors ought to be able to report on the effectiveness of internal controls, and that this is part of the responsibility and accountability expected of listed company directors. The debate is likely to continue over the next few years.

5 LAW AND REGULATION

5.1 The Codes of Best Practice discussed above are all voluntary codes of practice. However, companies are increasingly subject to laws and regulations with which they must comply as well. Some examples are given in the diagram below.

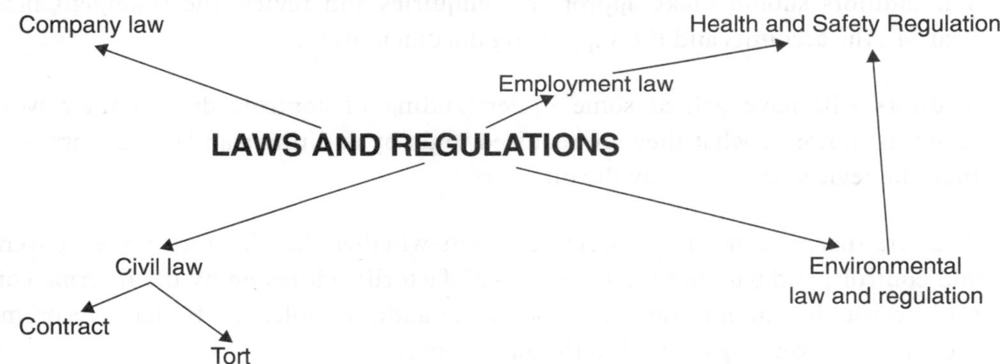

5.2 An auditor must be aware of the effect that non-compliance with the laws and regulations would have on the financial statements. Guidance is given in SAS 120 *Consideration of law and regulations*.

5.3 The statements of auditing standards in SAS 120 *Consideration of law and regulations* are as follows and these summarise the APB's approach to the subject.

SAS 120

Auditors should plan and perform their audit procedures, and evaluate and report on the results thereof, recognising that non-compliance by the entity with law or regulations may materially affect the financial statements. (SAS 120.1)

The auditors' consideration of compliance with law and regulations

The auditors should obtain sufficient appropriate audit evidence about compliance with those laws and regulations which relate directly to the preparation of, or the inclusion or disclosure of specific items in, the financial statements. (SAS 120.2)

The auditors should perform procedures to help identify possible or actual instances of non-compliance with those laws and regulations which provide a legal framework within which the entity conducts its business and which are central to the entity's ability to conduct its business and hence to its financial statements, by:

(a) obtaining a general understanding of the legal and regulatory framework applicable to the entity and the industry, and of the procedures followed to ensure compliance with that framework;

(b) inspecting correspondence with relevant licensing or regulatory authorities;

(c) enquiring of the directors as to whether they are on notice of any such possible instances of non-compliance with law or regulations; and

(d) obtaining written confirmation from the directors that they have disclosed to the auditors all those events of which they are aware which involve possible non-compliance, together with the actual or contingent consequences which may arise therefrom. (SAS 120.3)

When carrying out their procedures for the purpose of forming an opinion on the financial statements, the auditors should in addition be alert for instances of possible or actual non-compliance with law or regulations which might affect the financial statements. (SAS 120.4)

When the auditors become aware of information which indicates that non-compliance with law or regulations may exist, they should obtain an understanding of the nature of the act and the circumstances in which it has occurred and sufficient other information to evaluate the possible effect on the financial statements. (SAS 120.5)

When the auditors become aware of or suspect that there may be non-compliance with law or regulations, they should document their findings and, subject to any requirement to report them direct to a third party, discuss them with the appropriate level of management. (SAS 120.6)

The auditors should consider the implications of suspected or actual non-compliance with law or regulations in relation to other aspects of the audit, particularly the reliability or management representations. (SAS 120.7)

Reporting to management

The auditors should, as soon as practicable (save where SAS 120.15 applies) either:

(a) communicate with management, the board of directors or the audit committee, or
(b) obtain evidence that they are appropriately informed,

regarding any suspected or actual non-compliance with law or regulations that comes to the auditors' attention. (SAS 120.8)

If, in the auditors' judgement, the suspected or actual non-compliance with law or regulations is material or is believed to be intentional, the auditors should communicate the finding without delay. (SAS 120.9)

Reporting to addressees of the auditors' report on the financial statements

Where the auditors conclude that the view given by the financial statements could be affected by a level of uncertainty concerning the consequences of a suspected or actual non-compliance which, in their opinion, is fundamental, they should include an explanatory paragraph referring to the matter in their report. (SAS 120.10)

Where the auditors conclude that a suspected or actual instance of non-compliance with law or regulation has a material effect on the financial statements and they disagree with the accounting treatment or with the extent, or the lack, of any disclosure in the financial statements of the instance of its consequences they should issue an adverse or qualified opinion. If the auditors are unable to determine whether non-compliance with law or regulations has occurred because of limitation in the scope of their work, they should issue a disclaimer or a qualified opinion. (SAS 120.11)

Reporting to third parties

When the auditors become aware of a suspected or actual non-compliance with law and regulations which gives rise to a statutory duty to report, they should make a report to the appropriate authority without undue delay. (SAS 120.12)

Where the auditors become aware of a suspected or actual instance of non-compliance with law or regulations which does not give rise to a statutory duty to report to an appropriate authority they should:

(a) consider whether the matter may be one that ought to be reported to a proper authority in the public interest; and where this is the case

(b) except in the circumstances covered in SAS 120.15, discuss the matter with the board of directors including any audit committee. (SAS 120.13)

Where, having considered any views expressed on behalf of the entity and in the light of any legal advice obtained, the auditors conclude that the matter ought to be reported to an appropriate authority in the public interest, they should notify the directors in writing of their view and, if the entity does not voluntarily do so itself or is unable to provide evidence that the matter has been reported, they should report it themselves. (SAS 120.14)

Auditors should report a matter direct to a proper authority in the public interest and without discussing the matter with the entity if they conclude that the suspected or actual instance of non-compliance has caused them no longer to have confidence in the integrity of the directors. (SAS 120.15)

Overseas activities

Where any of the activities of a company or group are carried on outside the United Kingdom or the Republic of Ireland, the auditors should take steps to ensure that the audit work in relation to the detection and reporting of any non-compliance with local law and regulations is planned and carried out in accordance with the requirements of this SAS. (SAS 120.16)

5.4 The SAS draws a distinction between the responsibilities of the directors and the responsibilities of the auditors.

5.5 The directors should take the appropriate steps and establish arrangements to ensure compliance with law and regulations and to prevent and detect any non-compliance. In addition, they are responsible for the financial statements showing a true and fair view.

5.6 The auditors have no duty to prevent non-compliance with laws and regulations but they should 'plan, perform and evaluate their audit work in order to have a reasonable expectation of detecting material misstatement in the financial statements', including those arising from non-compliance with laws and regulations.

5.7 In an appendix to the SAS there is a list of examples of the type of information that may come to the auditors' attention and may indicate that non-compliance with law or regulations has occurred.

- **Investigation** by **government departments** or payment of fines or penalties
- **Payments** for **unspecified services** or loans to consultants, related parties, employees or government employees

- **Sales commissions** or **agents' fees** that appear excessive in relation to those normally paid by the entity or in its industry or to the services actually received
- **Purchasing** at **prices significantly above or below market price**
- **Unusual payments** in **cash, purchases** in the form of **cashiers' cheques** payable to bearer or **transfers** to **numbered bank accounts**
- **Unusual transactions** with **companies registered** in tax havens
- **Payments for goods or services** made **other than** to the **country** from which the goods or services originated
- **Existence** of an **accounting system** that fails, whether by design or by accident, to provide adequate audit trail or sufficient evidence
- **Unauthorised transactions** or improperly recorded transactions
- **Media comment**

Assessment of law and regulations in practice

5.8 SAS 120 has proved difficult for auditors to apply in practice. The Institute of Chartered Accountants in England and Wales recently issued a Technical Release on this area '*Consideration of law and regulations: Guidance and Questionnaire for Auditors.*' Significant aspects of applying SAS 120 in practice highlighted by the Technical Release were as follows.

Distinction between types of law

5.9 The most difficult distinction in practice is between:

- Laws which are **central** to the ability of the client to conduct its business
- Other laws and regulations

5.10 The Technical Release points out that:

(a) For some businesses, certain laws and regulations will be central, for other businesses the **same** laws and regulations will not be central.

(b) For some businesses, laws and regulations which were not central last year may be central this year, (for example where the maximum penalty for a first offence is a warning, but subsequent infringements may lead to closure of the business).

Procedures that should be performed

5.11 The Technical Release echoes the distinction that the SAS makes between checking systems of compliance and checking actual compliance. One example given is emissions from a chemical factory; auditors would review the company's systems for keeping these under control, and would also review correspondence with the environmental authority. However, the auditors would not be expected to check the actual emissions. The Technical Release poses the question how far checking compliance procedures might go.

Reporting

5.12 The Technical Release highlights various issues which procedures under SAS 120 may identify that may impact upon the audit report.

(a) The need for **possible provisions**:
- For fines, legal expenses, rectification costs
- For indirect costs, for example loss in value of stock

(b) **Going concern doubts** (because of uncertain future sales)

(c) **Scope limitation**, perhaps caused by unhelpful management responses to queries

5.13 Auditors should also consider whether they have a statutory duty to report breaches to third parties.

Money laundering

5.14 One area of laws and regulations which has caused auditors particular difficulty is money laundering. The APB issued Practice Notice 12 *Money Laundering* in May 1997 on the subject. Although this Practice Note is not listed as an examinable document, you do need to know what money laundering is and have a general awareness of how it impacts upon the audit.

KEY TERM

Money laundering covers any activity by which the apparent source and ownership of money representing the proceeds of income are changed so that the money appears to have been obtained legitimately.

5.15 There are five criminal offences which relate to money laundering.

- **Assisting** another to retain the proceeds of criminal conduct
- **Acquisition, possession or use** of the proceeds of criminal conduct
- **Concealing** the proceeds of criminal activity
- **Failure to disclose** knowledge or suspicion of money laundering (only money laundering related to drug trafficking or terrorism)
- **Tipping off** (disclosing information to any person if disclosure may prejudice an investigation into:
  - Drug trafficking
  - Drug money laundering
  - Terrorist related activities
  - Laundering the proceeds of criminal conduct)

5.16 The Practice Note suggests that the auditors are likely to be affected by money laundering legislation in the following ways.

Appointment

5.17 At minimum, auditors will seek to gain knowledge of the potential client's directors and management so as to fulfil the SAS 210 requirements of obtaining knowledge that is sufficient to enable them to understand the business.

5.18 In addition the money laundering regulations require auditors to carry out identity checks on the client if they are providing certain non-audit services (for example investment business advice) that constitute 'relevant financial business'. In practice many firms now extend these identification procedures to all new clients.

Planning and substantive testing

5.19 Auditor responsibilities under SAS 110 and 120 will influence the audit work that is planned and carried out.

5.20 The Practice Note lists a number of factors which may indicate both fraud and money laundering.

(a) **Factors arising from action by the entity or its directors**

These include:

- Complex corporate structure where complexity does not seem to be warranted
- Complex or unusual transactions, possibly with related parties
- Transactions with little commercial logic taking place in the normal course of business
- Transactions not in the normal course of business
- Transactions where there is a lack of information or explanations, or where explanations are unsatisfactory
- Transactions at an undervalue
- Transactions with companies whose identity is difficult to establish as they are registered in countries known for their commercial secrecy
- Extensive or unusual related party transactions
- Many large cash transactions when not expected
- Payments for unspecified services, or payments for services that appear excessive in relation to the services provided
- The forming of companies or trusts with no apparent commercial or other purpose
- Long delays in the production of company or trust accounts
- Foreign travel which is apparently **unnecessary** and **extensive**

(b) **Factors arising from action by a third party**

Circumstances which may indicate that third parties are using transactions with an entity to launder criminal proceeds include:

- A customer establishing a pattern of small transactions and then having one or two substantially larger ones
- Unusual transactions or a pattern of trading with one customer that is different from the norm
- A customer setting up a transaction that appears to be of no commercial advantage or logic
- A customer requesting special arrangements for vague purposes
- Unusual transactions with companies registered overseas
- Requests for settlement in bank accounts or jurisdictions which would be unusual for a normal commercial transaction

5.21 The Practice Note points out that these signs may not be apparent when assessing risk at the planning stage. Nevertheless auditors should be alert, particularly for a significant unusual pattern of activity.

5.22 As regards laws and regulations, the Practice Note draws a distinction between various types of entity.

(a) Entities where the money laundering laws and regulations are central to the business. These include:

  (i) **Financial sector entities** offering services that are governed by Money Laundering Regulations

  (ii) **Public sector entities** which are required to comply with specific regulations on money laundering.

(b) Entities where the money laundering laws and regulations are not central, but which may be more likely to be run for money laundering purposes or to be used to launder criminal proceeds. Examples given by the Practice Note include:

  (i) **Import/export companies**

  (ii) **Business** which are **cash-based** (for example, antique businesses, art dealers, auction houses, casinos or garages)

(c) Other entities

Reporting

5.23 Reporting money laundering can cause problems for auditors because of the possibility of breaching the laws relating to **tipping off**. Auditors will not only avoid reporting to management if they suspect management of being involved with money laundering, but they will also have to take care when carrying out audit procedures to avoid problems with tipping off.

5.24 The Practice Note suggests that **preliminary enquiries** to ascertain the precise nature of a transaction will not give rise to a tipping-off offence unless the auditors know or suspect an investigation is being mounted or is proposed, and that auditor enquiries may prejudice the investigation.

5.25 'It is important that auditors only go so far as to establish their own satisfaction whether there is a suspected case of money laundering involving the directors and to consider the consequences for the report on the financial statements.'

5.26 As regards the audit report on the financial statements, auditors potentially face a dilemma. An unqualified report may effectively legitimise an illegal business which may constitute assisting another to retain the proceeds of criminal conduct. On the other hand a qualified audit report or fundamental uncertainty paragraph may constitute tipping off. Legal advice, or advice from the Economic Unit of the National Criminal Intelligence Service (NCIS) may be necessary before the audit report is issued.

5.27 Auditors may also be required or wish to report suspicions of money laundering to appropriate authorities. Reports must be made in the following circumstances.

(a) For any client, if the auditor has knowledge or suspicions of **drug money laundering** or arrangements facilitating the retention or control of **terrorist funds** or the proceeds of terrorist related activities, or the provision of financial assistance for terrorism. Reports should be made to NCIS

(b) For financial services, reports to the appropriate regulators under SAS 620

(c) For public sector clients, to the appropriate authority

5.28 In other circumstances auditors may feel that suspicions should be reported in the public interest. The Practice Note points out that statutory immunity is granted, from any legal action for breach of confidence, for having notified the Economic Crime Unit of NCIS of suspicions of money laundering, provided the report is made in good faith.

Chapter roundup

- Corporate governance is the system by which companies are directed and controlled. It is important that management deal fairly with the investment of shareholders.
- Auditors report on the truth and fairness of the financial statements **only,** in their statutory role.
- However, it is increasingly perceived as important that assurance is given to shareholders concerning the corporate governance of their investment.
- The government have set up voluntary codes of best practice with regard to best practice, particularly the Cadbury Code.
- Listed companies are required to conform to the requirement of the combined code. This requires that companies set up audit committees.
- Audit committees are made up of non-executive directors. A key perceived benefit of audit committees is that they need to increase confidence in financial reports.
- Internal control is a key part of good corporate governance. **Directors** are **responsible** for maintaining a system of control that will safeguard the company's assets.
- Companies and directors are also subject to laws and regulations. Auditors' duties with regard to law and regulations are outlined in SAS 120, *Consideration of law and regulations.*
- Auditors must be aware of law and regulations as part of their planning. They must also be aware of their statutory duty to report non-compliance.

Quick quiz

1 Complete the definition.

The ____________ report defines ____________ ____________ as 'the system by which companies are directed or controlled'.

2 Which two items on the following list are not provisions on the Cadbury code?

(1) The **board of directors** must meet on a regular basis, retain full control over the company and monitor the executive management.

(2) A **clearly accepted division of responsibilities is necessary** at the head of the company, so no one person has complete power, answerable to no-one.

(3) Each listed company should have at least five executive directors, all of whom should be matched by a non-executive director.

(4) The report encourages **the separation of the posts of Chairman and a Chief Executive.**

(5) There should be a **formal schedule of matters which must be referred to the board** stating which decisions require a single director's signature and which require several signatures.

(6) The schedule should include all acquisitions and disposal of assets of the company and subsidiaries.

3 All companies must include a corporate governance statement in their annual report.

True ☐

False ☐

4 Name four potential duties of the audit committee.

(1) ________________

(2) ________________

(3) ________________

(4) ________________

5 Auditors are responsible for a company's system of internal controls

True ☐

False ☐

6 Name four areas of law which might affect a company.

(1) ________________

(2) ________________

(3) ________________

(4) ________________

7 Complete the following definition

Money ____________________ covers any activity by which the apparent source and ownership of - ________________ representing the proceeds of ________________ are ________________ so that the money appears to have been obtained ____________________.

Answers to quick quiz

1 Cadbury, corporate governance

2 (3) No minimum exists other than the legal minimum. Non-executives should generally be one third.

(6) Only **material** items.

3 False – only listed companies are required to.

4 (1) Review of financial statements
(2) Liaison with external auditors
(3) Review of internal audit
(4) Review of internal controls

5 False – this is the directors' duty

6 see Para 5.1

7 Laundering, income, income, changed, legitimately

Now try the question below from the Exam Question Bank

Number	Level	Marks	Time
5	Exam	15	27 mins

Part B
Audit process

Chapter 6

REVISION OF STATUTORY AUDIT

Topic list		Syllabus reference
1	**What is a statutory audit?**	**4(a)**
2	**What are the benefits and limitations of audit?**	**4(a)**
3	**Non-statutory audit**	**4(a)**
4	**Audit and small and medium sized entities**	**6(g)**
5	**Chronology of an audit**	**4(a)**
6	**Audit process**	**3**

Introduction

The statutory audit is still the most key audit which auditors undertake. You learnt about it in your earlier auditing studies, so a lot of this and the following chapters is revision. In Chapters 11 to 13 we shall introduce some advanced auditing areas which you will not have encountered previously.

The **threshold** was increased in 2000 to a turnover limit of £1,000,000 for exemption from audit. It is anticipated that it will rise further in the future. Given that environment, statutory audit is now only one area that audit firms are involved in.

There is **increasing interest in audit related and assurance services** as the number of companies requiring an audit reduces. Services other than statutory audit are explored in part C of this textbook. However, you should remember that many of the techniques and tests discussed in part B can also be used to carry out different engagements.

The **statutory audit** is still important. There are many companies whose turnover is still above the threshold and they will continue to have an annual audit. There is widespread belief that an **audit still has value** for smaller companies, and the government is considering the introduction of an audit alternative for smaller companies. In the absence of any good alternatives being finalised, it is anticipated that many smaller companies will continue to have an annual audit for the benefits it can bring.

These issues are all discussed in sections 1-5 of this chapter. The final section provides an introduction to the rest of part B.

Study guide

Section 14

- Explain the objectives and principal characteristics of statutory audit and discuss its value (eg in assisting management to reduce risk and improve performance)
- Distinguish between the respective responsibilities of auditors and management in relation to the audit of financial statements
- Describe the limitations of assurance provided by a statutory audit

Section 27

SMEs and audit exemption

- State the case for and against audit exemption for small businesses
- Discuss how the potential problems associated with the audit of small enterprises may be overcome

Exam guide

Statutory audit is one of the variety of services an accountant can provide. It is important to understand the nature, benefits and limitations of an audit.

1 WHAT IS A STATUTORY AUDIT?

1.1 We shall concentrate on the general guidance the APB gives on what constitutes an audit.

KEY TERM

An **audit** is an exercise whose objective is to enable auditors to express an opinion whether the financial statements give a true and fair view (or equivalent) of the entity's affairs at the period end and of its profit and loss (or income and expenditure) for the period then ended and have been properly prepared in accordance with the applicable reporting framework (for example relevant legislation and applicable accounting standards) or, where statutory or other specific requirements prescribe the term, whether the financial statements 'present fairly'.

1.2 This wording follows very closely that of the auditors' report on financial statements, which we will look at later.

1.3 First of all, though, we need to look at what an audit is really about. This is the subject matter of the APB's Statement of Auditing Standards SAS 100 *Objective and general principles governing an audit of financial statements*.The first 'Statement of Auditing Standards' in SAS 100 is as follows.

SAS 100.1

In undertaking an audit of financial statements auditors should:

(a) carry out procedures designed to obtain sufficient appropriate audit evidence, in accordance with Auditing Standards contained in SASs, to determine with reasonable confidence whether the financial statements are free of material misstatement;

(b) evaluate the overall presentation of the financial statements, in order to ascertain whether they have been prepared in accordance with relevant legislation and accounting standards; and

(c) issue a report containing a clear expression of their opinion on the financial statements.

1.4 The SAS's explanatory material highlights the credibility given to financial statements by the auditors' opinion; it provides '**reasonable assurance** from an **independent** source that they present a true and fair view'.

1.5 That is to say the audit report reassures readers of the accounts that the accounts have been examined by a **knowledgeable, impartial** professional. SAS 100 goes on to stress further the importance of auditors acting **independently** and **ethically.**

1.6 The assurance auditors give is governed by the fact that auditors use **judgement** in deciding what audit procedures to use and what conclusions to draw, and also by the limitations of every audit.

(a) The fact that auditing is **not** a purely **objective** exercise. Auditors have to make judgements in a number of areas including risk assessment, what constitutes a significant error, what tests to perform and ultimately what opinion to give.

(b) The fact that **auditors do not check every item** in the accounting records. We shall see that for many tests auditors only check a sample of items.

(c) The **limitations** of **accounting** and **internal control systems.** For example, the systems may not be able to deal with unusual transactions, and may not be flexible enough to cope well with changing circumstances.

(d) The possibility that **client management or staff** might **not tell the truth**, or **collude in fraud.** One important control may be a division of responsibilities so that one member of staff checks another's work, but the control will be ineffective if the two collude.

(e) The fact that audit **evidence indicates** what is **probable** rather than what is **certain**. Some figures in the accounts are estimates, some require a significant degree of judgement and some are affected by uncertainty.

(f) The fact that auditors are **reporting** generally **some months after** the balance sheet date. The client's position may be changing, and the position shown in the accounts at the last year-end may be significantly different from the up-to-date position. If on the other hand auditors do report soon after the balance sheet date, evidence about certain figures in the balance sheet may be insufficient.

(g) The **limitations** of the audit report. Although work has been done to make the report more informative, the standard format is unlikely to reflect all aspects of the audit. This is discussed further in Chapter 19.

Hence auditors can only express an opinion; they cannot certify whether accounts are completely correct.

1.7 Material misstatements may exist in financial statements and auditors will plan their work on this basis, that is with **professional scepticism.**

1.8 SAS 100 makes it clear that, even where auditors assess the risk of litigation or adverse publicity as very low, they must still perform sufficient procedures according to auditing standards, that is, there can never be a reason for carrying out an audit of a lower quality than that demanded by the auditing standards. This has been discussed in Chapter 4.

SAS 100.2

In the conduct of any audit of financial statements auditors should comply with the ethical guidance issued by their relevant professional bodies.

1.9 ACCA's ethical guidance has been discussed in Chapter 1.

1.10 Audits are required under statute in the case of a large number of undertakings, including the following:

Undertaking	Principal Act
Limited companies	Companies Act 1985
Building societies	Building Societies Act 1965
Trade unions and employer associations	Trade Union and Labour Relations Act 1974
Housing Associations	Various acts depending on the legal constitution of the housing association, including: Industrial and Provident Societies Act 1965 Friendly and Industrial and Provident Societies Act 1968 Housing Act 1980 Companies Act 1985 Housing Association Act 1985
Certain charities	Various acts depending on the status of the charity, including special Acts of Parliament.
Unincorporated investment businesses	Regulations made under the Financial Services Act 1986

1.11 Small limited companies are exempt from an audit. The new regulations are:

(a) A company is totally exempt from the annual audit requirement in a financial year if its turnover for that year is not more than £1million and its balance sheet total is not more than £1.4 million.

(b) The exemptions do not apply to public companies, banking or insurance companies or those subject to a statute based regulatory regime.

(c) A company that is part of a group can claim exemption provided the group of which it is a member is a small group which satisfies the conditions.

(d) Shareholders holding 10% or more of the capital of any company can veto the exemption.

(e) A dormant company which fulfils the criteria of s 249AA (that is it qualifies for exemption as a small company) does not need a special resolution to gain exemption from audit.

Responsibility

1.12 A key point that is made in SAS 100 is that auditors do not bear any responsibility for the preparation and presentation of the financial statements.

The responsibility for the preparation and presentation of the financial statements is that of the directors of the entity. Auditors are responsible for forming and expressing an opinion on the financial statements. The audit of the financial statements does not relieve the directors of any of their responsibilities.

1.13 Another key fact about responsibility which is often perceived incorrectly is that the **auditor does not have any responsibility with regard to prevention and detection of fraud.**

2 WHAT ARE THE BENEFITS AND LIMITATIONS OF AUDIT?

Benefits of audit

2.1 The key benefit of audit has been mentioned above. It is the fact that through an audit, the owners of the company (**members**) are given an **independent opinion** as to the **truth and fairness of the accounts** which have been prepared for them by the directors, giving them an impression of how their investment has performed in the period.

2.2 There are a number of subsidiary benefits however. Examples include:

- The financial statements can be used by **third parties such as banks**, to make decisions about the company. An audit will give them more **confidence in the financial statements**.
- The auditors can use their experience as business advisors to **help the directors improve the business** as a by-product of audit. This can be achieved by:
    - Management letter
    - Discussions during the audit
- Specifically, the existence of the auditor can help to **mitigate against risks**. A key example of this is the risk of fraud despite it not being the duty of the auditor to detect fraud.

Limitations of audit

2.3 Some of the limitations of audit were discussed at paragraph 1.6.

2.4 There are other provisos attached to the assurance given by the auditor. The auditors' opinion is **not** a **guarantee** of

- The **future viability** of the entity
- **Management's effectiveness and efficiency**
- No **fraud** having been perpetrated on the company

3 NON-STATUTORY AUDIT

3.1 **Non-statutory audits** are performed by independent auditors because the owners, proprietors, members, trustees, professional and governing bodies or other interested parties want them, rather than because the law requires them. In consequence, auditing may extend to every type of undertaking which produces accounts, including:

- Clubs
- Charities (assuming that an audit is not statutory)
- Sole traders
- Partnerships

3.2 Auditors may also give an **audit opinion** on **statements other than annual accounts**, including:

- Summaries of sales in support of a statement of royalties
- Statements of expenditure in support of applications for regional development grants
- The circulation figures of a newspaper or magazine

3.3 In all such audits the auditors must take into account any **regulations** contained in the internal rules or constitution of the undertaking. Examples of the regulations which the auditors would need to refer to in such assignments would include:

- The rules of clubs, societies and charities
- Partnership agreements

Advantages of the non-statutory audit

3.4 In addition to the advantages common to all forms of audit, including the verification of accounts, recommendations on accounting and control systems and the possible detection of errors and fraud, the audit of the accounts of a **partnership** may be seen to have the following advantages.

(a) It can provide a means of **settling accounts** between the partners.

(b) Where audited accounts are available this may make the **accounts more acceptable** to the **Inland Revenue** when it comes to agreeing an individual partner's liability to tax. The partners may well wish to take advantage of the auditors' services in the additional role of tax advisers.

(c) The **sale of** the business or the **negotiation of loan** or overdraft facilities may be facilitated if the firm is able to produce audited accounts.

(d) An audit on behalf of a '**sleeping partner**' is useful since generally such a person will have little other means of checking the accounts of the business, or confirming the share of profits due to him or her.

4 AUDIT AND SMALL AND MEDIUM SIZED ENTITIES

4.1 There has been a long-running debate in the UK as to whether small companies need a statutory audit. The audit exemption limit was recently raised, as discussed above, but the debate continues.

4.2 The case for retaining the small company audit rests on the value of the statutory audit to those who have an interest in audited accounts, that is, the users of accounts.

4.3 From the viewpoint of each type of user, the arguments for and against abolition are as follows.

(a) *Shareholders*

Against change: Shareholders not involved in management need the reassurance given by audited accounts. Furthermore, the existence of the audit deters the directors from treating the company's assets as their own to the detriment of minority shareholders.

Audited financial statements are invaluable in arriving at a fair valuation of the shares in an unquoted company either for taxation or other purposes.

For change: Where all the shareholders are also executive directors or closely related to them, the benefit gained from an audit may not be worth its cost.

(b) *Banks and other institutional creditors*

Against change: Banks rely on accounts for the purposes of making loans and reviewing the value of security.

For change — There is doubt whether banks rely on the audited accounts of companies to a greater extent than those of unincorporated associations of a similar size which have not been audited.

A review of the way in which the bank accounts of the company have been conducted and of forecasts and management accounts are at least as important to the banks as the appraisal of the audited accounts.

There is no reason why a bank should not make an audit a precondition of granting a loan.

(c) *Trade creditors*

Against change — Creditors and potential creditors should have the opportunity to assess the strength of their customers by examining audited financial statements either themselves or through a credit company.

For change — In practice, only limited reliance is placed on the accounts available from the Registrar of Companies as they are usually filed so late as to be of little significance in granting short term credit.

(d) *Tax authorities*

Against change — The Inland Revenue and Customs & Excise rely on accounts for computing corporation tax and checking VAT returns.

For change — There is little evidence to suggest that the tax authorities rely on audited accounts to a significantly greater extent than those, which, whilst being unaudited have been prepared by an independent accountant.

(e) *Employees*

Against change — Employees are entitled to be able to assess audited accounts when entering wage negotiations and considering the future viability of their employer.

For change — There is little evidence to suggest that, in the case of small companies, such assessments are made.

(f) *Management*

Against change — The audit provides management with a useful independent check on the accuracy of the accounting systems and the auditor is frequently able to recommend improvements in those systems.

For change — If the law were changed, the management of a company could, if they so desired, still elect to have an independent audit. It is likely, however, that a systems review accompanied by a management consultancy report would represent a greater benefit for a similar cost.

4.4 The government outlined a potential alternative to the audit for small companies, the **independent professional review**. This alternative is being considered by the major accountancy bodies at the present time.

Problems of small company audits

4.5 Small companies are different to large companies. They are often managed by their owners, which reduces the problems associated with corporate governance (discussed in Chapter 5) but may mean that there is a lack of accounting skill in the management.

4.6 They are also likely to have significantly more limited controls that a larger company. The minimum business controls were discussed in the 2.6, *Audit and Internal Review* textbook. You might find it helpful to refer to them here.

4.7 The APB have issued a practice note to help auditors overcome the problems associated with the audit of small businesses.

Application of SASs to small businesses

4.8 In July 1997 Practice Note 13 *The Audit of Small Businesses* was published. Although the detailed contents of this Practice Note are not examinable, it does make some important general points which you should remember.

4.9 The Practice Note states that the audit of small businesses is influenced by a number of factors. These include:

(a) The **characteristics of small businesses**. The most important characteristics are **concentration of ownership** and **management** in a few/single individual(s), the business having few sources of income and uncomplicated activities and limited internal controls and the potential for management override.

(b) The **professional relationship** between the business and its auditors. Auditors will often provide a range of **other services** as well as auditing, particularly accounting services. The Practice Note stresses the importance of the auditors maintaining objectivity despite providing other services, and not taking over the role of management.

(c) Audits of small businesses may also be affected by the fact that **small teams of auditors** may be **involved** and the rules governing the content of small businesses' financial statements.

4.10 The Practice Note then goes on to give a detailed commentary on how specific SASs impact upon the audit of small businesses.

SAS 110 Fraud and error

4.11 Amongst the signs of fraud that may be particularly relevant to small businesses are the owner-manager making no distinction between business and personal transactions and the owner-manager's lifestyle being materially inconsistent with remuneration levels.

SAS 130 Going concern

4.12 The Practice Note points out that a small business's continuation as a going concern may depend on a single factor, for example funds not being withdrawn.

SAS 230 Working papers

4.13 If accountancy work is being used as audit evidence, the work performed, the evidence obtained and the conclusions drawn are recorded as for normal audit work.

SAS 400 Audit evidence

4.14 The Practice Note emphasises that accountancy work can provide audit evidence for certain objectives, but is unlikely to provide sufficient evidence of completeness and valuation.

Question 1

The audit of small companies creates special problems for auditors

Briefly discuss the reasons why small companies create special problems for auditors and consider the reasons why auditors should direct their work more to verification of items by physical inspection and third party evidence than is the case when auditing larger companies.

Answer

The general principles to be applied to the audit of a small company are essentially the same as for any other audit. There are however, certain features about the audit of many small companies which can raise the difficulties in the application of those principles.

These problems arise because of certain features often presented in many companies employing a small number of administrative staff and controlled and managed by a single proprietor or at most by a small number of proprietors. These problems mainly derive from:

(i) Substantial domination of the accounting and financial management functions by one person

(ii) Limitations in the effectiveness from an audit point of view of the system of internal control rendered inevitable by the small number of employees.

The major difference from an audit point of view between a small company and a larger organisation will be the extent to which the system of internal control and the staff organisation provide a check whereby the work of one person is proved independently or is complementary to the work of another.

Whilst internal control, including internal check, in the small company may be effective for its primary purpose as a check for management use, the organisation will usually mean that it will be defective as a check on management itself.

These limitations in the effectiveness of internal control from an audit point of view may so reduce its value that the auditor will need to consider extending his/her audit procedures.

This will require him/her to increase the amount of testing of transactions and to intensify the procedures for the verification of liabilities and assets including for example attendance at stocktaking and confirmation of debtor balances by direct communication.

An auditor should always seek to obtain relevant and reliable audit evidence sufficient to enable him/her to draw reasonable conclusions. On the key question of 'reliability', the auditor of a small company is more likely to obtain sufficient evidence of which to base his opinion by concentrating his/her attention on those sources of evidence which are outside of the direct sphere of influence of the client.

It is for this reason that audit work should be directed more towards the verification of items by physical inspection and third party evidence than is the case when auditing larger companies.

---

5 CHRONOLOGY OF AN AUDIT

Determine audit approach

Stage 1 Determine the **scope** of the audit and the auditors' approach. For statutory audits the scope is laid down by the Companies Act 1985 and expanded by Auditing Standards.

The auditors should prepare an **audit plan,** which should be placed on file. The contents of the plan will be considered in Chapter 7.

Ascertain the system and controls

Stage 2 Determine the **flow of documents** and **extent of controls** in existence in the client's system.

This is a fact finding exercise which is achieved by discussing the accounting system and document flow with all the relevant departments (for example, sales, purchases, cash, stock and accounts personnel).

It is good practice to make a rough record of the system during this fact finding stage which will be converted to a formal record at Stage 3.

Stage 3 Prepare a **comprehensive record** of the **system to facilitate evaluation** of the systems. The records may be in various formats (for example, charts, narrative notes, internal control questionnaires and flowcharts).

Stage 4 Confirm that the **system recorded** is the same as that **in operation.**

This is achieved by performing walk-through tests. These involve tracing a handful of transactions through the system and observing the operation of controls over them.

This check is useful because sometimes client staff will tell the auditors what they **should be doing** rather than **what is actually done.**

Assess the system and internal controls

Stage 5 **Evaluate the systems** to gauge their reliability and formulate a basis for testing their effectiveness in practice.

Auditors will be able to recommend any improvements and also determine the extent of further tests at Stages 6 and 8 below.

Test the system and internal controls

Stage 6 *(This should only be carried out if the controls are evaluated as effective at Stage 5. If not, Steps 6 and 7 should be omitted.)*

If controls are effective, tests should are designed to establish compliance with the system should be selected and performed.

Tests of controls, which cover a larger number of items than walkthrough tests and cover a more representative sample of transactions through the period, should be carried out.

If **controls are strong**, the records should be reliable and the amount of detailed testing can be reduced. If **controls are ineffective** in practice, more extensive substantive procedures will be required.

Stage 7 After evaluating the systems and testing controls, auditors normally send an interim **report to management** identifying weaknesses and recommending improvements.

Test the financial statements

Stages 8 and 9 These tests are concerned with **substantiating the figures** given **in the final financial statements.**

Substantive tests also serve to assess the effect of errors, should errors exist.

Before designing a substantive procedure it is essential to consider whether any errors produced could be significant. If the answer is no, there is no point in performing a test.

Review the financial statements

Stage 10 The financial statements should be reviewed to determine the overall reliability of the account by making a **critical analysis of content and presentation.**

Express an opinion

Stage 11 The auditors evaluate the evidence that they have obtained and they **express their opinion** to members in the form of an **audit report.**

Stage 12 The **final report to management** is an important **non-statutory end product** of the audit. The purpose of it is to make further **suggestions for improvements** in the systems and to **place on record specific points** in connection with the audit and the accounts.

6 AUDIT PROCESS

6.1 The rest of part B deals with specific aspects of the audit process, as detailed in the table below.

Chapter 7	Revision of audit planning.
Chapter 8	Discussion about risk based auditing and other audit strategy.
Chapter 9	Revision of audit evidence.
Chapter 10	Revision of audit review.
Chapter 11	More advanced substantive testing issues in relation to assets.
Chapter 12	More advanced substantive testing issues in relation to liabilities.
Chapter 13	More advanced testing issues in relation to disclosure and other issues.

Specifically in Chapter 11-13, you should bear the following things in mind:

In the exam, you will be expected to evaluate certain matters pertaining to the audit of specific items in the financial statements. The key matters you should consider are:

- Materiality
- Risk
- Relevant accounting standards
- Audit evidence

Clearly the issues of risk and materiality will relate to details given in the question as these are unique to each situation. Little will be said about them in relation to each balance sheet area and issue.

Exam focus point

Although little is said about them in the last three chapters of this section, risk and materiality are key matters that an auditor has to consider in each given situation. It is absolutely vital that you remember to refer to them in an exam situation. Pertinent facts will be made in the question. You should be able to draw them out and explain their relevance.

Chapter roundup

- An audit is an exercise to give an independent opinion on the truth and fairness of financial statements
- It provides **reasonable** assurance. This is because:
  - Auditing is **not** purely an objective exercise
  - Auditors do **not** check each item
  - Limitations of control systems
- The benefits of an audit include:
  - Important third parties have more confidence in the financial statements
  - Auditors can help directors improve their business
  - Existence of auditor can mitigate against risks such as fraud
- Companies with turnover of less than £1m and balance sheet total of less than £1.4m are exempt from audit. There is a long-running debate in the UK on the benefits of audit for small companies.
- Small company audits can be problematic because:
  - The characteristics of small companies
  - The relationship with the auditor

Quick quiz

1 Name four limitations of an audit

(1) ____________________

(2) ____________________

(3) ____________________

(4) ____________________

2 There is a debate in the UK about the value of audit to smaller companies. Fill in the arguments for and against the audit

	FOR	AGAINST
Shareholders		
Banks		
Management		

3 Name the key benefits of an audit

(1) ____________________

(2) ____________________

(3) ____________________

Answers to quick quiz

1 see para 1.6

2

	FOR	AGAINST
Shareholders	Shareholders who are not management need the assurance given by an audit Audited financial statements can be used to obtain the fair value of shares	Where shareholders are directors the benefit gained from audit may not be worth its cost
Banks	Banks rely on the accounts for the purpose of making loans	An audit need not be a pre-condition of a loan
Management	Audit can be a useful independent check on accounting systems	Specialist systems review might be more helpful at little extra cost

3 see paras 2.1 + 2.2

Now try the question below from the Exam Question Bank

Number	Level	Marks	Time
6	Exam	20	36 mins

Chapter 7

AUDIT PLANNING

Topic list		Syllabus reference
1	**Revision: Overview of audit planning**	**3(b)**
2	**Materiality**	**3(b)**
3	**Risk**	**3(b)**
4	**General planning matters**	**3(b)**

Introduction

The issue of audit planning should not be new to you. You learnt how to plan an audit in your previous auditing studies. Why then is this chapter here? There are two answers:

- To **revise** the details that should be included in an **audit plan** and the general considerations included in planning
- To **consider** some of the **finer points of planning** from the point of view of the engagement partner, specifically to consider the issue of the **risk associated with the assignment** (which is a personal risk to the partner in the event of litigation arising)

Risk is an important factor in the audit. It falls into two categories:

- Specific **assignment risk** (known as audit risk) which you have studied previously
- **Business risk** associated with the client which is a part of inherent risk and therefore impacts on the audit

Risk is a key issue in an audit, and the most common approach to audits incorporates a recognition of those risks in the approach taken. It is called the **risk-based approach,** and we investigate it in Chapter 8.

Study guide

Section 9

General

- Identify and illustrate the matters to be considered in planning an assignment including:
  - Logistics (eg staff and client management, multiple locations, deadlines)
  - Use of IT in administration
  - Time budgets
  - Assignment objectives and reports required
  - Preliminary materiality
  - Financial statement or other assertions
  - Components of audit risk
  - Audit strategy

Materiality

- Define materiality and describe how it is applied in financial reporting and auditing
- Explain the criteria which determine whether or not a matter is material
- Discuss the use and limitations of prescriptive rules in making decisions about materiality

Risk Assessments

- Identify and distinguish between assignment (eg audit) and business risk
- Describe the factors which influence the assessment of a specified risk (eg inherent risk) for a given assignment
- Explain how and why the assessments of risks and materiality affect the nature, timing and extent of auditing procedures
- Critically appraise the audit risk model
- Recognise and assess the implications of a specified computer system (eg network) on an assignment

Section 26

- Explain how IT may be used to assist auditors and discuss the problems which may be encountered in automating the audit process.

Exam guide

The general area of planning was examined in two questions on the pilot paper. Planning audits is a key skill for an auditor. Specifically, identifying business risks was examined on the pilot paper.

1 REVISION: OVERVIEW OF AUDIT PLANNING — Pilot Paper

1.1 You learnt all the basics of audit planning in your studies for Paper 2.6, *Audit and Internal Review.* We shall review it here and then go on to look at adopting an **audit approach,** as that is a **key part of planning and audit.**

Question

You have been informed by the senior partner of your firm that you are to be in charge of the audit of a new client, Peppermint Chews Ltd, for the year ended 31 December 20X4. She tells you that the company is engaged in the manufacture and wholesaling of sweets and confectionery, with turnover of approximately £5,000,000 and a work force of about 150. The company has one manufacturing location, sells mainly to the retail trade but also operates 10 shops of its own. The senior partner asks you to draw up an outline audit plan for the assignment showing when you anticipate visits to the client will be made and what kind of work will be carried out during each visit. The deadline for your audit report is 28 February 20X5.

Required

Draw up an outline plan for the audit of Peppermint Chews for the year ended 31 December 20X4.

Your plan should include the following:

(a) Approximate timing in the company's year of each stage of the audit of this new client. State why you have selected the approximate timing

(b) The objective of each stage

(c) The kind of work that will be carried out at each stage

Answer

Initial visit

(a) Timing. As this is a new client, this visit should take place as soon as possible after the terms of engagement have been agreed with and accepted by the directors of Peppermint Chews plc.

(b) Objective. To build up a background knowledge of the company to assist in the more detailed planning of audit work that will be required at a later stage.

(c) Audit work. We shall need to obtain details of the following:

- The history and development of the company

- The nature of the commercial environment within which the company operates
- The nature of the company's products and manufacturing processes
- The plan of organisation within the company
- The accounting and internal control systems operating within the company
- The accounting and other records of the company and how they are maintained

The above will be obtained using such techniques as interview, observation, reviewing client's systems documentation, and so on.

We shall not at this stage carry out detailed tests of controls on the company's systems, but we should carry out 'walk-through' tests to gain confirmation that the systems outlined to them in theory appear to operate that way in practice.

Interim visit(s)

(a) Timing. As this is the first audit of Peppermint Chews plc, it may, in view of the extra work involved, be necessary to have more than one interim visit. If we decided that only one such visit would be needed, however, then ideally it should take place reasonably close to the year end, in, say, October 20X4. If it were decided that more than one visit were needed, then perhaps the first interim visit should take place in April/May 20X4.

(b) Objective. The purpose of interim audits is to carry out detailed tests on a client's accounting and internal control systems to determine the reliance that may be placed thereon.

(c) Audit work. Following the initial visit to the client, we should have completed their documentation of the client's systems using narrative notes and flowcharts. We should also have assessed the strengths and weaknesses of the systems and determined the extent to which they wish to place reliance on them.

Given effective controls, we shall select and perform tests designed to establish compliance with the system. We shall therefore carry out an appropriate programme of tests of controls. The conclusion from the results may be either:

(i) That the controls are effective, in which case we shall only need to carry out restricted substantive procedures; or

(ii) That the controls are ineffective in practice, although they had appeared strong on paper, in which case we shall need to carry out more extensive substantive procedures.

After carrying out tests of controls, it is normal practice, as appropriate, to send management a letter identifying any weaknesses and making recommendations for improvements.

Final visit

(a) Timing. This may well be split into a pre-final visit in December 20X4 and a final audit early in 20X5, or it could be a continuous process.

(b) Objective. We should visit the client prior to the year end to assist in the planning of the final audit so as to agree with the client detailed timings such as year end stock count and debtors circularisation, preparation of client schedules, finalisation of accounts and so forth.

The object of the final audit is to carry out the necessary substantive procedures, these being concerned with substantiating the figures in the accounting records and, eventually, in the financial statements themselves. The completion of these tests, followed by an overall review of the financial statements, will enable us to decide whether they have obtained 'sufficient appropriate audit evidence to be able to draw reasonable conclusions' so that they are in a position to express an opinion on the company's financial statements, the expression of an opinion in their audit report being the primary objective of the audit as required by s 236 Companies Act 1985.

(c) Audit work. The audit work to be carried out at this final stage would include the following:

- Consideration and discussion with management of known problem areas
- Attendance at stocktaking
- Verification of assets and liabilities/income and expenditure
- Following up interim audit work
- Carrying out review of post balance sheet events
- Analytical procedures
- Obtaining management representations
- Reviewing financial statements
- Drafting the audit report

1.2 An effective and efficient audit relies on proper planning procedures. The planning process is covered in general terms by SAS 200 *Planning.* More detailed areas are covered in other SASs, which you should be aware of.

SAS 200.1

Auditors should plan the audit work so as to perform the audit in an effective manner.

1.3 The SAS distinguishes between the general audit strategy and the detailed audit approach which must be formulated.

KEY TERMS

An **audit plan** is the formulation of the general strategy for the audit which sets the direction for the audit, describes the expected scope and conduct of the audit and provides guidance for the development of the audit programme.

An **audit programme** is a set of instructions to the audit team that sets out the audit procedures the auditors intend to adopt and may include references to other matters such as the audit objectives, timing, sample size and basis of selection for each area. It also serves as a means to control and record the proper execution of the work.

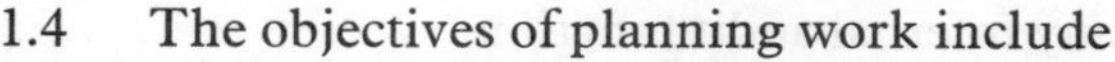

1.4 The objectives of planning work include:

- Ensuring that **appropriate attention is devoted** to the different areas of the audit
- Ensuring that **potential problems** are **identified**
- **Facilitating review**

1.5 Good planning also helps in assigning the proper tasks to the members of the audit team.

1.6 Audit procedures should be discussed with the client's management, staff and/or audit committee in order to co-ordinate audit work, including that of internal audit. However, all audit procedures remain the responsibility of the external auditors.

1.7 A structured approach to planning will include the following stages:

- **Updating knowledge of the client**
- **Preparing the detailed audit approach**
- Making **administrative decisions** such as staffing and budgets

1.8 The second bullet point above will be discussed in Chapter 8.

1.9 However, a brief reminder of all the other items which go into an audit plan are relevant here. The following table outlines the contents of a standard audit plan.

OVERALL AUDIT PLAN	
Knowledge of the entity's business	General economic factors and industry conditions Important characteristics of the client, (a) business, (b) principal business strategies, (c) financial performance, (d) reporting requirements, including changes since the previous audit The operating style and control consciousness of directors and management The auditors' cumulative knowledge of the accounting and control systems and any expected changes in the period
Risk and materiality	The setting of materiality for audit planning purposes The expected assessments of risks or error and identification of significant audit areas Any indication that misstatements that could have a material effect on the financial statements might arise because of fraud or for any other reason The identification of complex accounting areas including those involving estimates
Nature, timing and extent of procedures	The relative importance and timing of tests of control and substantive procedures The use of information technology by the client or the auditors The use made of work of any internal audit function Procedures which need to be carried out at or before the year end The timing of significant phases of the preparation of the financial statements The audit evidence required to reduce detection risk to an acceptably low level
Co-ordination, direction, supervision and review	The involvement of other auditors The involvement of experts, other third parties and internal auditors The number of locations Staffing requirements
Other matters	Any regulatory requirements arising from the decision to retain the engagement The possibility that the going concern basis may be inappropriate The terms of the engagement and any statutory responsibilities The nature and timing of reports or other communication with the entity that are expected under the engagement

2 MATERIALITY

KEY TERM

Materiality is an expression of the relative significance or importance of a particular matter in the context of financial statements as a whole.

2.1 Materiality considerations during **audit planning** are extremely important. The assessment of materiality at this stage should be based on the most recent and reliable financial information and will help to determine an effective and efficient audit approach. Materiality assessment will help the auditors to decide:

- **How many** and **what items** to examine
- Whether to use **sampling techniques**
- What **level of error** is likely to lead to a qualified audit opinion

2.2 The resulting combination of audit procedures should help to reduce audit risk to an appropriately low level.

Criteria of materiality

An item might be material due to its

Nature	Given the definition of materiality that an item would affect the readers of the financial statements, some **items** might **by their nature affect readers.** Examples include **transactions related to directors,** such as remuneration or contracts with the company.
Value	Some items will be significant in the financial statements by virtue of their **size,** for example, if the company had bought a piece of land with a value which comprised three-quarters of the asset value of the company, that would be material. That is why materiality is often expressed in terms of **percentages** (of assets, of profits).
Impact	Some **items may by chance have a significant impact** on financial statements, for example, a proposed journal which is not material in itself could convert a profit into a loss. The difference between a small profit and a small loss could be material to some readers.

Rules on materiality

2.3 It is clear from the points made about criteria for materiality that materiality is judgmental, and something that auditors must be aware of when approaching all their audit work.

2.4 However, you will know from your previous studies that generally accepted rules about materiality exist. Examples are:

- Items relating to directors are generally material
- Percentage guidelines are often given for materiality

2.5 While materiality **must always be a matter of judgement** for the auditor, it is **helpful to have some rules** to bear in mind. Reasons for this are:

- The rules give the auditor a **framework** within which to base his thoughts on materiality

- The rules provide a **benchmark** against which to assess quality of auditing, for example, in the event of litigation or disciplinary action.

3 RISK

3.1 The auditor must be aware of two types of risk.

- **Audit risk** (sometimes known as assignment risk)
- **Business risk**

Audit risk

KEY TERMS

Audit risk is the risk that auditors may give an inappropriate opinion on the financial statements. Audit risk has three components; inherent risk, control risk and detection risk.

Inherent risk is the suspectibility of an account balance or class of transactions to material misstatement, either individually or when aggregated with misstatements in other balances or classes, irrespective of related internal controls.

Control risk is the risk that a misstatement:

- Could occur in an account balance or class of transactions
- Could be material, either individually or when aggregated with misstatements in other balances or classes, and
- Would not be prevented, or detected and corrected on a timely basis, by the accounting and internal control systems.

Detection risk is the risk that the auditors' substantive procedures do not detect a misstatement that exists in an account balance or class of transactions that could be material, either individually or when aggregated with misstatements in other balances or classes.

3.2 Audit risk is the risk that the auditors given an unqualified opinion on the accounts when they should have given a qualified opinion, **or** they give an opinion qualified for a particular reason where that reason was not justified. SAS 300 *Accounting and internal control and audit risk assessments* covers audit risk.

3.3 You should be aware of the guidance given in SAS 300 from your earlier auditing studies.

Inherent risk

3.4 Inherent risk is the risk that items will be misstated due to characteristics of those items, such as the fact they are estimates or that they are important items in the accounts.

3.5 The auditors must use their professional judgement and all available knowledge to assess inherent risk. If not such information or knowledge is available then the inherent risk is **high.**

3.6 The results of the assessment must be properly documented and, where inherent risk is assessed as not high, then audit work may be reduced. The SAS lists the relevant factors to be considered under two headings.

- Risk associated with the entity as a whole
- Risk associated with the assertions of particular balances and classes of transactions

FACTORS AFFECTING CLIENT AS A WHOLE	
Integrity and **attitude to risk** of directors and management	Domination by a single individual can cause problems
Management experience and **knowledge**	Changes in management and quality of financial management
Unusual pressures on management	Examples include tight reporting deadlines, or market or financing expectations
Nature of business	Potential problems include technological obsolescence or over-dependence on single product
Industry factors	Competitive conditions, regulatory requirements, technology developments, changes in customer demand
Information technology	Problems include lack of supporting documentation, concentration of expertise in a few people, potential for unauthorised access

FACTORS AFFECTING INDIVIDUAL ACCOUNT BALANCES OR TRANSACTIONS	
Financial statement **accounts prone to misstatement**	Accounts which require adjustment in previous period or require high degree of estimation
Complex accounts	Accounts which require expert valuations or are subjects of current professional discussion
Assets at risk of being **lost or stolen**	Cash, stock, portable fixed assets (computers)
Quality of **accounting systems**	Strength of individual departments (sales, purchases, cash etc)
Unusual transactions	Transactions for large amounts, with unusual names, not settled promptly (particularly important if they occur at period-end) Transactions that do not go through the system, that relate to specific clients or processed by certain individuals
Staff	Staff changes or areas of low morale

Control risk

3.7 Control risk is the risk that client controls fail to detect material misstatements. SAS 300 requires a **preliminary assessment of control risk** at the planning stage of the audit if the auditors intend to rely on their assessment to reduce the extent to their substantive procedures. This assessment should be supported subsequently by tests of control. We will discuss a risk-based approach to the audit in Chapter 8.

Detection risk

3.8 Detection risk is the risk that audit procedures will fail to detect material errors. Detection risk relates to the inability of the auditors to examine all evidence. Audit evidence is usually persuasive rather than conclusive so some detection risk is usually present, allowing the auditors to seek 'reasonable confidence'.

3.9 The auditors' **inherent and control risk assessments** influence the **nature, timing and extent of substantive procedures** required to reduce detection risk and thereby audit risk.

(a) Auditors need to be careful when relying on their **assessment** of **control risk,** as good controls may impact upon some but not other aspects of audit areas. For example, good controls over the recording of sales and debtors would not reduce audit testing on bad debts, as the amounts recorded may represent amounts that will not be collected.

(b) To design an efficient audit strategy, auditors should not just consider reducing the number of items they test substantively, **extent** of testing, in inherent and control risks are low. They may also alter the tests they do, **design** of testing, by placing for instance more reliance on analytical procedures. They may also change the **timing** of tests, for example carrying out certain procedures such as circularisation at a date that is not the year-end, and placing reliance upon internal controls functioning at the year-end.

3.10 Misstatements discovered in substantive procedures may cause the auditors to modify their previous assessment of control risk.

Business risk

Pilot Paper

KEY TERMS

Business risk is the risk inherent to the company in its operations. It is risks at all levels of the business. It is split into three categories:

Financial risks are the risks arising from the financial activities or financial consequences of an operation, for example, cash flow issues or overtrading.

Operational risks are the risks arising with regard to operations, for example, the risk that a major supplier will be lost and the company will be unable to operate.

Compliance risk is the risk that arises from non-compliance with the laws and regulations that surround the business. The compliance risk attaching to environmental issues, for example, is discussed in Chapter 18.

3.11 In Chapter 5, we discussed the Turnbull guidelines that highlight the importance of risk management in a business. The above components of business risk are the risks that the company should seek to mitigate and manage.

3.12 The **process of risk management** for the business is as follows:

- Identify significant risks which could prevent the business achieving its objectives
- Provide a framework to ensure that the business can meet its objectives
- Review the objectives and framework regularly to ensure that objectives are met

3.13 This is discussed in more detail in Chapter 14.

3.14 A key part of the process is therefore to **identify the business risks**. There are various tools used to do this that you may have come across before. They are listed below.

- SWOT analysis
- The five forces model
- The PEST analysis
- Porter's value chain

> **Exam focus point**
>
> The study guide states that you should be able to identify business risks in a question. If you have previously used any of the above techniques, they may be useful to you, but in the exam, it will be better to use common sense as you work through any given question, bearing in mind the three components of business risk given above.

Relationship between business risk and audit risk

3.15 On the one hand, business risk and audit risk are completely unrelated:

- Business risk arises in the operations of a business
- Audit risk is focused on the financial statements of the business
- Audit risk exists only in relation to an opinion given by auditors

3.16 In other ways, the two are strongly connected. The strong links between them can be seen in the inherent and control aspects of audit risk. In audit risk these are limited to risks pertaining to the financial statements.

3.17 Business risk includes all risks facing the business. In other words, inherent audit risk is an aspect of business risk.

3.18 In response to business risk, the directors institute a system of controls. These will include controls to mitigate against the financial aspect of the business risk, which are the controls that audit control risk incorporates.

3.19 Detection risk is applicable to both the risk models from the point of view of the auditor. This is because whichever form of risk he chooses to base his audit on, there is still a risk arising that he will fail to detect material misstatement (that is, detection risk).

3.20 Therefore, although audit risk is very financial statements focused, business risk does form part of the inherent risk associated with the financial statements, not least, because if the risks materialise, the going concern basis of the financial statements could be affected.

4 GENERAL PLANNING MATTERS

4.1 The following administrative details of an audit will also need to be considered as part of the audit plan:

- Logistics
- Use of IT
- Time budgets
- Subsidiary objectives of the assignment

4.2 We shall consider these matters here.

Logistics

4.3 When planning an audit, the audit engagement partner or manager has to consider many practical things. We shall consider a few of them here:

- Staff
- Client management
- Locations of the audit
- Deadlines

Staff

4.4 There are several considerations with regard to audit staff, and these are shown in the diagram below.

Exam focus point

Bear in mind that not all will be relevant to all audits, and when answering questions, you should concentrate on the facts given in the question rather than listing all these factors regardless of information given in the question.

Client management

4.5 The management of the client company may have preferences regarding audit staff, for example, a finance director may be keen that there is continuity of audit staff on the assignment, so that last year's semi senior is this year's senior, or that the same staff are used from year to year.

4.6 This may not always be possible, but the person planning the audit will try and bear in mind the needs of the client in such matters. Consistency of audit staff may help audit efficiency in terms of knowledge of the business and its staff.

Locations

4.7 The person planning the audit will have to give consideration to the location of the audit. There are several issues that could arise.

Factor	Consideration
Location	Distance for audit staff to travel Mobility of audit staff Location of audit review by manager/engagement partner
Multiple locations	All the above considerations Determination of which locations to visit Allocation of audit staff to each site Liasing with client staff to ensure each site visit is convenient.

Deadlines

4.8 It is of vital importance that the audit team know the deadlines involved in the audit. The key dates that the team will need to know are likely to be:

- Date of stocktake
- Date the financial statements are due to have been drafted by
- Dates of main audit visit
- Date of manager review
- Date of engagement partner review
- Date of engagement partner's post audit meeting with client management
- Date on which the audit report is due to be signed
- Date of AGM

4.9 It is important that the audit team are aware of these dates and that the audit is planned so that the work can be achieved in relation to these dates. It is vitally important, for instance, that the audit is completed by the date on which the audit report is to be signed. It would be foolish to try and start detailed substantive testing before the financial statements had been drafted.

Use of IT

4.10 The use of IT is increasingly common in auditing. There are several factors which may need to be considered:

- Whether the client has a computerised system
- If so, whether the auditors will make use of CAATs
- Whether the auditor will use computers to complete his working papers
- If so, whether the members of the audit team are equipped with lap tops
- What specific audit tasks the engagement partner requires to be done on the computer, for example, analytical review
- Whether the partner wants to be able to contact the audit team electronically on site
- If so, whether the audit team are properly equipped with modems.

Time budgets

4.11 We discussed the importance of time estimation when we discussed setting the fee in Chapter 2. It is important to the engagement partner that the audit is completed in a cost effective manner. Therefore, the time taken to conduct each part of the audit will have been estimated and the fee set accordingly.

4.12 These time budgets are an important part of planning then.

- It is important that the time is estimated accurately
- It is important that the audit team is aware of the time budget
- It is important that the audit team record variances from the time budget

4.13 The time budget will be based on issues such as:

- Prior year time records
- Risk assessments
- Materiality considerations

4.14 In other words, if stock is the most material and risky item of the balance sheet, it will have a large estimate of time attached to it, especially if it took a long time last year.

4.15 In contrast an item such as long term bank loans could be material, but it is low risk due to the existence of good third party evidence and use can be made of procedures such as analytical review. It may therefore have less time budgeted to it.

Subsidiary objectives of the assignment

4.16 The key purpose of the audit, as you know, is to obtain sufficient, appropriate evidence to express an opinion on the financial statements.

4.17 However, there may be subsidiary (non-statutory) objectives of the audit assignment. An example would be the report to management. The audit plan should set out these subsidiary objectives and also set deadlines and any specific requirements for these.

Chapter roundup

- Auditors must plan their work so that it is undertaken in an effective manner. This will includes:
  - Ensuring attention aimed at potential problems
  - Determining audit approach
  - Facilitating preview
- Materiality considerations are important at the planning stage. An item might be material due to its nature, value or impact on readers of the financial statements.
- Risk falls into two components:
  - Audit risk: the risk that the auditor issues an inappropriate opinion
  - Business risk: the risk arising to the company through being in operations
- Business risk has three components:
  - Financial risk
  - Operational risk
  - Compliance risk
- Inherent audit risk and control audit risk can be seen as features of business risk.
- There are also general planning matters which the auditor must consider at the planning stage. These are:
  - Logistics
  - Use of IT
  - Time budgets
  - Subsidiary objectives

Quick quiz

1 What are the five components of an audit plan?

(1) ______________

(2) ______________

(3) ______________

(4) ______________

(5) ______________

2 Complete the definition:

____________________ is an expression of the ______________ ______________ or ____________________ of a particular matter in the context of financial statements.

3 Identify whether the following matters, which represent potential business risks to the company are financial, operational or compliance risks.

Item	**Potential business risk**
Going concern	
Physical disasters	
Breakdown of accounting systems	
Loss of key personnel	
Credit risk	
Breach of Companies Act	
VAT problems	
Currency risk	
Poor brand management	
Environmental issues	

4 Name four considerations relating to audit staff an audit plan should cover.

(1) ______________

(2) ______________

(3) ______________

(4) ______________

Answers to quick quiz

1 (1) Knowledge of the business
(2) Risk and materiality
(3) Nature, timing and extent of procedures
(4) Co-ordination, direction, supervision and review
(5) Other matters

2 Materiality, relative significance, importance

Item	Potential business risk
Going concern	Financial
Physical disasters	Operational
Breakdown of accounting systems	Financial
Loss of key personnel	Operational
Credit risk	Financial
Breach of Companies Act	Compliance
VAT problems	Compliance
Currency risk	Financial
Poor brand management	Operational
Environmental issues	Compliance

4 See diagram on para 4.4

Now try the question below from the Exam Question Bank

Number	Level	Marks	Time
7	Exam	20	36 mins

Chapter 8

AUDIT STRATEGY

Introduction

The issue of ensuring that the **correct approach** is taken to the audit is very important in planning, as we saw in Chapter 7.

Risk is a key issue in an audit, and the most common approach to audits incorporates a recognition of those risks in the approach taken. It is called the **risk-based approach,** and we look at two aspects of it in Sections 1 and 2.

There are **other approaches** to an audit, and other techniques which arise out of the risk-based approach. We shall look at these in Section 3 to 6. The risk based approach is the most commonly used. It may be used in conjunction with other approaches.

Lastly in this chapter, we have considered the issue of **analytical procedures.** Analytical procedures are important and useful at the planning stage. They are also relevant at the testing and review stages of an audit. Hence, it is useful to cover them at the outset. Do not forget the relevance of analytical review in the later stages of an audit, just because it is covered in detail in this section of the text.

Study guide

Section 7

General (approaches to auditing)

- Select and justify an appropriate approach to a given assignment
- Explain the circumstances in which a specified approach is not appropriate

Risk-based auditing

- Describe the business risk approach to auditing and its relationship to the audit risk model
- Outline the reasons why it is adopted in preference to other methodologies
- Describe the consequences of such a 'top down' approach to evidence gathering procedures (eg tests of controls, analytical procedures and test of details)

Systems audits

- Describe the components of an effective system of internal controls
- Identify the factors which contribute to a strong control environment
- Revise control objectives, control procedures, walk-through tests and tests of control ('compliance tests')

Section 8

Balance sheet approach

- Explain the importance of the balance sheet as a primary statement
- Discuss why this approach may be more appropriate for the audit of small businesses than a business risk approach
- Discuss the limitations of this approach

Revenue, expenditure and other cycles

- Illustrate how accounting transactions can be analysed into 'cycles' which correspond to line items in the balance sheet and profit and loss account
- Identify cycles relevant to a given situation (eg the conversion cycle for manufacturing enterprise)
- Describe the approach to each cycle

Directional testing

- Explain the concept of directional testing as a methodology
- Describe how this approach helps to detect misstatements and determines the populations from which samples are drawn
- Illustrate the use of directional testing within cycles
- Discuss the advantages and limitations of this approach

Analytical procedures

- Explain the nature and role of analytical procedures in the conduct of an assignment
- Recognise situations in which analytical procedures may be used extensively
- Describe the criteria for assessing the extent to which reliance can be placed on substantive analytical procedures

Section 10

- Select and explain substantive analytical procedures appropriate to given financial and other data

Exam guide

Audit strategy is a key syllabus area. You are likely to be presented with a scenario, and asked to choose and justify a particular strategy for the audit.

1 AUDIT RISK APPROACH

1.1 Risk-based auditing refers to the development of auditing techniques that are responsive to risk factors in an audit. The auditors apply judgement to determine what level of risk pertains to different areas of a client's system and devise appropriate audit tests.

1.2 This approach should ensure that the greatest audit effort is directed at the areas in which the financial statements are most likely to be misstated, so that the chance of detecting errors is improved and time is not spent on unnecessary testing of 'safe' areas.

1.3 The increased use of risk-based auditing reflects two factors.

(a) The growing complexity of the business environment increases the danger of fraud or misstatement. Factors such as the developing use of computerised systems and the growing internationalisation of business are relevant here.

(b) Pressures are increasingly exerted by audit clients for the auditors to keep fee levels down while an improved level of service is expected.

1.4 The auditors make an assessment of the various components of audit risk at the planning stage. This has been discussed in Chapter 7. They will then apply that assessment of risk and materiality assessment and determine the key audit areas, and the nature timing and extent of procedures.

1.5 The audit risk approach is the approach to audit which all your previous auditing studies have been based on.

2 BUSINESS RISK APPROACH

2.1 The business risk approach is a fairly recent development in auditing, growing out of the importance placed on risk management to a business. We discussed the elements of business risk in Chapter 7.

2.2 The approach develops the risk based approach by considering two issues:

- What factors lead to the problems which may cause material misstatements?
- What can the audit contribute to the business pursuing its goals?

2.3 The business risk approach was developed because it is believed that factors such as the way that the business is managed is more likely to have significance for the financial statements, in terms of accuracy, fraud and going concern.

Factors leading to material misstatements

2.4 The table below highlights some of the factors that exist.

Principal risk	Immediate Financial Statement Implications
Economic pressures causing reduced unit sales and eroding margins.	Stock values (SSAP 9) Going concern
Economic pressures resulting in demands for extended credit	Debtors' recoverability
Product quality issues related to inadequate control over supply chain and transportation damage.	Stock values – net realisable value and stock returns
Customer dissatisfaction related to inability to meet order requirements.	Going concern
Customer dissatisfaction related to invoicing errors and transportation damage.	Debtors' valuation
Unacceptable service response call rate related to poor product quality	Going concern Litigation – provisions and contingencies Stock – net realisable value
Out of date IT systems affecting management's ability to make informed decisions.	Anywhere

Question 1

State what category of business risk each of the risks in the above table falls under.

Answer

1 Financial
2 Financial
3 Operational
4 Operational
5 Operational
6 Operational
7 Operational

2.5 The business risk audit approach tries to mirror the risk management steps that have been taken by the directors. In this way, the auditor will **seek to establish that the financial statement objectives have been met**, through an investigation into whether all the other business objectives have been met by the directors.

2.6 This approach to the audit has been called a **'top-down' approach**, because it starts at the business and its objectives and works back down to the financial statements, rather than working up from the financial statements which has historically been the approach to audit.

2.7 The 'top-down approach' has an **effect on the procedures used in the audit**, as follows.

Audit procedure	Effect of 'top-down' approach
Tests of controls	As the auditor pays greater attention to the high level controls used by directors to manage business risks, controls testing will be focused on items such as the control environment and corporate governance than the detailed procedural controls tested under traditional approaches.
Analytical procedures	Analytical procedures are used more heavily in a business risk approach as they are consistent with the auditor's desire to understand the entity's business rather than to prove the figures in the financial statements.
Detailed testing	The combination of the above two factors, particularly the higher use of analytical procedures will result in a lower requirement for detailed testing, although substantive testing will not be eliminated completely.

2.8 The other key element of a business risk approach is that as it is focused on the business more fully, rather than the financial statements, there is greater opportunity for the auditor to add value to the client's business and to assist him in managing the risks that the business faces.

Advantages of business risk approach

2.9 There are a number of reasons why firms who use the business risk approach prefer it to historic approaches.

- Added value given to clients as the approach focuses on the business as a whole
- Audit attention focused on high level controls and high use of analytical procedures increase audit efficiency and therefore cost

- Does not focus on routine processes, which technological developments have rendered less prone to error than has historically been the case
- Responds to the importance that regulators and the government have placed on corporate governance in recent years
- Lower engagement risk (risk of auditor being sued) through broader understanding of the client's business and practices

3 SYSTEMS AND CONTROLS Pilot Paper

3.1 You should be familiar with the systems and controls approach to auditing, from your previous studies. It is always used in conjunction with another approach, because as you are aware, **substantive testing can never be eliminated completely**.

3.2 As you studied the concept of controls testing in detail in paper 2.6, *Audit and Internal Review*, (old paper 6), we shall only briefly revise it here.

Knowledge brought forward from paper 2.6

Management are required to institute a system of controls which is capable of fulfilling their duty of safeguarding the assets of the shareholders.

Auditors assess the system of controls put in place by the directors and ascertain whether they believe it is effective enough for them to be able to rely on it for the purposes of their audit.

If they believe that the system is effective, they carry out tests of controls to ensure that the control system operates as it is supposed to. If they believe that the control system is ineffective, they assess control risk as high and undertake higher levels of substantive testing (see Sections 4 and 5).

The key control objectives and procedures over the main cycles of sales, purchases and wages were studied at length at paper 2.6 (old paper 6). If you do not feel confident in what they are, you should go back to your textbook in these areas and revise them now.

4 CYCLES AND TRANSACTIONS

4.1 Cycles testing is in some ways closely linked to systems testing, because it is based on the same systems. However, while in Section 3 we considered the systems of the business in terms of controls testing, here we are looking at them in terms of substantive testing.

4.2 When auditors take a cycles approach, they test the transactions which have occurred, resulting in the entries in the profit and loss account (for example, sales transactions, stock purchases, asset purchases, wages payments, other expenses).

4.3 In which case, he would select a sample of transactions and test that the transaction was complete and processed correctly throughout the cycle. In other words, you are substantiating the transactions which appear in the financial statements.

Exam Focus Point

The auditors may assess the systems of a company as **ineffective.** In this case, they would carry out extensive substantive procedures. The substantive approach taken in this situation could a be cycles approach. In fact, if systems have been adjudged to be ineffective, the auditor is more likely to take a cycles approach, as it will be essential that the auditor substantiates that the transactions have been recorded properly, despite the poor systems.

4.4 The key business cycles are outlined below. Remember that you know what the processes should be in the cycle (you have assessed the system and controls in Section 3), under this approach, you are ensuring that individual transactions were processed correctly.

4.5 Hence, the cycles outlined below should correspond to the controls processes you are already aware of and which we discussed in Section 3.

Sales

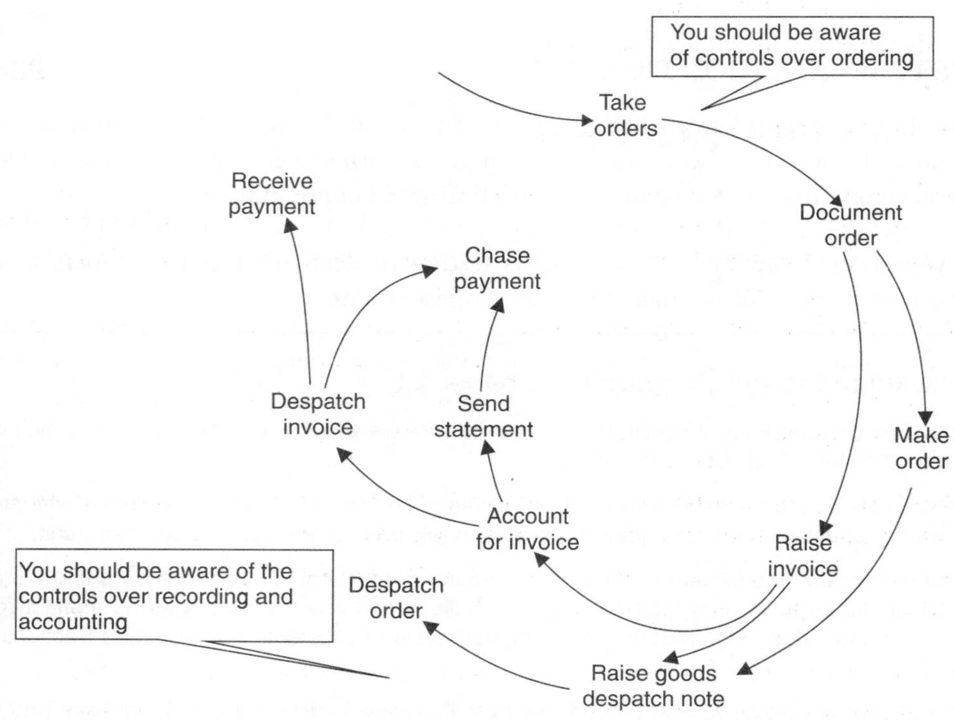

Purchases

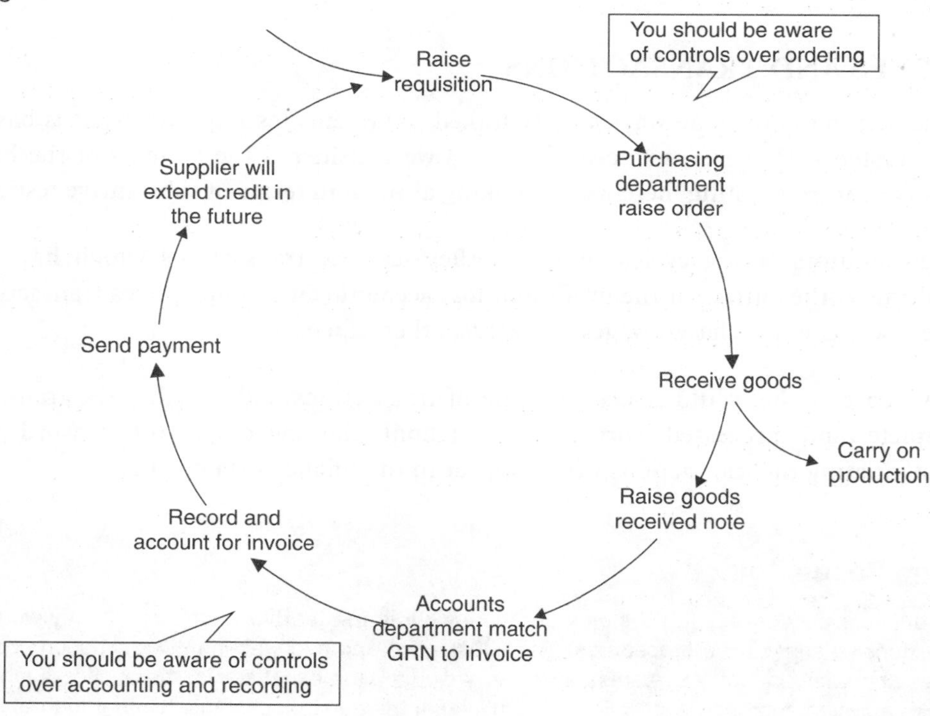

4.6 The auditor should be able to find an audit trail for each transaction consisting of (in the purchases cycle):

- Requisition
- Order
- GRN
- Invoice
- Ledger and daybook entries
- Payment in cashbook/cheque stub

5 BALANCE SHEET APPROACH

5.1 An alternative to the cycles (or transactions) approach to auditing is to take the balance sheet approach. This is the **most common approach to the substantive part of the audit**, after controls have been tested, whether a risk-based approach is being followed or not.

5.2 The balance sheet shows a snapshot of the financial position of the business at a point in time. It follows that it if is fairly stated and the previous snapshot was fairly stated then it is reasonable to undertake lower level testing the transactions which connect the two snapshots, for example, analytical review (examined in Section 7).

5.3 Under this approach, therefore, the auditors seek to concentrate efforts on substantiating the closing position in the year, shown in the balance sheet, having determined that the closing position from the previous year (also substantiated) has been correctly transferred to be the opening position in the current year.

5.4 You should be aware of the financial statement assertions and the substantive tests in relation to the major items on the balance sheet from your previous studies. Some further tests are detailed in Chapters 11 to 13.

Relationship with business risk approach

5.5 It is stated above that the substantive element of an audit undertaken under a business risk approach is restricted due to the high use of analytical procedures. However, the element of substantive testing which remains in a business risk approach can be undertaken under the balance sheet approach.

5.6 In some cases, particularly **small companies**, the business risks may be strongly connected to the fact that management is concentrated on one person. Another feature of small companies may be that their balance sheet is uncomplicated and contains one or two material items, for example, debtors or stock.

5.7 When this is the case, it is **often more cost-effective to undertake a highly substantive balance sheet audit than to undertake a business risk assessment**, as it is relatively simple to obtain the assurance required about the financial statements from taking that approach.

Limitations of the balance sheet approach

5.8 When not undertaken in conjunction with a risk based approach or systems testing, the **level of detailed testing** can be high in a balance sheet approach, rendering it **costly**.

6 DIRECTIONAL TESTING

6.1 Directional testing has been discussed in detail in your previous auditing studies. It is a product of detailed substantive testing. Substantive testing seeks to discover errors and omissions, and the discovery of these will depend on the direction of the test.

6.2 Broadly speaking, substantive procedures can be said to fall into two categories:

- Tests to discover **errors** (resulting in over- or under-statement)
- Tests to discover **omissions** (resulting in under-statement)

Tests designed to discover errors

6.3 These tests will start with the **accounting records** in which the transactions are recorded and check from the entries to supporting documents or other evidence. Such tests should detect any over-statement and also any under-statement through causes other than omission.

Case example: test for errors

If the test is designed to ensure that sales are priced correctly, the test would begin with a sales invoice selected from the sales ledger. Prices would then be checked to the official price list.

Tests designed to discover omissions

6.4 These tests must start from **outside the accounting records** and then check back to those records. Understatements through omission will never be revealed by starting with the account itself as there is clearly no chance of selecting items that have been omitted from the account.

Case example: tests for omission

If the test is designed to discover whether all raw material purchases have been properly processed, the test would start, say, with goods received notes, to be checked to the stock records or purchase ledger.

6.5 For most systems auditors would include tests designed to discover both errors and omissions. The type of test, and direction of the test, should be recognised before selecting the test sample. If the sample which tested the accuracy and validity of the sales ledger were chosen from a file of sales invoices then it would not substantiate the fact that there were no errors in the sales ledger. The approach known as 'directional testing' applies this testing discipline.

6.6 Directional testing is particularly appropriate when testing the financial statement assertions of existence, completeness, rights and obligations, and valuation.

Directional testing and double entry

6.7 The concept of directional testing derives from the principle of double-entry bookkeeping, in that for every **debit** there is a **corresponding credit**, (assuming that the double entry is complete and that the accounting records balance). Therefore, any **misstatement** of a **debit**

entry will result in either a corresponding **misstatement** of a **credit entry** or a **misstatement** in the opposite direction, of **another debit entry**.

6.8 By designing audit tests carefully the auditors are able to use this principle in drawing audit conclusions, not only about the debit or credit entries that they have directly tested, but also about the corresponding credit or debit entries that are necessary to balance the books.

6.9 Tests are therefore designed in the following way.

Test item	**Example**
Test debit items (expenditure or assets) for overstatement by selecting debit entries recorded in the nominal ledger and checking value, existence and ownership	If a fixed asset entry in the nominal ledger of £1,000 is selected, it would be overstated if it should have been recorded at anything less than £1,000 or if the company did not own it, or indeed if it did not exist (eg it had been sold or the amount of £1,000 in fact represented a revenue expense)
Test credit items (income or liabilities) for understatement by selecting items from appropriate sources independent of the nominal ledger and ensuring that they result in the correct nominal ledger entry	Select a goods despatched note and check that the resultant sale has been recorded in the nominal ledger sales account. Sales would be understated if the nominal ledger did not reflect the transaction at all (completeness) or reflected it at less than full value (say if goods valued at £1,000 were recorded in the sales account at £900, there would be an understatement of £100).

6.10 The matrix set out below demonstrates how directional testing is applied to give assurance on all account areas in the financial statements.

		Primary test also gives comfort on			
Type of account	**Purpose of primary test**	**Assets**	**Liabilities**	**Income**	**Expenses**
Assets	Overstatement (O)	U	O	O	U
Liabilities	Understatement (U)	U	O	O	U
Income	Understatement (U)	U	O	O	U
Expense	Overstatement (O)	U	O	O	U

6.11 Thus, a test for the overstatement of an asset simultaneously gives comfort on understatement of other assets, overstatement of liabilities, overstatement of income and understatement of expenses.

Question 2

Fill in the blank spaces.

(a) Based on double-entry bookkeeping, it can be seen from the matrix that assets can only be *understated* by virtue of:

(i) Other assets being __________; or
(ii) Liabilities being __________; or
(iii) Income being __________; or
(iv) Expenses being __________.

(b) Similarly, liabilities can only be *overstated* by virtue of:

(i) Assets being __________; or
(ii) Other liabilities being __________; or
(iii) Income being __________; or
(iv) Expenses being __________.

Answer

(a) (i) Overstated
(ii) Understated
(iii) Understated
(iv) Overstated

(b) (i) Overstated
(ii) Understated
(iii) Understated
(iv) Overstated

6.12 So, by performing the primary tests shown in the matrix, the auditors obtain audit assurance in other audit areas. Successful completion of the primary tests will therefore result in them having tested all account areas both for overstatement and understatement.

6.13 The major advantage of the directional audit approach is its cost-effectiveness.

(a) Assets and expenses are tested for overstatement only, and liabilities and income for understatement only, that is, items are not tested for both overstatement and understatement.

(b) It audits directly the more likely types of transactional misstatement, ie unrecorded income and improper expense (arising intentionally or unintentionally).

Exam focus point

Directional testing is particularly useful when there is a high level of detailed testing to be carried out, for example, when the auditors have assessed the company's controls and accounting system as ineffective.

7 ANALYTICAL PROCEDURES

7.1 You are familiar with analytical procedures and their various uses in an audit from your earlier auditing studies. This is revised briefly here.

Knowledge brought forward from 2.6 Audit and Internal Review

Guidance on analytical procedures is given in SAS 140, *Analytical Procedures.*

Analytical procedures can be used at three stages of the audit:

- Planning
- Substantive procedures
- Overall review

Analytical procedures consist of comparing items, for example, current year financial information with prior year financial information, and analysing predictable relationships, for example, the relationship between debtors and credit sales.

7.2 There are a number of occasions and assignments when an auditor will look to take an analytical procedures approach. One has already been mentioned in this chapter. When auditors use the business risk approach (para 2.7) they seek to use a high level of analytical procedures. Other examples include:

- Reviews (Chapter 15)
- Assurance engagements (Chapter 15)
- Prospective financial information (Chapter 17)

> **Exam focus point**
>
> You should note that whether or not auditors choose an analytical procedure approach for an audit, the knowledge you already have of analytical procedures **still applies**. In any audit, analytical procedures are used at the three stages. If the analytical procedures approach is taken, the use of analytical review at the second stage is expanded.

7.3 SAS 140 lists a number of factors which the auditors should consider when deciding whether to use analytical procedures as substantive procedures.

Factors to consider	Example
The **plausibility and predictability** of the relationships identified for comparison and evaluation	The strong relationship between certain selling expenses and turnover in businesses where the sales force is paid by commission
The **objectives** of the analytical procedures and the extent to which their results are reliable	
The **detail** to which information can be **analysed**	Analytical procedures may be more effective when applied to financial information or individual sections of an operation such as individual factories or shops
The **availability of information**	Financial: budgets or forecasts Non-financial: eg the number of units produced or sold
The **relevance of the information** available	Whether the budgets are established as results to be expected rather than as tough targets (which may well not be achieved)
The **comparability of the information** available	Comparisons with average performance in an industry may be of little value if a large number of companies differ significantly from the average
The **knowledge gained during previous audits**	The effectiveness of the accounting and internal controls The types of problems giving rise to accounting adjustments in prior periods

7.4 SAS 410 also identifies factors which should be considered when determining the reliance that the auditors should place on the results of substantive analytical procedures.

Reliability factors	Example
Other audit procedures directed towards the same financial statements assertions	Other procedures auditors undertake in reviewing the collectability of debtors, such as the review of subsequent cash receipts, may confirm or dispel questions arising from the application of analytical procedures to a profit of customers' accounts which lists for how long monies have been owed
The **accuracy** with which the expected results of analytical procedures can be predicted	Auditors normally expect greater consistency in comparing the relationship of gross profit to sales from one period to another than in comparing expenditure which may or may not be made within a period, such as research or advertising

The **frequency** with which a relationship is observed	A pattern repeated monthly as opposed to annually

7.5 Reliance on the results of analytical procedures depends on the auditors' assessment of the **risk** that the procedures may identify relationships (between data) do exist, whereas a material misstatement exists (that is, the relationships, in fact, do not exist). It depends also on the results of investigations that auditors have made if substantive analytical procedures have highlighted significant fluctuations or unexpected relationships (see below).

Practical techniques

7.6 When carrying out analytical procedures, auditors should remember that every industry is different and each company within an industry differs in certain aspects.

Important accounting ratios

Gross profit margin = $\frac{\text{Gross profit}}{\text{Turnover}} \times 100\%$

This should be calculated in total and by product, area and month/quarter if possible.

Debtors turnover period = $\frac{\text{Debtors}}{\text{Sales}} \times 365$

Stock turnover ratio = $\frac{\text{Cost of sales}}{\text{Stock}}$

Current ratio = $\frac{\text{Current assets}}{\text{Current liabilities}}$

Quick of acid test ratio = $\frac{\text{Current assets (excluding stock)}}{\text{Current liabilities}}$

Gearing ratio = $\frac{\text{Loans}}{\text{Share capital and reserves}} \times 100\%$

Return on capital employed = $\frac{\text{Profit before tax}}{\text{Total assests} - \text{current liabilites}}$

Significant items

Creditors and purchases

Stock and cost of sales

Fixed assets and depreciation, repairs and maintenance expense

Intangible assets and amortisation

Loans and interest expense

Investments and investment income

Debtors and bad debt expense

Debtors and sales

7.7 Ratios mean very little when used in isolation. They should be calculated for **previous periods** and for **comparable companies.** The permanent file should contain a section with summarised accounts and the chosen ratios for prior years.

7.8 In addition to looking at the more usual ratios the auditors should consider examining **other ratios** that may be **relevant** to the particular **clients' business,** such as revenue per passenger mile for an airline operator client, or fees per partner for a professional office.

> **Exam focus point**
>
> At this level, you are more likely to be required to **justify** why an analytical procedures approach should be taken then to calculate a series of ratios.
>
> However, if you are asked to perform analytical review in the exam, remember that it is vital that you analyse any calculation you have made in your answer. It is very important to make comments and draw conclusions.

7.9 Other analytical techniques include:

(a) **Examining related accounts** in conjunction with each other. Often revenue and expense accounts are related to balance sheet accounts and comparisons should be made to ensure relationships are reasonable.

(b) **Trend analysis.** Sophisticated statistical techniques (beyond the scope of this paper) can be used to compare this period with previous periods.

(c) **Reasonableness tests.** These involve calculating **expected value** of an item and comparing it with its actual value, for example, for straight-line depreciation.

$$(\text{Cost} + \text{Additions} - \text{Disposals}) \times \text{Depreciation \%} = \text{Charge in P \& L A/C}$$

Trend analysis

7.10 Trend analysis is likely to be very important if an analytical procedure approach is taken. Information technology can be used in trend analysis, to enable auditors to see trends graphically with relative ease and speed.

7.11 Methods of trend analysis include:

- 'Scattergraphs'
- Bar graphs
- Pie charts
- Any other visual representations
- Time series analysis
- Statistical regression

7.12 Time series analysis involves techniques such as eliminating seasonal fluctuations from sets of figures, so that underlying trends can be analysed. This is illustrated below.

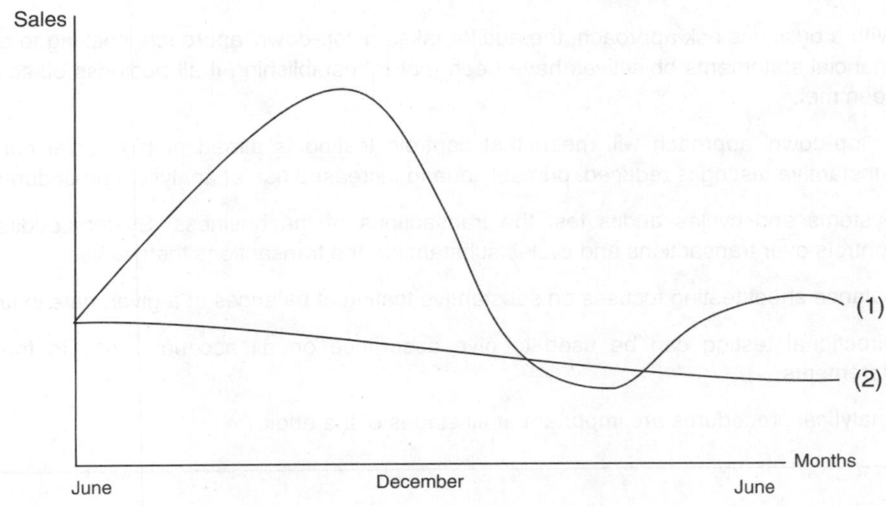

7.13 Line 1 in the diagram shows the actual sales made by a business. There is a clear seasonal fluctuation before Christmas. Line 2 shows a level of sales with 'expected seasonal fluctuations' having been stripped out. It shows that sales were lower than expected for December and continued to be low, despite December sales being higher than the other months.

7.14 Clearly, in this analysis, the seasonal fluctuations has been estimated. This analysis is useful however, because the estimate is likely to be based on past performance, so that conclusion from this is that there might be a problem:

- Sales are below the levels of previous years
- Sales are below expectation

Exam focus point

Audit approach has been identified as a key topic area. It is an area you should be familiar with from previous auditing studies, and most of the items looked at in this chapter should be revision.

A key point to remember when seeking to identify an appropriate strategy for a particular audit is that the approaches are linked and in some cases it may be best to use two or more together to achieve a good result. For example, directional testing would be used with a balance sheet approach because they are both substantive testing issues.

Remember also to focus on details given in the question to determine what approach is relevant. For example, if the question relates to a business which has a low level of large transactions, a cycles based approach might be relevant. A business with substantial numbers of sales transactions resulting in a balance sheet with substantial debtors in it might benefit from a balance sheet approach. It is likely that a risk approach would be taken in conjunction with these approaches. You should consider whether a business risk approach would be relevant.

The examiner has written two articles in the Student Accountant/Student's Newsletter which you should read:

- Directional testing, May 2001
- Analytical procedures, June 2000.

Chapter roundup

- Auditors usually take a risk based approach to an audit. This may be:
  - An audit risk based approach
  - A business risk approach
- With a business risk approach, the auditor takes a 'top-down' approach, seeking to establish if financial statements objectives have been met by establishing if all business objectives have been met.
- A 'top-down' approach will mean that controls testing is aimed at high level controls and substantive testing is reduced, primarily due to increased use of analytical procedures.
- Systems and cycles audits test the transactions of the business. System audits test the controls over transactions and cycles substantiate the transactions themselves.
- Balance sheet testing focuses on substantive testing of balances at a given date in time.
- Directional testing can be used to give assurance on all account areas in the financial statements.
- Analytical procedures are important at all stages of the audit.

Quick quiz

1 What are the effects of a 'top down' audit approach on:

(a) Tests of controls
(b) Analytical procedures
(c) Detailed testing

2 Name 4 key control objectives for sales.

(1) ____________________

(2) ____________________

(3) ____________________

(4) ____________________

3 When undertaking a cycles approach to auditing, the auditor is ensuring that transactions are processed through the cycle.

True ☐

False ☐

4 A balance sheet approach should never be combined with a business risk approach.

True ☐

False ☐

5 Complete the matrix.

		Primary test also gives comfort on			
Type of account	**Purpose of primary test**	**Assets**	**Liabilities**	**Income**	**Expenses**
Assets		U	O	O	U
Liabilities		U	O	O	U
Income		U	O	O	U
Expense		U	O	O	U

6 Name five significant relationships between items in the financial statements.

(1) ____________________

(2) ____________________

(3) ____________________

(4) ____________________

(5) ____________________

Answers to quick quiz

1 (a) Tests of control focused on high level controls
(b) Analytical procedures used more extensively
(c) Detailed testing consequently reduced

2 Any of:

Ordering and granting of credit

- **Goods** and **services** are **only supplied** to **customers** with **good credit ratings**
- **Customers** are encouraged to **pay promptly**
- **Orders** are **recorded correctly**
- **Orders** are **fulfilled**

Despatch and invoicing

- All **despatches** of goods are **recorded**
- All **goods and services** sold are **correctly invoiced**
- All **invoices** raised **relate to goods and services** that have been **supplied** by the business
- **Credit notes** are only given for **valid reasons**

Recording, accounting and credit control

- All sales that have been **invoiced** are **recorded** in the general and sales ledgers
- All **credit notes** that have been **issued** are **recorded** in the general and sales ledgers
- All **entries** in the sales ledger are **made** to the **correct** sales ledger **accounts**
- **Cut-off** is applied correctly to the sales ledger
- Potentially **doubtful debts** are **identified**

3 True

4 False

5

		Primary test also gives comfort on			
Type of account	**Purpose of primary test**	**Assets**	**Liabilities**	**Income**	**Expenses**
Assets	Overstatement (O)	U	O	O	U
Liabilities	Understatement (U)	U	O	O	U
Income	Understatement (U)	U	O	O	U
Expense	Overstatement (O)	U	O	O	U

6 See table at para 7.6

Now try the question below from the Exam Question Bank

Number	Level	Marks	Time
8	Exam	25	45 mins

Chapter 9

AUDIT EVIDENCE

Topic list		Syllabus reference
1	**Revision: Audit evidence**	3(c)
2	**Related parties**	3(c)
3	**Management Representations**	3(c)
4	**Using the work of others**	3(c)
5	**Revision: Documentation**	3(c)

Introduction

Audit evidence is a vital part of any audit. You have learnt the general issues relating to audit evidence in your previous studies. In this chapter we revise the basic relevant points about audit evidence and documentation. We then look in more detail at some areas where obtaining evidence can be complex.

The **basic issues** relating to **evidence** are that:

- **Auditors must obtain evidence** to support the assertions made by the directors in the financial statements.
- In order to support the audit opinion, this evidence must be **sufficient and appropriate.**
- For quality control reasons, the audit evidence must be **documented** sufficiently that
  - It can be referred to at a later date
  - Senior audit team members can **evaluate audit evidence** obtained prior to an audit opinion being issued.

Documentation and review are revised in Section 5 of this chapter.

Related parties are a difficult area to obtain audit evidence on. The auditor must bear certain points in mind when obtaining evidence on this area, specifically who it is from and how extensive it is. Obtaining evidence about related party transactions is considered in Section 2.

Often the auditors will have to rely on **management representations** about related parties. There are other occasions when this will be the case, when facts are confined to management or the matter is one of management judgement. Management representations are **subjective evidence**, and the auditor must proceed with caution when dealing with them. This is discussed in Section 3.

Sometimes, the **evidence** the auditor requires is **beyond the expertise of the auditor,** and he will need to **rely on the work of an expert.** The relevant procedures that the auditor must undertake are outlined in Section 4. The auditor may sometimes use the work of internal audit in gathering evidence. This is discussed in Chapter 16.

Study guide

Section 10 and 11

General

- Critically appraise the appropriateness and sufficiency of **different sources** of audit evidence and the procedures by which evidence may be obtained including
  - Management representations
  - The work of others (including internal auditors and specialists)
  - Sampling techniques and selection methods
  - Direct communication
  - Audit automation tools
- Identify and illustrate suitable investigative methods (eg audit procedures such as enquiry and observation) to obtain sufficient evidence from identified sources

Documentation

- Explain the reasons for preparing and keeping working papers and the importance of reviewing them

Related parties

- Explain the specific audit problems and procedures concerning related parties and related party transactions
- Recognise circumstances that may indicate the existence of unidentified related parties

Management representations

- Illustrate the use of written management representations as the primary source of audit evidence and as complementary audit evidence
- Discuss the implications of contradictory evidence being discovered

Using work of others

- Explain when it is justifiable to place reliance on the work of a specialist (eg a surveyor employed by the audit client)
- Assess the appropriateness and sufficiency of the work of internal auditors

Exam guide

Specific audit issues examined in 3.1 are likely to be at a higher level than in your previous auditing exams. Therefore, the more complex evidence issues of related parties, representations and using the work of others are important. You should consider how they link with specific accounting issues in Chapters 11-13.

1 REVISION: AUDIT EVIDENCE

1.1 You should be aware of the key points audit evidence from your previous auditing studies. We shall revise them briefly here.

1.2 Substantive procedures are designed to obtain evidence about the financial statement assertions.

KEY TERMS

Financial statement assertions are the representations of the directors that are embodied in the financial statements. By approving the financial statements, the directors are making representations about the information therein. These representations or assertions may be described in general terms in a number of ways, one of which is as follows.

Existence. An asset or liability exists at a given date.

Rights and obligations. An asset or liability pertains to the entity at a given date.

Occurrence. A transaction or event took place which pertains to the entity during the relevant period.

Completeness. There are no unrecorded assets, liabilities, transactions or events, or undisclosed items.

Valuation. An asset or liability is recorded at an appropriate carrying value

Measurement. A transaction or event is recorded in the proper amount and revenue or expense is allocated to the proper period.

Presentation and disclosure. An item is disclosed, classified and described in accordance with the applicable reporting framework (eg relevant legislation and applicable accounting standards).

1.3 An eighth assertion, **accuracy** that all assets, liabilities, transactions and events are **recorded accurately** is sometimes added.

1.4 Auditors obtain evidence by one or more of the following procedures.

PROCEDURES	
Inspection of assets	Inspection of assets that are recorded in the accounting records confirms **existence**, gives evidence of **valuation**, but does not confirm **rights and obligations** Confirmation that assets seen are recorded in accounting records gives evidence of **completeness**
Inspection of documentation	Confirmation to documentation of items recorded in accounting records confirms that an asset **exists** or a transaction **occurred**. Confirmation that items recorded in supporting documentation are recorded in accounting records tests **completeness** Cut-off can be verified by inspecting reverse population, that is, checking transactions recorded **after** the balance sheet date to supporting documentation to confirm that they occurred after the balance sheet date Inspection also provides evidence of **valuation/ measurement, rights and obligations** and the nature of items **(presentation and disclosure).** It can also be used to **compare** documents (and hence test **consistency** of audit evidence) and confirm **authorisation**

PROCEDURES	
Observation	Involves watching a procedure being performed (for example, post opening) Of limited use, as only confirms procedure took place when auditor watching
Enquiries	Seeking information from **client staff** or **external sources** Strength of evidence depends on knowledge and integrity of source of information
Confirmation	Seeking confirmation from another source of details in client's accounting records for example, confirmation from bank of bank balances
Computations	Checking arithmetic of client's records, for example, adding up ledger account
Audit automation tools	Auditors can make use of audit software to obtain evidence, for example: • Interrogation software • Comparison software • Resident code software to review transactions
Analytical procedures	See Chapter 8

1.5 In order to express an audit opinion, an auditor must obtain **sufficient, reliable audit evidence.**

Sufficient and appropriate audit evidence

1.6 'Sufficiency' and 'appropriateness' are interrelated and apply to both tests of controls and substantive procedures.

- **Sufficiency** is the measure of the **quantity** of audit evidence.
- **Appropriateness** is the measure of the **quality** or **reliability** of the audit evidence.

1.7 Auditors are essentially looking for enough reliable audit evidence. Audit **evidence usually indicates what is probable** rather than what is definite (is usually persuasive rather than conclusive) so different sources are examined by the auditors.

1.8 However, auditors can only give **reasonable assurance** that the financial statements are free from misstatement, so **not all sources of evidence will be examined**.

1.9 SAS 430 *Audit sampling* is based on the premise that auditors do not normally examine all the information available to them; it would be impractical to do so and using audit sampling will produce valid conclusions.

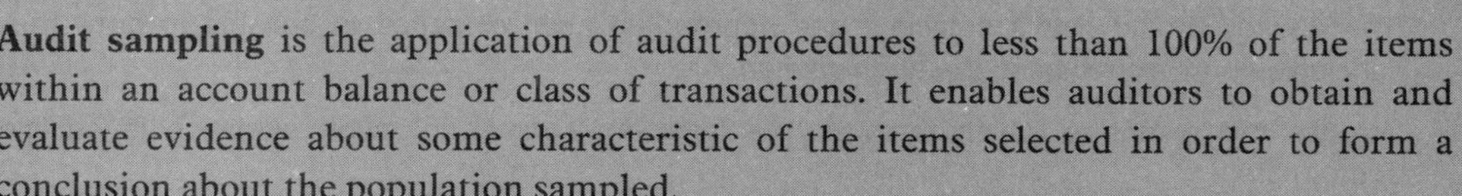

KEY TERMS

Audit sampling is the application of audit procedures to less than 100% of the items within an account balance or class of transactions. It enables auditors to obtain and evaluate evidence about some characteristic of the items selected in order to form a conclusion about the population sampled.

Sampling units are the individual items that make up the population.

Error is an unintentional mistake in the financial statements.

Tolerable error is the maximum error in the population that the auditors are willing to accept and still conclude that the audit objective has been achieved.

Sampling risk is the risk that the auditors' conclusion, based on a sample, may be different from the conclusion that would be reached if the entire population was subject to the same audit procedure.

Non-sampling risk is the risk that the auditors might use inappropriate procedures or might misinterpret evidence and thus fail to recognise an error.

1.10 The SAS points out that some testing procedures do **not** involve sampling, such as:

- Testing 100% of items in a population (this should be obvious)
- Testing all items with a certain characteristic (for example, over a certain value) as selection is not representative

1.11 The SAS distinguishes between **statistically based sampling,** which involves the use of random selection techniques from which mathematically constructed conclusions about the population can be drawn, and **non-statistical methods,** from which auditors draw a judgmental opinion about the population. However the principles of the SAS apply to both methods.

1.12 You should be aware of the major methods of statistical and non-statistical sampling.

Sufficiency of audit evidence

1.13 The auditors' judgement as to what is sufficient appropriate audit evidence is influenced by a number of factors.

- **Risk assessment**
- The **nature** of the **accounting and internal control systems**
- The **materiality** of the item being examined
- The **experience gained during previous audits**
- The auditors' **knowledge of the business** and **industry**
- The **results of audit procedures**
- The **source** and **reliability of information** available

1.14 If they are unable to obtain sufficient appropriate audit evidence, the auditors should **consider the implications for their report.**

Question 1

'The auditor should obtain sufficient and appropriate audit evidence to be able to draw reasonable conclusion on which to base the audit opinion.' (SAS 400.1)

Discuss the extent to which each of the following sources of audit evidence is sufficient and appropriate.

(a) Oral representation by management in respect of the completeness of sales where the majority of transactions are conducted on a cash basis

(b) Flowcharts of the accounting and control system prepared by a company's internal audit department

(c) Year-end supplier's statements

(d) Physical inspection of a fixed asset by an auditor, and

(e) Comparison of profit and loss account items for the current period with corresponding information for earlier periods.

Answer

Appropriate – Relevance

The relevance of audit evidence should be considered in relation to the overall audit objective of forming an opinion and reporting on the financial statements. The evidence should allow the auditor to conclude on the following:

Balance sheet items	- Completeness - Existence - Ownership - Valuation - Disclosure
Profit and loss account items	- Completeness - Existence - Valuation - Disclosure

(a) The representations by management in respect of the completeness of sales is relevant to the first of the objectives when gathering evidence on profit and loss account items. Depending on the system operated by the client and the controls over cash sales there may be no other evidence as to the completeness of sales.

(b) The flowcharts prepared by the internal audit department will not be directly relevant to the auditor's opinion on individual figures in the financial statements, but rather when the auditor is following the requirement in SAS 300 to ascertain the enterprise's system of recording and processing transactions. The auditor will wish to assess the adequacy of the system as a basis for the preparation of financial statements so the flowcharts will be relevant only if they are sufficiently detailed to allow the auditor to carry out this assessment. The auditor would also wish to make an initial assessment of internal controls at this stage so the flowcharts will be more relevant of control procedures are specifically identified.

(c) Year-end suppliers' statements provide evidence relevant to the auditor's conclusions on:

- The completeness of creditors, as omissions from the purchase ledger listing would be identified by comparing statements received to that listing
- The existence of creditors recorded in the purchase ledger
- The fact that the liabilities are properly those of the enterprise (for example, the statements are not addressed to, say, the managing director in his own name)
- The valuation of creditors at the year end with respect to cut-off of invoices and credit notes, and discounts or allowances.

(d) The physical inspection of a fixed asset is clearly relevant to the auditor's opinion as to the existence of the asset, and to some extent the completeness of recording of assets, that is, the auditor can check that all the assets inspected have been recorded. In certain circumstances evidence relevant to valuation might be obtained, for example, where a client has written down a building due to permanent diminution in value and the auditor sees it standing unused and derelict.

(e) The comparison of profit and loss account items with prior periods will provide evidence as to:

   (i) Completeness of recording, as omissions can be identified and investigated

   (ii) Valuation, in cases where the auditor has appropriate information on which to base expectations, for example, if the number of workers has doubled during the year and a set percentage wage increase had been effected in the year

   (iii) Disclosure, as the comparison should highlight any inconsistencies of classification and treatment from year to year.

Appropriate – Reliable

Reliability of audit evidence depends on the particular circumstances but the guideline offers three general presumptions

- Documentary evidence is more reliable than oral evidence
- Evidence obtained from independent sources outside the enterprise is more reliable than that secured solely from within the enterprise
- Evidence originated by the auditor by such means as analysis and physical inspection is more reliable than evidence obtained by others.

(a) The oral representations by management would be regarded as relatively unreliable using the criteria in the guideline, as they are oral and internal. In the absence of any external or auditor-generated evidence, the auditor should ensure that these representations are included in the letter of representation so that there is at least some documentary evidence to support any conclusions.

(b) The assessment of how reliable the flowcharts are would depend on the auditor's overall assessment of the internal audit department. The factor to be considered would include its degree of independence, the scope of its work, whether due professional care had been exercised, the technical competence and level of resource available to the internal audit department. This assessment should be documented by the external auditor of he is to make use of the flowcharts in his audit planning and design of tests.

(c) Suppliers' statements would generally be seen as reliable evidence, being documentary and form sources external to the enterprise. If the auditor had doubts as to the reliability of this evidence, it could be improved by the auditor originating similar evidence by means of a creditor's circularisation rather than relying on suppliers' statements received by the client.

(d) Physical inspection of a fixed asset is a clear example of auditor-originated evidence, so would usually be considered more reliable than that generate by others.

(e) Analysis such as this comparison of profit and loss items with the prior periods would again be terms auditor-generated evidence, and would be considered more reliable than evidence generated by others. Ultimately the reliability of such audit evidence depends on the reliability of the underlying data, this should be checked by compliance or substantive testing.

Sufficiency

The auditor needs to obtain sufficient relevant and reliable evidence to form a reasonable basis for his opinion on the financial statements. His judgements will be influenced by factors such as:

- His knowledge of the business and its environment
- The risk of misstatement
- The persuasiveness of the evidence

(a) To decide if the representations were sufficient with regard to concluding on the completeness of ales the auditor would consider:

   - The nature of the business and the inherent risk of unrecorded cash sales

- The materiality of the item; in this case it would appear that cash sales are material
- Any possible management bias
- The persuasiveness of the evidence in the light of other related audit work, for example, testing of cash receipts.

If the auditor believes there is still a risk of material understatement of sales in the light of the above, he should seek further evidence.

(b) Client-prepared flowcharts are **not** sufficient as a basis for the auditor's evaluation of the system. To confirm that the system does operate in the manner described, the auditor should perform 'walk through' checks, tracing a small number of transactions through the system. There is, however, no need for the auditor to prepare his own flowcharts if he is satisfied that those produced by internal audit are accurate.

(c) The auditor's decision as to whether the suppliers' statements were sufficient evidence would depend on his assessment of materiality and the risk of misstatement. Its persuasiveness would be assessed in conjunction with the results of other audit work, for example, substantive testing of purchases, returns, and cash payments, and compliance testing of the purchases system.

(d) Inspection of a fixed asset would be sufficient evidence as to the existence of the asset (provided it was carried out at or close to the balance sheet date). Before concluding on the fixed asset figure in the accounts, the auditor would have to consider the results of his work on other aspects as the ownership and valuation of the asset.

(e) In addition to the general considerations such as risk and materiality, the results of a 'comparison' alone would not give very persuasive evidence. It would have to be followed by a detailed investigation of variances (or lack of variances where they were expected). The results should be compared to the auditor's expectations based on his knowledge of the business, and explanations given by management should be verified. The persuasiveness of the evidence should be considered in the light on other relevant testing, for example, compliance testing of payments systems, or substantive testing of expense invoices.

---

2 RELATED PARTIES — Pilot Paper

2.1 The accounting for related party transactions is dealt with in FRS 8 *Related party disclosures*.

Knowledge brought forward from Paper 2.5 Financial Reporting

Related parties are defined as 'two or more parties, (where) at any time during the financial period:

(a) One party has either direct or indirect control of the other party, or

(b) The parties are subject to common control from the same source, or

(c) One party has influence over the financial and operating policies of the other party to an extent that that other party might be inhibited from pursuing at all times its own separate interests, or

(d) The parties, in entering a transactions, are subject to influence from the same source to such an extent that one of the parties to the transaction has subordinated its own separate interests.'

Related party transactions are the transfer of assets or liabilities or the performance of services by, to or for a related party irrespective of whether a price is charged.

SAS 460 *Related parties*

> **SAS 460.1**
>
> The auditors should plan and perform the audit with the objective of obtaining sufficient audit evidence regarding the adequacy of the disclosure of related party transactions and control of the entity in the financial statements.

Inherent difficulties of detection

2.2 It may **not** be **self-evident** to management whether a party is related. Furthermore, many accounting systems are **not designed** to either distinguish or summarise related party transactions, so management will have to carry out additional analysis of accounting information.

2.3 An audit cannot be expected to detect all material related party transactions. The risk that undisclosed related party transactions will not be detected by the auditors is especially high when:

- **Related party transactions** have **taken place without charge.**
- **Related party transactions** are **not self-evident** to the auditors.
- Transactions are with a party that the auditors could **not** reasonably be expected to **know** is **a related party.**
- **Active steps** have been taken by directors or management to **conceal** either the full terms of a transaction, or that a transaction is, in substance, with a related party.
- The **corporate structure** is **complex.**

Responsibilities of the directors

2.4 The directors are responsible for the **identification** of related party transactions. Such transactions should be **properly approved** as they are frequently not at arm's length. The directors are also responsible for the **disclosure** of related party transactions.

Quality of audit evidence

2.5 Such evidence may:

- Be limited
- Although not limited, be created by the related party

2.6 The auditors can, if other audit work does not indicate contrary evidence, accept **representations** from the directors (see section 3). The auditors should, however, have a degree of scepticism.

Identification of related parties and transactions

> **SAS 460.2**
>
> When planning the audit the auditors should assess the risk that material undisclosed related party transactions may exist.
>
> **SAS 460.3**
>
> The auditors should review for completeness information provided by the directors identifying material transactions with those parties that have been related parties for any part of the financial period.

2.7 The following examples are given of audit procedures.

- **Review minutes** of meetings of shareholders and directors and other relevant statutory records such as the register of directors' interests
- **Review accounting records** for large or unusual transactions or balances, in particular transactions recognised at or near the end of the financial period
- **Review confirmations of loans receivable** and payable and confirmations from banks. Such a review may indicate the relationship of guarantors to the client
- **Review investment transactions**, for example purchase or sale of an interest in a joint venture or other entity

2.8 The following substantive procedures are suggested, the extent of which should be determined as a result of tests of controls and the procedures listed above.

- **Enquire of management** and the directors as to whether transactions have taken place with related parties that are required to be disclosed
- **Review prior year working papers** for names of known related parties
- **Enquire** as to the **names** of all pension and other trusts established for the benefit of employees and the names of their management and trustees
- **Enquire** as to the **affiliation** of directors and officers with other entities
- **Review the register of interests in shares** to determine the names of principal shareholders
- **Enquire of other auditors** currently involved in the audit, or predecessor auditors, as to their knowledge of additional related parties
- Review the entity's tax returns, listing documents supplied to Stock Exchanges, returns made under companies legislation and other information supplied to regulatory agencies for evidence of the existence of related parties
- Review invoices and correspondence from lawyers for indications of the existence of related parties or related party transactions

SAS 460.4

The auditors should be alert for evidence of material related party transactions that are not included in the information provided by the directors.

2.9 The following evidence is suggested of the type mentioned in SAS 460.4.

- Transactions which have **abnormal terms of trade**, such as unusual prices, interest rates, guarantees and repayment terms
- Transactions which appear to **lack a logical business reason** for their occurrence
- Transactions in which **substance differs from form**
- Transactions **processed or approved in a non-routine manner** or by personnel who do not ordinarily deal with such transactions
- **Unusual transactions** entered into shortly before or after the end of the financial period

Examining identified related party transactions and disclosures

SAS 460.5

The auditors should obtain sufficient appropriate audit evidence that material identified related party transactions are properly recorded and disclosed in the financial statements.

2.10 The following procedures are suggested when the audit evidence about a related party transaction is limited.

- **Discuss** the **purpose** of **the transaction** with management or the directors
- **Confirm** the **terms** and **amount** of the **transaction** with the related party
- **Corroborate** with the **related party** the **explanation** of the purpose of the transaction and, if necessary, confirm that the transaction is **bona fide**

Disclosure relating to control of the entity

SAS 460.6

The auditors should obtain sufficient appropriate audit evidence that disclosures in the financial statements relating to control of the entity are properly stated.

Directors' representations

SAS 460.7

The auditors should obtain written representations from the directors concerning the completeness of information provided regarding the related party and control disclosures in the financial statements.

Audit conclusions and reporting

SAS 460.8

The auditors should consider the implications for their report if:

(a) they are unable to obtain sufficient appropriate audit evidence concerning related parties and transactions with such parties; or

(b) the disclosure of related party transactions or the controlling party of the entity in the financial statements is not adequate.

Problems with applying SAS 460

2.11 Problems auditors have had when applying SAS 460 include the following.

Identification of controlling party

2.12 Auditors may find it **very difficult to identify the controlling party** if the entity is part of a multi-national group. If the controlling party is a trust, auditors may have problems determining who if anyone controls the trust.

2.13 Alternatively the directors may state that they do not know the identity of the controlling party or that there is no controlling party. These statements may be difficult to disprove.

Materiality

2.14 This problem has two aspects:

(a) Auditors may not be able to determine whether **transactions** are **material** to **related parties** who are individuals (directors, key management and their families)

(b) Auditors may have particular problems **applying** the **definition** of **materiality** (an item is material if it affects the decisions of the users of the accounts). As materiality depends on **circumstances** as well as **amounts,** auditors have to decide whether the fact that certain transactions are on normal commercial terms influences whether they are disclosed.

Question 2

You are the senior in charge of the audit of AB Milton Ltd for the year ended 31 May 20X1. Details of AB Milton Ltd and certain other companies are given below.

AB Milton Ltd

A building company formed by Alexander Milton and his brother, Brian.

AB Milton Ltd has issued share capital of 500 ordinary £1 shares, owned as shown below.

Alexander Milton	210	42%	Founder and director
Brian Milton	110	22%	Founder and director
Catherine Milton (Brian's wife)	100	20%	Company secretary
Diane Hardy	20	4%	
Edward Murray	60	12%	Director

Edward Murray is a local business man and a close friend of both Alexander and Brian Milton. He gave the brothers advice when they set up the company and remains involved through his position on the board of directors. His own company, Murray Design Ltd, supplies AB Milton Ltd with stationery and publicity materials.

Diane Hardy is Alexander Milton's ex-wife. She was given her shares as part of the divorce settlement and has no active involvement in the management of the company. Alexander's girlfriend, Fiona Dyson, is the company's solicitor. She is responsible for drawing up and reviewing all key building and other contracts, and frequently attends board meetings so that she can explain the terms of a particular contract to the directors. Her personal involvement with Alexander started in May 20X1 and, since that time, she has spent increasing amounts of time at the company's premises.

Cuts and Curls Ltd

A poodle parlour, of which 50% of the issued shares are owned by Diane Hardy and 50% by Gillian Milton, who is Alexander and Diane's daughter.

Cuts and Curls operated from premised owned by AB Milton Ltd for which is pays rent at the normal market rate.

Campbell Milton Roofing Ltd

A roofing company owned 60% by AB Milton Ltd and 40% by Ian Campbell, the managing director.

Campbell Milton Roofing Ltd carries out regular work for AB Milton Ltd and also does roofing work for local customers. Alexander Milton is a director of Campbell Milton Roofing Ltd and Catherine Milton is the company secretary. All legal work is performed by Fiona Dyson.

(a) Based on the information given above, identify the potential related party transactions you expect to encounter during the audit of AB Milton Ltd and summarise, giving your reasons, what disclosure, if any, will be required in the full statutory accounts.

(b) Prepare notes for a training session for junior staff on how to identify related party transactions. Your notes should include:

  (i) A list of possible features which could lead you to investigate a particular transaction to determine whether it is in fact a related party transaction, and

  (ii) A summary of the general audit procedures you would perform to ensure that all material related party transactions have been identified.

Answer

Person/entity	Related party	Why	Transaction
Alex Milton	✓	Director	} No transactions mentioned
Brian Milton	✓	Director	
Brian's wife	✓	Wife of director	
Edward Murray	✓	Director	Purchases of stationery
Murray Designs	✓	Sub of Director	
Diane Hardy	×	No longer close family & ≥ 20%	
Fiona Dyson	✓	Presumed close family & shadow director	Contracts drawn
Cuts & Curls	?	(see below)	Rental agreement
Campbell Milton Roofing	✓	Sub of AB Milton	Work done for AB (see below)
Ian Campbell	✓/×	Could be considered key management of group	

Cuts & Curls is not clear cut. For it to be a related party Gillian Milton would need to be in a position to control Cuts & Curls and then due to her relationship with Alex Milton her company would come under the related party umbrella. Gillian only holds 50% and therefore holds joint control with her mother.

Disclosure

One a related party has been identified disclosure is required of any material transaction. Materiality is in most cases determined by considering both parties perspective. For instance, the contracts drawn by Fiona Dyson may be material to her even if not for AB Milton.

Transactions with subsidiaries, that is, Campbell Milton Roofing:

Disclosure is not required of transactions which are cancelled on consolidation. However, if group accounts are not prepared due to a small/medium group exemption material transactions between the two companies would need to be disclosed.

Disclosure should include:

- Names of the transacting related parties
- A description of the relationship
- A description of the transaction and the amounts included
- The amounts due to or form the related party at the end of the year
- Any other element of the transaction necessary for an understanding of the financial statements

(b) Notes for staff training sessions:

A logical place to start the audit of related party transactions would be to identify all possible related parties. This would always include

- Directors and shadow directors
- Group companies
- Pension funds of the company
- Associates

It is likely that the other related parties would include:

- Key management (perhaps identified by which staff have key man cover)
- Shareholder owning > 20% of the shares
- Close relatives associates of any of the above

A related party transaction need to be reported if it is a material either to the reporting entity on to the other party to the transaction.

Related party transactions do not necessarily have to be detrimental to the reporting entity, but those which are will be easier to find. Features which may indicate this may include:

- Unusually generous trade or settlement discounts
- Unusually generous payment terms
- Recorded in the nominal ledger code of any person previously identified as a related party (for example, director)
- Unusual size of transaction for customers (for example, if ABL were paying a suspiciously high legal bill for a building company)

Audit steps to find related party transactions may include:

- Identification of excessively generous credit terms by reference to aged debtors analysis
- Identification of excessive discounts by reference to similar reports
- Scrutiny of cash book/cheque stubs for payments made to directors or officers of the company (probably more realistic for smaller entities)
- Review of Board minutes for evidence of approval of related party transactions (directors are under a fiduciary duty to not make secret profits)
- Written representations from directors to give exhaustive list of all actual/potential related parties (that is, allow us to make the materiality assessment, not them)
- Review of accounting rewards for large transactions, especially near the year end and with non-established customers/suppliers
- Identification of any persons holding > 20% of the shares in the entity by reference of the shareholders' register

---

3 MANAGEMENT REPRESENTATIONS

3.1 The auditors receive many representations during the audit and some may be **critical to obtaining sufficient appropriate audit evidence.** Representations may also be required for general matters, for example, full availability of accounting records.

3.2 **Written confirmation** of oral representations **avoids confusion and disagreement.** The written confirmation may take the form of:

- A **representation letter** from **management** (see example below)
- A **letter from the auditors** outlining their understanding of management's representations, duly acknowledged and confirmed in writing by management
- **Minutes of meetings of the board** or directors, or similar body, at which such representations are approved

SAS 440 *Management representations* covers this area.

SAS 440.1

Auditors should obtain written confirmation of appropriate representations from management before their report is issued.

Acknowledgement by directors of their responsibility for the financial statements

SAS 440.2

The auditors should obtain evidence that the directors acknowledge their collective responsibility for the preparation of the financial statements and have approved the financial statements.

3.3 Auditors normally do this when they receive a signed copy of the financial statements which incorporate a relevant statement of the directors' responsibilities.

Representations by management as audit evidence

3.4 In addition to representations relating to responsibility for the financial statements, the auditors may wish to rely on management representations as **audit evidence.**

SAS 440.3

Auditors should obtain written confirmation of representations from management on matters material to the financial statements when those representations are critical to obtaining sufficient appropriate audit evidence.

3.5 Such matters should be **discussed** with those responsible for giving the written confirmation, to ensure that they **understand** what they are confirming. Written confirmations are normally required of **appropriately senior management**.

3.6 Only matters which are **material** to the financial statements should be included in a letter of representation.

3.7 When the auditors receive such representations they should:

- Seek **corroborative audit evidence**
- Evaluate whether the representations made by management appear **reasonable and are consistent** with other audit evidence obtained, including other representations

- Consider whether the individuals making the representations can be expected to be **well-informed** on the particular matters

3.8 The SAS then makes a very important point.

> 'Representations by management **cannot be a substitute for other audit evidence that auditors expect to be available**. If auditors are unable to obtain sufficient appropriate audit evidence regarding a matter which has, or may have, a material effect on the financial statements and such audit evidence is expected to be available, this constitutes a limitation in the scope of the audit, even if a representation from management has been received on the matter. In these circumstances it may be necessary for them to consider the implications for their report.'

3.9 There are two instances given in the SAS where management representations **may** be the only audit evidence available.

- **Knowledge of the facts is confined to management**, for example, the facts are a matter of management intention.
- **The matter is principally one of judgement or opinion**, for example, the trading position of a particular customer.

3.10 There may be occasions when the representations received do not agree with other audit evidence obtained.

> **SAS 440.4**
>
> If a representation appears to be contradicted by other audit evidence, the auditors should investigate the circumstances to resolve the matter and consider whether it casts doubt on the reliability of other representations.

Basic elements of a management representation letter

3.11 A management representation letter should:

- Be **addressed** to the **auditors**
- **Contain specified information**
- Be **appropriately dated**
- Be **approved by those with specific knowledge** of the relevant matters

3.12 The auditors will normally request that the letter is:

(a) Discussed and agreed by the board of directors (or equivalent)

(b) Signed on its behalf by the chairman and secretary before the auditors approve the financial statements.

3.13 The letter will usually be **dated on** the day the financial statements are **approved**, but if there is any significant delay between the representation letter and the date of the auditors' report, then the auditors should consider the need to obtain further representations.

Action if management refuses to provide written confirmation of representations

> **SAS 440.5**
>
> If management refuses to provide written confirmation of a representation that the auditors consider necessary, the auditors should consider the implications of this scope limitation for their report.

3.14 In these circumstances, the auditors should consider whether it is appropriate to rely on other representations made by management during the audit.

Example of a management representation letter

3.15 An **example** of a management representation letter is provided in an appendix to the SAS. It is **not** a standard letter, and representations do not have to be confirmed in letter form.

> (Company letterhead)
>
> (To the auditors) (Date)
>
> We confirm to the best of our knowledge and belief, and having made appropriate enquiries of other directors and officials of the company, the following representations given to you in connection with your audit of the financial statements for the period ended 31 December 20...
>
> (1) We acknowledge as directors our responsibilities under the Companies Act 1985 for preparing financial statements which give a true and fair view and for making accurate representations to you. All the accounting records have been made available to you for the purpose of your audit and all the transactions undertaken by the company have been properly reflected and recorded in the accounting records. All other records and related information, including minutes of all management and shareholders' meetings, have been made available to you.
>
> (2) The legal claim by ABC Limited has been settled out of court by a payment of £258,000. No further amounts are expected to be paid, and no similar claims have been received.
>
> (3) In connection with deferred tax not provided, the following assumptions reflect the intentions and expectations of the company:
>
> (a) capital investment of £450,000 is planned over the next three years;
>
> (b) there are no plans to sell revalued properties; and
>
> (c) we are not aware of any indications that the situation is likely to change so as to necessitate the inclusion of a provision for tax payable in the financial statements.
>
> (4) The company has not had, or entered into, at any time during the period any arrangement, transaction or agreement to provide credit facilities (including loans, quasi-loans or credit transactions) for directors or to guarantee or provide security for such matters.
>
> (5) There have been no events since the balance sheet date which necessitate revision of the figures included in the financial statements or inclusion of a note thereto.
>
> As minuted by the board of directors at its meeting on .... (date)
>
> ....
>
> Chairman Secretary

3.16 The following notes are provided by the SAS on the example.

(a) Other signatories may include those with specific knowledge of the relevant matters, for example the chief financial officer.

(b) Examples of other issues which may be the subject of representations from management include:

- The extent of the purchase of goods on terms which include reservation of title by suppliers

- The absence of knowledge of circumstances which could result in losses on long-term contracts
- The reasons for concluding that an overdue debt from a related party is fully recoverable
- Confirmation of the extent of guarantees, warranties or other financial commitments relating to subsidiary undertakings or related parties

Question 3

Management representations are an important source of audit evidence. These representations may be oral or written, and may be obtained either on an informal or formal basis. The auditors will include information obtained in this manner in their audit working papers where it forms part of their total audit evidence.

Required

(a) Explain the nature and role of the letter of representation.

(b) Explain why it is important for the auditors to discuss the contents of the letter of representation at an early stage of the audit.

(c) Explain why standard letters of representation are becoming less frequently used by the auditing profession.

Answer

(a) The letter of representation is a letter normally signed by appropriate directors normally on behalf of the whole board. Such a letter contains representations relating to matters which are material to the financial statements but concerning which knowledge of the facts is confined to management, or where the directors have used judgement or opinion in the preparation of the financial statements.

The precise scope and content of the letter of representation should be appropriate to the particular audit. An example of a typical situation in which representations may be required would be a case in which an employee's legal claim is settled out of court and the directors are asked to set out in writing their view that no further similar claims are expected to be paid. An absence of independent corroborative evidence and the fact that judgement on the part of directors is involved indicates the need for written evidence of the judgement in the letter of representation.

Representations are not a substitute for other necessary audit work, and they do not relieve the auditors of any of their responsibilities. Even where written representations are obtained, the auditors need to decide whether in the circumstances these representations, together with other audit evidence obtained, are sufficient to justify an unqualified opinion on the financial statements.

However, written representations by the directors do form part of the total audit evidence, and form part of the auditors' working papers. Their status as evidence is given weight by the fact that s 389 of the Companies Act 1985 makes it a criminal offence for directors knowingly or recklessly to make false statements to the auditors in the course of their duty.

One function which the letter of representation may also serve, although it is subsidiary to its central purposes, is that such a letter may act as a reminder to the directors of their responsibilities. For example, the letter will remind them of their responsibilities with regard to the truth and fairness of the accounts, and of their responsibility for statements made orally to the auditors but only recorded in writing in the letter of representation.

(b) The letter of representation should not be seen as an afterthought in the audit process, even though the letter should be finally approved and signed on a date as close as possible to the date of the audit report and after all other audit work has been completed.

Discussion of the contents of the letter early in the audit is an important part of the audit planning process. It makes the auditors aware at an early stage of the areas in which representations may be required. It also acts as prior warning to management of errors. This may usefully give management a chance to think carefully about the nature of any representations which are likely to be required in writing, and may encourage directors to become more fully aware of their responsibilities in relation to such written confirmations.

If discussion of the contents of the representation letter are left until the last stages of the audit, senior management may justifiably object that, the matters covered by the letter ought to have been raised earlier by the auditors. Management might object that if this had been done there would have been an opportunity to assemble appropriate corroborative evidence and thus avoid the need for written representations by the directors. Such objections may be made especially where audit deadlines are tight, which is often the case for companies which are part of a group.

Lengthy discussions of judgmental matters on which representations are being sought may, if left until the end of the audit process, detract from a good working relationship between the auditors and client management, and in extreme cases management may become reluctant to comply with the auditors' requests.

(c) Some audit firms make use of a standard form of letter of representation. The principal merit of using a standard letter is that, by using a standard for all audit work in the firm, the firm has more assurance that staff on each audit will have considered all of the typical kinds of matter on which written representations are normally sought from clients. Audit staff may benefit from using such a standard letter as a checklist of possible matters to include in a draft letter to discuss with management. However, in all cases there will be a need to 'tailor' the standard letter to suit the needs of the particular audit engagement. This may involve adapting paragraphs of a standard letter, or adding new paragraphs to cover matters special to the assignment.

Instead of using a full standardised letter, some firms make use of 'specimen paragraphs' to be included in draft letters of representation. Such specimen paragraphs offer the advantage of suggesting appropriate wording dealing with common matters on which representations are required. Given the judgmental nature of many such matters, careful wording is important.

As with all standardised audit documentation, there remains the danger that standardisation may encourage a 'mechanical' approach to audit work and this probably explains why many firms are becoming reluctant to use standard forms of letter. Where audit staff fail to use their initiative and imagination, the standard letter may be followed too closely, and important matters may be missed. However, it could be argued that the problem in such cases lies more with a lack of adequate training of audit staff than with the fact that standardised documentation is available.

In presenting a letter of representation to the directors, it is important that the letter is not treated as merely a standard formality. Even if the letter for a particular assignment contains only similar material to that included generally in such letters, and is little different from last year's letter for the same client, each point should be discussed with management in order to encourage the signatories to consider its contents fully.

4 USING THE WORK OF OTHERS

Experts

4.1 Professional audit staff are highly trained and educated, but their experience and training is limited to accountancy and audit matters. In **certain situations** it will therefore be necessary to employ someone else with **different expert knowledge** to gain sufficient, appropriate audit evidence.

KEY TERM

An **expert** is a person or firm possessing special skill, knowledge and experience in a particular field other than auditing.

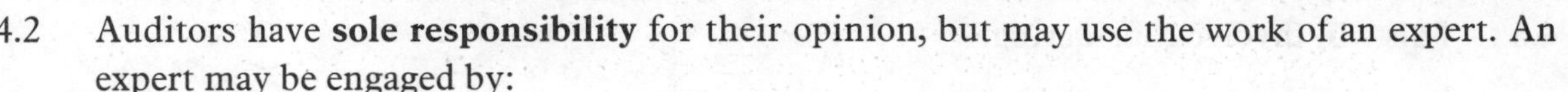

4.2 Auditors have **sole responsibility** for their opinion, but may use the work of an expert. An expert may be engaged by:

- A client to provide **specialist advice** on a particular matter which affects the financial statements
- The auditors in order to obtain **sufficient audit evidence** regarding certain financial statement assertions

SAS 520 *Using the work of an expert* covers this area.

Determining the need to use the work of an expert

> **SAS 520.1**
>
> When using the work performed by an expert, auditors should obtain sufficient appropriate audit evidence that such work is adequate for the purposes of an audit.

4.3 The following list of examples is given by the SAS of the audit evidence which might be obtained from the opinion, valuation etc of an expert.

- **Valuations of certain types of assets**, for example land and buildings, plant and machinery
- **Determination of quantities or physical condition of assets**
- **Determination of amounts** using specialised techniques, for example actuarial valuations
- **The measurement of work completed** and **work in progress** on contracts
- **Legal opinions**

4.4 When considering whether to use the work of an expert, the auditors should review:

- The **importance** of the matter being considered in the context of the accounts
- The **risk of misstatement** based on the nature and complexity of the matter
- The **quantity** and **quality** of other available **relevant audit evidence**

4.5 Once it is decided that an expert is required, the approach should be discussed with the management of the entity. Where the management is unwilling or unable to engage an expert, the auditors should consider engaging an expert themselves **unless sufficient alternative audit evidence can be obtained.**

Competence and objectivity of the expert

> **SAS 520.2**
>
> When planning to use the work of an expert the auditors should assess the objectivity and professional qualifications, experience and resources of the expert.

4.6 This will involve considering:

- The expert's **professional certification**, or licensing by, or membership of, an appropriate professional body
- The expert's **experience and reputation** in the field in which the auditors are seeking audit evidence

4.7 The risk that an expert's **objectivity is impaired** increases when the expert is:

- **Employed** by the entity
- **Related** in some other manner to the entity, for example, by being financially dependent upon, or having an investment in, the entity

4.8 If the auditors have **reservations** about the competence or objectivity of the expert they may need to carry out **other procedures** to obtain **evidence from another expert.**

The expert's scope of work

SAS 520.3

The auditors should obtain sufficient appropriate audit evidence that the expert's scope of work is adequate for the purposes of their audit.

4.9 Written instructions usually cover the expert's terms of reference and such instructions may cover such matters as follows.

- The **objectives** and **scope** of the expert's work
- A **general outline** as to the specific matters the expert's report is to cover
- The **intended use** of the expert's work including the possible communication to third parties of the expert's identity and extent of involvement
- The **extent** of the **expert's access** to appropriate records and files
- Information regarding the **assumptions and methods intended** to be used by the expert and their consistency with those used in prior periods

Assessing the work of the expert

SAS 520.4

The auditors should assess the appropriateness of the expert's work as audit evidence regarding the financial statement assertions being considered.

4.10 Auditors should assess whether the substance of the expert's findings is properly reflected in the financial statements or supports the financial statement assertions. It will also require consideration of:

- The **source data used**
- The **assumptions and methods used**
- **When** the expert carried out the work
- The reasons for any **changes in assumptions and methods**
- The **results** of the expert's work in the light of the auditors' overall knowledge of the business and the results of other audit procedures

4.11 The auditors do **not** have the expertise to judge the assumptions and methods used; these are the responsibility of the expert. However, the auditors should seek to obtain an understanding of these assumptions, to consider their reasonableness based on other audit evidence, knowledge of the business and so on.

4.12 **Where inconsistencies arise** between the expert's work and other audit evidence, then the auditors should attempt to resolve them by discussion with both the entity and the expert. Additional procedures (including use of another expert) may be necessary.

4.13 Where the **audit evidence** from the expert is **insufficient**, and there is no satisfactory alternative source of evidence, then the **auditors should consider the implications for their audit report.**

4.14 The SAS makes the following very important point (our bold).

> 'When the auditors are satisfied that the work of an expert provides appropriate audit evidence, **reference is not made to the work of the expert in their report**.'

Internal audit

4.15 If the client has an internal audit department, it may sometimes be possible for the external auditor to make use of their work in arriving at their audit opinion.

4.16 The methods by which the external auditors assess the adequacy and sufficiency of the work of internal audit is considered in Chapter 16.

5 REVISION: DOCUMENTATION

5.1 All audit work must be documented: the working papers are the **tangible evidence of all work done in support of the audit opinion.**

5.2 In the case of area where the evidence is difficult to obtain, such as related parties, and may arise through discussions with management, it is vital that notes are made of conversations and that, as discussed in Section 3, representations on material matters are confirmed in writing.

5.3 In your previous studies, you have learnt the practical issues surrounding how audit papers should be completed. There is a key general rule concerning what to include on a working paper to remember, which is:

> 'What would be necessary to provide an experienced auditor, with no previous connection with the audit, with an understanding of the work performed and the basis of the decisions taken.'

5.4 The key reason for having audit papers therefore is that they provide evidence of work done. They may be required in the event of litigation arising over the audit work and opinion given.

5.5 We shall briefly revise here the review of working papers. **Review** of working papers is important, as it allows a more senior auditor to **evaluate the evidence obtained** during the course of the audit for sufficiency and reliability, so that more evidence can be obtained to support the audit opinion, if required.

Review of audit working papers

5.6 Work performed by each assistant should be reviewed by personnel of appropriate experience to consider whether:

- The work has been **performed** in **accordance with the audit programme.**
- The work performed and the results obtained have been **adequately documented.**
- Any **significant matters** have been **resolved** or are reflected in audit conclusions.
- The **objectives** of the audit procedures have been **achieved.**

- The **conclusions** expressed are **consistent** with the results of the work performed and support the audit opinion.

5.7 The following should be reviewed on a timely basis.

- The **overall audit plan** and the **audit programme**
- The **assessments of inherent and control risks**
- The **results** of **control** and **substantive procedures** and the conclusions drawn therefrom including the results of consultations
- The **financial statements,** proposed audit adjustments and the proposed auditors' report

5.8 In some cases, particular in large complex audits, personnel not involved in the audit may be asked to review some or all of the audit work, the auditors' report etc. This is sometimes called a **peer review** or **hot review.**

Review of audit working papers: practical points

5.9 Throughout the audit, a system of review of all working papers will be used. In the case of a large audit, the work of assistants will be reviewed by the supervisor(s).

5.10 In turn, the audit manager will review the work of the supervisor and at least some , if not all, of the work performed by the assistants. The overall and final review will be undertaken by the audit engagement partner.

5.11 Each working paper should be initialled (or signed) and dated by the person who prepared it.

5.12 When a review takes place, the reviewer will often use a separate working paper to record queries **and** their answer.

5.13 The need to sign off all working papers and queries acts as an extra check, helping to ensure that all work has been carried out and completed.

5.14 After the supervisor has reviewed the work of the assistants there will usually be (in larger audit firms):

- A **manager review,** which will cover some of the assistants' work and an overall review of the audit work
- An **engagement partner review,** which will look at the manager's review, any controversial areas of the audit, the auditors' report etc

Question 4

Viewco Ltd is a manufacturer of TVs and video recorders. It carries out a full physical stocktake at its central warehouse every year on 31 December, its financial year end. Finished goods stocks are normally of the order of £3 million, with stocks of components and work in progress normally approximately £1 million.

You are the audit senior responsible for the audit of Viewco Ltd for the year ending 31 December 20X1. Together with a junior member of staff, you will be attending Viewco Ltd's physical stocktake.

(a) Explain why it is necessary for an auditor to prepare working papers.

(b) State, giving reasons, what information the working papers relating to this stocktaking attendance should contain.

Answer

(a) Working papers are necessary for the following reasons:

- So that the reporting partner can be satisfied that work delegated has been properly performed.
- To provide, for future reference, detail of problems encountered, evidence of work performed and conclusions drawn therefrom in arriving at the audit opinion.
- Their preparation encourages a methodical approach.
- To facilitate review.
- To provide evidence that Auditing Standards have been followed.

(b)

Information	*Reasons*
1. Administration	
Client name	• Enables an organised file to be produced.
Year end	
Title	
Date prepared	• Enables papers to be traced if lost
Initials of preparer	• Any questions can be addressed top the appropriate person
	• Seniority of preparer is indicated
Initials of senior to indicate review of junior's work	• Evidence that guideline on planning, controlling and recording is being followed
	• Evidence of adherence to auditing standards
2. Planning	
(i) Summary of different models of TV and Video held and the approximate value of each.	• Enables auditor to familiarise himself with different types of stock line
Summary of different types of raw material held and method of counting small components.	
Summary of different stages of WIP identified by client.	
(ii) Time and place of count.	• Audit team will not miss the count
(iii) Personnel involved.	• Auditor aware who to address questions/ problems to.
(iv) Copy of client's stocktake instructions and an assessment of them.	• Enables an initial assessment of the likely reliability of Viewco's count.
	• Assists in determining the amount of work audit team need to do.
	• Enables compliance work to be carried out, that is, checking Viewco staff follow the instructions.
(v) Plan of warehouse	• To ensure all areas covered at count
	• Clear where to find different models/components
	• Location of any 3rd party/moving stock clear.
(vi) Details of any known old or slow moving lines	• Special attention can be given to these at count, for example, include in test counts

(vii) Scope of tests counts to be performed, that is, number/value of items to be counted and method of selection. For Viewco probably more counting of higher value finished goods	• Ensures appropriate amount of work done based on initial assessment. • Clear plan for audit team.
3. Objectives of attendance, that is, to ensure that the quality of stock to be reflected in the financial statements is materially accurate.	• Reporting partner can confirm if appropriate/ adequate work done.
4. Details of work done	• Provides evidence for future reference and documents adherence to auditing standards. • Enables reporting partner to review the adequacy of the work and establish whether is meets the stated objective.
A. Details of **controls testing** work performed – observing Viewco's counters and ensuring they are following the instructions and conducting the count effectively, for example,	• Enable reassessment of likely reliability of Viewco's count. • Enables assessment of chances of items being double counted or omitted.
(i) Note of whether the area was systematically tided.	
(ii) Note of whether or how counted goods are marked.	
(iii) Note of how Viewco record and segregate any goods still moving on count day.	
(iv) Note of adequacy of supervision and general impression of counters.	• Enables assessment of overall of count and hence likely accuracy.
(v) Note whether counters are in teams of two and whether any check counts are performed.	• Evidence of independent checks may enhance reliability.
B. Details of **substantive** work performed	
(i) Details of items of raw materials or finished goods test counted:	
• From physical stock to client's count sheet.	• Evidence to support the accuracy and completeness of Viewco's count sheets
• From Viewco's count sheets to physical stock. For both of the above note stock code, description, number of units and quality. Use a symbol to indicate agreement with Viewco's records.	• Evidence to support the existence of stock recorded by Viewco.
(ii) Details of review for any old/ obsolete stock for example, dusty/damaged boxes. Note code, description, number of units and problem.	• Details can be followed up at final audit and the net realisable investigated.

(iii) Details of review of WIP • Assessment of volume of part complete items of each stage. • Assessment of appropriateness of degree of completion assigned to each stage by Viewco (could describe items at various stages).	• Evidence in support of accuracy of quantity of WIP • Details can be followed through at final audit to final stock sheets. • Basis for discussion of any description.
(iv) Copies of: • Last few despatch notes • Last few goods received notes • Last few material requisitions • Last few receipts to finished goods.	• Enables follow up at final audit to ensure cut-off is correct, that is, goods despatched are reflected as sales, goods received as purchases and items in WIP are not also in raw materials and finished goods.
(v) Copies of client's stock count sheets (where number makes this practical).	• Enables follow up at final audit to ensure that Viewco's final sheets are intact and no alterations have occurred.
5. Summary of Results In particular: (i) Details of any problems encountered. (ii) Details of any test count discrepancies and notes of investigation into their causes. (iii) Details of any representations by the management of Viewco.	• Senior/manager can assess any consequences for audit risk and strategy and decide any further work needed. • Provides full documentation of issues that could require a judgmental decision and could ultimately be the basis for a qualified opinion.
6. Conclusion	• Indicates whether or not the initial objective has been met and whether there are any implications for the audit opinion.

Chapter roundup

- Auditors need to obtain sufficient, appropriate audit evidence.
- Related party transactions can be a difficult area to gain audit evidence about. Evidence may be limited to representations by management.
- Management representations may be the only suitable evidence available when
  - Knowledge of facts is confined to management
  - The matter is principally one of judgement or opinion
- Oral representations should be confirmed in writing. Auditors should seek other evidence to corroborate statements made by management.
- Management representations can never be a substitute for evidence the auditors expected to be available.
- Sometimes auditors may need to use the work of an expert to obtain sufficient appropriate audit evidence.
- They should follow the guidance of SAS 520 when doing so.
- All evidence obtained should be documented. Working papers should be prepared in accordance with accepted standards.
- Working papers should be reviewed by a more senior audit staff member before an audit conclusion is drawn.

Quick quiz

1 List the financial statement assertions.

(1) 

(2) ____________

(3) ____________

(4) ____________

(5) ____________

(6) ____________

(7) ____________

2 Which of the following is not an auditor's method of obtaining evidence?

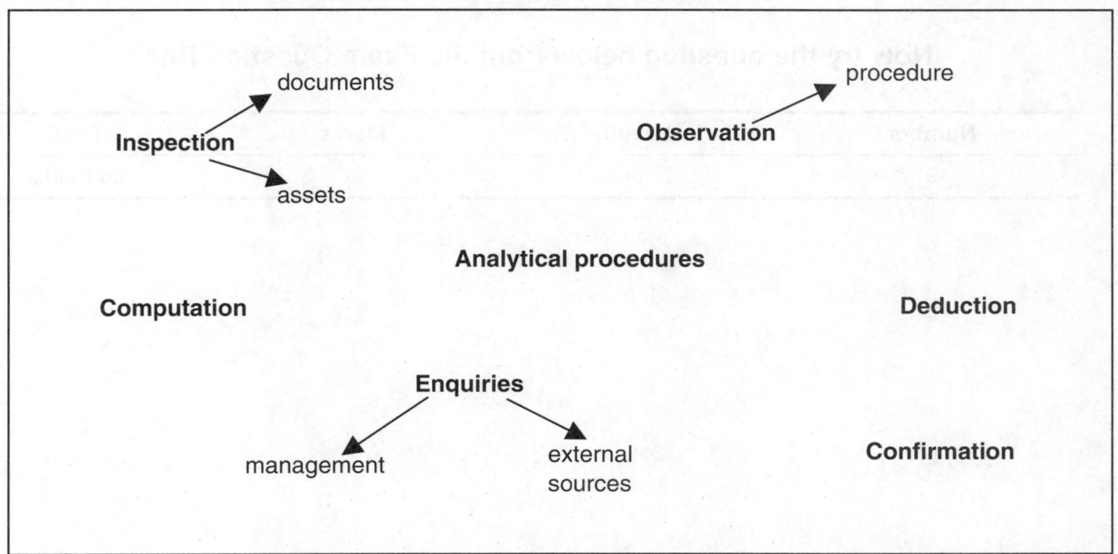

3 Give five instances where the risk of undisclosed related party transactions going undiscovered by the auditors is high.

(1) ____________________

(2) ____________________

(3) ____________________

(4) ____________________

(5) ____________________

4 Management representations might take the form of a letter from the auditors acknowledged and signed by the director.

True ☐

False ☐

5 Complete the definition

An ____________________ is a person or firm possessing ____________________ ____________________, knowledge and experience in a particular field other than ________________.

6 Give three examples of audit evidence which can be obtained from an expert.

(1) ____________________

(2) ____________________

(3) ____________________

7 What is a hot review?

Answers to quick quiz

1 See para 1.2

2 deduction

3 See para 2.3

4 True

5 Expert, special skill, accountancy

6 See para 4.3

7 A hot review is when a member of staff who has not been involved in the audit is asked to review all the working papers

Now try the question below from the Exam Question Bank

Number	Level	Marks	Time
9	Exam	20	36 marks

Chapter 10

AUDIT EVALUATION AND REVIEW

Topic list		Syllabus reference
1	Revision: Review procedures	3(d)
2	Revision: Opening balances and Comparatives	3(d)
3	Revision: Other information	3(d)
4	Revision: Subsequent events	3(d)
5	Revision: Going concern	3(d)

Introduction

Towards the end of an audit, a series of review and evaluations are carried out. You should be familiar with them from you previous auditing studies.

One types of review that takes place at the end of an audit was discussed in the previous chapter. This is the review that the audit engagement partner undertakes in order to establish his audit opinion. This is usually after a review by an audit manager to evaluate whether sufficient, reliable audit evidence has been obtained, in accordance with the audit plan.

This chapter deals with the remaining reviews that are undertaken.

Section 1 outlines the **overall review** which is undertaken on the financial statements as a whole and the review of errors and potential errors which have emerged during the course of an audit.

In Section 2, the issue of **opening balances and comparatives** is discussed. In the event of a recurring audit, both these items are audited by review. In special circumstances, notably the first audit, different considerations and procedures must be followed.

The audit report is usually sent out by the company in the form of a large annual report. The audit report does not relate to all of the information contained within it. However, the auditor has some responsibilities with regard to this information, primarily to ensure that it does not contradict audited material. He must review the **other information** to establish whether this is the case. The detailed procedures and requirements are discussed in Section 3.

Lastly, the auditor conducts reviews of the **going concern** presumption and the period between the balance sheet and the signing of the audit report **(subsequent events)**. There is guidance given on both these areas in SASs, and they are dealt with in Sections 5 and 4 respectively.

Study guide

Section 12 and 13

General

- Explain review procedures (including the use of analytical procedures and checklists)
- Evaluate findings quantitatively and qualitatively, for example:
  - The results of audit tests and procedures
  - The effect of actual and potential misstatements

Opening balances and comparatives

- Describe how the auditor's responsibilities for corresponding figures and comparative financial statements are discharged
- Describe the further considerations and audit procedures relevant to initial engagements

Other information

- Explain the auditor's responsibilities for 'other information'
- Discuss the course of action available to an auditor if a material inconsistency exists

Subsequent events

- Specify the nature and timing of audit procedure designed to identify subsequent events that may require adjustments to, or disclosure in, the financial statements.

Going concern

- Give examples of indicators that the going concern basis may be in doubt and recognise mitigating factors
- Evaluate the evidence which might be expected to be available and assess the appropriateness of the going concern basis in given situations
- Describe the disclosures in financial statements relating to going concern
- Understand the implication for the auditors' report where doubts about the going concern basis
    - Have been resolved
    - Remain unresolved
- Comment on the auditors' responsibilities in respect of going concern statements

Exam guide

Going concern is a particularly important audit review. Bear in mind the links with planning, knowledge of the business and analytical procedures. Comparatives were examined in the pilot paper.

1 REVISION: REVIEW PROCEDURES

1.1 Once the bulk of the substantive procedures have been carried out, the auditors will have a draft set of financial statements which should be supported by appropriate and sufficient audit evidence. SAS 470 *Overall review of financial statements* covers the beginning of the end of the audit process.

SAS 470.1

Auditors should carry out such a review of the financial statements as is sufficient, in conjunction with the conclusions drawn from the other audit evidence obtained, to give them a reasonable basis for their opinion on the financial statements.

1.2 This review requires appropriate skill and experience on the part of the auditors.

Compliance with accounting regulations

> **SAS 470.2**
>
> Auditors should consider whether the information presented in the financial statements is in accordance with statutory requirements and that the accounting policies employed are in accordance with accounting standards, properly disclosed, consistently applied and appropriate to the entity.

1.3 The SAS goes on to list the factors which the auditors should consider when examining the **accounting policies**.

- Policies **commonly adopted** in **particular industries**
- Policies for which there is substantial **authoritative support**
- Whether any **departures from applicable accounting standards are necessary** for the financial statements to give a true and fair view
- Whether the **financial statements reflect** the **substance** of the underlying transactions and not merely their form

1.4 The SAS suggests that, when compliance with statutory requirements and accounting standards is considered, the auditors may find it useful to use a **checklist**.

Review for consistency and reasonableness

> **SAS 470.3**
>
> Auditors should consider whether the financial statements as a whole and the assertions contained therein are consistent with their knowledge of the entity's business and with the results of other audit procedures, and the manner of disclosure is fair.

1.5 The SAS lists the principal considerations:

(a) Whether the financial statements adequately reflect the **information** and **explanations** previously obtained and conclusions previously reached during the course of the audit

(b) Whether it reveals any **new factors** which may affect the presentation of, or disclosure in, the financial statements

(c) Whether **analytical procedures** applied when completing the audit, such as comparing the information in the financial statements with other pertinent data, **produce results** which assist in arriving at the overall conclusion as to whether the financial statements as a whole are consistent with their knowledge of the entity's business

(d) Whether the **presentation** adopted in the financial statements may have been **unduly influenced by the directors' desire** to present matters in a favourable or unfavourable light

(e) The potential impact on the financial statements of the **aggregate of uncorrected misstatements** (including those arising from bias in making accounting estimates) identified during the course of the audit and the preceding period's audit, if any

Analytical procedures

1.6 In Chapter 8 we discussed how analytical review procedures can be used as substantive tests. There are also used as part of the overall review procedures at the end of an audit.

1.7 Remember the areas that the analytical review at the final stage must cover:

- Important accounting ratios
- Related items
- Changes in products; customers
- Price and mix changes
- Wages changes
- Variances
- Trends in production and sales
- Changes in material and labour content of production
- Other profit and loss account expenditure
- Variations caused by industry or economy factors

1.8 As at other stages, significant fluctuations and unexpected relationships must be investigated and documented.

Summarising errors

> **SAS 220.3**
>
> In evaluating whether the financial statements give a true a fair view, auditors should assess the materiality of the aggregate of uncorrected misstatements.

1.9 The aggregate of uncorrected misstatements comprises:

(a) **Specific misstatements** identified by the auditors, including uncorrected misstatements identified during the audit of the previous period if they affect the current period's financial statements

(b) Their **best estimate** of **other misstatements** which cannot be quantified specifically

1.10 If the auditors consider that the aggregate of misstatements may be material, they must consider reducing audit risk by extending audit procedures or requesting the directors to adjust the financial statements (which the directors may wish to do anyway).

1.11 The auditors should consider the implications for their audit report if:

- The directors refuse to adjust.
- The extended audit procedures do not enable the auditors to conclude that the aggregate of uncorrected misstatements is not material.

1.12 The summary of errors will not only list errors from the current year, but also those in the previous year(s). This will allow errors to be highlighted which are reversals of errors in the previous year, such as in the valuation of closing/opening stock. Cumulative errors may also be shown, which have increased from year to year.

SCHEDULE OF UNADJUSTED ERRORS

	20X2				20X1			
	P&L account		*Balance sheet*		*P&L account*		*Balance sheet*	
	Dr	*Cr*	*Dr*	*Cr*	*Dr*	*Cr*	*Dr*	*Cr*
	£	£	£	£	£	£	£	£
(a) ABC Ltd debt unprovided	10,470			10,470	4,523			4,523
(b) Opening/ closing stock under-valued*	21,540			21,540		21,540	21,540	
(c) Closing stock undervalued		34,105	34,105					
(d) Opening unaccrued expenses								
Telephone*		453	453		453			453
Electricity*		905	905		905			905
(e) Closing unaccrued expenses								
Telephone	427			427				
Electricity	1,128			1,128				
(f) Obsolete stock write off	2,528			2,528	3,211			3,211
Total	36,093	35,463	35,463	36,093	9,092	21,540	21,540	9,092
*Cancelling items	21,540			21,540				
		453	453					
		905	905					
	14,553	34,105	34,105	14,553				

1.13 The schedule will be used by the audit manager and partner to decide whether the client should be requested to make adjustments to the financial statements to correct the errors.

Completion checklists

1.14 Audit firms frequently use checklists which must be signed off to ensure that all final procedures have been carried out, all material amounts are supported by sufficient appropriate evidence, etc. An example is shown in the appendix.

2 REVISION: OPENING BALANCES AND COMPARATIVES

KEY TERMS

Opening balances are those account balances that exist at the beginning of the period. Opening balances are based upon the closing balances of the preceding period and reflect the effect of transactions of preceding periods and accounting policies applied in the preceding period.

Comparatives are the corresponding amounts and other related disclosures from the preceding period which are part of the current period's financial statements as required by relevant legislation and applicable accounting standards. Such comparatives are intended to be read in relation to the amounts and other disclosures related to the current period.

2.1 SAS 450 *Opening balances and comparatives* covers this area. It is appropriate to consider such matters at the planning stage as well as the final stages of the audit as the outcome of the relevant audit procedures could have a substantial impact on the audit of current year transactions and balances.

SAS 450.1

Auditors should obtain sufficient appropriate audit evidence that amounts derived from the preceding period's financial statements are free from material misstatements and are appropriately incorporated in the financial statements for the current period.

2.2 Note that the preceding period accounts, when new auditors are appointed, may have been reported on by the predecessor auditors or they may have been **unaudited**.

Opening balances

SAS 450.2

Auditors should obtain sufficient appropriate audit evidence that:

(a) opening balances have been appropriately brought forward;

(b) opening balances do not contain errors or misstatements which materially affect the current period's financial statements; and

(c) appropriate accounting policies are consistently applied or changes in accounting policies have been properly accounted for and adequately disclosed.

2.3 If the auditors are unable to obtain sufficient appropriate audit evidence, then they should consider the implications for their audit report.

2.4 The SAS goes on to look at opening balances from the point of view of both **continuing auditors** and **incoming auditors**.

KEY TERMS

Continuing auditors are the auditors who audited and reported on the preceding period's financial statements and continue as the auditors for the current period.

Predecessor auditors are the auditors who previously audited and reported on the financial statements of an entity, and who have been replaced by the incoming auditors.

Incoming auditors are the auditors who are auditing and reporting on the current period's financial statements, not having audited and reported on those for the preceding period.

Continuing auditors

2.5 Audit procedures need not extend beyond ensuring that opening balances have been **appropriately brought forward** and the current accounting policies have been consistently applied, **if**:

- The continuing auditors issued an unqualified report on the preceding periods' financial statements.
- The audit of the current period does not reveal any matters which cast doubt on those financial statements.

2.6 If a **qualified audit report** was issued on the preceding period's financial statements then the auditors should consider whether the matter which gave rise to the qualification has been **adequately resolved** and properly dealt with in the **current period's financial statements**. This is in addition to the procedures above.

Incoming auditors

2.7 This situation is obviously more difficult. Appropriate and sufficient audit evidence is required on the opening balances and this depends on matters such as the following.

- The **accounting policies** followed by the entity
- Whether the **preceding period's financial statements were audited** and, if so, whether the auditors' report was **qualified**
- The **nature of the opening balances,** including the risk of their misstatement
- The **materiality of the opening balances** relative to the current period's financial statements

2.8 The **procedures given** for continuing auditors should be carried out. Other procedures suggested by the SAS are as follows.

- **Consultations with management** and review of records, working papers and accounting and control procedures for the preceding period
- **Substantive testing of any opening balances** in respect of which the results of other procedures are considered unsatisfactory

2.9 Consultations with predecessor auditors will not normally be necessary as the above procedures will be sufficient. Predecessor auditors have no legal or ethical duty to provide information and would not normally be expected to release relevant working papers. However:

> 'they are expected to cooperate with incoming auditors to provide clarification of, or information on, specific accounting matters where this is necessary to resolve any particular difficulties.'

Comparatives

2.10 Opening balances will, in the current year's financial statements, become comparative figures which must be disclosed.

SAS 450.3

Auditors should obtain sufficient appropriate audit evidence that:

(a) the accounting policies used for the comparatives are consistent with those of the current period and appropriate adjustments and disclosures have been made where this is not the case;

(b) the comparatives agree with the amounts and other disclosures presented in the preceding period and are free from errors in the context of the financial statements of the current period; and

(c) where comparatives have been adjusted as required by relevant legislation and accounting standards, appropriate disclosures have been made.

2.11 The SAS then goes on to discuss the status of comparatives from an audit perspective.

> 'The comparatives form part of the financial statements on which the auditors express an opinion, although they are not required to express an opinion on the comparatives as such. Their

responsibility is to establish whether the comparatives are the amounts which appeared in the preceding period's financial statements or, where appropriate, have been restated.'

2.12 Where the auditors are unable to obtain sufficient appropriate audit evidence to support the comparatives they must consider the implications for their report. The SAS then discusses these implications in various situations.

Continuing auditors

2.13 The extent of audit procedures for comparatives will be significantly less then those for current year balances; normally they will be limited to a **check that balances have been brought forward correctly**. Materiality of any misstatements should be considered in relationship to **current** period figures.

2.14 The auditors' report on the previous period financial statements may have been qualified. Where the qualification matter is still **unresolved**, two situations may apply.

(a) If the matter is material in the context of the current period's opening balances as well as comparatives, the report on the current period's financial statements should be **qualified regarding opening balances and comparatives**.

(b) If the matter does not affect opening balances but is material in the context of the current period's financial statements, the report on the current period's financial statements should **refer to the comparatives**.

- If comparatives are **required by law or regulation**, the reference will be in the form of a **qualification on the grounds of non-compliance** with that requirement.
- If comparatives are presented solely as **good practice**, the reference should be in the form of an **explanatory paragraph**.

2.15 Where a previous qualification has been resolved and dealt with properly in the financial statements then no mention of the qualification needs to be made in the current audit report. If, however, the matter was material to the current period, then it should be mentioned in the current report, including an explanation of how it has been resolved.

2.16 It is also possible that a qualification will still be necessary, for example if a provision has been made in the current year which should have been made in the previous period.

Incoming auditors: audited comparatives

2.17 In this situation, the preceding period's financial statements have been audited by other auditors. The incoming auditors only bear audit responsibility for the comparatives in the context of the financial statements as a whole. The incoming auditors will use the knowledge gained in the current audit to decide whether the previous period's financial statements have been properly reflected as comparatives in the current period's financial statements.

2.18 The procedures described above should be considered should such a situation arise.

Incoming auditors: unaudited comparatives

2.19 In this situation (for example, where the company took advantage of the small company audit exemption in the previous period) the auditors should check that there is clear **disclosure** in the current financial statements that the comparatives are unaudited. They must still undertake the duties mentioned above as far as is appropriate. If there is not sufficient appropriate evidence, or if disclosure is inadequate, the auditors should consider the implications for their reports.

Question 1

An auditing standard has been issued on *Opening balances and comparatives*, and one of the matters it considers is where one firm of auditors takes over from another firm. You have recently been appointed auditor of Lowdham Castings Ltd, a company which has been trading for about thirty years, and are carrying out the audit for the year ended 30 September 20X6. The company's turnover is about £500,000 and its normal profit before tax is about £30,000.

Required

Discuss your responsibilities in relation to the comparatives included in the accounts for the year ended 30 September 20X6. You should also consider the information you would require from the retiring auditors.

Answer

Consideration of the financial statements of the preceding period is necessary in the audit of the current period's financial statements in relation to three main aspects.

(a) **Opening position**: obtaining satisfaction that those amounts which have a direct effect on the current period's results or closing position have been properly brought forward

(b) **Accounting policies**: determining whether the accounting policies adopted for the current period are consistent with those of the previous period

(c) **Comparatives:** determining that the comparatives are properly shown in the current period's financial statements

The auditors' main concern will therefore be to satisfy themselves that there were no material misstatements in the previous year's financial statements which may have a bearing upon their work in the current year.

The new auditors do not have to 're-audit' the previous year's financial statements, but they will have to pay more attention to them than would normally be the case where they had themselves been the auditors in the earlier period. A useful source of audit evidence will clearly be the previous auditors, and, with the client's permission, they should be contacted to see if they are prepared to co-operate. Certainly, any known areas of weakness should be discussed with the previous auditors and it is also possible that they might be prepared to provide copies of their working papers (although there is no legal or ethical provision which requires the previous auditors to co-operate in this way).

3 REVISION: OTHER INFORMATION

3.1 The APB's SAS 160 *Other information in documents containing audited financial statements* provides guidance for auditors in this area.

3.2 The SAS uses the term 'other information' by which it means financial and non-financial information **other than** the audited financial statements and the auditors' report, which an entity may include in its annual report, either by custom or statute. Examples are:

- A directors' report (required by statute)
- A chairman's statement
- An operating and financial review
- Financial summaries

3.3 Auditors have no responsibility to report that other information is properly stated because an audit is only an expression of opinion on the truth and fairness of the financial statements. However, they may be engaged separately, or required by statute, to report on elements of other information, for example, review the directors' statement of compliance with the Cadbury Code.

3.4 The SAS then moves on to the auditors' general responsibilities towards 'other information'.

> **SAS 160.1**
>
> Auditors should read the other information. If as a result they become aware of any apparent misstatements therein, or identify any material inconsistencies with the audited financial statements, they should seek to resolve them.

Auditors' consideration of other information

> **SAS 160.2**
>
> If auditors identify an inconsistency between the financial statements and the other information, or a misstatement within the other information, they should consider whether an amendment is required to the financial statements or to the other information and should seek to resolve the matter through discussion with the directors.

3.5 A **misstatement** within other information exists when it is stated incorrectly or presented in a misleading manner.

3.6 An **inconsistency** exists when the other information contradicts, or appears to contradict information contained in the financial statements. This could lead to doubts about audit evidence or even the auditors' opinion.

Unresolved misstatements and inconsistencies

> **SAS 160.3**
>
> If, after discussion with the directors, the auditors conclude
>
> (a) that the financial statements require amendment and no such amendment is made, they should consider the implications for their report;
>
> (b) that the other information requires amendment and no such amendment is made, they should consider appropriate actions including the implications for their report.

3.7 The auditors have a statutory duty to consider a company's directors' report. S 235 Companies Act 1985 states that:

> 'the auditors shall consider whether the information given in the directors' report for the financial year for which the accounts are prepared is consistent with those accounts; and if they are of opinion that it is not they shall state that fact in their report.'

3.8 Matters which may require resolution or reference in an explanatory paragraph within the auditors' report include:

(a) An **inconsistency between amounts or narrative** appearing in the financial statements and the directors' report

(b) An **inconsistency between the bases of preparation** of related items appearing in the financial statements and the directors' report, where the figures themselves are not directly comparable and the different bases are not disclosed

(c) An **inconsistency between figures** contained in the financial statements **and a narrative interpretation** of the effect of those figures in the directors' report

3.9 Other information may contain misstatements or inconsistencies with the financial statements and the auditors may be unable to resolve them by discussion with the directors. They may need to use an **explanatory paragraph** within the auditors' report to describe the apparent misstatement or material misconsistency.

Timing considerations

3.10 SAS 600 *Auditors' reports on financial statements* (see Chapter 19) requires all other information to be approved by the entity, and the auditors to consider all necessary evidence, before the audit opinion is expressed.

4 REVISION: SUBSEQUENT EVENTS

4.1 Before describing the steps taken by the auditors to obtain reasonable assurance in respect of subsequent events (also called post balance sheet events - the terms are interchangeable) we need to revise the accounting requirements of the relevant accounting standard SSAP 17 *Accounting for post balance sheet events.*

SSAP 17

KEY TERMS

Post balance sheet events are those events, both favourable and unfavourable, which occur between the balance sheet date and the date on which the financial statements are approved by the board of directors.

Adjusting events are post balance sheet events which provide additional evidence of conditions existing at the balance sheet date. They include events which because of statutory conventional requirements are reflected in financial statements.

Non-adjusting events are post balance sheet events which concern conditions which did not exist at the balance sheet date.

4.2 Standard practice in respect of the disclosure of post balance sheet events is as follows.

> 'Financial statements should be prepared on the basis of conditions existing at the balance sheet date.
>
> A material post balance sheet event requires changes in the amounts to be included in financial statements where:
>
> (a) it is an adjusting event; or
>
> (b) it indicates that application of the going concern concept to the whole or a material part of the company is not appropriate.
>
> A material post balance sheet event should be disclosed where:
>
> (a) it is a non-adjusting event of such materiality that its non-disclosure would affect the ability of the users of financial statements to reach a proper understanding of the financial position; or
>
> (b) it is the reversal or maturity after the year end of a transaction entered into before the year end, the substance of which was primarily to alter the appearance of the company's balance sheet.'

4.3 In respect of each disclosable post balance sheet event, the notes to the financial statements should state:

(a) The **nature** of the event

(b) An **estimate** of the financial effect, or a statement that it is not practicable to make such an estimate

Exam focus point

Knowledge of the relevant accounting requirements is particularly important when dealing with post balance sheet events.

Audit procedures

PROCEDURES TESTING SUBSEQUENT EVENTS	
Enquiries of management	Status of items involving **subjective judgement**/ accounted for using preliminary data
	New **commitments**, borrowings or guarantees
	Sales or destruction of **assets**
	Issues of **shares/debentures** or changes in business structure
	Developments involving **risk areas, provisions** and **contingencies**
	Unusual accounting adjustments
	Major events (for example going concern problems) affecting appropriateness of accounting policies for estimates
Other procedures	**Consider procedures** of management for identifying subsequent events
	Read minutes of general board/committee meetings
	Review latest accounting records and financial information

4.4 These procedures should be performed as near as possible to the date of the auditors' report. Reviews and updates of these procedures may be required, depending on the length of the time between the procedures and the signing of the auditors' report and the susceptibility of the items to change over time.

Subsequent events discovered after the date of the auditors' report but before the financial statements are issued

4.5 The financial statements are the directors' responsibility. The directors should therefore inform the auditors of any material subsequent events between the date of the auditors' report and the date the financial statements are issued. The auditors do **not** have any obligation to perform procedures, or make enquires regarding the financial statements **after** the date of their report.

SAS 150.3

When, after the date of their report but before the financial statements are issued, auditors become aware of subsequent events which may materially affect the financial statements, they should establish whether the financial statements need amendment, should discuss the matter with the directors and should consider the implications for their report, taking additional action as appropriate.

4.6 When the financial statements are amended, the auditors should extend the subsequent events procedures discussed above to the date of their new report, carry out any other appropriate procedures and issue a new audit report dated the day it is signed.

4.7 The situation where the statements are not amended but the auditors feel that they should be is discussed below.

Subsequent events discovered after the financial statements have been issued but before their laying before the members, or equivalent

4.8 Auditors have no obligations to perform procedures or make enquiries regarding the financial statements **after** they have been issued.

SAS 150.4

When, after the financial statements have been issued, but before they have been laid before the members or equivalent, auditors become aware of subsequent events which, had they occurred and been known of at the date of their report, might have caused them to issue a different report, they should consider whether the financial statements need amendment, should discuss the matter with the directors, and should consider the implications for their report, taking additional action as appropriate.

4.9 The SAS gives the appropriate procedures which the auditors should undertake when the directors revise the financial statements.

- **Carry out the audit procedures** necessary in the circumstances
- **Consider,** where appropriate, whether Stock Exchange or financial services regulations require the **revision to be publicised** or a regulator informed
- **Review the steps taken by the directors** to ensure that anyone in receipt of the previously issued financial statements together with the auditors' report thereon is informed of the situation
- **Issue a new report** on the revised financial statements

4.10 When the auditors issue a **new report** they:

- **Refer in their report to the note to the financial statements** which more extensively discusses the reason for the revision of the accounts
- **Refer to the earlier report** issued by them on the financial statements
- **Date** their new report **not earlier** than the date the revised financial statements are approved
- **Have regard** to the **guidance** relating to reports on revised annual financial statements and directors' reports as set out in APB's Practice Note 8 *Reports by auditors under company legislation in the United Kingdom*

4.11 Where the directors do **not** revise the financial statements but the auditors feel they should be revised, and where the statements have been issued but not yet laid before the members; or if the directors do not intend to make an appropriate statement at the AGM, then the auditors should consider steps to take, on a timely basis, to prevent reliance on their report eg a statement at the AGM. The auditors have no right to communicate to the members directly in writing.

Question 2

You are auditing the financial statements of Hope Engineering Ltd for the year ending 31 March 20X8. The partner in charge of the audit instructs you to carry out a review of the company's activities since the financial year end. Mr Smith, the managing director of Hope Engineering Ltd, overhears the conversation with the partner and is surprised that you are examining accounting information which relates to the next accounting period.

Mr Smith had been appointed on 1 March 20X8 as a result of which the contract of the previous managing director, Mr Jones, was terminated. Compensation of £500,000 had been paid to Mr Jones on 2 March 20X8.

As a result of your investigations you find that the company is going to bring an action against Mr Jones for the recovery of the compensation paid to him, as it had come to light that two months prior to his dismissal, he had contractually agreed to join the board of directors of a rival company. The company's solicitor had informed Hope Engineering Ltd that Mr Jones' actions constituted a breach of his contract with them, and that an action could be brought against the former managing director for the recovery of the moneys paid to him.

Required

(a) Explain the nature and purpose of a review of the period after the balance sheet date.

(b) List the audit procedures which would be carried out in order to identify any material subsequent events.

(c) Discuss the audit implications of the company's decision to sue Mr Jones for the recovery of the compensation paid to him.

Answer

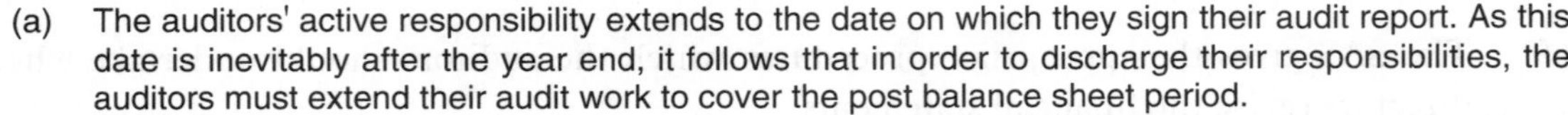

(a) The auditors' active responsibility extends to the date on which they sign their audit report. As this date is inevitably after the year end, it follows that in order to discharge their responsibilities, the auditors must extend their audit work to cover the post balance sheet period.

The objective of the audit of the post balance sheet period is to ascertain whether the directors have dealt correctly with any events, both favourable and unfavourable, which occurred after the year end and which need to be reflected in the financial statements, if those statements are to show a true and fair view and comply with the Companies Act.

The general rule is that, in the preparation of year end financial statements, no account should be taken of subsequent events unless to do so is required by statute or to give effect to retrospective legislation, or to take account of an adjusting event. In accordance with SSAP 17, a material subsequent event may be an *adjusting event* where it provides information about a condition existing at the balance sheet date, for example realisable values of stock, or indicates that the going concern concept is no longer applicable. Additionally, *non-adjusting events* may have such a material effect on the company's financial condition, for example a merger, that disclosure is essential to give a true and fair view.

(b) The audit procedures which should be carried out in order to identify any material subsequent events consist of discussions with management, and may also include consideration of the following.

(i) Procedures should be implemented by management to ensure that all events after the balance sheet date have been identified, considered and properly evaluated as to their effect on the financial statements.

(ii) Relevant accounting records should be reviewed, specifically to identify subsequent cash received from debtors, to check items uncleared at the year end on the bank reconciliation, to check NRV of stocks from sales invoices, and so on. However, window dressing also may be identified.

(iii) Budgets, profit forecasts, cash flow projections and management accounts for the new period should be reviewed to assess the company's trading position.

(iv) Known 'risk' areas and contingencies, whether inherent in the nature of the business or revealed by previous audit experience, or by solicitors' letters, should be considered.

(v) Minutes of shareholders', directors' and management meetings and correspondence and memoranda relating to items included in the minutes should be reviewed.

(vi) Relevant information which has come to the auditors' attention from sources outside the enterprise, including public knowledge of competitors, suppliers and customers, should be taken into account.

The subsequent events review should be carried out to a date as near as practicable to that of the audit report by making enquiries of management and considering the need to carry out further tests. It should be fully documented and, where appropriate, a letter of representation should be obtained from management.

(c) The compensation paid to Mr Smith would be disclosed as part of directors' emoluments for the year ended 31 March 20X8. However, the question then arises as to whether or not the financial statements need to take any account of the possible recovery of the compensation payment.

The auditors should first ascertain from the board minutes that the directors intend to proceed with the lawsuit and should then attempt to assess the outcome by consulting the directors, the company's legal advisors and perhaps by taking Counsel's opinion. Only if it seems probable that the compensation will be recovered should a contingent asset be disclosed in the notes to the accounts, along with a summary of the facts of the case. A prudent estimate of legal costs should be deducted.

It could be argued that Mr Smith's breach of contract existed at the balance sheet date and that the compensation should therefore be treated as a current asset, net of recovery costs. However, this would not be prudent, given the uncertainties over the court case.

---

5 REVISION: GOING CONCERN

5.1 SAS 130 *Going concern basis in financial statements* was developed separately from the bulk of the other auditing standards because of its importance. This arises from the exposure of the auditors should they miss the going concern problems of a client and the difficulties surrounding the determination of going concern status in any given situation.

Going concern as an accounting concept

KEY TERMS

The **going concern** concept: the enterprise will continue in operational existence for the foreseeable future. This means in particular that the profit and loss account and balance sheet assume no intention or necessity to liquidate or curtail significantly the scale of operation.

5.2 This definition is supported by legal requirements. Under these requirements, the financial statements of an entity are assumed to be prepared on a going concern basis.

5.3 Where the going concern basis is **not** appropriate:

- The entity may not be able to recover the amounts recorded in respect of assets.
- There may be changes in the amounts and dates of maturities of liabilities.

Therefore, if material, the amounts and classification of assets and liabilities would need to be adjusted.

5.4 Consequently, the **directors** must satisfy themselves that the going concern basis is appropriate. Even where it is, further disclosure may be required to give a true and fair view.

The applicability and scope of this SAS

> **SAS 130.1**
>
> When forming an opinion as to whether financial statements give a true a fair view, the auditors should consider the entity's ability to continue as a going concern, and any relevant disclosures in the financial statements.

5.5 The SAS gives guidance to auditors in the context of the going concern basis in financial statements which are required to be properly prepared under CA 1985 and to show a true and fair view. The SAS does **not** give guidance relating to the going concern in any other context, for example *Cadbury Report* matters.

Foreseeable future

5.6 Accounting guidance uses the term 'foreseeable future' but does not define it. The SAS recognises that any consideration of foreseeable future involves 'making a judgement, at a particular point in time, about future events which are inherently uncertain'. The SAS suggests that the degree of **uncertainty increases significantly** the **further into the future** the consideration is taken and the 'foreseeable future' depends on the specific circumstances at a point in time.

5.7 As a consequence there can never be any certainty in relation to going concern. The auditors' judgement is only valid at that time and can be 'overturned by subsequent events'.

Consideration of going concern by the directors

5.8 The directors must assess going concern by looking at a period into the future and considering all available and relevant information. The SAS states that a minimum length for this period cannot be specified; it would be 'artificial and arbitrary' as there is no 'cut off point' after which the directors would change their approach.

Audit procedures

5.9 The audit procedures will be based on the directors' deliberations and the information they used. The auditors must assess whether the audit evidence is sufficient and appropriate and whether they agree with the directors' judgement. They should consider:

- The nature of the entity (its size and the complexity of its circumstances, for instance)
- Whether the information relates to future events, and if so how far into the future those events lie

A lengthy appendix to the SAS gives examples of how auditors might apply the SAS in different circumstances.

Audit evidence

> **SAS 130.2**
>
> The auditors should assess the adequacy of the means by which the directors have satisfied themselves that:
>
> (a) it is appropriate for them to adopt the going concern basis in preparing the financial statements; and
>
> (b) the financial statements include such disclosures, if any, relating to going concern as are necessary for them to give a true and fair view.
>
> For this purpose:
>
> (i) the auditors should make enquiries of the directors and examine appropriate available financial information; and
>
> (ii) having regard to the future period to which the directors have paid particular attention in assessing going concern, the auditors should plan and perform procedures specifically designed to identify any material matters which could indicate concern about the entity's ability to continue as a going concern.

Preliminary assessment

5.10 The auditors' approach includes a preliminary assessment, when the overall audit plan is being developed, of the risk that the entity may be unable to continue as a going concern. The auditors should consider.

(a) **Whether the period** to which the directors have paid particular attention in assessing going concern is **reasonable** in the client's circumstances

(b) The **systems**, or other means (formal or informal), **for timely identification of warnings of future risks** and uncertainties the entity might face

(c) **Budget and/or forecast information** (cash flow information in particular) produced by the entity, and the quality of the systems (or other means, formal or informal) in place for producing this information and keeping it up to date

(d) Whether the **key assumptions** underlying the budgets and/or forecasts appear appropriate in the circumstances, including consideration of:

- Projected profit
- Forecast levels of working capital
- The completeness of forecast expenditure
- Whether the client will have sufficient cash at periods of maximum need
- The financing of capital expenditure and long-term plans

(e) The **sensitivity of budgets and/or forecasts** to variable factors both within the control of the directors and outside their control

(f) Any **obligations, undertakings or guarantees** arranged with other entities (in particular, lenders, suppliers and group companies)

(g) The **existence, adequacy and terms of borrowing facilities,** and supplier credit

(h) The **directors' plans** for resolving any matters giving rise to the concern (if any) about the appropriateness of the going concern basis. In particular, the auditors may need to consider whether:

- The plans are realistic.
- There is a reasonable expectation that the plans are likely to resolve any problems foreseen.
- The directors are likely to put the plans into practice effectively.

5.11 The auditors' and directors' procedures can be very simple in some cases, particularly in the case of smaller companies, where budgets and forecasts are not normally prepared and no specific systems are in place to monitor going concern matters.

The auditors' examination of borrowing facilities

5.12 The auditors will usually:

- Obtain confirmations of the existence and terms of bank facilities
- Make their own assessment of the intentions of the bankers relating thereto

5.13 These procedures will become more important if (for example) there is a **low margin** of **financial resources** available to the entity, correspondence between the bankers and the entity reveals that the **last renewal** of facilities was **agreed with difficulty** and a **significant deterioration in cash flow** is projected.

5.14 If the auditors cannot satisfy themselves then, in accordance with the audit reporting standard (SAS 600), they should consider whether the relevant matters need to be:

- **Disclosed in the financial statements** in order that they give a true and fair view
- **Referred to in the auditors' report** (by explanatory paragraph or qualified opinion)

Determining and documenting the auditors' concerns

SAS 130.3

The auditors should determine and document the extent of their concern (if any) about the entity's ability to continue as a going concern. In determining the extent of their concern, the auditors should take account of all relevant information of which they have become aware during their audit.

5.15 The following are given as examples of indicators of an entity's inability to continue as a going concern.

Going concern	
Financial	An excess of liabilities over assets
	Net current liabilities
	Necessary borrowing facilities have not been agreed
	Default on terms of loan agreements, and potential breaches of covenant
	Significant liquidity or cash flow problems
	Major losses or cash flow problems which have arisen since the balance sheet date and which threaten the entity's continued existence
	Substantial sales of fixed assets not intended to be replaced
	Major restructuring of debts
	Denial of (or reduction in) normal terms of trade credit by suppliers

	Major debt repayment falling due where refinancing is necessary to the entity's continued existence
	Inability to pay debts as they fall due
Operational	Fundamental changes to the market or technology to which the entity is unable to adapt adequately
	Externally forced reductions in operations (for example, as a result of legislation or regulatory action)
	Loss of key management or staff, labour difficulties or excessive dependence on a few product lines where the market is depressed
	Loss of key suppliers or customers or technical developments which render a key product obsolete
Other	Major litigation in which an adverse judgement would imperil the entity's continued existence
	Issues which involve a range of possible outcomes so wide that an unfavourable result could affect the appropriateness of the going concern basis

Exam focus point

Any question on going concern is likely to ask you to identify signs that a particular client may not be a going concern.

5.16 Auditors may still obtain sufficient appropriate audit evidence in such situations to conclude that the going concern basis is still appropriate. Further procedures such as discussions with the directors and further work on forecasts may be required.

5.17 Where auditors consider that there is a significant level of concern about the going concern basis, they might write to the directors suggesting the need to take suitable advice.

Written confirmations of representations from the directors

SAS 130.4

The auditors should consider the need to obtain written confirmations of representations from the directors regarding:

(a) the directors' assessment that the company is a going concern; and

(b) any relevant disclosures in the financial statements.

5.18 Representations may be critical in terms of audit evidence. If they do *not* receive such representations the auditors should consider whether:

- There is a limitation of scope in their work and a qualified opinion is required in 'except for' or 'disclaimer' terms.
- The failure of the directors to provide written confirmation could indicate concern.

Assessing disclosures in the financial statements

> **SAS 130.5**
>
> The auditors should consider whether the financial statements are required to include disclosures relating to going concern in order to give a true and fair view.

5.19 The main concern here is **sufficiency** of disclosure where:

- There are going concern worries.
- The future period the directors have considered is less than one year.

5.20 The auditors must assess whether the statements show a true and fair view and hence whether their opinion should be qualified, as well as whether all matters have been satisfactorily disclosed.

Reporting on the financial statements

5.21 The SAS summarises, in flowchart form, how auditors formulate their opinion as to whether the financial statements give a true and fair view and this is shown on the next page.

> **SAS 130.6**
>
> Where the auditors consider that there is a significant level of concern about the entity's ability to continue as a going concern, but do not disagree with the preparation of the financial statements on the going concern basis, they should include an explanatory paragraph when setting out the basis of their opinion. They should not quality their opinion on these grounds alone, provided the disclosures in the financial statements of the matters giving rise to the concern are adequate for the financial statements to give a true and fair view.

5.22 The following matters must be included in the financial statements for disclosure to be regarded as adequate.

- A statement that the financial statements have been prepared on the **going concern basis**
- A statement of the **pertinent factors**
- The **nature** of the concern
- A statement of the **assumptions** adopted by the directors, which should be clearly distinguishable from the pertinent facts
- (Where appropriate and practicable) a statement regarding the directors' **plans for resolving the matters** giving rise to the concern
- Details of any **relevant actions** by the directors

Going concern and reporting on the financial statements

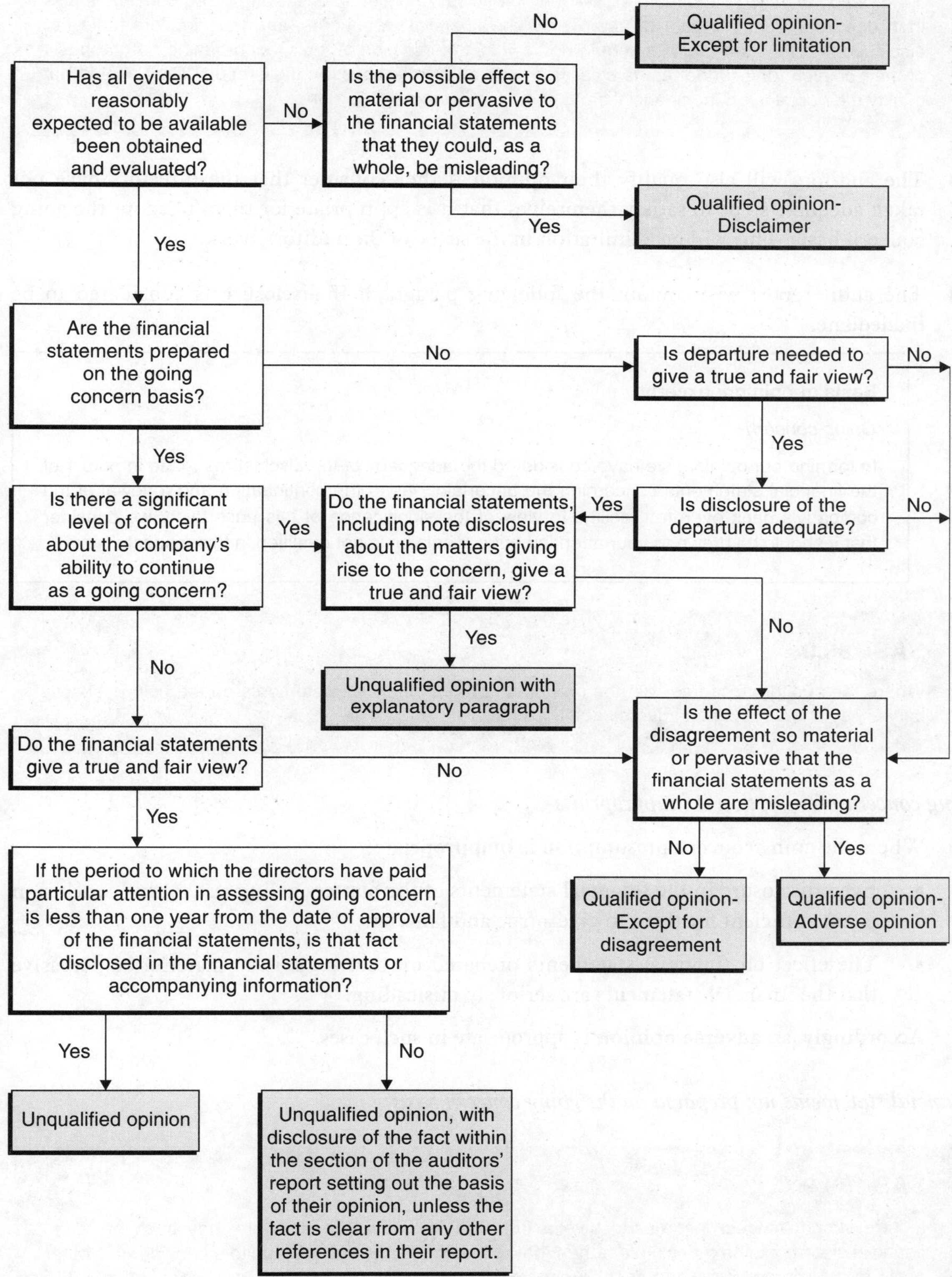

SAS 130.7

If the period to which the directors have paid particular attention in assessing going concern is less than one year from the date of approval of the financial statements, and the directors have not disclosed that fact, the auditors should do so within the section of their report setting out the basis of their opinion, unless the fact is clear from any other references in their report. They should not qualify their opinion on the financial statements on these grounds alone.

5.23 The auditors will also qualify their opinion if they consider that the directors have not taken adequate steps to satisfy themselves that it is appropriate for them to adopt the going concern basis. This will be a limitation in the scope of the auditors' work.

5.24 The audit report will contain the following paragraph if disclosure is considered to be inadequate.

Basis of opinion: excerpt

Going concern

In forming our opinion, we have considered the adequacy of the disclosures made in note 1 of the financial statements concerning the uncertainty as to the continuation and renewal of the company's bank overdraft facility. In view of the significance of this uncertainty we consider that it should be drawn to your attention but our opinion is not qualified in this respect.

SAS 130.8

Where the auditors disagree with the preparation of the financial statements on the going concern basis, they should issue an adverse audit opinion.

Going concern presumption is inappropriate

5.25 Where the going concern presumption is **inappropriate**:

- Even disclosure in the financial statements of the matters giving rise to this conclusion is **not** sufficient for them to give a true and fair view.
- The effect on financial statements prepared on that basis is so material or pervasive that the financial statements are seriously misleading.

Accordingly, an **adverse opinion** is appropriate in such cases.

Financial statements not prepared on the going concern basis

SAS 130.9

In rare circumstances, in order to give a true and fair view, the directors may have prepared financial statements on a basis other than that of a going concern. If the auditors consider this other basis to be appropriate in the specific circumstances, and if the financial statements contain the necessary disclosures, the auditors should not qualify their opinion in this respect.

5.26 Under such circumstances, the accounts may be prepared on a basis that reflects the fact that assets may need to be realised other than in the ordinary course of operations. The auditors may wish to refer to the basis on which the financial statements are prepared.

5.27 Section summary

- Director and auditor assessment of the going concern basis should take place over the **foreseeable future.**
- Auditors should make a **preliminary assessment** of going concern and be alert during the audit for **signs of going concern problems.**
- Specific audit procedures include **assessment** of **client forecasts,** examination of **borrowing facilities** and obtaining **representations** from the directors.
- Auditors may **qualify** the audit report because they disagree with the use of the **going concern basis** or **extent of disclosure.**
- Alternatively auditors may consider it appropriate to give an unqualified opinion with a **fundamental uncertainty** paragraph.

Question 3

You are planning to audit of Truckers Ltd whose principal activities are road transport and warehousing services, and the repair of commercial vehicles. You have been provided with the draft accounts for the year ended 31 October 20X5

	Draft 20X5	Actual 20X5
	£'000	£'000
Summary profit and loss account		
Turnover	10,971	11,560
Cost of sales	(10,203)	(10,474)
Gross profit	768	1,086
Administrative expenses	(782)	(779)
Interest payable and similar charges	(235)	(185)
Net (loss) profit	(249)	122

	Draft 20X5	Actual 20X5
	£'000	£'000
Summary balance sheet		
Fixed assets	5,178	4,670
Current assets		
Stock of parts and consumables	95	61
Debtors	2,975	2,369
	3,070	2,430
Creditors falling due within one year		
Bank loan	250	-
Overdraft	1,245	913
Trade creditors	1,513	1,245
Lease obligations	207	-
Other creditors	203	149
	3,481	2,307
Creditors falling due after more than one year		
Bank loan	750	1,000
Lease obligations	473	-
	1,223	1,000
Net assets	3,544	3,793

You have been informed by the managing director that the fall in turnover is due to:

(1) The loss, in July, of a long-standing customer to a competitor, and

(2) A decline in trade in the repair of commercial vehicles.

Due to the reduction in the repairs business, the company has decided to close the workshop and sell the equipment and spares stock. No entries resulting from this decision are reflected in the draft accounts.

During the year, the company replaced a number of vehicles funding them by a combination of leasing and an increased overdraft facility. The facility is to be reviewed in January 20X6 after the audited accounts are available.

The draft accounts show a loss for 20X5 but the forecasts indicate a return to profitability in 20X6 as the managing director is optimistic about generating additional turnover from new contracts.

(a) State the circumstances particular to Truckers Ltd which may indicate that the company is not a going concern. Explain why these circumstances given cause for concern.

(b) Describe the audit work you would undertake in order to ascertain whether Truckers Ltd is a going concern.

Answer

(a)

Circumstances	**Why cause for concern?**
Fall in gross profit % achieved	Whilst the fall in absolute turnover has been explained the fall in gross profit margin is more serious. This will continue to be a problem as expenses seem constant and interest costs are growing. This will make a future return to profitability difficult.
Losses £249,000	Such levels of losses by comparison to 20X4 profits will make negotiations with bank difficult. Especially with the loss of a major customer
Increased debtor balance and increased ageing 20X5 96.7 days 20X4 74.8 days	Worsening debt collection is bad news when the company is making losses and has a deteriorating liquidity position. The increase in average debt collection period may be due to a bad debt on the account of the major customer lost in the year. A bad debt write-off would cause much increased losses.
Worsening liquidity ratio 20X4 1.03 20X5 0.85	This is a significant fall which will worsen further if a bad debt provision is required The company has loan and lease commitments which possibly may not be met.
Increasing reliance on short term finance	This does not secure the future. With the company going through so much change this may cause difficulties for the bank overdraft facility negotiations
Gearing will have increased	This leads to an interest commitment which is a drain on future profits. This may also cause a problem in negotiating new finance arrangements.
Loss of major customers to competitor	Risk of unprovided bad debts in the accounts Other customers could follow suits worsening the company's future prospects.
Loss of commercial customers	Commercial customers normally provide regular income which is important for a company with repayment commitments.
Draft Accounts - final adjustments are outstanding	The company's net asset position could be worsened considerably if fixed assets are written down to recoverable amount, repairs stock written down to net realisable value.

Circumstances	Why cause for concern?
	As mentioned before further bad debt provisions may be necessary. The closure may necessitate redundancy provisions. All of these factors could increase losses considerably.
Overdraft facility to be reviewed 3 months after the year end	This time period is probably not long enough to see a real improvement in the company's fortunes. As auditors we will be reporting when faced with fundamental uncertainty. Trying to anticipate the banks likely reactions to the financial statements will be high risk.
Future return to profits anticipated at a time when competitors are achieving success	The concern should be whether this is over optimistic. If so too much reliance being placed upon management representation would be high risk strategy. Summary – If the company is not a going concern the accounts would be truer and fairer if prepared in a break-up basis. Material adjustments may then be required to the accounts.

(b) 1. Try to establish the true and fair assets position. Look specifically in the post balance sheet period at sale proceeds for fixed assets and repairs stock, cash received from debtors.

Detailed review of debtors ageing and cash recovery is vital. Any amount outstanding from the lost customer must be investigated with the directors.

2. The optimistic view of likely future contracts must be discussed with the MD and a representation requested. Orders in the post balance sheet period should be investigated.

3. Obtain the management's view of the company's main competitor, specifically discussing the lost customer. Look out for media coverage of the competitors' business.

4. Check the extent to which the company has met its loan and lease commitments in the post balance sheet period. Review transactions in the post balance sheet period for evidence of further lost custom.

5 Obtain cashflow and profit forecasts:

- Discuss assumptions with the directors.
- Perform sensitivity analysis flexing the key assumptions ie interest rates, date of payment of creditors and receipts from debtors.
- Check all commitments have been cleared in accordance with legal agreements.
- Agree budgets to any actual results achieved in the post balance sheet period.
- Assess reasonableness of assumptions in the light of the success of the achievement of the company's budgets set for 20X5. Discuss with the directors any targets not achieved.
- Rework calculations
- Check future profits are expected to meet likely interest charges.

6. Check that the company is operating within its overdraft facility in the post balance sheet period. Review bank certificate for terms and conditions of the facility. Review bank correspondence for any suggestion the bank is concerned about its current position.

7. Discuss the extent to which the new vehicle fleet is attracting new contracts as anticipated. Scrutinise any new contracts obtained and check improved gross profit margins will be achieved.

8. Obtain management representation as to the likelihood of the company operating for twelve months from the date of approval of the financial statements.

Chapter roundup

- The auditors must perform and document an **overall review** of the financial statements before they can reach an opinion, covering:
  - Compliance with statute and accounting standards
  - Consistency with audit evidence
  - Overall reasonableness
- As part of their completion procedures, auditors should consider whether the **aggregate of uncorrected misstatements** is material.
- **Analytical procedures** should be used at the final stage of audit. The review should cover:
  - Key business ratios
  - Related items in accounts
  - The effect of known changes on the accounts
- Specific procedures must be applied to **opening balances** at a new audit client.
- The auditors' responsibilities for **comparatives** relate mainly to **consistency**, although comparatives and opening balances can have an impact on current results.
- **Unaudited published information** includes the **directors' report,** and other statements such as the **chairman's statement** and an **operating and financial review.** Auditors have a statutory responsibility to report inconsistencies between the directors' report and accounts.
- Auditors should consider the effect of **subsequent events** (after the balance sheet date) on the accounts.
- Auditors have a responsibility to **review subsequent events** before they sign their audit report, and may have to take action if they become aware of subsequent events between the date they sign their audit report and the date the financial statements are laid before members.
- Evaluation of going concern is most important. Auditors should consider the **future plans** of directors and any signs of **going concern problems** which may be noted throughout the audit. **Bank facilities** may have to be confirmed.
- When reporting on the accounts, auditors should consider whether the going concern basis is **appropriate,** and whether **disclosure** of going concern problems is **sufficient**.

Quick quiz

1 Name eight items that analytical review at the final stage must cover.

1.	__________	5.	__________
2.	__________	6.	__________
3.	__________	7.	__________
4.	__________	8.	__________

2 The auditor will maintain a schedule of unadjusted errors. This will include:

- Specific misstatements identified by the auditors
- Best estimate of other misstatements

True ☐

False ☐

3 Two situations might exist in the current period where a previous qualification matter is still unresolved. Name one.

4 Which of the items on the following list are not part of the 'other information' within the scope of SAS 160?

- Directors' report
- Chairman's report
- Cashflow statement
- Operating and financial review
- Auditors' report
- Financial summaries

5 Link the term to the definition

(a) Relevant events

(b) Subsequent events

(i) Relevant events which occur between the period end and the laying of the accounts.

(ii) Events which provide additional evidence relating to conditions at the balance sheet date, or which did not exist at the balance sheet date but are material.

6 List five enquiries which may be made of management in testing subsequent events.

1. ____________________
2. ____________________
3. ____________________
4. ____________________
5. ____________________

7 Complete the definition

The ______________ concept: The enterprise will continue in existence for the ________ ________.

8 The 'foreseeable future' is always a period of 12 months

True ☐

False ☐

Answers to quick quiz

1 See para 1.7

2 True

3 See para 2.14

4 Cashflow statement and auditors' report

5 (a)(ii), (b)(i)

6 See table above para 4.4

7 Going concern, foreseeable future

8 False

Now try the question below from the Exam Question Bank

Number	Level	Marks	Time
10	Exam	20	36 mins

Chapter 11

AUDIT OF FINANCIAL STATEMENTS I (ASSETS)

Introduction

Chapters 11-13 explore some aspects of audit testing in relation to some of the more advanced aspects of accounting practice, and some audit issues you have not encountered previously.

This chapter deals with assets. There are two categories of asset, as you are aware; fixed and current. You studied aspects of the audit of all categories of current asset for paper 2.6, *Audit and Internal Review.* In this chapter we shall look at a more complex area of stock, that is, **long term contracts.** We shall also consider the implications of a **standard cost system** for the audit.

In previous auditing studies, you have looked at the audit of tangible fixed assets. We shall revise that here. There are two further categories of fixed asset.

- **Intangibles**
- **Investments**

We shall look at the audit of these categories in Sections 3 and 4.

Remember that you are supposed to be able to consider four key matters in relation to items appearing in the accounts. These are:

- Risk
- Materiality
- Relevant accounting standards
- Audit evidence

In the following three chapters we shall concentrate on the latter two. You should always bear in mind the issues of risk and materiality, but these factors often depend on the question, as they are unique in every case.

You should also bear in mind the **financial statement assertions** relating to **assets** as you work through this chapter. In general terms, they are:

- Existence
- Completeness
- Valuation
- Rights and obligations

Study guide

Sections 14 and 15

- Evaluate the matters (for example, materiality, risk, relevant accounting standards, audit evidence) relating to:
  - Stock
  - Standard costing systems
  - Long term contracts
  - Investments
  - Impairment
  - Goodwill
  - Brand valuations
  - Research and development
  - Other intangible assets

  This list is not exhaustive, in particular, the audit transactions, balances and other events examined in Paper 2.6 is now assumed knowledge.)

Exam guide

You should note the point in brackets in the Study Guide. The basic details relating to auditing financial statements are **not** reproduced here and in the following two chapters. However, they are examinable. You should revise them from your previous text book. Investments were examined on the pilot paper.

1 STOCKS AND LONG TERM CONTRACTS

1.1 The key accounting standard relating to stocks and long term contracts is SSAP 9. You should be aware of its provisions, but the key points are summarised here.

SSAP 9 Stocks and long term contracts

Stock must be **valued** at the lower of cost and net realisable value

Net realisable value is the actual or estimated selling price less trade discounts, further costs to completion and costs to be incurred in marketing, selling or distribution.

Cost is the expenditure which has been incurred in the normal course of business in bring the product to its present location and condition. (Purchase price + costs of conversion.) **Standard costing** is an acceptable alternative where prices fluctuate.

A **long-term contract** is 'a contract entered into for the design, manufacture or construction of a single substantial asset or the provision of a service (or of a combination of assets or services which together constitute a single project) where the time taken substantially to complete the contract is such that the contract activity falls into different accounting periods.'

Stocks

1.2 You studied the audit of stocks in detail in your studies for 2.6, *Audit and Internal Review* (old paper 6). You should be able to design procedures to verify the existence and valuation of stock. Try the following question to make sure.

Question 1

Bathsheba Ltd is a manufacturer of a large range of bathroom fittings made from bought-in steel components which are chromed in small vats. The year end stock mainly consists of components and finished items. The total stock was valued at £50,400 out of total assets of £160,000. This stock figure was obtained by count at the year-end and valuation by reference to purchase invoices and manufacturing cost estimates.

Required

State what work you would do to put yourself in a position to be able to conclude that the amount attributed to stock was fairly stated in respect of:

(a) Quantities
(b) Identification
(c) Condition
(d) Cut-off
(e) Valuation

Answer

The work to be undertaken to satisfy the auditors that stocks of Bathsheba Ltd were fairly stated in respect of the stated matters would be as follows.

(a) **Quantities**

(i) Prior to the statutory date, obtain a copy of the company's stocktaking instructions and evaluate so as to consider whether, if followed, these would be likely to result in a an accurate count. If necessary, suggestions should be made to improve the instructions.

(ii) Attend the client's premises at the date of the stocktake to observe whether or not the client's stocktaking procedures are being properly applied.

(iii) During attendance, carry out test counts as well as supervising recounts by client's staff and make notes of entries on rough stock sheets for subsequent verification to final inventory.

(iv) Also, at stocktake, ensure that there are adequate controls over the issue and return of all stock sheets.

(v) After the stocktaking date ensure that the final inventory has been properly prepared from the rough stock sheets, and in particular follow up own notes made during attendance.

(b) **Identification**

Procedures here will be similar to (a) above as regards evaluation of client's stocktaking instructions and attendance. However, the following procedures are particularly important:

(i) Ensure that staff responsible for counting include those with necessary expertise to identify properly all stocks.

(ii) Test identification, so far as is possible, with catalogues etc of both the client and suppliers.

(iii) Compare, on a sample basis, descriptions on final inventory with those on rough stock sheets.

(c) **Condition**

Once again, similar considerations will apply as to the review of client's instructions and attendance at stocktaking. It will also be necessary to ensure that staff are available who are capable of properly assessing the condition of all stocks. In addition the auditors should:

(i) Test the condition of a sample of items, in particular making note of any stock which appears to be damaged or slow moving.

(ii) Ensure that those items noted as being of other than A1 condition at the time of the stocktake are properly noted as such in the final inventory.

(d) **Cut-off**

Cut-off is vitally important so far as stocks are concerned and particular attention should be paid to reviewing that part of the client's stocktaking instructions which relates to this. Whenever possible, there should be no movement of goods in or out, or processing, whilst stocktaking is in progress. The auditors should:

(i) When attending the stocktake ensure that there is no movement of goods during the counting in accordance with the instructions.

(ii) Make a note of the details of the last goods received notes and last despatch notes.

(iii) Carry out follow up procedures to ensure that all sales and purchases are accounted for in the right period. These include matching up goods received notes with purchase invoices and matching up despatch notes with sales invoices to ensure they are recorded in the correct period.

(e) **Valuation**

So far as bought-in components are concerned, the auditors should ensure that the method of valuation used is consistent with that applied in earlier years. The question suggests that these are valued by reference to purchase invoices and to be in accord with SSAP 9 these could be valued either by using unit cost, FIFO or average cost. The auditors should determine which method is in fact being used and test to see that it is being properly applied. A sample of stock prices should be tested against purchase invoices to ensure that the stock valuation is an approximation to actual costs as required by SSAP 9.

The question states that the other method used for determining stock valuation is by reference to manufacturing cost estimates. It is assumed that this will relate to WIP and stocks of finished goods. To determine whether the valuation of such stock is reasonable, it will be necessary to:

(i) Examine the costing records and ensure that they include all necessary costs of conversion.

(ii) Select a sample of finished goods lines and WIP and verify that the value has been properly assessed from the costing records.

As regards all stock, it will be necessary to consider the adequacy of the method for determining the net realisable value of those goods identified as being damaged, obsolete or slow moving.

Finally, the auditors should consider the adequacy of the disclosure of the stock in the financial statements and ensure that stock values and classification are confirmed in the letter of representation.

1.3 An additional thing to consider in the audit of stock is what **evidence** to obtain about **cost**, when there is a **standard costing system** in operation. Remember that SSAP 9 allows standard costs to be used where prices are fluctuating.

1.4 Where standard costing is being used the auditor will have **two objectives**:

- Ensure that standard costing is an **appropriate basis** for valuing stock
- Ensure that the **calculation** of the standard cost is **reasonable**

1.5 In evaluating whether standard costs are an appropriate basis, the auditor must

- **Establish whether prices have fluctuated.** This can be done by reviewing purchase invoices, consulting a price index and enquiry of management.
- **Consider if the use of standard costing is the best accounting policy to use.** This should be discussed with the directors.
- If the accounting policy has changed from the previous year, he must **consider the comparability of the accounts** under FRS 18.
- Under FRS 18, there should also be **disclosure** about any changes of accounting policy in the accounts, which he should ensure is sufficient.

1.6 In ensuring that the calculation of the standard cost is reasonable, the auditor must

- Obtain a copy of the calculation of standard cost
- Check the additions and calculations
- Consider whether the calculation is reasonable (for example, based on averages of costs over the year)
- Verify elements of the calculation to appropriate documentation, for example,
  - Purchase prices to invoices
  - Wages and salaries to personnel records
  - Overheads to expenses in the financial statements where possible
- Alternatively, the standard cost may be verifiable by analytical review with comparison to total expense figures in the profit and loss account, for example,
- Wages should be based on the total wage cost divided by the production total for the year.

Long term contracts

1.7 Before addressing the issue of audit evidence with regard to long-term contracts, it is valuable to revise the accounting requirements of SSAP 9 in more detail.

SSAP 9 Stocks and long term contracts

Turnover and profit recognised must reflect the proportion of work carried out at the accounting date. (This can be calculated on a sales or cost basis)

Where the outcome of a project cannot be foreseen with any reasonable certainty, profit should not be taken up. An expected loss should be provided for in full.

The balance sheet entries could therefore be:

- **Stocks** (costs to date, less costs recognised)
- **Debtors** (turnover recognised less payments on account)
- **Creditors** (payments on account)
- **Provisions** (for any foreseeable losses)

1.8 The auditor will have to audit the calculation of attributable profit or loss and assess if it is reasonable. He will then have to verify all the movements on the balance sheet accounts to that calculation.

1.9 The auditor should undertake the following procedures:

- Obtain a copy of the calculation and check the additions and calculations
- Assess whether the basis of calculation is comparable with prior years (FRS 18)
- He should then verify the figures in the calculation:
  - Turnover to certification of work completed to date
  - Total contract price to original contract

- Cost of work completed to invoices
- Payments on account to remittance advices

- **He should discuss with management if there is any chance of a loss arising on the contract**

2 TANGIBLE FIXED ASSETS

2.1 You covered all the key aspects relating to tangible fixed assets in your studies for 2.6, *Audit and Internal Review* (old paper 6). Try the following question to ensure that you remember the key issues.

Question 2

You have been asked to carry out the audit of the fixed assets of Simons Engineering Ltd for the year ended 31 March 20X7. The draft accounts show the following movements on fixed assets in the year.

	Freehold land and buildings	*Plant & machinery*	*Motor vehicles*	*Total*
Cost or valuation	£	£	£	£
At 1 April 20X6	353,000	406,000	173,000	932,000
Additions	392,000	86,000	65,000	443,000
Disposals	-	(29,000)	(47,000)	(76,000)
At 31 March 20X7	654,000	463,000	191,000	1,299,000
Depreciation				
At 1 April 20X6	132,000	187,000	74,000	393,000
Charge for the year	12,900	43,000	42,000	97,900
On disposals	-	(25,000)	(32,000)	(57,000)
At 31 March 20X7	144,900	205,000	84,000	433,900
NBV at 31 March 20X7	500,100	258,000	107,000	865,100

During the year ended 31 March 20X7 the company purchased some land and built a new factory, which was completed during the year.

The company maintains a fixed asset register for all fixed assets, and it depreciates its fixed assets at the following rates.

Land and buildings	2% on cost
Plant and machinery	10% on cost
Motor vehicles	25% on cost

It is company's policy to charge a full year's depreciation on assets in the year of purchase and no depreciation in the year of sale.

(a) List and describe the audit tests you would perform to verify the amounts shown in fixed assets in the company's accounts for the year ended 31 March 20X7.

(b) If the company did not maintain a fixed asset register, describe the problems you would experience and how it would affect your audit work and opinion.

Answer

(a) The following series of tests summarise the substantive procedures that the auditors might perform in respect of tangible fixed assets.

General

(i) Reconcile opening position per last year's audit working papers with accounting records and fixed asset register.

(ii) Obtain or prepare a summary of tangible fixed assets under categories, showing how the figures of gross book value, accumulated depreciation and net book value appearing in the draft accounts reconcile with the opening position. Check client-prepared summary to accounting records.

(iii) Scrutinise general ledger accounts and fixed asset register, and enquire into any unusual items.

Rights and obligations

(i) Verify title and hence rights and obligations to land and buildings by inspection of title deeds and land registry certificates.

(ii) Obtain a certificate from solicitors temporarily holding deeds, stating the purpose for which they are being held and that they hold them free from any mortgage or lien. Where deeds are held by bankers, obtain a similar certificate stating also that the deeds are held for safe custody only.

(iii) Inspect vehicle registration documents or verify sale proceeds if sold since the balance sheet date, and reconcile opening and closing vehicles by numbers as well as amounts.

(iv) Obtain or prepare a list of additions during the year and verify ownership by inspection of architect's certificates, solicitors' completion statements, suppliers' invoices etc. Check purchases have been authorised.

(v) Review for evidence of charges in statutory books and by company search.

(vi) Examine invoices received after year-end, orders and minutes for evidence of capital commitments.

Valuation

(i) Verify costs of additions to suppliers' invoices etc. as above.

(ii) Check that costs have been capitalised correctly.

(iii) Where the clients have used their own labour force to construct assets, ensure that materials, labour and overheads, if appropriate, have been correctly analysed and are properly charged to capital.

(iv) Review depreciation rates applied in relation to:

(1) Asset lives
(2) Replacement policy
(3) Past experience of gains or losses on disposal
(4) Consistency with prior years and accounting policy

(v) For revalued assets, ensure that the charge for depreciation is based on the revalued amount.

(vi) Compare ratios of depreciation to fixed assets by category with:

(1) Previous years
(2) Depreciation policy rates

(vii) Ensure no further depreciation has been provided on fully depreciated assets.

(viii) Check valuation by inspecting any recent valuation certificate and considering experience of valuer, scope of work and methods and assumptions. Consider other evidence of valuation eg inspection. Confirm that treatment of revaluation gains and losses complies with FRS 15.

(ix) Review insurance policies in force for all categories of tangible fixed assets and consider the adequacy of their insured values and check expiry dates.

(x) Consider any evidence of permanent diminution in value eg physical inspection, asset no longer used etc.

Existence

Make physical inspection of any item over £... and random selection of others.

Completeness

(i) Select of sample of fixed assets seen and confirm that they are recorded in the fixed asset register and the accounting records.

(ii) Reconcile fixed asset register and accounting records.

(iii) Check records of income yielding assets to confirm that all income to which the client is entitled has been collected.

Occurrence

Obtain or prepare a list of disposals and scrappings from fixed assets during the year. Reconcile original cost with sale proceeds and verify book profits and losses. Check assets have been deleted from the fixed asset register.

Presentation and disclosure

Consider whether disclosure complies with Companies Act and FRS 15.

(b) If a fixed asset register is not kept, the auditors should obtain a schedule for the permanent file of the major items of fixed assets showing the original cost and estimated present depreciated value, or update the existing schedule. They should attempt to reconcile both the total cost and total depreciated value with the figures appearing in the draft accounts. They should also prepare their own schedule of the items inspected and file this on the current audit file.

The auditors should be able to vouch additions during the year to supporting documentation in the normal way; however, they will, in the absence of an asset register, be faced with more of a problem in relation to disposals. Where they have a schedule of major items from previous years the continuing existence of assets may be checked to this schedule, but where this is not the case, the auditors will have to rely more on a scrutiny of the cash book for any large unexplained receipts, and management representations.

At the end of the day the auditors may well conclude that there is material uncertainty as to the existence and valuation of fixed assets and be forced to give an appropriate qualification in their audit report in that they will not have received all the information and explanations considered necessary for the purposes of their audit.

2.2 **FRS 11 states that fixed assets (tangible and intangible) should be recorded in the financial statements at no more than their recoverable amount. In certain circumstances, assets should be subject to an impairment review.**

Exam focus point

You should revise what indicators of impairment are from your 2.5 studies if you are not sure what they are.

2.3 The audit approach towards impairment should be as follows.

Planning

- Assess whether impairment reviews might be necessary from knowledge of the business.

Testing

- Obtain the client's workings of the impairment loss
- Consider whether they are reasonable
- Recalculate, to ensure they are arithmetically correct
- If possible, verify new value to documentation, for example valuers' report

3 INTANGIBLE FIXED ASSETS

3.1 Accounting guidance for intangibles is given in FRSs 10 and 11 and SSAP 13.

3.2 The types of asset we are likely to encounter under this heading include patents, licences, trade marks, development costs and goodwill. All intangibles have a finite economic life and should hence be amortised.

> **FRS 10**
>
> Positive purchased goodwill should be capitalised and classified as an asset on the balance sheet. Internally generated goodwill should not be capitalised.
>
> An intangible purchased separately from the business should be capitalised at cost. If purchased as part of a business, an intangible should only be capitalised separately if its value can be measured reliably or it becomes part of the price attributed to goodwill.
>
> Internally generated intangibles may be capitalised if they have a readily ascertainable market value. Brands are specifically excluded from this description.
>
> Goodwill and intangibles with a limited useful life should be amortised. Assets may also require impairment reviews under FRS 11.

3.3 The auditor should carry out the following procedures

Completeness

- Prepare analysis of movements on cost and amortisation accounts

Rights and obligations

- Obtain confirmation of all patents and trademarks held by a patent agent
- Verify payment of annual renewal fees

Valuation

- **Review specialist valuations** of intangible assets, considering:
  - Qualifications of valuer
  - Scope of work
  - Assumptions and methods used
- **Confirm carried down balances** represent **continuing value**, which are proper charges to future operations

Additions (rights and obligations, valuation and completeness)

- **Inspect purchase agreements, assignments** and **supporting documentation** for intangible assets acquired in period
- **Confirm purchases** have been **authorised**
- **Verify amounts capitalised** of patents developed by the company with supporting costing records

Amortisation

- **Review amortisation**
  - Check computation
  - Confirm that rates used are reasonable

Income from intangibles

- **Review sales returns** and **statistics** to verify the reasonableness of income derived from patents, trademarks, licences etc
- **Examine audited accounts** of third party sales covered by a patent, licence or trademark owned by the company

Goodwill

3.4 Key tests are as follows.

- Agree consideration to a sales agreement
- **Confirm valuation** of assets acquired is reasonable
- **Check purchased goodwill** is **calculated correctly** (it should reflect the difference between the fair value of the consideration given and the aggregate of the fair values of the separable net assets acquired)
- Check goodwill does not include non-purchased goodwill
- Review amortisation
  - Test calculation
  - Assess whether amortisation rates are reasonable
- **Ensure valuation** of **goodwill** is **reasonable** and that impairment is not required by reviewing prior year's accounts and discussion with the directors

Development costs

Companies Act 1985

- Development costs can be included in the balance sheet only in special circumstances.
- Development costs capitalised must be amortised.
- Accounts must disclose reasons for capitalisation and period over which the expenditure is to be written off.

SSAP 13

Definitions

Pure (or basic) research

Experimental or theoretical work undertaken primarily to acquire new scientific or technical knowledge for its own sake rather than directed towards any specific aim or application.

Applied research

Original or critical investigation undertaken in order to gain new scientific or technical knowledge and directed towards a specific practical aim or objective.

Development

'Development' is defined as:

'the use of scientific or technical knowledge in order to produce new or substantially improved materials, devices, products or services, to install new processes or systems prior to the commencement of commercial production or commercial applications, or to improving substantially those already produced or installed.'

Expenditure on pure and applied research (other than on fixed assets) is required to be written off in the year of expenditure.

The special circumstances which must be satisfied to justify deferral of development expenditure are:

- There is a clearly defined project.
- The related expenditure is separately identifiable.
- The outcome of such a project has been assessed with reasonable certainty as to:
    - Its technical feasibility
    - Its ultimate commercial viability considered in the light of factors such as likely market conditions (including competing products), public opinion, consumer and environmental legislation
    - The aggregate of the deferred development costs, any further development costs, and related production, selling and administration costs is reasonably expected to be exceeded by related future sales or other revenues
- Adequate resources exist, or are reasonably expected to be available, to enable the project to be completed and to provide any consequential increases in working capital.

3.5 The key audit tests largely reflect the criteria laid down in SSAP 13.

- **Check accounting records** to confirm:
    - **Project** is **clearly defined** (separate cost centre or nominal ledger codes)
    - **Related expenditure** can be **separately identified**, and certified to invoices, timesheets
- **Confirm feasibility** and **viability.**
    - Examine market research reports, feasibility studies, budgets and forecasts
    - Consult client's technical experts.
- **Review budgeted revenues** and **costs** by examining results to date, production forecasts, advance orders and discussion with directors.
- **Review calculations** of **future cash flows** to ensure resources exist to complete the project.
- **Review previously deferred expenditure** to ensure SSAP 13 criteria are still justified.
- **Check amortisation:**
    - Commences with production
    - Charged on a systematic basis

3.6 The good news for the auditors in this audit area is that many companies adopt a prudent approach and write off research and development expenditure in the year it is incurred. The auditors' concern in these circumstances is whether the profit and loss account charge for research and development is complete, accurate and valid.

4 INVESTMENTS **Pilot Paper**

4.1 This section applies to companies where dealing in investments is secondary to the main objectives of the company. Under the general heading of 'investments' four distinct items are considered:

- Investment properties (not on your syllabus)
- Investments in companies, whether listed or unlisted, fixed interest or equity
- Income arising from the above investments
- Investment in subsidiary and associated companies

(*Note*. The following comments apply equally to investments treated as fixed or current. An investment in subsidiary or associate can be audited in the same way as any other investment in an unlisted company. However, you should be mindful of related party transactions when dealing with these.)

Internal control considerations

4.2 The key controls are:

(a) **Authorisation** over investment dealing (which should be from high level management).

(b) **Segregation of duties:**

- The **recording** and **custody** roles should be kept separate.
- As investments may be misappropriated by being pledged as collateral, those responsible for custody should not have access to cash.

Existence and rights and obligations

4.3 Stockbrokers should not normally be entrusted with the safe custody of share certificates on a continuing basis since they have ready access to the Stock Exchange. Auditors should not therefore rely on a certificate from a broker stating that he holds the company's securities.

4.4 If securities are being transferred over the year-end the auditors should obtain a broker's certificate. The transaction should be further verified by examining contract notes, and in the case of purchases, examination of the title documents after the year-end.

4.5 Substantive tests

- **Examine certificates of title** to investments listed in investment records and confirm that they are:
  - Bona fide complete title documents
  - In the client's name
  - Free from any charge or lien
- **Examine confirmation** from **third party investment custodians** (such as banks) and check:
  - Investments are in client's name
  - Investments are free from charge or lien

- **Inspect certificates** of **title** which are held by third parties who are not bona fide custodians
- **Inspect blank transfers** and **letters of trust** to confirm client owns shares in name of nominee
- **Review minutes** and **other statutory books** for evidence of charging and pledging

Additions (rights and obligations, valuation and completeness)

- **Verify purchases** to agreements, contract notes and correspondence
- **Confirm purchases** were **authorised**
- **Check** with Stubbs, Extel or appropriate financial statements that all **reported capital changes** (bonus or rights issues) have been correctly **accounted for** during the period

Disposals (rights and obligations, valuation and completeness)

- **Verify disposals** with contract notes, sales agreements correspondence etc.
- **Check** whether investment **disposals** have been **authorised**
- **Confirm** that **profit** or **loss** on sale of investments has been **correctly calculated** taking account of:
  - Bonus issue of shares
  - Consistent basis of identifying cost of investment sold
  - Rights issues
  - Accrued interest
  - Taxation

Valuation

4.6 The auditors should establish that the company's policy on valuing investments has been correctly applied and is consistent with previous years, for example cost or market value.

4.7 Substantive tests

- **Confirm** the **value** of **listed investments** by reference to the Stock Exchange Daily Lists or the quotations published in the Financial Times or Times. The middle market value should be used
- Review accounts of unlisted investments and:
  - **Calculate** the **net assets value** of the shares and value the investment on a yield basis
  - **Ensure** that the **valuation** of the investment is **reasonable**
- **Check** that **no substantial fall** in the value of the investments has taken place since the balance sheet date
- **Consider** whether there are any **restrictions** on **remittance** of **income** and ensure these are properly disclosed
- **Check** whether **current asset investments** are included at the **lower of cost** or **net realisable value**

Investment income

4.8 The basis of recognising investment income may vary from company to company particularly for dividends, for example:

- Credit taken only when received (cash basis)
- Credit taken when declared
- Credit taken only after ratification of the dividend by the investee's shareholders in general meeting

A consistent basis must be applied from year to year.

4.9 **Completeness, occurrence and measurement**

- **Check** that all **income** due has been **received,** by reference to Stubbs or Extel cards for listed investments, and financial statements for unlisted investments
- **Review investment income** account for **irregular** or unusual **entries**, or those not apparently pertaining to investments held (particular attention should be paid to investments bought and sold during the year)
- **Ensure** that the **basis** of **recognising** income is **consistent** with previous years
- **Compare investment income** with **prior years** and **explain** any **significant fluctuations**
- **Consider whether** there are likely to be any **restrictions** on **realisation** of the investment or remittance of any income due (especially for investments abroad) and ensure these are properly disclosed in the financial statements

If the client is a charity or a pension scheme, auditors should check that tax deducted at source has been reclaimed from the Inland Revenue.

Other tests

4.10 Other tests that are likely to be carried out include the following.

- **Obtain** or prepare a **statement** to be placed on the current file **reconciling the book value** of listed and unlisted investments at the last balance sheet date and the current balance sheet date (tests **completeness**)
- **Ensure** that the **investments** are **properly categorised** in the financial statements into listed and unlisted

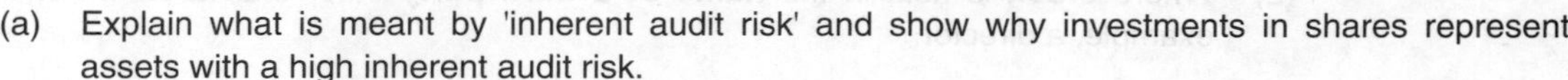

Question 3

For many companies investments in shares represent a substantial portion of total assets, for others investments are only temporary assets, or merely reflect incidental aspects of company operations. For the auditors, investments in shares can represent assets with high inherent audit risk.

(a) Explain what is meant by 'inherent audit risk' and show why investments in shares represent assets with a high inherent audit risk.

(b) Describe the audit procedures which would verify the existence and the rights and obligations of investments in shares.

(c) Describe how the auditors would determine that all investment income from shares had been properly recorded in the accounting records.

Answer

(a) Inherent risk is the **susceptibility** of an **account balance** or **class of transactions** to **intentional** or **unintentional misstatement** that could be material, either individually or when aggregated with misstatements in other balances or classes.

Inherent risk is assessed before considering the effects of internal controls, and must be assessed in order to determine the most effective audit approach. The number and size of errors which could occur depend partly on the client's type of **business**, how it is **managed**, the **quality of personnel** and the **accounting practices** in use.

Investments represent assets with a high inherent audit risk because the following factors are present.

(i) **Complexity** of **accounting estimates** and **calculations**, for instance the dates and amounts of investment income. Receipts are difficult to schedule and control.

(ii) A high degree of **subjectivity in valuation**, requiring judgement and decision by management. The auditors must verify that proper assets values are reported for each category of investments.

For all categories, a measure of current market value is required. For **quoted shares** held as current assets, the value will be the lower of **cost** and **net realisable value**, while for longer term holdings as **fixed assets**, the value will be cost or market value. The **market value** at the balance sheet date should be using the **mid-market price** provided in the Stock Exchange Daily Official List (SEDOL).

Unquoted shares are more difficult to value because they have no established market price and must be valued using the most appropriate 'ad hoc' method. The choices are **yield bases** (earnings and dividend), **earning capacity** and **net assets**, but none of these will give a definitive answer because of the numerous factors affecting the valuation.

(iii) **Susceptibility** to **material fraud** and **misappropriation**. Many securities are readily negotiable, and documents of title may be subject to unauthorised use. Ideally, securities should be held by independent custodians. Undue reliance should not be placed upon certificates without supporting evidence, especially where the auditors do not audit all companies within a group. Securities may not be specifically identifiable, or may be registered in a name other than that of the beneficial owner.

(iv) The **experience** and **competence** of **accounting personnel** responsible for the preparation of the sections of the accounts involving investments needs to be extensive, but may be deficient in the absence of outside advice by technical experts.

(b) The existence and rights and obligations of investments in shares would be verified using the following audit procedures.

(i) **Inspect share certificates** and **contract notes**. All documents should be inspected together at the same time, and should be in the name of the client.

(ii) **Examine documentary evidence** to **verify all purchases and sales** during the year, including **authorisation minutes**. Purchase cost and sales income would be vouched and traced to the bank.

(iii) **Ask third parties** holding share certificates pending delivery, whether for safe custody or as collateral, to **confirm directly** to them their holding on behalf of the client. **Verification** is **unsatisfactory** in the following cases and the matter would be referred for action to the audit manager.

(1) Where **stock** is being held by **brokers** for **safe custody** and not merely pending delivery (since brokers are not considered to be appropriate as custodians except in the event of purchase or sale of investment).

(2) Where **stock** is held in the **name of a third party** other than a bank nominee, for example, a director.

(iv) Examine agreements, board minutes and supporting correspondence in respect of unquoted shares.

(v) Review investment income received, as it is *prima facie* evidence of the existence and beneficial ownership of the securities.

(c) To determine that all investment income had been properly recorded the auditors would carry out the following work.

(i) **Check** to Extel or stock exchange lists, or company accounts in respect of unquoted companies, to **determine** the **dividends** that should have been received in the period.

(ii) **Obtain information** on all **bonus** and **rights issues** during the year and investigate action taken and shares received.

(iii) Check that the **interest due is received** on the **due date** and that it relates correctly to the nominal value of the security.

(iv) **Verify** the **correctness of calculation** and recording of **capital gains and losses**, and their treatment in the financial statements.

(v) **Review** the **reasonableness** of **investment income accounts**, taking into consideration the amounts budgeted for and the amounts received in previous years. Material variations would need to be explained, taking into account purchases, bonus issues and sales in the period.

Chapter roundup

- Stocks are accounted for in accordance with SSAP 9. It allows standard costing to be used where prices are fluctuating. Auditors may need to amend their normal valuation procedures a little when auditing standard costs.
- To audit long term contracts, the auditor must access the reasonableness of the calculation of attributable profit and loss.
- Accounting guidance on intangibles is given in FRSs 10 and 11. Intangibles are only permitted to be capitalised if their value is separately identifiable. The auditor should therefore be able to audit valuation fairly easily.
- When auditing investments, the auditor may have to audit both
  - Asset
  - Income

Quick quiz

1 Match the accounting item with the relevant accounting standard(s)

(a)	Long term contracts	(i)	FRS 11
(b)	Intangible fixed assets	(ii)	FRS 15
(c)	Tangible fixed assets	(iii)	SSAP 9
		(iv)	SSAP 13
		(v)	FRS 10

2 Name four procedures to test for the existence of investments.

(1) ____________________

(2) ____________________

(3) ____________________

(4) ____________________

3 Why might investments have high inherent risk?

4 Complete the definition.

A ____________________-________________ ______________________ is a contract entered into for the ____________________, __________________ or _________________ of a single substantial asset where the time later substantially to ___________________ the contract is such that contract activity falls into ____________________ _______________________.

5 Brands may never be capitalised.

True ☐

False ☐

Answers to quick quiz

1 (a) (iv)

(b) (i) (iv) (v)

(c) (ii) (i)

2 See para 4.5

3 See answer to question 3a

4 Long-term contract, design, manufacture, construction, complete, different accounting periods

5 False. Internally generated brands may never be capitalised. Purchased brands with a separately identifiable value may be capitalised.

Now try the question below from the Exam Question Bank

Number	Level	Marks	Time
11	Exam	25	45 mins

Chapter 12

AUDIT OF FINANCIAL STATEMENTS II (LIABILITIES)

Introduction

This chapter deals with liabilities. Liabilities can be categorised as follows:

- Creditors: amounts falling due within one year (current liabilities)
- Creditors: amounts falling due in more than one year (long-term liabilities)
- Provisions

You studied the basic auditing procedure in relation to current and long-term liabilities in your studies at 2.6, *Audit and Internal Review* (old paper 6). In this chapter we are going to look at some specialised liabilities (**leases and deferred tax**) and also the audit of **provisions. Contingencies** are linked with provisions as they are all accounted for under FRS 12.

In general terms the relevant financial statement assertions for liabilities are:

- Completeness
- Rights and obligations
- Existence

It is important to test liabilities for **understatement.**

Study guide

Sections 14 and 15

- Evaluate the matters (eg materiality, risk, relevant accounting standards, audit evidence) relating to:
  - Deferred taxation
  - Leases
  - Provisions, contingent liabilities and contingent assets

  (This list is not exhaustive, in particular, the audit of transactions, balances and other events examined in Paper 2.6 is now assumed knowledge.)

Exam guide

Provisions were examined on the pilot paper. These liabilities are complex issues because accounting for them is complex. Note also the specific materiality issues arising as you work through the chapter.

1 LEASES

1.1 First we shall look at the audit of **leases**. The relevant accounting standard for leases is SSAP 21, but the provisions of FRS 5 are also relevant. This is because leases are accounted for according to their **substance**.

> **SSAP 21**
>
> A finance lease is one where substantially all the risks and rewards of ownership are transferred to the lessee. SSAP 21 provides that such a lease should be recognised on the balance sheet, as is the associated asset.
>
> An operating lease is any lease which is not a finance lease. These are accounted for as the payments are due (in other words, the commitment to future liability is not recognised).

1.2 You can see that the **classification** of the lease is **likely to have a material effect on the financial statements.** If the lease is a finance lease, the balance sheet will show substantial assets and liabilities. The net effect will be minimal, but the face of the balance sheet will be materially different to if it was an operating lease.

1.3 It is important that the auditor ensures that the **classification** (which would fall under the assertion existence) is correct. Other important assertions are valuation, and rights and obligations.

1.4 The following audit procedures are relevant.

Classification and rights and obligations

- Obtain a copy of the lease agreement
- Review the lease agreement to ensure that the lease has been correctly classified according to SSAP 21

Valuation (finance leases)

- Obtain a copy of the client's workings in relation to finance leases
- Check the additions and calculations of the workings
- Ensure that the interest has been accounted for in accordance with SSAP 21
- Recalculate the interest
- Agree the opening position
- Agree any new assets to lease agreements
- Verify lease payments in the year to the bank statements

Valuation (operating leases)

- Agree payments to the bank statements (if material)

Disclosure

- The auditor should ensure the finance leases have been properly disclosed in the financial statements

2 DEFERRED TAXATION

2.1 Deferred tax is accounted for under FRS 19.

FRS 19

Full provision must be made for deferred tax assets and liabilities arising from timing differences between the recognition of gains and losses in the financial statements and their recognition in a tax computation, such as:

- Accelerated capital allowances
- Accruals for pension costs and other post-retirement benefits that will be deducted for tax purposes only when paid
- Elimination of unrealised intragroup profits on consolidation
- Unrelieved tax losses
- Other sources of short-term timing differences

The FRS permits but does not require entities to adopt a policy of discounting deferred tax assets and liabilities.

The FRS includes other requirements regarding the measurement and presentation of deferred tax to be:

- Measured using tax rates that have been enacted or substantively enacted
- Presented separately on the face of the balance sheet if the amounts are so material that, in the absence of such disclosure, readers may misinterpret the accounts.

2.2 Deferred tax is the **tax attributable to timing differences**. Where a company 'saves tax' in the current period by having accelerated capital allowances, a **provision for the tax charge** is **made in the balance sheet.**

2.3 The provision is made is because over the course of the asset's life, the tax allowances will reduce until the depreciation charged in the accounts is higher than the allowances. This will result in taxable profit being higher than reported profit and the company will be 'suffering higher tax' in this period.

2.4 **The provision may or may not be material depending on** the entity's **future plans** and therefore the extent to which it is **estimated that tax liabilities will crystallise.**

2.5 As part of the **planning process**, if the client receives tax services from the firm, the auditor should consult the tax department as to the companies future tax plans, to ascertain whether they expect a deferred tax liability to arise. This will assist any analytical review they carry out on the deferred tax provision.

2.6 As has been discussed above, there is a **degree of estimation involved** in the deferred tax provision. The auditor should approach it bearing in mind that this is an area which **could be manipulated by the directors.**

2.7 Remember that **manipulating the deferred tax figure will not affect the actual tax position**. However, a **deferred tax charge** (the other part of the double entry for the balance sheet provision) **is charged on the profit and loss account before dividends**, even if it is not actually paid to the Inland Revenue.

2.8 As there is estimation involved, when auditing the deferred tax provision, the auditor should bear in mind the guidance given in SAS 420 *Audit of Accounting Estimates*.

2.9 The following procedures will be relevant:

- Obtain an copy of the deferred tax workings and the corporation tax computation
- Check the arithmetical **accuracy** of the deferred tax working
- Agree the **figures used** to calculate timing differences to those on the **tax computation** and the **financial statements**
- Discuss the **assumptions made about future events** with the directors and/or the tax specialists to ensure that they are reasonable
- Consider the assumptions made in the light of your knowledge of the business and any other evidence gathered during the course of the audit to ensure reasonableness
- Agree the opening position on the deferred tax account to the prior year financial statements
- Review the basis of the provision to ensure:
    - It is line with accounting practice under FRS 19
    - It is suitably comparable to practice in previous years, and
    - Any changes in accounting policy have been disclosed

3 PROVISIONS AND CONTINGENCIES **Pilot Paper**

3.1 Provisions are accounted for under FRS 12.

FRS 12

A **provision** is a liability that is of uncertain timing or amount, to be settled by the transfer of economic benefits.

A **contingent liability** is either

(a) A possible obligation arising from past events whose existence will be confirmed only by the occurrence of one or more uncertain future events not wholly within the entity's control; or

(b) A present obligation that arises from past events but is not recognised because it is not probable that a transfer of economic benefits will be required to settle the obligation or because the amount of the obligation cannot be measured with sufficient reliability.

A **contingent asset** is a possible asset arising from past events whose existence will be confirmed only by the occurrence of one or more uncertain future events not wholly within the entity's control.

FRS 12 states that a provision should be **recognised** as a liability in the financial statements when:

- An entity has a **present obligation** (legal or constructive) as a result of a past event
- It is probable that a **transfer of economic benefits** will be required to settle the obligation
- A **reliable estimate** can be made of the obligation

3.2 The audit tests that should be carried out on provisions and contingent assets and liabilities are as follows.

- **Obtain details** of all **provisions** which have been included in the **accounts** and all **contingencies** that have been disclosed
- **Obtain** a **detailed analysis** of all **provisions** showing opening balances, movements and closing balances
- **Determine** for each material provision **whether** the **company** has a **present obligation** as a result of past events by:
  - **Review** of **correspondence** relating to the item
  - **Discussion** with the **directors,** have they created a valid expectation in other parties that they will discharge the obligation?
- **Determine** for each material provision **whether** it is **probable** that a **transfer of economic benefits** will be required to settle the obligation by:
  - **Checking** whether any **payments** have been **made** in the post balance sheet period in respect of the item
  - **Review of correspondence** with solicitors, banks, customers, insurance company and suppliers both pre and post year end
  - **Sending** a **letter** to the **solicitor** to obtain their views (where relevant)
  - **Discussing** the **position** of similar **past provisions** with the directors. Were these provisions eventually settled
  - **Considering** the **likelihood** of **reimbursement**
- **Recalculate** all **provisions** made
- **Compare** the **amount provided** with any post year end payments and with any amount paid in the past for similar items
- In the event that it is not possible to estimate the amount of the **provision,** check that this **contingent liability** is **disclosed** in the accounts
- **Consider** the **nature** of the **client's business.** Would you expect to see any other provisions, for example, warranties?
- **Consider** whether disclosures of **provisions, contingent liabilities and contingent assets** are correct and sufficient

Representations from solicitors

3.3 In appropriate circumstances, the auditors may decide to obtain written representations in respect of legal actions from the company's legal advisers.

3.4 Requests for such confirmation should be kept within the solicitor-client relationship and should thus be issued by the client with a request that a copy of the reply be sent direct to the auditors. As with a debtors' circularisation it should be appreciated that the auditors do not have a right to communicate with third parties directly.

3.5 If the enquiries lead to the discovery of significant matters not previously identified, the auditors will wish to extend their enquiries and to request their client to address further enquiries to, and arrange a meeting with, the solicitors, at which the auditors will wish to be present.

3.6 If, having regard to all the circumstances, the auditors are unable to satisfy themselves that they have received all the information they require for the purpose of their audit, they must qualify their report.

Exam focus point

You should appreciate that the problems of accounting for contingencies makes their audit difficult.

Question 1

In February 20X7 the directors of Newthorpe Engineering plc suspended the managing director. At a disciplinary hearing held by the company on 17 March 20X7 the managing director was dismissed for gross misconduct, and it was decided the managing director's salary should stop from that date and no redundancy or compensation payments should be made.

The managing director has claimed unfair dismissal and is taking legal action against the company to obtain compensation for loss of his employment. The managing director says he has a service contract with the company which would entitle him to two years' salary at the date of dismissal.

The financial statements for the year ended 30 April 20X7 record the resignation of the director. However, they do not mention his dismissal and no provision for any damages has been included in the financial statements.

Required

(a) State how contingent losses should be disclosed in financial statements according to FRS 12 *Provisions, Contingent Liabilities and Contingent Assets.*

(b) Describe the audit work you will carry out to determine whether the company will have to pay damages to the director for unfair dismissal, and the amount of damages and costs which should be included in the financial statements.

Note. Assume the amounts you are auditing are material.

Answer

(a) FRS 12 states that a provision should be recognised in the accounts if:

- An entity has a **present obligation** (legal or constructive) as a result of a past event
- A **transfer** of **economic benefits** will **probably** be **required** to settle the obligation
- A **reliable estimate** can be **made** of the amount of the obligation.

Under FRS 12 contingent liabilities should not be recognised. They should however be disclosed unless the prospect of settlement is remote. The entity should disclose:

- The **nature** of the liability
- An estimate of its **financial effect**
- The **uncertainties** relating to any possible payments
- The likelihood of any **re-imbursement**

(b) The following tests should be carried out to determine whether the company will have to pay damages and the amount to be included in the financial statements.

(i) **Review** the director's **service contract** and **ascertain** the **maximum amount** to which he would be entitled and the **provisions** in the service contract that would **prevent** him making a **claim**, in particular those relating to grounds for justifiable dismissal.

(ii) **Review** the results of the **disciplinary hearing. Consider** whether the company has acted in accordance with **employment legislation** and its **internal rules,** the **evidence** presented by the **company** and the defence made by the **director.**

(iii) **Review correspondence** relating to the case and **determine** whether the **company** has **acknowledged** any **liability** to the director that would mean that an amount for compensation should be accrued in accordance with FRS 12.

(iv) **Review correspondence** with the company's **solicitors** and **obtain legal advice**, either from the company's solicitors or another firm, about the likelihood of the claim succeeding.

(v) **Review** correspondence and contact the company's solicitors about the likely **costs** of the case.

(vi) **Consider** the **likelihood** of **costs** and **compensation** being **re-imbursed** by **reviewing** the company's **insurance arrangements** and contacting the insurance company.

(vii) **Consider** the **amounts** that should be **accrued** and the **disclosures** that should be made in the accounts. Legal costs should be accrued, but compensation payments should only be accrued if the company has admitted liability or legal advice indicates that the company's chances of success are very poor. However the claim should be disclosed unless legal advice indicates that the director's chance of success appears to be remote.

Chapter roundup

- The classification of a lease can have a material effect on the financial statements. If a lease is classified as a **financial lease** it will be recognised on the balance sheet, as will the asset to which it relates.
- The auditor should review the lease agreement to ensure it has been classified in accordance with SSAP 21.
- Deferred tax should be provided for in full to the extent that tax liabilities are expected to crystallise under FRS 19. Deferred tax is the tax attributable to timing differences.
- The auditor needs to audit the movement on the deferred tax provision. To do this he will need to:
  - Agree figures in the calculation to the tax computation and the financial statements
  - Review assumptions made for reasonableness.
- Provisions are accounted for under FRS 12, as are contingencies. A provision is a liability, whereas a contingent liability is only a potential liability, only requiring disclosure.
- The auditors should assess whether provisions represent present obligations arising from past events by reviewing relevant correspondence and discussion with directors. The auditors may also seek representations from the clients solicitors.

Quick quiz

1 Complete the definition

A ____________ lease is one where substantially all the ________________ and ________________ of ownership are transferred to the lessee.

2 Sort the following valuation tests into those relevant for finance leases and those relevant to operating leases.

- Obtain client's workings
- Ensure interest calculated in accordance with SSAP 21
- Agree the opening position
- Agree new assets to lease agreements
- Verify payments to bank statements

3 What key issue related to deferred tax may affect its size and therefore materiality?

4 Name four timing differences which must be provided for under FRS 19.

(1) ________________

(2) ________________

(3) ________________

(4) ________________

5 What are the FRS 12 recognition criteria for a provision?

(1) ________________

(2) ________________

(3) ________________

6 The auditor may request information directly from the client's solicitors.

True ☐

False ☐

Answers to quick quiz

1 Finance, risks, rewards

2
- Obtain client's workings — F
- Ensure interest calculated in accordance with SSAP 21 — F
- Agree the opening position — F
- Agree new assets to lease agreements — F
- Verify payments to bank statements — F and O

3 The future capital expenditure plans of the entity.

4 See the grey box at para 2.1

5 See the grey box at para 3.1

6 False. The client should request the information

Now try the question below from the Exam Question Bank

Number	Level	Marks	Time
12	Exam	20	36 mins

Chapter 13

AUDIT OF FINANCIAL STATEMENTS III (DISCLOSURE AND OTHER ISSUES)

Introduction

There are a series of disclosure and other miscellaneous issues that arise in financial statements which the auditor must consider before he issues his report. Some are only relevant to larger companies. Refer to your accounting notes to ensure that you are aware the size and company that some of these disclosures are relevant to.

There is not necessarily any relationship between any of the items discussed in this chapter, so do not assume links that do not exist. The auditor might have to bear some of these issues in mind as he carried out his substantive audit work, or as part of an overall review of financial statements.

Study guide

- Evaluate the matters (eg materiality, risk, relevant accounting standards, audit evidence) relating to:
  - Cash flow statements
  - Segmental information
  - Revenue recognition
  - Government grants and assistance
  - Borrowing costs
  - Earnings per share
  - Discontinued operations

  (This list is not exhaustive, in particular, the audit of transactions, balances and other events examined in Paper 2.6 is now assumed knowledge.)

Exam guide

Another important disclosure issue is related party transactions (see Chapter 9) which was examined in the pilot paper.

BPP PUBLISHING

1 SEGMENTAL INFORMATION

1.1 The disclosure of segmental information is governed by the Companies Act 1985 and by SSAP 25.

> **SSAP 25**
>
> **This extends the Companies Act requirements** on analysis of turnover and profits as follows:
>
> - The result as well as turnover must be disclosed for all segments.
> - 'Result' for these purposes is profit or loss before tax, minority interests and extraordinary items.
> - Each segment's net assets should be disclosed (so that return on capital employed can be calculated).
> - Segmental turnover must be analysed between sales to customers outside the group and inter-segment sales/transfers (where material).
>
> Like the CA 1985, SSAP 25 requires analysis by two types of segment, class of business and geographical market.

1.2 The following procedures are relevant:

> - Obtain a client schedule of turnover workings
> - Discuss with management the basis for the segmentation
> - Verify a sample of items to backing documentation (invoices) to ensure disclosure is correct

2 EARNINGS PER SHARE

2.1 Accounting for Earnings per Share is governed by FRS 14. It requires that companies of a certain size disclose their earning per share for the year. This is the profit in pence attributable to each share. FRS 14 describes the various possible complications to calculating earnings per share, but auditing it is straightforward.

2.2 The size of the figure is unlikely to be material in itself, but it is key investor figure. As it will be of **interest to all the investors** who read it, it is **material by its nature**.

2.3 When considering earnings per share, the auditor must consider **two issues**:

- Whether it been disclosed on a comparable basis to the prior year, and have any changes in accounting policy been disclosed in accordance with FRS 18, and
- Whether it has been calculated correctly.

2.4 The audit procedures are as follows:

> - Obtain a copy of the client's workings for earnings per share. (If a simple calculation has been used, this can be checked by re-doing the fraction on the face of the profit and loss account.)
> - Compare the calculation with the prior year calculation to ensure that the basis is comparable

- Discuss the basis with the directors if it has changed to ascertain if it is the best basis for the accounts this year and whether the change has been adequately disclosed
- Recalculate to ensure that it is correct.

3 DISCONTINUED OPERATIONS

3.1 Discontinued operations are accounted for under FRS 3. The FRS requires that discontinued operations are disclosed separately on the face of the balance sheet. This may well be material for the following reasons:

- Potentially material through **size**
- May be **inherently material** if the change in operations is a sign of management policy or a major change in focus of operations

3.2 Essentially, the fact that some operations have been discontinued is of interest to shareholders, which is why the FRS 3 disclosures came about. The auditor must be aware of the implications of FRS 3 for the financial statements at all stages of the audit:

(a) At the **planning stage**, if the auditor is aware of an operation being discontinued in the year or in the following period.

(b) While he is doing his **substantive testing**, he must be aware if evidence points to the fact that operations have been discontinued

(c) The issue of discontinued operations is important at the **review stage** of the audit in terms of:

- **Subsequent events** (disclosure requirements of FRS 3 extend beyond the balance sheet date)
- **Going concern** (the discontinued operations may cast doubt on the ability of the company to continue in the foreseeable future)
- Review of financial statements (the auditor needs to be satisfied that the correct **disclosures** have been made)

3.3 To audit whether the disclosures have been made correctly, the auditor should undertake the following procedures:

- Discuss the disclosure with management, to ensure that FRS 3 has been correctly applied.
- Review board minutes and any relevant correspondence to ascertain details of the operation being discontinued.
- Obtain a copy of the client's workings to disclose the discontinued operations.
- Review the workings to ensure that the figures are reasonable and agree to the financial statements.
- Trace a sample of items disclosed as discontinuing items to backing documentation (invoices) to ensure that they do related to discontinued operations.

4 CASHFLOW STATEMENTS

4.1 Cash flows are accounted for under the provisions of FRS 1. The cash flow statement is essentially a reconciliation exercise between items on the profit and loss account (operating profit) and the balance sheet (cash).

4.2 As such, the **cash flow statement is often audited by the auditor reproducing it from the audited figures in the other financial statements.** This can be done quickly and easily in the modern era by use of computer programmes.

4.3 However, if the auditor wished to audit it another way, he could check and recalculate each reconciliation with the financial statements. This would involve checking each line of the statement by working through the client's workings and agreeing items to the accounting records and backing documentation (for example, tax paid to the bank statements) and the other financial statements.

Question 1

Why is the cash flow statement relevant to the auditors?

Answer

Report on the cash flow statement

The cash flow statement is not specified in the audit report, but the auditors are in effect reporting on it because financial reports are obliged to include a cash flow statement under FRS 1 in order to show a true and fair view. The auditors must therefore assess the truth and fairness of the cash flow statement as required by the revised FRS 1.

Analytical review

The information in the cash flow statement will be used by the auditors as part of their analytical review of the accounts, for example, by adding further information on liquidity. This will be particularly helpful when comparing the statement to previous periods.

Going concern

The cash flow statement may indicate going concern problems due to liquidity failings, overtrading and overgearing. However, the statement is an historical document, prepared well after the year end, and is therefore unlikely to be the first indicator of such difficulties.

Audit evidence

The auditors will obtain very little direct audit evidence from the cash flow statement. It has been prepared by the company (not the auditors or an independent third party) from records which are under scrutiny by the auditors in any case. Thus the auditors will already have most of this information, although in different format.

However, the cash flow statement should provide additional evidence for figures in the accounts, for example, the purchase or sale of tangible fixed assets. Consistency of evidence will be important and complementary evidence is always welcome.

5 REVENUE RECOGNITION

5.1 We mentioned an important example of revenue recognition earlier, and that was as part of long-term contracts. When assessing what income to recognise from a long term contract, the person accounting for them should bear in mind the provisions of FRS 5.

5.2 As you are aware, FRS 5 deals with the substance of transactions and thus revenue recognition falls within its specification. Revenue recognition is an issue that is pervasive to financial statements, so is something that the auditor should be aware of when conducting his audit rather than to seek to audit it of itself.

5.3 Turnover (or revenue), is commonly audited by analytical review. This is because turnover should be predicable and there are good bases on which to base analytical review, such as:

- Plenty of information, for example, last year's accounts, budget, monthly analyses (companies tend to keep a lot of information about sales)
- Logical relationships with items such as stock and debtors

5.4 Unless complex transactions arise where revenue is not as clear cut as a product being supplied and invoiced for, revenue recognition is generally not an issue. However, in some companies, for example, those that deal primarily in long term contracts, revenue recognition can be a **material** issue. Examples of industries where this might be true:

- Building industry
- Engineering industry
- Long term service industries, for example caterers with yearly contracts

5.5 In such industries, auditing revenue recognition will be similar to auditing long-term contracts. The auditor should

- Consider whether the basis for recognition is reasonable
- Agree turnover recognised to relevant documents (for example, work certificates or contracts)

Question 2

The senior partner of JLPN, a firm of auditors, has issued as 'Audit Risk Alert' letter to all partners dealing with key areas of concern which should be given due consideration by his firm when auditing public companies. The letter outlines certain trends in audit reporting that, if not scrutinised by the auditors, could lead to a loss of reliability and transparency in the financial statements. The following three key concerns were outlined in the letter.

(a) Audit committees play a very important role together with the financial director and auditor in achieving high quality financial control and auditing. Recently the efforts of certain audit committees have been questioned in the press.

(b) The Stock Exchange had reported cases of inappropriate revenue recognition practises including:

 (i) Accelerating revenue prior to the delivery of the product to the customer's site, or prior to the completion of the terms of the sales arrangement

 (ii) Recognition of revenue when customers have unilateral cancellation or termination provisions, other than the normal customary product return provisions

(c) It has been reported that the management of companies had intentionally violated UK Generally Accepted Accounting Practice by immaterial amounts. The reason for this has been the sensitivity of reported earnings per share in a market place where missing the market's expectation of earnings per share by a small amount could have significant consequences.

Required

(a) Explain the importance if the role of an 'Audit Risk Alert' letter to a firm of auditors.

(b) Discuss the way in which the auditor should deal with each of the key concerns outlined in the letter in order to ensure that audit risk is kept to an acceptable level.

Answer

(a) The '**risk alert letter**' is a memorandum used by the reporting partner to notify fellow partners of concerns emerging from dealings with clients, regulatory authorities or the Stock Exchange. It ensures that:

- Key audit risk areas are reviewed
- Significant trends and irregularities are identified
- Quality is maintained
- Litigation risk is reduced
- Investor confidence is maintained as it reduces manipulation

(b) (i) **Audit Committees** are held to secure good a quality of **internal control** and financial reporting in plc's. If the auditor has doubts about the effectiveness of an audit committee then he should **review its structure, independence and membership** to ensure it meets its objectives. Any shortcomings should be reported to the board and/or the members.

(ii) **Revenue acceleration** is a **creative accounting device**. Revenue should **not** be **recognised until earned and realised** (realisable), so the practices described are not acceptable. Only if the risks of ownership have fully transferred to the buyer and the seller has not retained any specific performance obligation should revenue be recognised earlier.

Extended audit tests concerning revenue recognition and 'cut off' tests may be appropriate if the auditor suspects anomalies.

(iii) Where **intentional GAAP violations** have occurred, **materiality judgement** may be affected. The auditor must ensure the audit team is aware that violations of GAAP **can affect EPS** for certain clients, and that staff are sufficiently experienced and trained in order to detect such violations. It may be that the errors are individually immaterial, but the **aggregate effect** must be considered. Furthermore, the practice of intentional misstatements may indicate that the **management** of the company **lacks integrity** and the auditor should consider whether the client should be retained.

6 BORROWING COSTS

6.1 FRS 4 gives guidance on how to account for capital instruments. 'Capital instruments' includes debt, so it also gives guidance on how to account for borrowing costs.

FRS 4

The **finance cost** of debt is the difference between the total payments required to be made and the initial carrying value of the debt (that is the interest cost or the dividends plus any premium payable on redemption or other payments).

The carrying amount of debt should be increased by the finance cost in respect of the reporting period **and reduced by payments made in respect of the debt** in that period.

6.2 Payments made in the period will consist of interest and may include an element of capital repayment. Generally, there is unlikely to be a material difference between the way that the lender allocates the finance cost and the way that the entity should allocate it under FRS 4.

6.3 If there is no **material** difference, borrowing costs are simple to audit. The **cost of borrowing is interest,** which is disclosed in the profit and loss account.

6.4 Interest can often be audited by **analytical review,** as it has a predicable relationship with loans (for example, bank loans or debentures).

6.5 Alternatively it can be **verified to payment records** (bank statements) **and loan agreement** documents.

6.6 However, if borrowing costs are so substantial that there is likely to be a material difference between the methods, the auditor should carry out the following procedures:

- Obtain the client workings in relation to borrowing costs
- Review them to ensure the method of allocation is in accordance with FRS 4
- Agree relevant figures to accounting information or the financial statements
- Agree figures in respect of interest payments made to statements from lender and/or bank statements

7 GOVERNMENT GRANTS AND ASSISTANCE

7.1 Government grants and assistance are accounted for under SSAP 4. They may be either revenue or capital grants.

7.2 **Revenue grants** offer no difficulties to account for or to audit. To audit them, the auditor should:

- Obtain documentation relating to the grant and ensure that it should be classified as revenue
- The value may be agreed to the same documentation (for example, a letter outlining the details of the grant, or a copy of an application form sent by the client)
- The receipt of the grant can be agreed to bank statements

7.3 **Capital grants** can be more difficult to account for. This can raise auditing issues as well.

SSAP 4

Capital grants are cash grants to cover a proportion of the costs of certain items of capital expenditure (for example buildings, plant and machinery).

Grants relating to fixed assets should be credited to revenue over the expected useful life of the assets and this can be done in one of two ways:

(a) **By reducing the acquisition cost of the fixed asset** by the amount of the grant, and providing depreciation on the reduced amount.

(b) By **treating** the amount of the grant **as a deferred credit and transferring a portion of it to revenue** annually.

7.4 Audit procedures:

- Consider whether the basis of accounting is comparable to the previous year.
- Discuss the basis of accounting with the directors to ensure that the method used is the best method
- Ensure that any changes in accounting method are disclosed.
- If method (a) above is used, no further audit work is necessary
- If method (b) is used, the transfer to revenue should be audited, if material. The methods used to audit this would be as for depreciation.

Chapter roundup

- The auditor should review a client's workings for segmental information under SSAP 25 for reasonableness. Information may be vouched to backing documentation such as invoices.
- EPS is material in that it is of interest to readers. The auditor must ensure that it has been calculated properly, and on a comparable basis to previous years.
- Discontinued operations may be material due to their size or nature. The auditor should consider them
  - At the planning stage
  - During substantive testing
  - At the review stage (going concern/subsequent events)
- Evidence concerning discontinued operations is likely to primarily be found in board minutes and correspondence (for example, with solicitors).
- Cash flow statements should be consistent with information given in the rest of the financial statements. They may provide the auditors with useful analytical evidence.
- Revenue recognition can be a material issue if the entity undertakes complex transactions.
- Accounting for borrowing costs under FRS 4 can be complex. The auditor should review the client's workings.
- Capital grants may be an issue for auditors. They should consider whether the basis of capitalisation is comparable to previous years. Any transfers should be audited in a similar way to depreciation.

Quick quiz

1 Link the disclosure issue with the accounting guidance

(a)	Segmental information	(i)	FRS 5
(b)	EPS	(ii)	SSAP 25
(c)	Discontinued operations	(iii)	FRS 3
(d)	Revenue recognition	(iv)	FRS 14

2 Why is EPS disclosure likely to be material?

3 Which of the following is not a reason why turnover is often audited by analytical review?

(1) Availability of good, comparable evidence
(2) Profit and loss account is not as important as balance sheet
(3) It is quicker than detailed substantive testing
(4) Turnover has logical relationships with other items in the financial statements

4 Which of the following audit procedures relate to capital grants and which to revenue grants?

- Obtain relating documentation and ensure classification is correct.
- Agree value receipt of grant to:
  - Documentation (above)
  - Bank Statements
- Consider reasonableness of transfers to revenue
- Ensure capitalisation method is comparable

5 Auditors do not report on the cash flow statement (only the balance sheet and profit and loss as recorded in the opinion section of the report).

True ☐

False ☐

Answers to quick quiz

1 (a)(ii), (b)(iv), (c)(iii), (d)(i).

2 It is of interest to the key readers of accounts – the shareholders.

3 (2) The profit and loss account **is just as important.** However, (3) **is true,** because it is cost effective to use analytical review as a substantive procedure where good evidence is available.

4
- Obtain relating documentation and ensure classification is correct. C/R
- Agree value receipt of grant to: C/R
  - documentation (above)
  - bank statements
- Consider reasonableness of transfers to revenue C
- Ensure capitalisation method is comparable C

5 False

Now try the question below from the Exam Question Bank

Number	Level	Marks	Time
13	Exam	15	27 mins

Chapter 14

GROUP AUDITS

Introduction

This is a new auditing topic for you, one which is concerned with practical difficulties of communication between auditors and the problems of geography.

In auditing group accounts, as in so many other areas, the auditors require detailed accounting knowledge in order to fulfil their responsibilities. Your studies in financial accounting should have made you familiar with the extensive statutory and professional requirements governing the preparation of group accounts.

Study guide

Section 16

- Identify the specific matters to be considered before accepting appointment as principal auditor to a group
- Explain the organisation, planning, management and administration issues specific to group and joint audits
- Identify the specific audit problems and describe audit procedures in relation to:
  - The correct classification of investments
  - Acquisitions and disposals
  - Related party transactions
  - Inter-company balances
  - Goodwill on consolidation
  - Enterprises in developing countries
- Discuss support letters as audit evidence
- Describe the matters to be considered and the procedures to be performed when a principal auditor uses the work of another auditor
- Explain the implications for the auditors' report on a financial statements of an entity where the opinion on a component is qualified.

Exam guide

Planning associated with a group audit was examined on the pilot paper.

1 GROUP ACCOUNTING AND THE HOLDING COMPANY AUDITORS

Knowledge brought forward from Paper 2.6

FRS 2 *Accounting for subsidiaries.*

FRS 6 *Acquisitions and mergers*

FRS 7 *Fair values in acquisition accounting*

FRS 9 *Associates and joint ventures*

Companies Act 1989 provisions relating to groups

KEY TERMS

Principal auditors are the auditors with responsibility for reporting on the financial statements of an entity when those financial statements include financial information of one or more components audited by other auditors.

Other auditors are auditors, other than the principal auditors, with responsibility for reporting on the financial information of a component which is included in the financial statements audited by the principal auditors. Other auditors include affiliated firms, whether using the same name or not, and correspondent firms, as well as unrelated auditors.

Component is a division, branch, subsidiary, joint venture, associated undertaking or other entity whose financial information is included in financial statements audited by the principal auditors.

Responsibility of principal auditors

1.1 The duty of the principal auditors is:

> 'To report on whether in their opinion the group accounts give a true and fair view of the state of affairs as at the end of the year, and the profit and loss for the year, of the undertakings included in the consolidation as a whole, so far as concerns members of the company' (s 235 Companies Act 1985).

1.2 The principal auditors have **sole responsibility** for this opinion even where the group financial statements include amounts derived from accounts which have not been audited by them. As a result, they cannot discharge their responsibility to report on the group financial statements by an unquestioning acceptance of component companies' financial statements, whether audited or not.

Rights of principal auditors

1.3 The principal auditors have all the statutory rights and powers in respect of their audit of the holding company that we identified in the context of the audit of non-group companies in earlier chapters (for example right of access at all times to the holding company's books, accounts and vouchers).

1.4 The principal auditors also have the following rights:

(a) The **right to require from the other auditors** of a UK-incorporated company such **information and explanations** as they may reasonably require (s 389A(3) CA 1985)

(b) The right to **require the parent company** to take all reasonable steps to **obtain reasonable information** and explanations from the subsidiary and this will include foreign subsidiaries (s 389A(4) CA 1985)

1.5 Even where their responsibilities in this regard are not set down by statute (for example where the component company is an associated company not a subsidiary), the other auditors should appreciate that the component company's financial statements will ultimately form a part of the group financial statements. In principle, the other auditors should therefore be prepared to **co-operate** with the **principal auditors** and make available such information as the principal auditors may require.

2 PRINCIPAL AUDITORS AND OTHER AUDITORS

2.1 The principal auditors must decide how to take account of the work carried out by the other auditors.

2.2 The APB has produced an auditing standard on this subject: SAS 510 *The relationship between principal auditors and other auditors.*

SAS 510.1

When using the work of other auditors, principal auditors should determine how that work will affect their audit.

Acceptance as principal auditors

SAS 510.2

Auditors should consider whether their own participation is sufficient to enable them to act as principal auditors.

2.3 The principal auditors should not be so far removed from large parts of the group audit that they are unable to form an opinion. The SAS suggests that, in this context, the principal auditors should consider the following.

- The **materiality** of the portion of the financial statement which they do not audit
- The **degree of their knowledge** regarding the business of the components
- The **nature of their relationship** with the firms acting as other auditors
- Their **ability** where necessary to **perform additional procedures** to enable them to act as principal auditors
- The **risk of material misstatements** in the financial statements of the components audited by other auditors

Exam focus point

In addition to these points, the prospective auditor should also consider the general points relating to acceptance of appointment discussed in Chapter 2.

Principal auditors' procedures

> **SAS 510.3**
>
> When planning to use the work of other auditors, principal auditors should consider the professional qualifications, experience and resources of the other auditors in the context of the specific assignment.

2.4 The initial enquires of this nature will be concerned with:

- The other auditors' **membership of a professional body**
- The **reputation** of any firm to which the other auditors are affiliated. A review of the previous audit work by the other auditor may be required

> **SAS 510.4**
>
> Principal auditors should obtain sufficient appropriate audit evidence that the work of the other auditors is adequate for the principal auditors' purposes.

2.5 In order to obtain such evidence at the planning stage, the principal auditors should advise the other auditors of the use they intend to make of their work and make arrangement for the co-ordination of their audit efforts. The principal auditors will inform the other auditors about the following matters.

- **Areas** requiring **special consideration** (key risks, control environment)
- Procedures for the **identification** of **discloseable inter-entity transactions**
- Procedures for notifying principal auditors of **unusual circumstances**
- The **timetable** for completion of the audit
- The **independence requirements**
- The **relevant accounting, auditing** and **reporting requirements**

2.6 The nature, timing and extent of the principal auditors' procedures will depend on the individual circumstances of the engagement, and their assessment of the other auditors. Factors that may be taken into account include the following.

- **Assessment** of other auditors
- **Risks**
- **Materiality** of components
- **Relationships** with the client

2.7 Procedures that the principal auditors may use include the following.

- **Discussions** with the other auditors about their audit procedures
- **Review** of a **written summary** of those procedures (perhaps using a questionnaire)
- **Review** of the other auditors' **working papers**

2.8 These procedures may be considered unnecessary if evidence has already been obtained of adequate quality control over the other auditors' work.

2.9 Having received the agreed work, documentation etc from the other auditors:

> **SAS 510.5**
>
> The principal auditors should consider the significant findings of the other auditors.

2.10 This consideration may involve:

- **Discussions** with the other auditors and with the directors or management
- **Review** of copies of **reports** to **directors** or **management** issued by the other auditors
- **Supplementary tests,** performed by the principal auditors or by the other auditors

Co-operation between auditors

> **SAS 510.6**
>
> Other auditors, knowing the context in which the principal auditors intend to use their work, should co-operate with and assist the principal auditors.

Information supplied by other auditors

2.11 Where the component is a subsidiary the other auditors will have a **statutory** duty to co-operate as mentioned in Section 1 above.

2.12 If there is no such statutory obligation, but the principal auditors state their intention to use the other auditors' work, then the other auditors may need to obtain permission from the component to communicate with the principal auditors on the auditing matters.

2.13 Where this permission is refused, the other auditors should inform the principal auditors of the refusal, so that the principal auditors can agree with the directors of the entity they audit what action to take.

2.14 The other auditors should draw to the attention of the principal auditors any matters they discover in their audit which they feel is likely to be relevant to the principal auditors' work.

2.15 If the other auditors are unable to perform any aspect of their work as requested, they should inform the principal auditors.

Information supplied by principal auditors

2.16 The other auditors have sole responsibility for their audit opinion on the financial statements of the component they audit. They should **not** rely on the principal auditors informing them of matters which might have an impact on the financial statements of the component. If they wish to do so, they should seek representations directly from the directors or management of the entity audited by the principal auditors.

2.17 The principal auditors have no obligation, statutory or otherwise, to provide information to other auditors. Where during the course of their audit, they discover matters which they consider may be relevant to the other auditors' work, they should discuss and agree an appropriate course of action with the directors of the entity which they audit. This may involve the principal auditors communicating directly with the other auditors, or the directors informing the component or the other auditors.

2.18 If the circumstances are such that the information cannot be passed to the other auditors, for example due to sensitive commercial considerations, the principal auditors should take **no further action**. To divulge such information in these situations would be a breach of client confidentiality.

Other aspects of the audit requiring consideration in a group context

Support letters

2.19 It is sometimes the case that a subsidiary, when considered in isolation, does not appear to be a going concern. In the context of group accounts, the parent and the subsidiary are seen to be a complete entity, so if the group as a whole is a going concern, that is sufficient.

2.20 When auditing the incorporation of the single company into the group accounts however, the audit will need assurance that the subsidiary is a going concern.

2.21 In such a case, the auditor may request a 'support letter' from the director of the parent company. This letter states that the intention of the parent is to continue to support the subsidiary, which makes it a going concern. A support letter is sufficient, appropriate audit evidence on this issue.

Developing countries

2.22 Consolidating a subsidiary from a developing country may be a problem for a UK company, as the basis of preparation of the subsidiary's accounts may be so different to UK GAAP that the principal auditor will not be able to conclude that the accounts show a true and fair view.

2.23 This is only a problem if the accounts, or the differences caused by the basis of preparation are **material to the group.**

2.24 The problem can be averted by asking the directors to restate the accounts under UK GAAP. The principal auditors might require that this restatement process is audited to ensure it is accurate.

2.25 Increased inernationalisation of accounting practice is **reducing the risk** of this problem arising.

Control environment and systems

2.26 Assessment of the control environment and systems in accordance with SAS 300 *Accounting and internal control systems and audit risk assessments* will include assessment of the overall group control environment. Factors to consider include:

- Organisational structure of the group
- Level of involvement of the parent company in components
- Degree of autonomy of management of components
- Supervision of components' management by parent company
- Information systems, and information received centrally on a regular basis
- Role of internal audit in review of components

Reports to directors or management

2.27 When reporting to management in a group situation, SAS 610 *Reports to directors or management* states that the directors or management of the parent undertaking of a group of companies may wish to be informed of significant points arising in the reports to the directors or management to its subsidiary undertakings.

2.28 In these circumstances, **permission** is **required** from the directors or management of the subsidiary undertakings to disclose the contents of any reports to directors or management of the parent undertaking or the principal auditors.

Question 1

You are the main auditor of Mouldings Holdings plc, which has subsidiaries in the UK and overseas, many of which are audited by other firms. All subsidiaries are involved in the manufacture or distribution of plastic goods and have accounting periods coterminous with that of the holding company.

You are required to state why you would wish to review the work of the auditors of the subsidiaries not audited by you and to detail the work you would wish to carry out in performing such a review.

Answer

(a) Reasons for reviewing the work of other auditors

The main consideration which concerns the audit of all group accounts is that the holding company's auditors (the 'principal' auditors) are responsible to the members of that company for the audit opinion on the whole of the group accounts.

It may be stated (in the notes to the financial statements) that the financial statements of certain subsidiaries have been audited by other firms, but this does not absolve the principal auditors from any of their responsibilities.

These responsibilities are imposed by statute. S 235 (2) Companies Act 1985 requires the auditors of a holding company to report to its members on the truth and fairness of the view given by the financial statements of the company and its subsidiaries dealt with in the group accounts. Furthermore, the Act provides the principal auditors with powers (389A) to obtain such information and explanations as they reasonably require from the subsidiary companies and their auditors, or from the parent company in the case of overseas subsidiaries, in order that they can discharge their responsibilities as holding company auditors.

The auditing standard SAS 510 The relationship between principal auditors and other auditors clarifies how the principal auditors can carry out a review of the audits of subsidiaries in order to satisfy themselves that, with the inclusion of figures not audited by themselves, the group accounts give a true and fair view.

The scope, standard and independence of the work carried out by the auditors of subsidiary companies (the 'other' auditors) are the most important matters which need to be examined by the principal auditors before relying on financial statements not audited by them. The principal auditors need to be satisfied that all material areas of the financial statements of subsidiaries have been audited satisfactorily and in a manner compatible with that of the principal auditors themselves.

(b) Work to be carried out by principal auditors in reviewing the other auditors' work

(i) Send a questionnaire to all other auditors requesting detailed information on their work, including:

(1) An explanation of their general approach (in order to make an assessment of the standards of their work)

(2) Details of the accounting policies of major subsidiaries (to ensure that these are compatible within the group)

(3) The other auditors' opinion of the subsidiaries' overall level of internal control, and the reliability of their accounting records

(4) Any limitations placed on the scope of the auditors' work

(5) Any qualifications, and the reasons for them, made or likely to be made to their audit reports

(ii) Carry out a detailed review of the other auditors' working papers on each subsidiary whose results materially affect the view given by the group financial statements. This review will enable the principal auditors to ascertain whether (*inter alia*):

(1) An up to date permanent file exists with details of the nature of the subsidiary's business, its staff organisation, its accounting records, previous year's financial statements and copies of important legal documents.

(2) The systems examination has been properly completed, documented and reported on to management after discussion.

(3) Tests of controls and substantive procedures have been properly and appropriately carried out, and audit programmes properly completed and signed.

(4) All other working papers are comprehensive and explicit.

(5) The overall review of the financial statements has been adequately carried out, and adequate use of analytical procedures has been undertaken throughout the audit.

(6) The financial statements agree in all respects with the accounting records and comply with all relevant legal requirements and accounting standards.

(7) Minutes of board and general meetings have been scrutinised and important matters noted.

(8) The audit work has been carried out in accordance with approved auditing standards.

(9) The financial statements agree in all respects with the accounting records and comply with all relevant legal and professional requirements.

(10) The audit work has been properly reviewed within the firm of auditors and any laid-down quality control procedures adhered to.

(11) Any points requiring discussion with the holding company's management have been noted and brought to the principal auditors' attention (including any matters which might warrant a qualification in the audit report on the subsidiary company's financial statements).

(12) Adequate audit evidence has been obtained to form a basis for the audit opinion on both the subsidiaries' financial statements and those of the group.

If the principal auditors are not satisfied as a result of the above review, they should arrange for further audit work to be carried out either by the other auditors on their behalf, or jointly with them. The other auditors are fully responsible for their own work; any additional tests are those required for the purpose of the audit of the group financial statements.

---

3 THE CONSOLIDATION

3.1 After receiving and reviewing all the subsidiaries' (and associates') accounts, the principal auditors will be in a position to audit the consolidated accounts.

3.2 An important part of the work on the consolidation will be checking the consolidation adjustments. Consolidation adjustments generally fall into two categories:

- **Permanent consolidation adjustments**
- **Consolidation adjustments** for the **current year**

3.3 The audit steps involved in the consolidation process may be summarised as follows.

Step 1. Check the **transposition** from the audited accounts of each subsidiary/associate to the consolidation schedules

Step 2. Check that adjustments made on consolidation are appropriate and comparable with the previous year. This will involve:

- **Recording** the **dates** and **costs** of **acquisitions** of subsidiaries and the assets acquired
- **Calculating goodwill** and **pre-acquisition reserves** arising on consolidation
- **Preparing** an overall **reconciliation** of movements on reserves and minority interests

Step 3. Check for acquisitions:

- Whether **acquisition** or **merger accounting** has been **appropriately used**
- The **appropriateness** of the **date** used as the date for acquisition
- The **treatment** of the **results** of **investments** acquired during the year
- If acquisition accounting has been used, that the **fair value** of acquired **assets** and **liabilities** is reasonable (to ascertainable market value by use of an expert)
- **Goodwill** has been **calculated correctly** and if amortised, period of amortisation is reasonable

Step 4. Check for disposals:

- The **appropriateness** of the **date** used as the date for disposal. This can be agreed to sales documentation
- Whether the **results** of the **investment** have been **included** up to the date of disposal, and whether figures used are reasonable

(Audited figures may not be available, and management accounts may have to be used).

Step 5. **Consider** whether **previous treatment** of **existing subsidiaries** or **associates** is still **correct** (consider level of influence, degree of support)

Step 6. Verify the **arithmetical accuracy** of the consolidation workings

Step 7. **Review** the **consolidated accounts** for **compliance** with the Companies Act 1985, SSAPs, FRSs and other relevant regulations. Care will need to be taken where:

- Group companies do not have coterminous accounting periods.
- Subsidiaries are not consolidated.
- Accounting policies of group members differ because foreign subsidiaries operate under different rules.

Other important areas include:

- Treatment of participating interests and associates
- Treatment of goodwill and intangible assets
- Foreign currency translation
- Treatment of loss-making subsidiaries
- Treatment of restrictions on distribution of profits of a subsidiary

Step 8. **Review** the **consolidated accounts** to confirm that they give a true and fair view in the circumstance

3.4 The audit of related party transactions was considered in Chapter 9. Remember that when auditing a consolidation, the relevant related parties are those related to the **consolidated**

group. Transactions with consolidated subsidiaries need **not** be disclosed, as they are incorporated in the financial statements

3.5 The principal auditors are often requested to carry out the consolidation work even where the accounts of the subsidiaries have been prepared by the client. In these circumstances the auditors are of course acting as accountants **and** auditors and care must be taken to ensure that the **audit** function is carried out and evidenced.

Question 2

Your firm is the auditor of Beeston Industries plc, which has a number of UK subsidiaries (and no overseas subsidiaries), some of which are audited by other firms of professional accountants. You have been asked to consider the work which should be carried out to ensure that inter-company transactions and balances are correctly treated in the group accounts.

Required

(a) List and briefly describe the audit work you would perform to check that inter-company balances agree, and to state why inter-company balances should agree, and the consequences of them not agreeing.

(b) List and briefly describe the audit work you would perform to verify that inter-company profit in stock has been correctly accounted for in the group accounts.

Answer

(a) Inter-company balances should agree because, in the preparation of consolidated accounts, it is necessary to cancel them out. If they do not cancel out then the group accounts will be displaying an item which has no value outside of the group and profits may be correspondingly under or over-stated. The audit work required to check that inter-company balances agree would be as follows.

(i) Obtain and review a copy of the holding company's instructions to all group members relating to the procedures for reconciliation and agreement of year end inter-company balances. Particular attention should be paid to the treatment of 'in transit' items to ensure that there is a proper cut-off.

(ii) Obtain a schedule of inter-company balances from all group companies and check the details therein to the summary prepared by the holding company. The details on these schedules should also be independently confirmed in writing by the other auditors involved.

(iii) Confirmation of nil balances should also be confirmed by both the group companies concerned and their respective auditors.

(iv) The details on the schedules in (iii) above should also be agreed to the details in the financial statements of the individual group companies which are submitted to the holding company for consolidation purposes.

(b) Where one company in a group supplies goods to another company at cost plus a percentage, and such goods remain in stock at the year end, then the group stocks will contain an element of unrealised profit. In the preparation of the group accounts, best accounting practice requires that a provision should be made for this unrealised profit.

In order to verify that inter-company profit in stock has been correctly accounted for in the group accounts, the audit work required would be as follows.

(i) Confirm the group's procedures for identification of such stocks and their notification to the parent company who will be responsible for making the required provision.

(ii) Obtain and review schedules of inter-group stock from group companies and confirm that the same categories of stock have been included as in previous years.

(iii) Select a sample of invoices for goods purchased from group companies and check to see that as necessary these have been included in year end inter-group stock and obtain confirmation from other auditors that they have satisfactorily completed a similar exercise.

(iv) Check the calculation of the provision for unrealised profit and confirm that this has been arrived at on a consistent basis with that used in earlier years, after making due allowance for any known changes in the profit margins operated by various group companies.

(v) Check the schedules of inter-group stock against the various stock sheets and consider whether the level of inter-group stock appears to be reasonable in comparison with previous years, ensuring that satisfactory explanations are obtained for any material differences.

---

4 REPORTING ON GROUP ACCOUNTS

4.1 The principal auditors should **not** ordinarily refer in their report to the name of any other auditors, or to the fact that other companies have been audited by other auditors. The principal auditors cannot delegate the responsibility for their opinion; any such reference might mislead the reader into believing otherwise.

4.2 If the principal auditors form an unqualified opinion on the group accounts, the report wording and presentation would be as shown in Chapter 19 but would vary in referring to a group rather than a company. Such a report would be appropriate irrespective of whether the principal auditors are also auditors of all or any of the subsidiary and associated companies within the group.

4.3 In the event of any **restriction in the scope of their audit** of the group financial statements, including inability to obtain evidence about the work of other auditors, the principal auditors should consider **qualifying their report**.

4.4 The reports of other auditors on the component's financial statements may contain a qualified opinion or an explanatory paragraph referring to an uncertainty. In such cases the principal auditors should consider whether the subject of the qualification or fundamental uncertainty is of **such nature and significance**, in relation to the financial statements of the entity on which they are reporting, that it should be reflected in their audit report.

5 JOINT AUDITS

5.1 The relationship between principal and other auditors discussed in the previous sections is **not** the same as that between the auditors involved in a joint audit.

5.2 A joint audit can be defined as one 'where two or more auditors are responsible for an audit engagement and jointly produce an audit report to the client'.

Reasons for joint audits

5.3 Two or more firms of accountants could act as joint auditors for a number of reasons.

(a) **Takeover**. The holding company may insist that their auditors act jointly with those of the new subsidiary.

(b) **Locational problems**. A company operating from widely dispersed locations may find it convenient to have joint auditors.

(c) **Political problems**. Overseas subsidiaries may need to employ local auditors to satisfy the laws of the country in which they operate. It is sometimes found that these local auditors act jointly with those of the holding company.

(d) Companies preferring to use **local accountants**, while at the same time enjoying the wider range of services provided by a large national firm.

5.4 There are several practical points that must be borne in mind before accepting a joint audit. In particular it will be necessary to assess the **experience** and **standards** of the other firm by looking at the audit techniques used, by scrutinising their working papers and establishing whether they have had experience in similar jobs.

5.5 Joint audits are not mentioned by the new SAS on engagement letters, but the old operational guideline *Engagement letters* advised that, where there are joint auditors, the audit engagement should be explained in similar terms by each set of auditors.

5.6 Once a joint position has been accepted the **programme** to be adopted and the **split** of the **detailed work** will have to be discussed.

5.7 One of the major criticisms of joint audits is that they may be expensive. This is probably true, but if the two firms have organised the work between them properly the difference should be minimal. Furthermore, an increase in the fees may be justified by improved services not least because the two firms of accountants are likely to work as efficiently as possible from a sense of professional pride.

5.8 Both firms must sign the audit report and both are responsible for the whole audit whether or not they carried out a particular area of the audit programme. It follows that both firms will be **jointly liable** in the event of litigation.

6 AUDITING FOREIGN SUBSIDIARIES

6.1 When a UK auditing firm has a UK client which owns overseas subsidiaries, the UK client may:

- Choose to have the foreign subsidiaries audited by local firms (as has been assumed in Sections 1 to 4 above)
- Request that the UK auditors undertake the audit of the foreign subsidiaries

6.2 Even when the UK auditors are a large firm, and local offices audit the foreign subsidiaries, the 'principal' auditors at the client's UK head office often undertake an audit visit to a major foreign subsidiary each year. This is particularly the case with world-wide clients, such as major airlines.

6.3 A summary of the difficulties and possible solutions involved in auditing foreign subsidiaries would include the following.

Language difficulties might be overcome by finding a member of the UK office who speaks the relevant language, or a translator.
Cultural differences should be tackled by the UK auditors learning as much as possible about the country before leaving the UK.
Differences in local accounting and auditing conventions, as well as legislation, can again be tackled by study before the audit begins (as discussed in Section 2).
Some countries may have very **specific problems,** including civil unrest, high inflation or hyper inflation, currency restrictions and so on. The auditors will need to consider how such issues should be tackled in the audit (as well as the eventual consolidation).
The auditors may face difficulties obtaining the necessary **permit to work** or even enter the country in question. The client company should help the auditors as much as possible in this respect.

> The auditors must ensure that they have **sufficient support** in their base office in the UK to help them if any difficulty arises.

6.4 Audit firms may also have an international network (as discussed in Chapter 4) and may be able to use an affiliated partnership to audit the foreign subsidiary.

Chapter roundup

- Principal company auditors have a duty to report on the truth and fairness of group accounts. They have the right to require from auditors of subsidiaries the **information** and **explanations** they require, and to require the principal company to obtain the necessary **information** and **explanations** from subsidiaries.
- Principal auditors should consider whether their **involvement** in the group audit is **sufficient** for them to act as principal auditors.
- The reliance placed on other auditors will depend on a variety of factors.
  - **Assessment** of the other firms' **independence** and **competence**
  - **Reviews** of other firms' work
- Consolidation procedures include:
  - Checking **consolidation adjustments** have been correctly made
  - Checking **treatment of additions and disposals** has been correct
  - **Arithmetical** checks
- Auditing a **foreign subsidiary** can pose practical problems for auditors. An appreciation of the features of doing business and auditing in the country concerned is vital.

Quick quiz

1 Match the auditors with the correct definition.

(a) Principal auditors

(b) Other auditors

(i) The auditors with responsibility for reporting on the financial statements of an entity when those financial statements include financial information of one or more components by others.

(ii) Auditors with responsibility for reporting on the financial information of a component which is included in the financial statements audited by another firm. This includes affiliated firms, whether using the same name or not, and correspondent firms, as well as unrelated auditors.

2 List three rights of principal auditors

(1) ____________________

(2) ____________________

(3) ____________________

3 Complete the matters which the principal auditors must consider in relation to a group audit.

- The ____________________ of the portion of the financial statements which they do no audit.
- The ________________ ____ ____________ ____________ regarding the business of the component.
- The ______________ of their __________________ with the other auditors.
- Their ability, where necessary, to__________________ __________________ ________________.

- The risk of ______________ ______________ in the financial statements not audited by them.

4 Name four factors the principal auditors should take into account when planning the nature, timing and extent of their procedures.

(1) ______________

(2) ______________

(3) ______________

(4) ______________

5 What is a support letter?

6 List the eight steps involved in auditing a consolidation.

(1) ______________

(2) ______________

(3) ______________

(4) ______________

(5) ______________

(6) ______________

(7) ______________

(8) ______________

7 If two firms undertake a joint audit, they shall be jointly liable in the event of litigation.

True ☐

False ☐

8 Name four difficulties which might arise from the audit of a foreign subsidiary.

(1) ______________

(2) ______________

(3) ______________

(4) ______________

Answers to quick quiz

1 (a)(i), (b)(ii)

2 (1) Statutory rights and duties in relation to audit of holding company

(2) Right to require information and explanations of auditors of a UK incorporated company included in the consolidation

(3) Right to require the parent company to take all reasonable steps to obtain information and explanations from the subsidiary.

3 Materiality, degree of their knowledge, nature, relationship, perform additional procedures, material misstatements.

4 See para 2.6

5 See para 2.21

6

STEP ONE	Check the transposition from individual audited accounts to the consolidation workings.
STEP TWO	Check consolidation adjustments are correct and comparable with prior years
STEP THREE	Check for, and audit, acquisitions
STEP FOUR	Check for, and audit, disposals
STEP FIVE	Consider whether previous treatment of subsidiaries and associates is still correct
STEP SIX	Verify the arithmetical accuracy of the workings
STEP SEVEN	Review the consolidated accounts for compliance with the Companies Act 1985
STEP SEVEN	Review the consolidated accounts to ensure they give a true and fair view

7 True

8 See the table at para 6.3

Now try the question below from the Exam Question Bank

Number	Level	Marks	Time
14	Exam	25	45 mins

Part C
Other services

Chapter 15

ASSURANCE AND AUDIT RELATED SERVICES

Topic list	Syllabus reference
1 Assurance engagements	4(d)
2 Risk assessments	4(d)
3 Performance measurement	4(d)
4 Systems reliability	4(d)
5 Electronic commerce	4(d)
6 Audit related services	4(c)

Introduction

The auditing environment has been subject to changes recently. As discussed in Chapter 5, there is a perceived need for improved corporate governance, and a **need for assurance** to be given to shareholders concerning it. A focus on quality performance, perhaps inspired by increasing regulation, has led to a need for performance measurement.

Business systems have evolved. While financial systems are still important to the shareholder, other systems, such as computer systems are now vitally important in business.

A recent report by one of the bodies of professional accountants, the ICAEW, predicted a future where accountants pursued fields other than traditional assignments of audit and tax. The truth of this can be seen by reviewing the current focus of major audit firms on fields other than audit.

Assurance and non-audit services have evolved with this environment. They include services which include some of the issues discussed above, particularly IT, and also services which give levels of assurance regarding given questions where an audit as such is not required.

There is currently no UK guidance in these areas, so our study of this area will include a review of the international requirements. Assurance engagements are covered by ISAE 100, *Assurance Engagements*, and guidance on audit related services (also called non audit services) can be found in ISA 920, *Engagements to perform agreed-upon procedures*, and ISA 930, *Engagements to compile financial information*.

Study guide

Sections 17, 18 and 19

17 'Audit-related' services

General

- Distinguish between audit and audit-related services and the comparative levels of assurance provided by the auditor.

Reviews

- Distinguish between an attestation engagement and a direct reporting engagement

- Describe, for example:
  - a review of interim financial information
  - 'due diligence' (when acquiring a company, business or other asset)
- Explain and illustrate the importance of inquiry and analytical procedures
- Discuss the effectiveness of the current 'negative assurance' form of reporting

Agreed-upon procedures

- Explain why these and compilation engagements do not (usually) meet the requirements for an assurance engagement
- Illustrate the form and content of a report of factual findings

Compilations

- Describe the general principles and procedures relating to a compilation engagement (eg to prepare financial statements)
- Illustrate the form and content of a compilation report.

18, 19 Assurance services

General

- Explain the need for a range of assurance services and discuss to what extent these can be provided by auditors
- Explain the effects of assurance services being provided by the external auditor
- Describe how the level of assurance (high or moderate) provided by an engagement depends on the subject matter evaluated, the criteria used, the procedures applied and the quality and quantity of evidence obtained
- Describe the form and content of the professional accountant's report for an assurance engagement
- Discuss the situations in which it would be appropriate to express a reservation or deny a conclusion

Risk assessment

- Distinguish between management risk assessment and auditor risk assessment
- Explain the meaning of risk and the importance of risk thresholds
- Describe and illustrate different types of risk, (eg financial, operational, information/IT, environmental)
- Describe the ways in which risks may be identified and analysed (eg in terms of their significance, the likelihood of occurrence and how they should be managed)
- Discuss the relative advantages and disadvantages of qualitative and quantitative risk assessment methods
- Explain the different ways in which management can respond to risk (eg manage it, eliminate it, develop a recovery plan)

Performance measurement

- Describe the benefits of providing assurance on business performance measures
- Discuss the relevance of traditional financial accounting performance measures and operational measures
- Describe how the reliability of performance information systems is assessed (including benchmarking)
- Describe the elements of a value for money audit (ie economy, efficiency and effectiveness) and give examples of its use

Systems reliability

- Describe the need for information integrity and controls
- Discuss the demand for reliable and more timely reporting and explain the benefits of providing assurance to management and external users
- Describe the procedures for assessing internal control effectiveness (eg in real-time systems)

Electronic commerce

- Describe and illustrate the ways in which organisations are using core technologies (eg EDI, E-mail, Internet, World Wide Web)
- Explain how e-commerce affects the business risk of an entity
- Describe the issues of privacy and security of information for transactions and communications
- Outline and illustrate the principles and criteria which underlie web assurance

Exam guide

Assurance and audit related services are extremely important areas for auditors in practice. Areas such as e-commerce are also particularly topical.

1 ASSURANCE ENGAGEMENTS

KEY TERM

An **assurance engagement** is one where a professional accountant evaluates or measures a subject matter that is the responsibility of another party against suitable criteria, and expresses an opinion which provides the intended user with a level of assurance about that subject matter.

1.1 An assurance assignment is a professional service designed to give specific opinions about representations made by a party about a certain item.

1.2 It therefore has both similarities and dissimilarities to an audit.

Similarities to an audit	Dissimilarities to an audit
It provides a user with a level of **assurance**.	It is **not statutorily required**.
Similar **techniques** for finding evidence to support the opinion may be used.	Level of **assurance** may be **lower** than for an audit, so evidence may be less comprehensive.
It is a **reporting** assignment.	The end user is likely to be more pro-active in its **relationship with the accountant**.
It is an evidence gathering exercise **based on assertions/representations** made.	It does not have to be based on a financial assertion.

Why have assurance engagements?

1.3 As stated above, an assurance engagement is not a statutory necessity (in comparison to an audit, which is required for most companies). It is important to understand why an assurance engagement might be required.

1.4 An assurance engagement **improves the quality of decision-making** for users. It gives an knowledgeable opinion on factors which decision-makers are interested in.

1.5 Assurance engagements are of increasing importance for other reasons too:

- The decline in audit (turnover threshold now £1m)
- The increased importance of computer systems in business

1.6 The next question, inevitably is, what has this to do with auditors? The table above shows some generalised comparisons between audit and assurance services. The two services are different, but in many ways are comparable. The techniques and skills involved may be similar.

1.7 The decline in audit apparent in recent times leaves an 'assurance gap'. Readers of accounts still require assurance about assertions made within financial statements, and investors still need knowledgeable guidance when making investment decisions.

1.8 Auditors are in a good position to provide assurance services, being **respected business advisers** possessing **relevant skills**.

Elements of an assurance engagement

1.9 A definition of an assurance engagement is given above. It is also helpful to consider what ISAE 100 *Assurance engagements* **excludes from being assurance engagements**:

- Agreed-upon procedures (see section 6)
- Compilation of financial or other information (see section 6)
- Preparation of tax returns where no conclusion is expressed, and tax consulting
- Management consulting
- Other advisory services

1.10 The ISAE states that an assurance engagement will display all the following elements.

ISAE 100.8

Whether a particular engagement is an assurance engagement will depend upon whether it exhibits all the following elements:

(a) a three party relationship involving:

- a professional accountant
- a responsible party; and
- an intended user;

(b) a subject matter;

(c) suitable criteria;

(d) an engagement process; and

(e) a conclusion

Assurance given

1.11 The ISAE refers to 'high level assurance engagements'. High level is given to mean high, but not absolute assurance. This can be compared to the 'reasonable assurance' given in an audit.

1.12 Reasonable assurance is given about the truth and fairness of the financial statements. The assurance takes into account a concept of materiality, so that the opinion given is reasonable, rather than correct.

1.13 In a high-level assurance engagement, the accountant is drawing a conclusion based on stated representations. Such an answer can be given in more 'correct' terms, although the nature of evidence collection means that absolute assurance cannot be given.

1.14 The ISAE outlines the basic principles associated with a high level assurance engagement. They are similar to the requirements for an audit. They are outlined here. (Note that the word 'practitioner' is used to mean accountant here.)

Accepting appointment and planning

ISAE 100.34

A practitioner who performs an assurance engagement should be independent.

ISAE 100.35/36/37

These requirements state that a practitioner should only accept an assurance engagement if all the elements of an assurance engagement are present.

ISAE 100.38

The practitioner should agree on the terms of the assurance engagement with the party who engages the practitioner.

ISAE 100.40

The practitioner should implement quality control policies and procedures designed to ensure that all assurance engagements are conducted in accordance with applicable standards issued by the International Federation of Accountants.

ISAE 100.41

The practitioner should plan and conduct the assurance engagement in an effective manner to meet the objective of the engagement.

ISAE 100.42

The practitioner should plan and conduct an assurance service engagement with an attitude of professional scepticism.

ISAE 100.43

The practitioner should have or obtain knowledge of the engagement circumstances sufficient to identify and understand the events, transactions and practices that nay have a significant effect on the subject matter and engagement.

ISAE 100.44

The practitioner should assess whether the criteria are suitable to evaluate the subject matter.

ISAE 100.48

The practitioner should consider materiality and engagement risk when planning and conducting an assurance engagement in order to reduce the risk of expressing an inappropriate conclusion that the subject matter conforms in all material respects with suitable criteria.

1.15 You can see the acceptance and planning procedures for an assurance agreement are very similar to those for an audit. Differences are:

- Ensuring all the criteria laid out in ISA 100.8 are present
- Assessing whether the criteria are suitable to evaluate the subject matter

Obtaining evidence on assurance engagements

ISAE 100.52

The practitioner should obtain sufficient appropriate evidence on which to base the conclusion.

ISAE 100.57

The practitioner should document matters that are important in providing evidence to support the conclusion expressed in the practitioner's report, and in providing evidence that the assurance engagement was performed in accordance with applicable standards.

ISAE 100.60

The practitioner should consider the effects of subsequent events up to the date of the practitioner's report. When the practitioner becomes aware of events that materially affect the subject matter and the practitioner's conclusion, the practitioner should consider whether the subject matter reflects those events properly or whether those events are addressed properly in the practitioner's report.

ISAE 100.61

When an expert is used in the collection and evaluation if evidence, the practitioner and the expert should, on a combined basis, possess adequate knowledge of the subject matter and have adequate proficiency in the subject matter for the practitioner to determine that sufficient appropriate evidence has been obtained.

ISAE 100.65

When an expert is involved, the practitioner should have a level of involvement in the engagement and an understanding of the aspects of the subject matter for which the expert has been used, sufficient to enable the practitioner to accept the responsibility for expressing a conclusion on the subject matter.

ISAE 100.67

When an expert is involved, the practitioner should obtain sufficient appropriate evidence that the work of the expert is adequate for the purposes of the assurance engagement.

1.16 Similarly, the procedures for obtaining evidence are very similar to an audit. The accountant must obtain sufficient, appropriate evidence.

1.17 What constitutes sufficient, appropriate evidence will depend on the nature of the assignment and the criteria being reported on. This is a matter for professional judgement on the accountant's part.

Reporting on assurance engagements

ISAE 100.68

The report should express an opinion that conveys a high level of assurance about the subject matter, based on the results of the work performed. The practitioner's opinion about a subject matter based on the identified suitable criteria and the evidence obtained in the course of the assurance engagement.

1.18 The standard **does not issue a standard format** for an assurance report. Instead it outlines the items required to be included in such a report as a minimum.

1.19 The form of the conclusion to be reached by the practitioner is determined by the nature of the assignment.

ISAE 100.68

The report should express a conclusion that conveys a high level of assurance about the subject matter, based on the results of the work performed. The practitioner's report should contain a clear expression of the practitioner's opinion about a subject matter based on the identified suitable criteria and the evidence obtained in the course of the assurance engagement.

1.20 The form of the report can vary. It can be written or oral, or be delivered in 'symbolic representation'.

Content of the report

1.21 The ISAE outlines the standard content of an assurance report thus:

ISAE 100.71

The practitioner's report should include:

(a) title

(b) an addressee

(c) a description of the engagement and identification of the subject matter

(d) a statement to identify the responsible party and describe the practitioner's responsibilities

(e) when the report is for a restricted purpose, identification if the parties to whom the report is restricted and for what purpose it was prepared

(f) identification of the standards under which the engagement was conducted

(g) identification if the criteria

(h) the practitioner's conclusion, including any reservations of denial of a conclusion

(i) the report date

(j) the name of the firm or the practitioner and the place of issue of the report

1.22 There may be occasion when the practitioner feels that he cannot reach a conclusion about the subject matter, or when the conclusion is that the subject matter is not in all ways in accordance with the representations. The ISAE makes the following provisions:

ISAE 100.73

The conclusion should clearly express circumstances where:

(a) the practitioner is of the view that one, some of all aspects of the subject matter do not conform to the identified criteria;

(b) the assertion prepared by the responsible party is inappropriate in terms of the identified criteria; or

(c) the practitioner is unable to obtain sufficient appropriate evidence to evaluate one or more aspects of the subject matter's conformity with the identified criteria.

Exam focus point

This ISAE is very new. It is not effective until 31 December 2001, although earlier application is encouraged. It has been reproduced in detail here because there is currently no UK guidance on this issue. You should not need a detailed knowledge of this ISAE in the exam, just an awareness of the general principles surrounding assurance engagements, and reporting on assurance engagements. The examiner has written an article 'Rest Assured' in the June 2001 issue of *Student Accountant*, which you should ensure you read.

1.23 In the following sections we shall consider some examples of areas where the accountant can provide assurance services.

2 RISK ASSESSMENTS

2.1 We discussed business risk in Chapter 7. It had three elements; financial, operational and compliance. There are a number of specific risks within these elements, some of which are shown the diagram below.

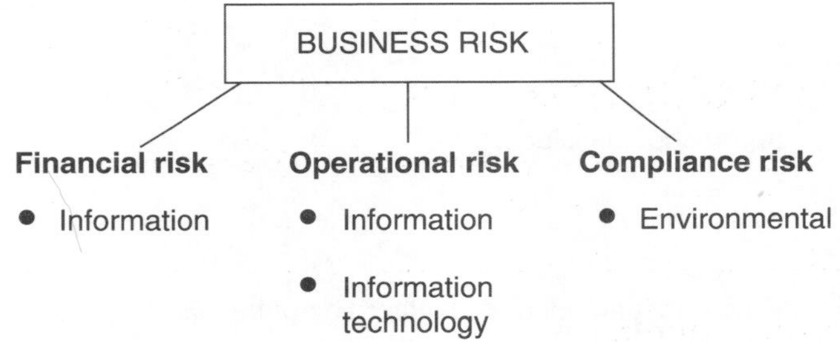

Responsibility for risk assessment

2.2 In Chapters 5 and 7, we discussed the various responsibilities that exist for assessing risk in companies. There are three sets of people involved in risk assessments:

- Directors/management
- Internal audit
- External audit

2.3 The first two sets (directors and internal audit) can be bracketed together because, as we shall see in Chapter 16, internal audit are employed by directors to assist them in carrying out their duties one of which, under the Turnbull guidelines, is risk management.

Risk assessment	
Directors	Are responsible for assessing the **business risk** pertaining to the company.
Auditors	Are responsible for assessing the **audit risk** pertaining to the audit of the company. If they choose to take the business risk approach to the client, they will also assess the **business risk**. However, it is **not** their responsibility to do so. Professional requirements mean they **must** assess audit risk.

Responses to risk

2.4 There are several responses that management can take to risk:

- **Avoid risk**, for example, by not entering a certain market
- **Mitigate risk**, for example, by entering markets which have complementary effects for the company
- **Accept risk**

2.5 If management choose to accept risk, they must set the **risk thresholds**, that is, determine levels of risk where they will stop accepting risk and choose one of the other strategies. These thresholds are important because if directors or management are reckless with regard to risk, they may not be carrying out their fiduciary duties.

2.6 Some methods for identifying risk were mentioned in Chapter 7.

Assurance services

2.7 The auditor can provide assurance services on management or internal audit's risk assessments.

3 PERFORMANCE MEASUREMENT

3.1 Before we consider the benefits of performance measurement we should revise it itself. This is a topic studied at papers 2.4 and 3.3.

Performance measurement

Earlier in this text, we discussed how recently measures have been taken to improve the accountability of management to shareholders.

Performance measurement includes a series of measures within the company designed to ensure that people who work in the company are **accountable** to management for their performance.

Here are some benefits of performance measurement.

- Clarifies the objectives of the organisation
- Develops agreed measures of activity
- Gives greater understanding of processes
- Facilitates comparison of performance in different organisations
- Facilitates the setting of targets for the organisation and its managers
- Promotes the accountability of the organisation to its stakeholders

3.2 The above points refer to the **benefits of performance measurement in itself**. The last bullet point above hints at the benefits of giving assurance on performance measurement.

3.3 Performance measurement is aimed at providing benefits to stakeholders. **Assurance services** can provide an **independent opinion** as to whether the company's business performance measures are providing the benefit they are intended to.

Traditional performance measures

Financial

3.4 You should be aware of the key financial ratios used to measure performance from your studies at 2.4, *Financial Management and Control.*

3.5 The traditional financial ratios give indicators about:

- Profitability
- Liquidity
- Gearing
- Investment

3.6 These areas are all performance measures that **shareholders** will be interested in as they will indicate the strength of the investment, the likelihood of income from the investment, the future existence of the investment.

3.7 Whilst these measures are relevant to shareholders, they are measures which investors would expect companies to calculate as a matter of course, and also to calculate them correctly. Therefore, there should not be any need for assurance services in these areas.

3.8 Assurance services relating to management accounting issues are likely to offer more value to shareholders. This would include assurance services relating to:

- Detail behind figures in financial statements, for example:
  - Sales by product
  - Sales by region
  - Sales by division
- Timeliness of information, in other words, are shareholders receiving the information quickly enough to make good investment decisions.
- Comparisons between the performance of the company and its competitors, or its budgets, or its historic performance.

Operational

3.9 Operational performance measures are more designed to provide quality service to a different stakeholder, the **customer**.

3.10 Remember that assurance services are between an accountant and a third party. This third party does not have to be a shareholder (as was the case in traditional audit), so an assurance engagement could be undertaken for potential or existing customers, or suppliers, on the operational performance of a company.

3.11 Clearly, indicators of operational performance will vary with each business. Measures could include:

- Sales per salesperson
- Number of new products launched each year

3.12 The issue performance is measured on will be the key drivers of operation for that particular business.

Value for money audits

3.13 Value for money audits were introduced in paper 2.6, *Audit and Internal Review* (old paper 6), as an example of an assurance service that could be undertaken by internal audit. We shall revise them briefly here.

3.14 Although much has been written about value for money (VFM), there is no great mystique about the concept. The term is common in everyday speech and so is the idea.

To drive the point home, think of a bottle of Fairy Liquid. If we believe the advertising, Fairy is good 'value for money' because it washes half as many plates again as any other washing up liquid. Bottle for bottle it may be more expensive, but plate for plate it is cheaper. Not only this but Fairy gets plates 'squeaky' clean. To summarise, Fairy gives us VFM because it exhibits the following characteristics.

- **Economy** (more clean plates per pound)
- **Efficiency** (more clean plates per squirt)
- **Effectiveness** (plates as clean as they should be)

3.15 The **assessment** of economy, efficiency and effectiveness should be a part of the normal process of any organisation, public or private. Management should carry out **performance reviews** as a regular feature of their control responsibilities.

3.16 Assurance can be given by auditors in the form of independent assessments of management performance, known as **value for money audits (VFM audits).**

3.17 In a VFM audit, the objectives of a particular programme or activity need to be specified and understood in order for the auditor to make a proper assessment of whether value for money has been achieved.

(a) In a **profit seeking organisation,** objectives can be expressed financially in terms of target profit or return. The organisation, and profit centres within it, can be judged to have operated **effectively** if they have **achieved a target profit** within a given period.

(b) In **non-profit seeking organisations,** effectiveness cannot be measured this way, because the organisation has non-financial objectives. The **effectiveness** of performance in such organisations could be measured in terms of whether **targeted non-financial objectives have been achieved,** but as we have seen there are several problems involved in trying to do this.

3.18 **Public sector organisations** are now under considerable **pressure** to prove that they operate economically, efficiently and effectively, and are encouraged from many sources to draw up **action plans** to achieve value for money as part of the continuing process of good management.

3.19 Value for money is important **whatever level of expenditure** is being considered. Negatively it may be seen as an approach to spreading costs in public expenditure fairly across services but positively it is necessary to ensure that the desired impact is achieved with the minimum use of resources.

Revision of value for money terminology

Economy

3.20 Economy is concerned with the cost of inputs, and it is achieved by **obtaining those inputs at the lowest acceptable cost**. Economy **does not mean straightforward cost-cutting,** because resources must be acquired which are of a suitable **quality** to provide the service to the desired standard. Cost-cutting should not sacrifice quality to the extent that service standards fall to an unacceptable level. Economising by buying poor quality materials, labour or equipment is a 'false economy'.

Efficiency

3.21 Efficiency means the following.

(a) **Maximising output for a given input,** for example maximising the number of transactions handled per employee or per £1 spent.

(b) **Achieving the minimum input for a given output**. For example, the Department of Social Security is required to pay Unemployment Benefit to millions of people. Efficiency will be achieved by making these payments with the minimum labour and computer time.

Effectiveness

3.22 Effectiveness means ensuring that the **outputs** of a service or programme have the **desired impacts**; in other words, finding out whether they **succeed in achieving objectives**, and if so, to what extent.

Studying and measuring the three Es

3.23 Economy, efficiency and effectiveness can be studied and measured with reference to the following.

(a) **Inputs**

- Money
- Resources - the labour, materials, time and so on consumed, and their cost

For example, a VFM audit into state secondary education would look at the efficiency and economy of the use of resources for education (the use of schoolteachers, school buildings, equipment, cash) and whether the resources are being used for their purpose: what is the pupil/teacher ratio and are trained teachers being fully used to teach the subjects they have been trained for?

(b) **Outputs**, in other words the **results of an activity**, measurable as the services actually produced, and the quality of the services.

In the case of a VFM audit of secondary education, outputs would be measured as the number of pupils taught and the number of subjects taught per pupil; how many examination papers are taken and what is the pass rate; what proportion of students go on to further education at a university or college.

(c) **Impacts**, which are the **effect that the outputs** of an activity or programme have in **terms of achieving policy objectives.**

Policy objectives might be to provide a minimum level of education to all children up to the age of 16, and to make education relevant for the children's future jobs and careers. This might be measured by the ratio of jobs vacant to unemployed school leavers. A VFM audit could assess to what extent this objective is being achieved.

3.24 As another example from education, suppose that there is a programme to build a new school in an area. The **inputs** would be the **costs of building** the school, and the resources used up; the **outputs** would be the **school building** itself; and the **impacts** would be the **effect that the new school has on education in the area** it serves.

4 SYSTEMS RELIABILITY

4.1 A huge number of businesses now use computer systems to run their businesses, and financial information is processed on a computer system.

4.2 This means that a number of the controls which the directors are required to put into place to safeguard the assets of the shareholders are incorporated into computer systems.

4.3 You learnt about building controls into a computer system in your studies for paper 2.1, *Information Systems*.

Knowledge brought forward from Paper 2.1, Information Systems

It is possible to build controls into computerised processing. A balance must be struck between the degree of control and the requirement for a user friendly system.

Controls can be classified into:

- Security controls
- Integrity controls
- Contingency controls

Integrity controls can be subdivided into two areas:

- Data integrity is preserved when data is the same as it is in source documents and has not been accidentally or intentionally altered, destroyed or disclosed.
- Systems integrity refers to system operation conforming to the design specification despite attempts (deliberate or accidental) to make it behave incorrectly.

4.4 When auditors undertake their assessment and testing of controls for the purposes of the statutory audit, they focus on the general and application controls of the system, which relate to security and policies for data input.

4.5 In other words, when undertaking the work for the statutory audit, the auditor is interested in the data integrity, as it is the data which is incorporated into the financial statements.

4.6 However, it is also important to stakeholders in the company that the system used, which will often impact on operation as well as financial information operates reliably and that risks are mitigated against.

4.7 The **two key risks** are:

- The system being put at risk by a virus or some other fault or breakdown which spreads across the system
- The system being invaded by an authorised user who could then
  - Affect the smooth operation of the system
  - Obtain commercial sensitive information

4.8 The client is likely to have contingency plans in the event of the system being affected by the risks outlined above. However, it is also important to know that the original system is as reliable as could be expected, and whether it is the best system that the company could be using, at the given cost.

4.9 The company might seek such assurances from its service provider. However, the service provider has a vested interest in the company believing that its system is reliable and the best available, because he is paid to supply it.

4.10 This means that the directors might seek an assurance service from its auditors or another firm of accountants, to undertake work to ascertain if the assertions of the service provider are correct.

4.11 If a firm of accountants were to consider taking on such an assurance engagement, they should ensure that they had sufficient skill to undertake the procedures required to ascertain if the assurances were correct. They would have to ensure that they had an IT specialist on the team.

Assessing internal control effectiveness

4.12 Internal control effectiveness is generally assessed by means of undertaking a systems audit.

Systems audit

4.13 You have studied systems audits extensively in your previous auditing studies. As part of any audit, auditors assess the quality and effectiveness of the accounting system. Increasingly, this necessarily includes a consideration of computer systems.

4.14 Auditors could accept an assurance engagement to undertake this task outside of the audit and to report specifically on findings. The following are the key areas they are likely to concentrate on to establish how reliable the systems are:

- Management policy
- Segregation of duties
- Security

4.15 You should be aware that these are important control considerations in a computer environment. The details that the reporting accountant will consider are outlined below.

Management policy

- Does management have a written statement of policy with regard to computer systems?
- Is it compatible with management policy in other areas?
- Is it adhered to?
- Is it sufficient and effective?
- Is it updated when the systems are updated?
- Does it relate to the current system?

Segregation of duties

- Is there adequate segregation of duties with regard to data input?
- Are there adequate system controls (eg passwords) to enforce segregation of duties?

Security

- Is there a security policy in place:
  - Physical security (locked doors/windows)
  - Access security (passwords
  - Data security (virus shields)
- Is it adhered to?
- Is it sufficient and effective?

Reporting

4.16 It is vital that **management** receive information on the effectiveness of their controls systems and systems reliability generally. This is because, as stated earlier, the operations of the company are likely to rely heavily if not completely on computer systems, and if problems arise, operations could be severely affected.

4.17 Problems could arise in terms of:

- No production being possible
- No invoicing being possible
- Invoicing being duplicated or omitted

4.18 Other stakeholders, such as customers and suppliers, will also be interested in the reliability of the company's systems, as they will not want to deal with a company who makes mistakes and cannot operate properly.

4.19 It is because of the vital importance of this area to business that management may also want to obtain assurance concerning the information it receives on systems reliability.

5 ELECTRONIC COMMERCE

KEY TERMS

The Internet is a global network connecting millions of computers.

The World Wide Web (WWW) is a system of Internet servers that support specially formatted documents. A group of documents accessed from the same base web site is known as a website.

Electronic data interchange (EDI) is a form of computer to computer data transfer. Information can be transferred in electronic form, avoiding the need for the information to be re-inputted somewhere else.

Electronic mail (e-mail) is a system of communicating with other connected computers or via the internet in written form.

Electronic commerce (e-commerce) means conducting business electronically via a communications link.

5.1 The items described above are all now commonly used in business. You are probably familiar with most, if not all of them.

5.2 All the items discussed above are (or can be) used in e-commerce. As this is an exceedingly fast growing area of business, it is a very important area for everyone, including accountants, today. You should be familiar with the idea of e-commerce from Paper 2.1 *Information systems* (old Paper 5).

5.3 The need for assurance services relating to e-commerce arise from some of its disadvantages, which are revised here.

Disadvantages of e-commerce

5.4 E-commerce involves an unusual mix of people – security people, web technology people, designers, marketing people – and this can be very difficult to manage. The e-business needs supervision by expensive specialists.

5.5 At present, in spite of phenomenal growth the market is still fuzzy and undefined. Many e-businesses have **yet to make a profit**, the best-known example being **Amazon.com** the Internet book-seller.

5.6 Unless the e-business is one started completely from scratch, any new technology installed will probably **need to link up with existing business systems**, which could potentially take years of programming. Under-estimating the time and effort involved is a common obstacle.

5.7 The international availability of a website means that the laws of all countries that transactions may be conducted from have to be considered. The legal issues surrounding e-commerce are complex and still developing.

Lack of trust

5.8 Above all, however, the problem with e-commerce is one of **trust**. In most cultures, consumers grant their trust to business parties that have a close **physical presence**: buildings, facilities and people to talk to. On the Internet these familiar elements are simply not there. The seller's reputation, the size of his business, and the level of customisation in product and service also engender trust.

5.9 Internet merchants need to elicit consumer trust when the level of **perceived risk** in a transaction is high. However, research has found that once consumers have built up trust in an Internet merchant such concerns are reduced.

5.10 Internet merchants need to address issues such as fear of **invasion of privacy** and abuse of customer information (about their **credit cards**, for example) because they stop people even considering the Internet as a shopping medium.

5.11 The parties involved in e-commerce need to have confidence that any communication sent gets to its target destination **unchanged**, and **without being read by anyone else.**

Web assurance

5.12 As discussed above it has been a feature of electronic commerce that people seem to be happy to browse on line, but less happy to make purchases, due to a lack of knowledge about the company they were dealing with. This led to concerns about

- Processing of the transaction
- Use of the personal information that must be given to complete the sale

- Poor business practices by the company (late delivery/errors in order etc)

5.13 Web assurance seeks to remove this barrier by providing assurance to the users of the service. An example of an assurance service developed in relation to e-commerce is WebTrust.

5.14 An assurance assignment under WebTrust would involve looking at the assertions of the company relating to the concerns above, and seeking evidence as to whether what they say about their service is true, and whether their systems comply with pre-determined criteria.

5.15 The outcome of the exercise is that if the accountant has assurance that the systems comply and the representations made about the service is fair, the Website can be WebTrust accredited.

6 AUDIT RELATED SERVICES

6.1 Audit related services are another area in which there is currently no UK guidance. We shall consider the guidance given in international standards to get an outline of what is involved in audit related services (sometimes called non audit services).

KEY TERMS

Audit related services are reviews, agreed-upon procedures and compilations. These things are specifically excluded from being assurance engagements by ISAE 100.

Review engagements. The objective of a review engagement is to enable an auditor to state whether, on the basis of procedures which do not provide all the evidence that would be required in an audit, anything has come to the auditor's attention that causes the auditor to believe that the financial statements are not prepared, in all material respects, in accordance with an identified financial reporting framework.

Agreed-upon procedures audit. In an engagement to perform agreed-upon procedures, an auditor is engaged to carry out those procedures of an audit nature to which the auditor and the entity and any appropriate third parties have agreed and to report on factual findings. The recipients of the report must form their own conclusions form the report by the auditor. The report is restricted to those parties that have agreed to the procedures to be performed since others, unaware of the reasons for the procedures may misinterpret the results.

Compilation engagement. In a compilation engagement, the accountant is engaged to use accounting expertise as opposed to auditing expertise to collect, classify and summarise financial information.

6.2 These services are known as 'audit related services' due to their connections with audit.

Reviews	Reviews are extremely similar to audit, in that similar work is undertaken. The key difference between them is that a review is **designed to give less assurance** than an audit on similar issues.
Agreed-upon procedures	This is again similar to audit in that similar work will be undertaken. The key difference here is **that amount and direction of work undertaken** to draw conclusions will **be agreed in advance** between two parties. The conclusions drawn will be specific to the work done.

Compilations	Of all the three types of audit related service, this is the least like audit. It involves an auditor using another of his skills **in putting together financial information.**

Reviews **Pilot Paper**

6.3 There are two types of review assignment:

- An **attestation** engagement where the accountant declares that a given premise is either correct or not
- A **direct reporting** engagement, where the accountant reports on issues that have come to his attention during the course of his review

6.4 These types of review assignment can be illustrated in the following way.

6.5 EXAMPLE: ATTESTATION ENGAGEMENT

Auditors may sometimes be asked to review interim financial information. In such an engagement, the auditor is being asked to attest whether

- The accounting policies used are consistent with those used in the prior year financial statements, and
- Any material modifications should be made to the interim financial information as it has been presented.

6.6 EXAMPLE: DIRECT REPORTING ENGAGEMENT

An example of a direct reporting engagement is a 'due diligence' engagement. This is where an accountant is asked to review the accounts and systems of a target company in the event of a prospective business purchase.

In such an event, the accountant is asked simply to report on issues arising.

6.7 In a review engagement, the auditor will rely more heavily on procedures such as enquiry and analytical review than on more detailed substantive testing. The reasons for this are as follows:

- He is seeking a lower level of assurance than for a statutory audit, so these forms of evidence seeking are sufficient due to risk being lower
- Such techniques can provide indicators to direct work and from which to draw conclusions, and they are quick and, therefore, cost-effective to undertake

6.8 ISA 910 *Engagements to review financial statements* contains guidance of review engagements.

> **ISA 910.7**
>
> For the purpose of expressing negative assurance in the review report, the auditor should obtain sufficient appropriate evidence primarily through inquiry and analytical procedures to be able to draw conclusions.

ISA 910.8

The procedures required to conduct a review of financial statements should be determined by the auditors having regard to the requirements of this ISA, relevant professional bodies, legislation, regulation and, where appropriate, the terms of the review engagement and reporting requirements.

6.9 As we noted when we considered assurance services, many of the requirements of the ISA are similar to the requirements of an audit.

- Planning
  - Obtain knowledge of the business
  - Same materiality requirements
  - Using the work of others
- Evidence
  - Document all important matters
  - Apply judgement in determining nature, timing and extent of procedures
  - Enquire about subsequent events
  - Extend procedures if material misstatements are suspected

Reporting

6.10 The nature of reporting on reviews was outlined in paper 2.6. However, as it was not covered in the old paper 6, it is covered here.

6.11 An external review is an exercise similar to an audit, which is designed to give a reduced degree of assurance concerning the proper preparation of a set of financial statements.

6.12 As you know from your 2.6 studies negative assurance is given on review assignments. Negative assurance is defined on page 309.

ISA 910.25/26

The review report should contain a clear written expression of **negative assurance.** The auditor should review and assess the conclusion drawn from the evidence obtained as the basis for the expression of negative assurance.

Based on the work performed, the auditor should assess whether any information obtained during the review indicates that the financial statements do not give a true and fair view (or 'are not presented fairly, in all material respects,') in accordance with the identified financial reporting framework.

No matters have come to the attention of the auditor

6.13 In this case, the auditor should give a clear expression of negative assurance in his report. An example of an unqualified review report is given in the appendix to the ISA, and it is reproduced here.

Form of Unqualified Review Report

REVIEW REPORT TO...

We have reviewed the accompanying balance sheet of ABC Company at December 31, 20XX, and the related statements of income and cash flows for the year then ended. These financial statements are the responsibility of the Company's management. Our responsibility is to issue a report on these financial statements based on our review.

We conducted our review in accordance with the International Standard on Auditing (or refer to relevant national standards or practices) applicable to review engagements. This Standard requires that we plan and perform the review to obtain moderate assurance as to whether the financial statements are free of material misstatement. A review is limited primarily to inquiries of company personnel and analytical procedures applied to financial data and thus provides less assurance than an audit. We have not performed an audit and, accordingly, we do not express an audit opinion.

Based on our review, nothing has come to our attention that causes us to believe that the accompanying financial statements do not give a true and fair view (or 'are not presented fairly, in all material respects,') in accordance with International Accounting Standards.

Date *AUDITOR*

Address

Matters have come to the attention of the auditor

6.14 If matters have come to the attention of the auditor, he should **describe those matters**. The matters may have the following effects.

Impact	Effect on report
Material	Express a **qualified** opinion of negative assurance
Pervasive	Express an **adverse** opinion that the financial statements do not give a true and fair view

6.15 The auditor may feel there has been a limitation in the scope of the work he intended to carry out for the review. If so, he should **describe the limitation.** The limitation may have the following effects.

Impact	Effect on report
Material to one area	Express a **qualified** opinion of negative assurance due to amendments which might required if the limitation did not exist
Pervasive	Do not provide any assurance

Agreed-upon procedures

6.16 As discussed above, the international standard on assurance engagements, ISAE 100, specifically excludes both agreed upon-procedures and compilation engagements from being assurance engagements.

6.17 The reasons for this exclusion are:

Agreed-upon procedures	While a degree of assurance is likely to be received by the user of a report resulting from agreed-upon procedures, the **purpose of the report is not to give assurance**. The **purpose** of the report **is** for the accountant to **draw specific conclusions** about the issue which has been investigated in the assignment.
Compilation	In a compilation engagement, **the accountant does not offer an opinion**, so by virtue of this, it **cannot be an assurance engagement**. It is simply a collation exercise.

6.18 Agreed upon procedures assignments are discussed in ISA 920 *Engagements to perform agreed upon procedures regarding financial statements*.

Accepting appointment

ISA 920.9

The auditor should ensure with representatives of the entity, and ordinarily, other specified parties who will receive copies of the report of factual findings, that there is a clear understanding regarding the agreed procedures and the conditions of the engagement.

Carrying out procedures

6.19 The auditors should plan the assignment. They should carry out the agreed upon procedures, documenting his process and findings.

Reporting

6.20 As there is no current UK guidance on agreed-upon procedures engagements, we shall look at the report structure suggested by the international guidance, ISA 920, *Engagements to perform agreed upon procedures*.

ISA 920.18

The report of factual findings should contain:

(a) title;

(b) addressee (ordinarily the client who engaged the auditor to perform the agreed-upon procedures)

(c) identification of specific financial or non-financial information to which the agreed-upon procedures have been applied;

(d) a statement that the procedures performed were those agreed upon with the recipient;

(e) a statement that the engagement was performed in accordance with the International Standard on Auditing applicable to agreed-upon procedure engagements, or with relevant national standards or practices;

(f) when relevant a statement that the auditor is not independent of the entity;

(g) identification if the purpose for which the agreed-upon procedures were performed;

(h) a listing of the specific procedures performed;

(i) a description of the auditor's factual findings including sufficient details of errors and exceptions found;

(j) statement that the procedures performed do not constitute either an audit or a review, and, as such, no assurance is expressed;

(k) a statement that had the auditor performed additional procedures, an audit or a review, other matters might have come to light that would have been reported;

(l) a statement that the report is restricted to those parties that have agreed to the procedures to be performed;

(m) a statement (when applicable0 that the report relates only to the elements, accounts, items or financial and non-financial information specified and that it does not extend to the entity's financial statements taken as a whole;

(n) date of the report;

(o) auditor's address;

(p) auditor's signature.

Compilations

6.21 A compilation engagement is one where the accountant is engaged to compile information. Examples include:

- Preparing financial statements
- Preparing tax returns

6.22 The information to be compiled does not have to be financial information.

6.23 The international guidance on compilation engagements is found in ISA 930 *Engagements to compile financial information*. The most relevant piece of guidance that it contains for us is the guidance on reporting, which is reproduced below.

Reporting

6.24 The information compiled by the accountant should contain a reference to the fact that it has not been audited.

ISA 930.18

Reports on compilation engagements should contain the following:

(a) title

(b) addressee

(c) a statement that the engagement was performed in accordance with the ISA applicable to compilation engagements, or with national standards and practices;

(d) when relevant, a statement that the accountant us not independent of the entity;

(e) identification if the financials information noting that it is based on information provided by management;

(f) a statement that neither an audit nor a review has been carried out and that accordingly no assurance is expressed on the financial information;

(g) a statement that neither an audit nor a review has been carried out and that accordingly no assurance is expressed on the financial information;

(h) a paragraph, when considered necessary, drawing attention to the disclosure of material departures from the identified financial reporting framework;

(i) date of the report;

(j) accountant's address;

(k) accountant's signature.

Chapter roundup

- An assurance engagement is one where the accountant evaluates a subject matter which is the responsibility of another party against suitable criteria, and express an opinion which provides the intended user with a level of assurance.
- Assurance services improve the quality of decision making for users.
- An assurance engagement must include:
  - A three-party relationship
  - A subject matter
  - Suitable criteria
  - An engagement process
  - A conclusion
- The nature of the assignment means that 'more correct' assurance can be given than for audit, particularly specific assurance can be given, but absolute assurance is still impossible due to the nature of evidence collection.
- Accountants can provide assurance services in the following areas:
  - Risk assessment
  - Performance measurement
  - Systems reliability
  - E-commerce
- Audit related services are reviews, agreed-upon procedures and compilations.
- Reviews can be divided into two types:
  - Attestation engagements
  - Direct reporting engagements
- There is international guidance in issue about agreed-upon procedure engagements and compilation engagements.

Quick quiz

1 Assurance services are required by statute.

True ☐

False ☐

2 Which of the following are expressly not excluded from being assurance engagements by ISAE 100.

- Agreed-upon procedure assignments
- Preparation of tax returns where no conclusion is expressed
- Review assignments
- Management consulting
- Compilation assignments
- Tax consulting

3 What five elements are required for an engagement to be an assurance engagement?

(1) ____________________

(2) ____________________

(3) ____________________

(4) ____________________

(5) ____________________

4 The assurance report has a standard, written format

True ☐

False ☐

5 What three concerns does WebTrust seek to allay?

(1) ____________________

(2) ____________________

(3) ____________________

6 Name the three types of engagement which comprise audit-related services.

(1) ____________________

(2) ____________________

(3) ____________________

7 Link the review assignment with its description.

(a) Attestation engagement

(b) Direct reporting engagement

(i) The accountant is required to confirm whether:
- Accounting policies are consistent with those in prior year financial statements
- Any material modifications to the presented information are required.

(ii) The accountant is required to conduct a review and report on issues arising.

Answers to quick quiz

1 False

2 Review assignments. The rest are specifically excluded.

3 See para 1.10

4 False

5 See para 5.12

6 Review assignments, agreed-upon procedures assignments and compilation assignments.

7 (a)(i)

(b)(ii)

Now try the question below from the Exam Question Bank

Number	Level	Marks	Time
15	Exam	20	36 mins

Chapter 16

INTERNAL AUDIT AND OUTSOURCING

Introduction

In this chapter we **revise internal audit** which you studied in some detail in your studies for 2.6, *Audit and Internal Review* (old paper 6). Internal auditors provide services to the management of a company. In section two, we **compare the services** that internal auditors provide, **to the assurance and audit-related services we introduced in the previous chapter.** We also introduce a **practical issue,** the internal auditors' approach to **multi-site operations.**

In the second half of the chapter, we look at outsourcing. **Outsourcing is a key issue in business today.** It is commonly used in both the private and the public sectors. It can be used for a range of activities, and to whatever extent the management of the company want to use it. There are, of course, practical considerations for management, such as the potential redundancies they would have to make with certain functions outsourced. However, the key issues for management are **cost and control.**

The two issues are linked simply because the **question of outsourcing has become a key issue in internal audit.** Businesses are being encouraged to invest in internal audit, because of the benefits that the internal audit department can provide to corporate governance.

However, setting up an internal audit department can be costly and difficult and these problems may seem to outweigh the benefits suggested and the requirements of a voluntary code. Outsourcing can overcome these problems, leading to the adoption of **good practice in corporate governance.**

Study guide

Section 21

- Revise internal audit and
    - Its role in corporate governance
    - Its relationship (eg with audit committees, external auditors)
    - The factors which determine the extent to which reliance can be placed on its work
- Compare the objectives and principal characteristics on internal audit with other assurance engagements
- Compare and contrast operational and compliance audits
- Describe possible approaches to multi-site operations (eg cyclical compliance audits)

- Discuss the provision of outsourced internal auditing services

Section 22

- Explain the different approaches to 'outsourcing' and compare with 'insourcing'
- Discuss the advantages and disadvantages of outsourcing finance and accounting functions including:
  - data (transaction) processing
  - pensions
  - information technology (IT)
  - internal auditing
  - due diligence work
  - taxes
- Explain the impact of outsourced functions on the conduct of an audit

Exam guide

Outsourcing and internal audit could be examined together or separately. Either or both could feature in a planning scenario question.

1 REVISION: INTERNAL AUDIT

1.1 The internal audit function was considered in detail in the textbook for 2.6, *Audit and Internal Review.* Work through the following question to ensure that you remember the basic principles of internal auditing.

Question 1

(a) Describe the principal differences between internal and external auditors, considering the following factors.

(i) Eligibility

(ii) Security of appointment

(iii) Main objectives and limitations on the scope of their work

(b) Explain how external auditors would evaluate specific work carried out by internal auditors.

Answer

(a) **Eligibility**

Under the Companies Act 1985, a person is ineligible to act as external auditor if he is an officer or employee of the company, a partner or employee of such a person or a partnership in which such a person is a partner. An internal auditor is an employee of the company.

The Companies Act also requires external auditors to belong to a recognised supervisory body, and this means they must hold an appropriate qualification, follow technical standards and maintain competence.

By contrast anyone can act as an internal auditor even if they do not have a formal accounting qualification. It is up to the company's management who they appoint.

Security

Under the Companies Act, the external auditors are appointed to hold office until the conclusion of the next general meeting. They can be dismissed by an ordinary resolution of shareholders with special notice in general meeting, and have the right to make representations.

External auditors cannot be dismissed by individual directors or by a vote of the board. The only influence directors can have on the removal of external auditors is through their votes as shareholders. The rules on security of tenure are there because of the need for external auditors to protect the interests of shareholders by reporting on directors' stewardship of the business.

By contrast, as internal auditors are employees of the company, they can be dismissed by the directors or lower level of management, subject only to their normal employment rights.

Objectives and limitations on the scope of the audit work

The primary objective of external auditors is laid down by statute, to report on whether the company's accounts show a true and fair view of the state of the company's affairs at the period-end, and of its profit or loss for the period. External auditors are also required to report if certain other criteria have not been met, for example the company fails to keep proper accounting records or fails to make proper disclosure of transactions with directors.

Internal auditors' objectives are whatever the company's management decide they should be. Some of the objectives may be similar to those of external audit, for example to confirm the quality of accounting systems. Other objectives might be in areas which have little or no significance to the external auditor, for example recommending improvements in economy, efficiency and effectiveness.

Statutory rules mean that management cannot limit the scope of external auditors' work. External auditors have the right of access to all a company's books and records, and can demand all the information and explanations they deem necessary. As the objectives of internal audit's work are decided by management, management can also decide to place limitations on the scope of that work.

(b) External auditors should consider whether:

- The work is performed by persons having adequate technical training and proficiency as internal auditors
- The work of assistants is properly supervised, reviewed and documented
- Sufficient appropriate audit evidence is obtained to afford a reasonable basis for the conclusions reached
- The conclusions reached are appropriate in the circumstances
- Any reports prepared by internal audit are consistent with the results of the work performed
- Any exceptions or unusual matters disclosed by internal audit are properly resolved
- Amendments to the external audit programme are required as a result of matters identified by internal audit work
- There is a need to test the work of internal audit to confirm its adequacy.

1.2 Hopefully you could answer that question. If you struggled, you might want to refer back to your notes from 2.6, *Audit and Internal Review*, but here is a summary of the key revision points on internal audit in this syllabus.

Role of internal audit in corporate governance

Internal audit are placed perfectly to assist management in the assessment of risks and internal controls required by the Hampel and Turnbull reports. The Turnbull report in particular highlights the role internal audit can have in providing objective assurance and advice on risk and control.

The Turnbull report sets out some key guidelines for the Board.

TURNBULL GUIDELINES

- Have a **defined process** for the **review** of effectiveness of **internal control.**
- Review **regular** reports on **internal control.**
- Consider **key risks** and how they have been **managed.**
- Check the **adequacy** of **action taken** to remedy weaknesses and incidents.

- Consider the **adequacy** of **monitoring.**
- Conduct an **annual assessment** of risks and the effectiveness of internal control.
- Make a **statement** on this process in the **annual report.**

The traditional definition of internal audit given at the start of the section shows how internal audit can help the directors achieve these objectives; the traditional purpose of internal audit was to review controls.

The third of the Turnbull guidelines refers to risk. All companies face risks arising from their operational activities. Risks arise in different areas.

- Risk the company will go bankrupt
- Risks arising from regulations and law
- Risks arising from publicity

Turnbull requires that risk be managed. This gives rise to another role for the internal audit function, **risk management.**

Risk awareness and management should be the role of everyone in the organisation. The extended role of internal audit with regard to risk is the monitoring of integrated risk management within a company, and the reporting of results to the Board to enable them to report to shareholders.

Internal auditor relationships

Internal auditors have relationships with the following people:

- **Management**: by whom they are employed and may report to
- **Audit committee**: whom they report to
- **External auditors**: who may make use of their work

Reliance on the work of internal auditors by external auditors

The external auditors may make use of the work of internal audit. The guidance over when this appropriate is given to them in SAS 500 *Considering the work of internal audit.*

The SAS states that the external auditors must give consideration first to the scope and organisation of the internal audit department and then evaluate the specific audit work they are interested in.

The following factors must be considered.

- Proficiency and training of the people who have undertaken the work
- Level of supervision, review and documentation of the work of assistants
- Sufficiency and appropriateness of evidence to draw conclusions
- Appropriateness of conclusions drawn
- Consistency of any reports prepared with the work performed
- Whether the work necessitates amendment to the external audit programme

Internal auditors and risk management

1.3 The issue of the Turnbull guidance and internal audit's role in relation to risk management was touched on briefly in the box.

1.4 In response to the Turnbull guidance, directors need to ensure three steps are taken in their business.

- Identify risks
- Control risks
- Monitor risks

1.5 If an internal audit department exists, it is likely to be involved in all stages of this process due to some key skills it has. These will be drawn out as we consider the stages below.

Identify risks

1.6 Firstly, a detailed review of specific systems will be required. These systems are:

- Recording information supply
- Establishing a document trail
- Verifying the above processes

1.7 Internal auditors, with their knowledge of a company's systems, are likely to be involved in this process.

1.8 Once the system has been reviewed, the person designated as risk manager will assess the system and identify the risks which may arise. These risks could include, for example:

- Contractual risks (important customers not agreeing to given contractual terms)
- Operational risks (scarce raw materials, risks arising through storage and use)
- Physical risks (for example, health and safety compliance)
- Product distribution (logistics, networks, outlets)
- Regulation (different jurisdictions, internet trading)
- Reputation (brands and staff profile)

Control risks

1.9 Once risks have been identified, the business needs to control the risks. The methods used to control the risks will depend on the risks themselves, but the following broad measures may be taken:

- Training staff in particular areas
- Communication of risk avoidance measures to all staff
- Constant risk awareness and opportunity identification at all levels of the business

Monitor risks

1.10 After risks have been identified and controlled the entire process needs to be monitored, to ensure that the process is followed continuously, and that new risks which arise are identified.

1.11 Internal auditors are well placed in the organisation to monitor the process of continuous risk management as an extension of their other compliance duties.

1.12 Equally, external auditors could undertake such a monitoring role as an assurance engagement, discussed in Chapter 15.

2 OTHER INTERNAL AUDIT ISSUES

2.1 For 3.1, there are some additional issues to consider in relation to internal audit as a result of the further emphasis of other types of audits and assurance services in this syllabus. They are:

- Internal audit and assurance engagements
- Operational and compliance audits
- Multi-site operations
- Outsourcing

2.2 Outsourcing relates to areas other than internal audit, so this will be considered later in the chapter. At this stage, we shall consider the first three issues.

Internal audit and assurance engagements

REMEMBER

The definition of an **assurance engagement** is:

An assignment where a professional accountant evaluates or measures a subject matter that is the responsibility of another party against suitable criteria, and expresses an opinion which provides the intended user with a level of assurance about that subject matter.

Internal audit can be described as follows:

An independent appraisal function established within an organisation to examine and evaluate its activities.

2.3 It is clear from the above definitions that internal audit is in many ways an **assurance function**. Internal auditors, like accountants undertaking an assurance engagement, will evaluate and measure the performance of certain aspects of the company against pre-ordained criteria.

2.4 However, in some ways, internal audit can also be compared to an **agreed-upon procedures assignment**, which, as you know from the chapter on audit related services, is not an assurance engagement. This is because the work the internal audit function perform may be pre-ordained by management.

Operational and compliance audits

KEY TERMS

Operational audits are audits of the operational processes of the organisation and check not only compliance with controls but also the effectiveness of controls as part of the risk management process.

Compliance audits are audit checks intended to determine whether the actions of employees are in accordance with company policy or laws and regulations.

2.5 Compliance audits are the traditional realm of internal auditors. They involve having a knowledge of the company policy and carrying out tests to ensure that company policy is being followed in practice.

2.6 As such, compliance audits tend to fall into the category of internal audit providing assurance services, as discussed above. This is because management are employing them to give them assurance that certain criteria have been met.

2.7 However, the work is not assurance in the strict sense of ISAE 100, because internal audit are not really checking 'assertions' of the employees of the company. They are checking that procedures have been complied with.

2.8 Operational audits are different to compliance audits in that the scope is more extensive. As part of an operational audit, the internal audit department might undertake a compliance audit, but the scope **also includes an assessment of the effectiveness** of the procedures that are being audited.

2.9 As such, an operational audit is more like an agreed-upon procedures engagement. While an element of assurance is given (particularly with regard to the compliance elements of the assignment), the audit is designed with the intention of the internal auditor drawing his own conclusions about the systems from the work he has done.

Multi-site operations

2.10 Some organisations have several outlets which all operate the same systems. A good example of this would be a retail chain, which would have a number of shops where systems relating to stock and cash, for example, would be the same.

2.11 The objective of audits of multi-site operations is the same as the objective of single site operations. However, as results might vary across the different location, the internal auditor has to take a different approach. Some possible approached to multi-site operations audits are set out below.

(a) **Compliance based audit approach**

With a compliance based audit approach, a master audit programme is drawn up which is used to check the compliance of the branches with the set procedures, after which the results from the branches are compared. There are two possible ways of undertaking the compliance based approach:

- **Cyclical**. This approach is based on visiting all of the sites within a given timeframe.
- **Risk based approach**. This alternative determines which branches are to be visited based on the risk attached to them.

(b) **Process based audit approach**

With a process based audit approach, the audit is planned so that specific key processes are audited. In a retail operation, for example, this could involve the important process of cash handling being audited. This approach can also be undertaken in two ways:

- **Cyclical**. Aims to audit all processes in a business within a set timeframe.
- **Risk-based**. The processes to be audited are determined with reference to the risk attached to them.

Practical considerations

2.12 The practical issues to consider in relation to multi-site operations are:

- Which sites to visit
- How often to visit various sites
- Whether to conduct routine or surprise visits and what mix of these types of visit.

2.13 Remember that the considerations behind which sites to visit will **not** be the same as for external auditors. Internal auditors may consider issues (among others) such as:

- Size of operation
- History of systems compliance

- Quality/experience of staff on site
- Past results of testing
- Management interest in particular sites

3 OUTSOURCING

KEY TERMS

Outsourcing is the process of purchasing key functions from an outside supplier. In other words, it is **contracting-out** certain functions, for example, internal audit or information technology.

Insourcing, by contrast, is the practice of operating such functions within the company, in other words, running your own information technology department. Some companies who develop a particular specialism in operating a key function (which is not their sole business) may extend insourcing, by operating the function for other businesses, as a sideline to their major business.

3.1 Generally, if a company chooses to outsource, it will outsource functions which are not perceived to be key competencies. The different approaches which can be taken to outsourcing depend on the extent to which a company contracts out non-core functions. This can be seen by way of an example.

Case example

The Toy Company Limited

The Toy Company Limited is a small company, owned and run by Edward T. Bear. It was left to him by his father, T. Bear, who was a skilled toy maker. The business began as a one man operation in the garage and is now has 250 employees and technical computerised processes and is run from its own factory complex.

Edward joined the company on leaving school. He worked alongside his father for ten years. Last year his father died and left the shares in the company to Edward and his sister Victoria. Victoria has never had any role in the company, and is keen to continue that.

The company employed an accountant twenty years previously, and he is still an employee of the firm. In the intervening years, the accounts department has grown to now incorporate five other employees, with one having specific payroll duties. The accounts department has a computer system which is separate from the computer system used in operations.

In operations, there are several divisions: design, manufacture, packaging, sales and marketing.

The company also employs a part time human resources manager who deals with staff matters and recruitment. The office cleaner is the longest serving member of staff. She has worked for Mr Bear since he set up in his first work shop forty years ago.

3.2 In the example of the Toy Company, there are several areas where management could consider outsourcing. We will consider the advantages and disadvantages of this below. Here we are only looking to see where the potential lies.

3.3 The core competency of the company is the manufacture of toys. This means that there are several functions which do not fall within this competency:

- Accounting
- Human Resources

- Cleaning

3.4 Of the above areas, cleaning would be the least risky to outsource because the cleaning does not directly impact on the operation of the business. Cleaning is a common outsourced function in the private sector.

3.5 However, we are more interested in the accounting function, being accountants. The accounts department is not part of the core competency, so potentially, it could be outsourced. Within this decision, there are several others. The company could outsource:

- Pension functions
- Tax related functions (VAT, PAYE)
- The entire payroll function
- Invoicing
- Credit control
- The entire accounting function

3.6 When considering **the extent to which the company wants to adopt outsourcing**, it will must consider the risk involved and the control which management want to maintain over the function. There is less risk involved in outsourcing a part of the payroll function (for example, pensions) than in outsourcing the whole finance function.

3.7 Similar subdivisions can be seen when considering the outsourcing of other functions:

Human Resources	Welfare
	Health and safety
	Recruitment
	The entire department
Information Technology	Maintenance
	Project management
	Network management
	The entire IT function

3.8 Just to extend the point about outsourcing to its furthest extremes, it is possible to consider outsourcing more of the business than has been discussed above.

3.9 In the first instance, Edward could critically appraise the core competency of his business (the manufacture of toys) and subdivide it further. He might decide that the production processes are the core competency and that functions such as design and sales and marketing should be outsourced.

3.10 In an extreme case, it is possible to create a **virtual organisation**. For example, Edward could decide that he has no particular personal interest in toy manufacture, but that he does wish to retain the business. In which case, he could outsource all the different functions of the business, but maintain control of the contracts and therefore ultimately the business.

3.11 An example of an industry where this could be the case is the airline industry, where it is possible to contract out the aircraft and their maintenance and the crew to fly them.

Advantages and disadvantages of outsourcing

3.12 We will look in detail at the advantages and disadvantages of outsourcing some specific functions in the following sections. For now, however, we shall consider some general advantages and disadvantages of outsourcing that apply to them all.

Advantages of outsourcing
Cost. A key advantage of outsourcing is that it is often cheaper to contract a service out than it is to conduct it in house.
Specialist service. Outsourcing results in specialist being used to provide the service when that would not have been the case if the function was performed in house.
Indemnity. The service organisation may provide indemnity in the event of problems arising. If problems arise in house, there is no such comfort zone.
Cash flow. Obtaining the service through a contract may assist with cash flow, as the contract will represent a flat fee, whereas the cost of providing the service in house might have led to fluctuating costs (for example, if temporary staff are required in a busy period).

Disadvantages of outsourcing
The single biggest disadvantage of outsourcing, is the extent to which the company loses **control** over the function.
The **initial cost** of outsourcing may be **substantial,** if an aspect of the decision is to close a current department of the business. The question of **potential redundancies** may dissuade companies from considering outsourcing.
The contract has to be **managed** to ensure that the service being provided is appropriate and in accordance with the contract. This may take a disproportionate amount of **time**.
The contract might limit the **liability** of the contractor, leading to problems if the contract is not performed well. This might even result in **court action** being required.
Should these disadvantages be realised, the **cost** of outsourcing could outweigh the benefit, even though in theory outsourcing should reduce cost.

4 OUTSOURCING INTERNAL AUDIT

4.1 Internal audit is rarely a core competency of a company. However, it is a valuable service to management. The corporate codes of recent years that we discussed in chapter five have emphasised the importance of internal audit in assessing controls and monitoring risks.

4.2 There are **problems associated with setting up an internal audit department,** however. These are:

- Cost of recruiting staff.
- Difficulty of recruiting staff of sufficient skill and qualification for the company's preference or need.
- The fact that management are not accounting specialist and therefore might struggle to direct the new department in their duties.
- The time frame between setting up the department and seeing the results of having the department.

- The fact that the work required may not be enough to justify engaging full time staff
- The fact that a variety of skills and seniority levels are required, but only one member of full time staff can be justified.

4.3 The advantage of outsourcing internal audit is that outsourcing can overcome all these problems:

- Staff need not be recruited, as the **service provider has good quality staff**.
- The service provider has **specialist skill** and can assess what management require them to do. As they are external to the operation, this will not cause operational problems.
- Outsourcing can provide an **immediate** internal audit department.
- The service contract can be for the **appropriate time scale** (a two week project, a month, etc)
- Because the **time scale is flexible**, **a team of staff** can be provided if required.
- The service provider could also provide less than at team, but, for example, could provide one member of staff on a full-time basis for a short period, as a **secondment**.

4.4 Outsourced internal audit services are provided by many audit firms, particularly the big five. This can range from a team of staff for a short term project, or a single staff member on a long term project.

4.5 However, the fact that internal audit services are typically provided by external auditors can raise problems as well:

- The company might wish to **use the same firm** for internal and external audit services, but this may lead to **complications for the external auditors**.
- The **cost** of sourcing the internal audit function might be high enough to make the directors choose not to have an internal audit function at all.

4.6 A key advantage of outsourcing internal audit is that **outsourcing can be used on a short term basis,** to:

- Provide immediate services
- Lay the basis of a permanent function, by setting policies and functions
- Prepare the directors for the implications of having an internal audit function
- Assist the directors in recruiting the permanent function.

5 OUTSOURCING FINANCE AND ACCOUNTING FUNCTIONS

5.1 Various functions will be considered in the table below. Remember, however, the key advantages and disadvantages set out in Section 3, they are all likely to be true of the functions discussed more specifically below.

FUNCTION	
Data processing	
Disadvantages	There may be logistical difficulties in outsourcing data processing, due to the high level of paper involved (invoices, goods received notes etc). This information will have to be given to the service organisation. A secondary, and more important, effect is that the company might not always have control of their key accounting documentation and records. It is a legal requirement that the directors maintain this information. While they may delegate the practicalities, they are still responsible for maintaining the records.
Pensions	
Advantages	Pensions are a specialist area and there is merit in getting a specialist to operate the company's pension provision.
Disadvantages	Pensions are closely related to the payroll and the company will need to share sensitive information with the pension provider, which may make the situation complicated
Information technology	
Advantages	A key advantage of outsourcing all, or elements of, the IT function is that this will enable the company to keep pace with **rapid technological advances.** It also allows the company to take advantage of the work of specialist in a field that many people still find difficult but which they use regularly to carry out their business. Outsourcing can provide a useful **safety net** of a technical helpline or indemnity in the event of computer disaster. It is also possible that through outsourcing, the company will be able to obtain **added-value,** such as new ways of doing business identified (for example, e-commerce)
Due diligence	
Advantages	A key advantage in relation to outsourcing due diligence is the high level of **expertise** that can be brought in. The company can expect **quality** from its service contractor, and can seek **legal compensation** from them in the event of negligence.
Taxes	
Advantages	In relation to taxes, the key advantage is also the buying in of **expertise**.
Disadvantages	The disadvantage of outsourcing tax work is that while the work can be outsourced, the **responsibility** cannot. The tax authorities will deal with the responsible person, not the agent, so the loss of control is particularly risky in this case

6 IMPACT OF OUTSOURCING ON AN AUDIT

6.1 The impact of outsourcing on an external audit is considered in SAS 480 *Service organisations*.

6.2 You were introduced to this SAS in the text for 2.6, *Audit and Internal Review*. However, as it was not examined in the old syllabus at paper 6, *The Audit Framework*, it is set out in detail here.

KEY TERM

A **service organisation** is an organisation that provides services to another organisation.

6.3 As we have discussed above, some companies choose to outsource activities necessary to the running of their business to service organisations. SAS 480 gives examples of such activities that may be outsourced:

- Information processing
- Maintenance of accounting records
- Facilities management
- Asset management (for example, investments)
- Initiation or execution of transactions on behalf of the other entity

6.4 Some outsourced activities may be directly relevant to the audit. The most obvious example above is the maintenance of accounting records, but most of them actually could impact on the audit.

6.5 Auditors need to obtain sufficient, appropriate audit evidence to express an opinion on financial statements. they therefore need to consider an approach towards the parts of the audit affected by the service organisation.

Audit planning

6.6 As part of their audit planning, auditors need to obtain a knowledge of the business. Understanding what functions are outsourced is a part of that.

SAS 480.2

In planning the audit, user entity auditors should determine whether activities undertaken by service organisations are relevant to the audit.

KEY TERM

The **user entity** is the organisation which is outsourcing any of its activities to the service organisation.

6.7 The SAS lists the following activities as relevant activities. (This is not an exclusive list.)

- Maintenance of accounting records
- Other finance functions
- Management of assets
- Undertaking or making arrangements for transactions as agent of the user entity.

6.8 It is important for the auditor to understand the terms of the agreement between the service organisation and the user entity.

SAS 480.3

User entity and auditors should obtain and document an understanding of:

(a) the contractual terms which apply to relevant activities undertaken by service organisations; and

(b) the way that the user entity monitors those activities so as to ensure that it meets its fiduciary and other legal responsibilities.

6.9 The SAS gives a list of things the auditor should consider.

Whether the terms contain an adequate specification of the information to be provided to the user entity and responsibilities for initiating transactions relating to the activity undertaken by the service organisation.
The way that accounting records relating to relevant activities are maintained.
Whether the user entity has right to access to accounting records prepared by the service organisation concerning the activities undertaken, and relevant underlying information held by it, and the conditions in which such access may be sought.
Whether the terms take proper account of any applicable requirements of regulatory bodies concerning the form of records to be maintained, or access to them.
The nature of relevant performance standards.
The way in which the use entity monitors performance of relevant activities and the extent to which its monitoring process relies on controls operated by the service organisation.
Whether the service organisation has agreed to indemnify the user entity in the event of a performance failure.
Whether the contractual terms permit the user entity auditors access to source of audit evidence including accounting records of the user entity and the information necessary for the conduct of the audit.

Assessing audit risk and designing audit procedures

6.10 It is important that the auditor considers the impact that the client's use of a service organisation has on the risk of the audit.

SAS 480.4

User entity auditors should determine the effect of relevant activities on their assessment of inherent risk and the user entity's control environment.

6.11 The auditor should consider:

- The **nature** of the service
- The degree of **authority** delegated
- The arrangements for ensuring **quality**
- Whether assets prone to loss or misappropriation are involved
- The **reputation** of the service organisation

6.12 In relation to control risk, the auditor should consider the monitoring that the user entity has in place over the service organisation's activities.

6.13 The appendix to the SAS outlines a number of control considerations.

6.14 Having considered the risk attached to the use of the service organisation, the auditor should design audit procedures to obtain sufficient, appropriate audit evidence.

Accounting records

> **SAS 480.5**
>
> If a service organisation maintains all or part of user entity's accounting records, user entity auditors should assess whether the arrangements affect their reporting responsibilities in relation to accounting records arising from law or regulations.

6.15 This is because it is a legal requirement (under the Companies Act 1985) that directors are responsible for maintaining accounting records.

Obtaining audit evidence

> **SAS 480.6**
>
> Based on their understanding of the aspects of the user entity's accounting system and control environment relating to relevant activities, user entity auditors should:
>
> (a) asses whether sufficient appropriate audit evidenced concerning the relevant financial statement assessment is available from records held at the user entity; and if not
>
> (b) determine effective procedures to obtain evidence necessary for the audit, either by direct access to records kept by service organisations or through information obtained from the service organisations or their auditors.

6.16 The SAS outlines a series of procedures which the auditors should evaluate for efficiency and effectiveness:

- Inspecting records and documents held by the user entity
- Establishing the effectiveness of controls
- Obtaining representations to confirm balance and transactions from the service organisation
- Performing analytical review on
  - The records maintained by the user entity, or
  - The returns received from the service organisation
- Inspecting records and documents held by the service organisation
- Requesting specified procedures re performed by
  - The service organisation
  - The user entity's internal audit department
- Reviewing information from the service organisation or its auditors concerning the design and operation of its control systems.

SAS 480.7

When using a report issued by the service organisation's auditors, the user entity's auditors should consider the scope of the work performed and assess whether the report is sufficient and appropriate for its intended use.

6.17 The new entity's auditors should consider whether the information contained in the report is:

- Relevant
- Adequate
- Covers the right time period

6.18 The auditor is always **solely responsible** for the audit opinion. He must be assured that he has gained sufficient, appropriate advice to have an opinion on the financial statements, he must then express his opinion.

Impact on internal audit

6.19 External auditors will be affected when outsourced functions impact on the financial statements. Internal audit will be interested in outsourced functions which affect the business (that is, any outsourced function).

6.20 Internal audit will be interested in the contractual arrangements made with the service organisation. They may want to pay a visit to the organisation and undertake a review of its systems to ensure that they are sufficient for the business's needs.

Chapter roundup

- Internal audit have a key role in corporate governance, providing objective assurance on control and risk management.
- External auditors may use the work of internal audit during the course of their audit. However, they must assess the proficiency and quality of the staff and work done.
- The work undertaken by internal auditors has some similarities and some dissimilarities with both assurance services and audit related services.
- There are four possible approaches internal auditors may take to multi-site operations these are:
  - Compliance based - cyclical
    - risk based
  - Process based - cyclical
    - risk based
- Outsourcing is the contracting out of certain functions. A business can outsource a small part of the function, or the entire function, or practically all its functions!
- The key advantage of outsourcing are the cost benefits it can provide and the use of specialist skills. Some specific-function advantages are:
  - IT – keeping up with technological advance
  - IT/Due diligence – indemnity against poor quality
  - Internal audit – speed of set up, time scale needs met
- The key disadvantage is loss of **control.**
- The impact on the audit of one is discussed in SAS 480, *Service Organisations.*

Quick quiz

1 List six factors which the external auditors should consider in relation to the work of internal audit.

(1) ____________________

(2) ____________________

(3) ____________________

(4) ____________________

(5) ____________________

(6) ____________________

2 Complete the definitions

________________ audits are audits of the ____________ ____________ of the organisation and check not only compliance with controls but also the ____________ of controls as part of the risk management process.

________________ audits are audit checks intended to determine whether the actions of employees are in __________________ with company ____________ or ____________ and ____________.

3 Outsourcing is another term that means staff recruitment

True ☐

False ☐

4 Name five elements of the accounts function which could be outsourced.

(1) ____________________

(2) ____________________

(3) ____________________

(4) ____________________

(5) ____________________

5 Complete the table, putting the advantages made under the right headings and naming the specific function, if relevant.

General advantages	Function-specific advantages

- Cost
- Keeping pace with technological advance
- Liability/indemnity
- Cashflow
- Specialist service
- Indemnity
- Flexibility (particularly with regard to time scale)

6 The auditor may refer to the responsibility of the service organisation when giving his opinion in financial statements.

True ☐

False ☐

Answers to quick quiz

1 (1) Proficiency and training of staff
(2) Level of supervision, documentation and review of the work
(3) Sufficiency and appropriateness of evidence
(4) Appropriateness of conclusion
(5) Consistency of reports with work performed
(6) Whether work necessitates amendment to original audit plan

2 Operational, operational processes, effectiveness

Compliance, accordance, policy, law, regulations

3 False. It is contracting-out functions

4 See para 3.5

5

General advantages	Function-specific advantages
• Cost • Liability/indemnity • Cashflow • Specialist service • Flexibility	• Technological advance (IT) • Liability/indemnity (IT/due diligence) • Immediacy (IA) • Flexibility/time scale (IA)

6 False

- Responsibility for accounting records still lies with directors
- Responsibility for auditing them still lies with auditors

Now try the question below from the Exam Question Bank

Number	Level	Marks	Time
16	Exam	20	36 mins

Chapter 17

PROSPECTIVE FINANCIAL INFORMATION

Introduction

There is currently **no existing UK guidance** on reporting on prospective financial information (PFI). There was a draft standard issued in 1990 by the APC and a discussion paper issued in 1998 by the APB.

However, there is **guidance in issue internationally,** with ISA 810, *The examination of prospective financial information*. We shall use this as a basis for our studies on PFI, in the absence of any definitive UK perspective.

There is no statutory requirement in the UK to report on PFI other than a requirement for listed companies to obtain an auditors' report on profit forecasts included in listing particulars (outside the scope of this syllabus). However, **forecasts are of significant interest to users.** Some would say that PFI is of more interest to users of accounts than historic information (HFI), which of course, auditors do report on in the statutory audit.

This is an area in which the **auditors can therefore provide an alternative service to audit, in the form of a review or assurance engagement.** This chapter therefore looks at the considerations that the auditor should consider when taking on such an engagement. The basis for this chapter has been laid in Chapter 15, but in this chapter, we consider issues specific to PFI.

Study guide

Section 20

- Define 'prospective financial information' and distinguish between a 'forecast' and a 'projection'
- Describe the matters to be considered before accepting an engagement to report on prospective financial information
- Discuss the level of assurance which the auditor may provide and explain the other factors to be considered in determining the nature, timing and extent of examination procedures
- Describe examination procedures to verify forecasts and projections relating to
  - capital expenditure
  - profits
  - cashflows
- Discuss the basis on which auditors should form an opinion on prospective financial information

Exam guide

The difficulties of reporting on PFI and the points raised in the APB's discussion paper could be relevant as a 'current issue' in the exam.

1 REPORTING ON PROSPECTIVE FINANCIAL INFORMATION

KEY TERM

Prospective financial information is information based on assumptions about events that may occur in the future and possible actions by an entity.

1.1 From the definition given above, you can see that prospective financial information is highly subjective. This makes it a difficult area to examine and report on.

1.2 There has never been any auditing guidance on prospective financial information in the UK. A draft auditing guideline was issued in 1990 by the Auditing Practices Committee, but it did not become a final guideline.

1.3 The purpose of this exposure draft was to give **general guidance** to accountants reviewing and reporting on such information, which may be prepared:

- As an internal management tool for decision making, or
- For the use of third parties, such as:
  - In a prospectus issued to raise capital, in order to provide potential investors with information about future expectations
  - In a document issued in connection with a public take-over, and
  - In a document for the information of lenders (for example statements of cash flow showing the funds expected to be available for payment of interest and principals)

1.4 What is called 'prospective financial information' may take various forms, from a statement such as 'profits will be somewhat higher that last year' to a detailed monthly cash flow statement. It may also comprise profit and loss accounts, cash flows, working capital statements and balance sheets or any combinations of them.

1.5 There has recently been renewed interest in the reporting of prospective financial information (PFI), with the ICAEW issuing a discussion paper about PFI in the Autumn of 2000.

1.6 There is an international auditing standard on the issue, which is ISA 810 *The examination of prospective financial information*.

1.7 In this chapter we will consider points contained within the APC draft on the issue of prospective financial information. However, as it is dated and was never formalised into auditing guidance, we shall also consider the more recent debate about the subject, and particularly, the international guidance on the matter.

1.8 The ISA gives the following definitions of the two key components of PFI.

> **KEY TERMS**
>
> A **forecast** means prospective financial information prepared on the basis of assumptions as to future events which management expects to take place and actions management expects to take as of the date the information is prepared (best estimate assumptions).
>
> A **projection** means prospective information prepared on the basis of
>
> (a) Hypothetical assumptions about future events and management actions which are not necessarily expected to take place, such as when some entities are in a start-up phase or are considering a major change in the nature of operations; or
>
> (b) A mixture of best estimate and hypothetical assumptions
>
> (ISA 810)

1.9 The recent discussion paper in the UK on PFI suggested **a departure from the international definitions,** on the grounds that prospective information is always based to an extent on future expectations.

1.10 It suggests the following definitions:

- **Forecast**. Something about which the directors are prepared to say 'this is highly likely to happen'.
- **Projection**. Something about which the directors are prepared to say 'this is reasonably likely to happen'.

1.11 It lists a series of factors that will help to distinguish between the two. They include:

- The activities involved
- The time scale
- The discretion over decision-making involved
- The relationship with overall management strategy

APB's discussion paper

1.12 In April 1998 the Auditing Practices Board issued a discussion paper on *Prospective Financial Information*. The discussion paper considers a number of issues including:

(a) The fact that many **assumptions go beyond accountants' expertise,** for example projecting future market size or share of a projects or evaluating the natural resources to be obtained from a mine. Additionally even independent experts may have difficulties reaching unequivocal opinions on these issues.

(b) Whether accountants should be required to **report explicitly** on whether assumptions made when the information was prepared are reasonable. The APB is concerned that the potential scope of this opinion is so wide as to render it of limited value.

1.13 The paper also considers whether accountants should report on whether the forecast is likely to be achieved; this option is not favoured by the APB on the grounds that the work needed to reach an opinion on achievability would have a substantial cost (if indeed such an opinion could be reached).

1.14 The paper points out that factors affecting the reliability of prospective financial information include the future period to which the information relates, and whether the

information is about an established business or a newly started up business. The paper proposes a system of categorisation depending on whether the directors believe the predicted outcome will take place, hope it will take place or are just illustrating a possible outcome. A system of categorisation may prove significant if accountants report on different types of information in different ways.

1.15 The paper discusses the level of detail that should be included, and the desirability of disclosing the sensibilities used when preparing the information.

1.16 The paper also considers the question of **liability.** The APB sees this as tied in with what the subject is of the accountant's report. The paper raises the possibility that reports on certain categories of information should only be given in terms that limit the accountants' liability. The paper suggests that an accountants' review with limited liability would be better than no review at all.

1.17 The paper also notes that in the USA there is '**safe harbour**' legislation relating to reports on prospective financial information. This gives protection from forward-looking statements being used as a basis for liability if certain cautionary words accompany the statements, and the plaintiffs fail to establish that those making the statement knew they were false and misleading. In other countries prospective financial information is often not published because of the **liability risks** involved.

1.18 The paper points out that increases in the information provided will reduce investors' risk, and investors are after all seeking a return from a **risk-based** investment. It may be inequitable therefore for the liability of accountants (and directors and sponsors) to increase because of efforts they are making to reduce investors' risk. This paper does though acknowledge the contrary argument, that giving protection from liability may mean that forecasts and projections are recklessly included in investment circulars.

1.19 The key issues that projections relate to are:

- Capital expenditure
- Profits
- Cashflows

These are the key areas which we will focus on in the procedure part of this chapter.

2 ACCEPTING AN ENGAGEMENT

2.1 ISA 810 gives the following guidance about accepting an engagement to examine PFI.

> **ISA 810.11**
>
> The auditor should not accept, or should withdraw from, an engagement when the assumptions are clearly unrealistic or when the auditor believes that the prospective financial information will be inappropriate for its intended use.
>
> **ISA 810.12**
>
> The auditor and the client should agree on the terms of the engagement.

2.2 The ISA also lists the following **factors** which the auditor should consider:

- The **intended use** of the information

- Whether the information will be for general or limited **distribution**
- The **nature of the assumptions**, that is, whether they are best estimate or hypothetical assumptions
- The **elements** to be **included** in the information
- The **period covered** by the information

2.3 It also states that the auditor should have sufficient knowledge of the business to be able to evaluate the significant assumptions made.

3 PROCEDURES

3.1 In carrying out their review, the general matters to which attention should be directed are:

- The nature and background of the company's business
- The accounting policies normally followed by the company
- The assumptions on which the forecast is based
- The procedures followed by the company in preparing the forecast.

3.2 **The nature and background of the company's business**. The accountants will review the company's character and recent history, with reference to such matters as the nature of its activities and its main products, markets, customers, suppliers, divisions, locations, and trend of results.

3.3 **The accounting policies normally followed by the company.** The accountant will wish to establish the accounting principles normally followed by the company and ensure that they have been consistently applied in the preparation of forecasts.

3.4 **The procedure followed by the company in preparing the forecast.** In carrying out their review of the accounting bases and calculations for forecasts, and the procedures followed by the company for preparing them, the main points which the reporting accountants will wish to consider include the following:

(a) Whether the forecast under review is based on forecasts regularly prepared for the purpose of management or whether it has been separately and specially prepared for the immediate purpose.

(b) Where forecasts are regularly prepared for management purposes, the degree of accuracy and reliability previously achieved, and the frequency and thoroughness with which estimates are revised.

(c) Whether the forecast under review represents the management's best estimate of results which they reasonably believe can and will be achieved as distinct from targets which the management have set as desirable.

(d) The extent to which forecast results for expired periods are supported by reliable interim accounts.

(e) The details of the procedures followed to generate the forecast and the extent to which it is built up form detailed forecasts of activity and cash flow.

(f) The extent to which profits are derived from activities having a proved and consistent trend and those of a more irregular, volatile or unproved nature.

(g) How the forecast takes account of any material extraordinary items and prior year adjustments, their nature, and how they are presented.

(h) Whether adequate provision is made for foreseeable losses and contingencies and how the forecast takes account of factors which may cause it to be subject to a high degree of risk, or which may invalidate the assumptions.

(i) Whether working capital appears adequate for requirements; (normally this would require the availability of properly prepared cash-flow forecasts) and where short-term or long-term finance is to be relied on, whether the necessary arrangements have been made and confirmed.

(j) The arithmetical accuracy of the forecast and the supporting information and whether forecast balance sheets and sources and applications of funds statements have been prepared as these help to highlight arithmetical inaccuracies and inconsistent assumptions.

ISA 810.17

When determining the nature, timing and extent of examination procedures, the auditor's considerations should include:

(a) the likelihood of material misstatement;

(b) the knowledge obtained during any previous engagement;

(c) management's competence regarding the preparation of prospective financial information;

(d) the extent to which the prospective financial information is affected by the management's judgement; and

(e) the adequacy and the reliability of the underlying data

3.5 The ISA goes on to say that the auditor should **seek appropriate evidence** on those areas which are **particularly sensitive to variation** and have a **material effect** in the information.

3.6 The following list of procedures are procedures which may also be relevant when assessing prospective financial information. The auditor should undertake the review procedures discussed above in addition to these.

Profit forecasts

- Verify projected **income** figures to suitable evidence. This may involve:
  - Comparison of the basis of projected income to similar existing projects in the firm
  - Review of current market prices for that product or service, that is, what competitors in the market charge successfully
- Verify projected **expenditure** figures to suitable evidence. There is likely to be more evidence available about expenditure in the form of:
  - Quotations or estimates provided to the firm
  - Current bills for things such as services which can be used to reliably estimate
  - Market rate prices, for example, for advertising
  - Interest rate assumptions can be compared to the bank's current rates
  - Costs such as depreciation should correspond with relevant capital expenditure projections

Capital expenditure

The auditor should check the capital expenditure for **reasonableness**. For example, if the projection related to buying land and developing it, it should include a sum for land.

- Projected costs should be **verified to estimates and quotations** where possible
- The projections can be reviewed for **reasonableness**, including a comparison prevailing **market rates** where such information is available (such as for property)

Cash forecasts

- The auditors should review cash forecasts to ensure the **timings involved** are **reasonable** (for example, it is not reasonable to say the building will be bought on day 1, as property transactions usually take longer than that).
- The auditor should check the cash forecast for **consistency with the any profit forecasts** (income/expenditure should be the same, just at different times)
- If there is no comparable profit forecast, the income and expenditure items should be verified as they would have been on a profit forecast.

4 EXPRESSING AN OPINION

Level of assurance

4.1 It is clear that as prospective financial information is subjective information, it is **impossible** for an auditor **to give the same level of assurance** regarding it, as he would on **historic financial information.**

4.2 In their discussion paper of 1998, the **APB did not favour** the idea that auditors should **report on whether the projections are achievable**. This is because they felt that if this were even possible, it would take time and therefore be prohibitively expensive.

4.3 The ISA suggests that the auditor express an opinion including

- A statement of **negative assurance** that as to whether the **assumptions** provide a reasonable basis for the prospective financial information
- An opinion as to whether the prospective financial information is **properly prepared** on the basis of the assumptions and the relevant reporting framework
- Appropriate **caveats as to the achievability** of the forecasts.

KEY TERM

Negative assurance is assurance of something in the absence of any evidence arising to the contrary. In effect, this means the auditor is saying, 'I believe that this is reasonable because I have no reason to believe otherwise.'

Report outlined in the APC's 1990 exposure draft

4.4 The draft guideline emphasises that **responsibility** for any prospective financial information **lies with management.**

4.5 The exposure draft proposes that in making his report, the reporting accountant should ensure that the report including his opinion:

(a) Identifies the prospective financial information under review

(b) Draws attention to his work having been carried out in accordance with the auditing guideline *Prospective financial information*

(c) Includes a statement of management's responsibility for the prospective financial information and for the assumptions

(d) If profit estimates are included, indicates that such estimates are unaudited

(e) Includes appropriate caveats.

Report under ISA 810

ISA 810.27

The report by an auditor on an examination of prospective financial information should contain the following:

(a) title;

(b) addressee;

(c) identification of the prospective financial information;

(d) a reference to the International Standards on Auditing or relevant national standards or practices applicable to the examination of prospective financial information;

(e) a statement that management is responsible for the prospective financial information including the assumptions on which it is based;

(f) when applicable, a reference to the purpose and/or restricted distribution of the prospective financial information;

(g) a statement of negative assurance as to whether the assumptions provide a reasonable basis for the prospective financial information;

(h) an opinion as to whether the prospective financial information is properly prepared on the basis of the assumptions and is presented in accordance with the relevant financial reporting framework;

(i) appropriate caveats concerning the achievability of the results indicated by the prospective financial information;

(j) date of the report which should be the date procedures have been completed;

(k) auditor's address

(l) signature

ISA 810.31

When the auditor believes that the presentation and disclosure of the prospective financial information is not adequate, the auditor should express a qualified or adverse opinion in the report on the prospective financial information, or withdraw from the engagement as appropriate.

ISA 810.32

When the auditor believes that one or more significant assumptions do not provide a reasonable basis for the prospective financial information prepared on the basis of best-estimate assumptions or that one or more significant assumptions do not provide a reasonable basis for the prospective financial information given the hypothetical assumptions, the auditor should either express an adverse opinion and describe the scope limitation in the report on the prospective financial information.

Question 1

A new client of your practice, Peter Lawrence, has recently been made redundant. He is considering setting up a residential home for old people as he is aware that there is an increasing need for this service with an ageing population (more people are living to an older age). He has seen a large house, which he plans to convert into an old people's home. Each resident will have a bedroom, there will be a communal sitting-room and all meals will be provided in a dining-room. No long-term nursing care will be provided, as people requiring this service will either be in hospital or in another type of accommodation for old people.

The large house is in a poor state of repair, and will require considerable structural alterations (building work), and repairs to make it suitable for an old people's home. The following will also be required:

- New furnishings (carpets, beds, wardrobes and so of for the resident's rooms; carpets an furniture for the sitting-room and dining-room)
- Decoration of the whole house (painting the woodwork and covering the walls with wallpaper)
- Equipment (for the kitchen and for helping disabled residents)

Mr Lawrence and his wife propose to work full-time in the business, which he expects to be available for residents six months after the purchase of the house. Mr Lawrence has already obtained some estimates of the conversion costs, and information on the income and expected running costs of the home.

Mr Lawrence has received about £30,000 from his redundancy. He expects to receive about £30,000 from the sale of his house (after repaying his mortgage). The owners of the house he proposes to buy are asking £50,000 for it, and Mr Lawrence expects to spend £50,000 on conversion on the house (building work, furnishing, decorations and equipment).

Mr Lawrence has prepared a draft capital expenditure forecast, a profit forecast and a cash flow forecast which he has asked you to check before he submits them to the bank, in order to obtain finance for the old people's home.

You are required to list and briefly describe the checks you would make, and the factors you would consider in checking:

(a) The capital expenditure forecast
(b) The profit forecast
(c) The cash flow forecast

Answer

All three of the forecasts to be reviewed should be prepared on a monthly basis and the following work would be required in order to consider their reasonableness.

(a) **Capital expenditure forecast**

(i) The forecast should include all costs relating to the acquisition of the house and these should be checked against relevant documentation such as solicitor's correspondence and estate agent's details. The expenditure should include:

- Sale price agreed by the seller
- Survey fees
- Legal costs
- Stamp duty

(ii) Cost of new furnishings should be checked against suppliers price lists and any written confirmation of discounts available for 'bulk' purchases of beds and so on.

(iii) The cost of the required structural alternations, repairs and redecoration's should be checked against the estimates obtained by Mr Lawrence.

(iv) Cost of specialised equipment should be checked against suppliers' price lists and any written confirmation of discounts available for 'bulk' purchases.

(v) The completeness of the capital expenditure should be assessed in the light of the firm's experience, if any, or similar ventures. It would also be expedient to visit the house which Mr Lawrence is intending to purchase to gain some 'feel' for the level of repairs required and the amount of furniture which it would reasonably be able to accommodate.

(b) **Profit forecast**

(i) As a first step it will be necessary to recognise that the residential home will not be able to generate any income until the bulk of the capital expenditure has been incurred in order to make the home 'habitable'. However, whilst no income can be anticipated the business will have started to incur expenditure in the form of loan interest, rates and insurance.

(ii) The only income from the new building will be rent receivable from residents. The rentals which Mr Lawrence is proposing to charge should be assessed for reasonableness in the light of rental charged to similar homes in the same area. In projecting income it would be necessary to anticipate that it is likely to take some time before the home could anticipate full occupancy and also it would perhaps be prudent to allow for some periods where vacancies arise because of the 'loss' of some of the established residents.

(iii) The expenditure of the business is likely to include the following.

(1) **Wages and salaries.** Although Mr and Mrs Lawrence intend to work full-time in the business, they will undoubtedly need to employ additional staff to care for residents, cook, clean and tend to the gardens. The numbers of staff and the rates of pay should be assessed for reasonableness against the projected levels of occupancy and the rates paid in similar local businesses of which the firm has knowledge.

(2) **Rates and water rates.** An estimate of the likely cost of these should be available from the local council and/or the estate agents dealing with the sale of property.

(3) **Food.** The estimate of the expenditure for food should be based in the projected levels of staff and residents, with some provision for wastage.

(4) **Heat and light.** The estimates for heat, light and cooking facilities should be assessed in the light of experience of similar clients.

(5) **Insurance.** Mr Lawrence should have obtained estimates of the premium costs for both employers and public liability insurance and it will be necessary to ensure that adequate cover has been provided against all risks.

(6) **Advertising.** There is likely to be quite high initial advertising costs for both residents and staff. The costs of newspaper and brochure advertising costs should be checked against quotes obtained by Mr Lawrence.

(7) **Repairs and renewals.** Adequate provision should be made for replacement of linen, crockery and such like and maintenance of the property.

(8) **Depreciation.** The depreciation charge should be assessed for reasonableness, with the capital costs involved being charged to the capital expenditure forecast.

(9) **Loan interest and bank charges.** These should be checked against the bank's current rates and the amount of the principal agreed to the cash forecast.

(c) **Cash flow forecast**

(i) The timing of the capital expenditure will need to be estimated accurately in order to determine when the funds will be needed.

(ii) The timing of cash flows and revenue expenditure will be closely related to the details within the profit forecast:

- Income from residents would normally be receivable weekly/monthly in advance
- The majority of expenditure for wages etc would be payable in the month in which it is incurred
- Payments to the major utilities (gas, electricity, telephone) will normally be payable quarterly, as will the bank charges
- Rates and taxes are normally paid half-yearly
- Insurance premiums will normally be paid annually in advance.

(iii) The castings on the cash forecast should be checked and the details agreed to the capital expenditure and profit forecasts.

Question 2

Gunthorpe Plumbing Supplies Limited ('Gunthorpe') is a wholly owned subsidiary of Lucknow Builders Merchants plc ('Lucknow') and has been trading at a loss for a number of years. The recent bleak economic climate has led the directors of Lucknow to decide to put Gunthorpe into liquidation and make all the employees redundant, including its three directors.

The three directors of Gunthorpe have decided to form a new company, Gunthorpe Plumbing Supplies (2001) Limited ('Gunthorpe (2001)'), and use their redundancy pay and personal savings to purchase all the shares in the company.

The board of directors of Lucknow have agreed to sell the following assets and liabilities of Gunthorpe to the new company.

- All the fixed assets except for one warehouse (see below)
- Trading stock, and
- Trade debtors and creditors

The price for the fixed assets has been agreed and the value of the trading stock, debtors and creditors will be confirmed at the date of transfer by an independent valuer.

The directors of Gunthorpe (2001) propose to obtain additional finance in the form of a long term loan from a merchant bank and working capital will be financed by a bank overdraft from their existing bankers.

The directors have asked you to assist them in preparing a profit forecast and cash flow forecast for submission to the two banks. They have provided you with copies of the detailed accounts of Gunthorpe for the past five years, and they point out the following changes which, in their opinion, will enable the new company to trade at a profit.

(a) The substantial management charge imposed by Lucknow will disappear. However, additional costs will have to be incurred for services which were provided by the parent company, such as maintaining the accounting records and servicing the company's vehicles

(b) Initially fewer staff will be employed

(c) Only one of the company's two premises is being taken over – the premises which are not being taken over will be sold by Lucknow on the open market.

The directors have provided you with the following brief details of Gunthorpe's trade. It currently has a turnover of about £1 million and is a wholesaler of plumbing equipment (copper pipes, pipe connections, water taps etc) which are sold mainly on credit to plumbers and builders. Trade discount is given to larger customers. There are some cash sales to smaller customers, but these represent no more than 10% of total sales.

Required

Describe the work you would perform to:

(a) Verify that the value of items included in the profit forecast are reasonable
(b) Verify that the value of items included in the cash flow forecast are reasonable.

Answer

(a) **Verification of items in profit forecast**

The main items appearing in the profit forecast and the required work in relation to them would be as follows:

(i) The budgeted sales income should be considered against that which has actually been achieved in recent years. If the new management are forecasting any increase in the level of sales, the justification for this must be carefully reviewed. Tests should be made to ensure that all expenditure directly related to income is properly accounted for. Confirmation should be sought that the projected income takes proper account of the trade discounts that it is assumed will have to be granted.

(ii) The major term of expenditure is likely to be the purchase of goods for resale. Enquiry should be made as to whether suppliers will continue to grant the new company the same level of trade discounts as the old company and also whether the volume of purchases is such that a similar mark-up will be attained. Management explanations should be sought for any material differences in the anticipated gross profit rate, such explanations being fully investigated as to their plausibility.

(iii) The wages and salaries payable by the new company should be checked by asking management how many people they intend to employ and at what rates. The reasonableness of the projected charge for wages and salaries should be assessed by comparison with the figure for wages and salaries most recently paid by the old company.

(iv) All other major items of expenditure included in the profit forecast (ie selling expenses, finance expenses and administration expenses) should be considered by comparison with the figures of the old company in previous years, ensuring that a reasonable allowance is made for the effects of inflation.

(v) The charges for items previously covered by the management charge should be checked for their completeness and reasonableness.

(vi) An overall review of the projected profits should be undertaken to ensure that it appears to be a realistic forecast and not merely an idealistic target figure.

(b) **Verification of items in the cash flow forecast**

As well as generally checking to ensure that the cash flow forecast appears to be consistent with the profit forecast, specific checks should be made as follows.

(i) The timing of payments due to the parent company.

(ii) The period of credit granted to debtors by the old company as it is unlikely that the new company will be in a position to insist on prompter payment by customers.

(iii) The period of credit taken from suppliers should be dealt with in a similar way, although enquiry should be made as to whether creditors are prepared to trade with the new company on the same terms as the old.

(iv) The timing of payment for overhead expenditure should be checked to see that it is reasonable and consistent with established practice.

(v) Although in the early months one would not expect there to be any major purchase or sale of fixed assets, the position here should be confirmed by discussion with management of their prolonged plans.

Chapter roundup

- The internationally accepted definition of a forecast is:
  - A **forecast** means prospective financial information prepared on the basis of assumptions as to future events which management expects to take place and actions management expects to take as of the date the information is prepared (best estimate assumptions)
- UK opinion currently defines it a little differently:
  - **Forecast.** Something about which the directors are prepared to say 'this is highly likely to happen'.
- The two definitions of projection can also be compared:
  - (Int'l) A **projection** means prospective information prepared on the basis of
    - (a) Hypothetical assumptions about future events and management actions which are not necessarily expected to take place, such as when some entities are in a start-up phase or are considering a major change in the nature of operations, or
    - (b) A mixture of best estimate and hypothetical assumptions.
  - (UK) **Projection.** Something about which the directors are prepared to say 'this is reasonably likely to happen'.
- The auditor should agree the terms of the engagement with the directors, and should withdraw from the engagement if the assumptions made to put together the PFI are untreatable.
- The auditor should **review** the information to ensure:
  - Accounting policies are comparable to published HFI
  - Forecast is mathematically accurate
- Potential additional procedures could include:
  - Analytical review (against similar historic projects)
  - Verification of projected expenditure to quotes or estimates
- It is impossible to give the same level of assurance about PFI as it is on HFI, **negative assurance** may be given.
- Reports on PFI should include (amongst other things)
  - Statement of management's responsibilities
  - Appropriate caveats

Quick quiz

1 Complete the definition

A ______________ means PFI prepared on the basis of ____________ as to ______________ events which management expects to take place and __________________ management expects to take as of __________ the __________ is __________

2 List four factors which will help distinguish between a projection and a forecast.

(1) __________________

(2) __________________

(3) __________________

(4) __________________

3 Complete the matters an auditor should consider when undertaking a PFI engagement.

- The intended _______________ of the information
- Whether the information will be general or limited _______________
- The nature of the _______________
- The _______________ to be included in the information
- The _______________ to be covered by the information

4 Identify whether the following procedures are relevant to profit forecasts, capital expenditure forecasts or cash forecasts.

- Ensure the timings are reasonable
- Projected costs should be verified to estimates and quotations
- Analytical review on income (based on comparable projects)
- Review for reasonableness
- Review for consistency with profit forecast.

5 Complete the definition.

_______________ _______________ is assurance of something in the ____________ of any evidence arising to the _________.

6 Reporting accountants are responsible for the PFI they are giving an opinion on.

True ☐

False ☐

Answers to quick quiz

1 Forecast, assumptions, future, actions, date, information, prepared.

2 (1) Activities involved
(2) Time scale
(3) Discretion over decision-making involved
(4) Relationship with overall management strategy

3 Use, distribution, assumptions, elements, period.

4

• Ensure the timings are reasonable	C
• Projected costs should be verified to estimates and quotations	P/CapEx
• Analytical review on income (based on comparable projects)	P
• Review for reasonableness	P/CapEx/C
• Review for consistency with profit forecast.	CapEx/C

5 Negative assurance, absence, contrary

6 False

Now try the question below from the Exam Question Bank

Number	Level	Marks	Time
17	Exam	25	45 mins

Chapter 18

SOCIAL AND ENVIRONMENTAL AUDITS

Introduction

In this chapter we investigate the impact of social and environmental issues on the auditor. This takes two distinct forms:

- Impact of social and environmental issues on the **statutory audit**
- Impact of social and environmental issues on the provision of **assurance services** by the auditor.

Increasing importance is placed on social and environmental issues in business. Recent years have seen a substantial weight of environmental legislation passed which puts a **significant burden of compliance** on companies.

This is dangers of non-compliance (fines, bad publicity, impact on going concern) is an aspect of the **environmental risk** which faces companies.

As we discussed in Chapter 5, recent government reports have placed a burden on the directors of companies to assess and manage risks as part of **good corporate governance.** It is part of their duty to implement internal controls which mitigate against the risks arising from social and environmental issues. The impact of social and environmental issues is discussed in the first half of this chapter (Sections 1, 2 and 3).

Secondly in this chapter, we turn to the issued raised for the auditor. As stated above, these are two-fold.

As environmental and social issues are a risk to the business, they **must be considered as part of the audit process**. They will impact on the audit in many ways. These include **planning** the audit (knowledge of the business and risk assessment), **conducting substantive work** (considering accounting issues arising, such as impairment and provisions), and **final reviews** (going concern particularly, but possibly also things like subsequent events).

The increased public awareness of the issues and the importance of social and environmental issues in corporate governance brings further opportunities for the auditor however. In Chapter 15 we discussed **assurance services**. Environmental and social issues are a concern to the stakeholders in a company. They are increasingly reported on by directors in annual reports, a trend which is likely to continue. In such a situation, there is an opportunity for auditors to provide assurance services, that the assertions made by the directors are borne out in practice.

Study guide

Section 23

- Discuss the increasing importance of policies which govern the relationship of an organisation to its employees, society and the environment
- Describe the difficulties in measuring social and environmental performance and give examples of targets and sustainability indicators
- Explain the auditor's main considerations with respect to social and environmental matters and give examples of how they impact on companies and their financial statements (eg impairment of assets, provisions and contingent liabilities)
- Discuss how control over social and environmental risks may be exercised by management and evaluated by the auditor
- Describe substantive procedures to detect potential misstatements in respect of socio-environmental matters
- Explain what action may be taken by the auditor in situations of non-compliance with relevant laws and regulations (eg environmental acts and health and safety regulations)
- Discuss the form and content of an independent verification statement (eg on an environmental management systems (EMS) and a report to society)

Exam guide

This topic was the subject of an essay question on the pilot paper, for 15 marks.

1 STAKEHOLDERS

1.1 To recap, there are various **stakeholders** in a company. Traditionally auditors are concerned with one set, the shareholders, to whom they report on the financial statements.

1.2 The diagram below shows various other stakeholders that a company might have.

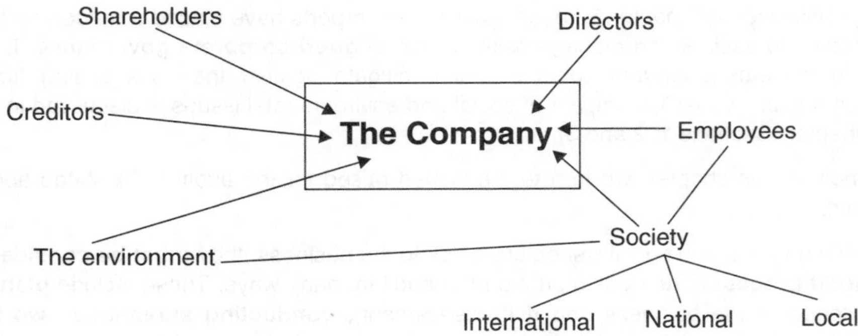

1.3 In this chapter we are concerned with the needs of three of the above categories; employees, the environment and society, and the knock on impact this has on the shareholders, directors and the company itself.

1.4 The diagram links the first three because in this context they are inextricably linked.

The environment The environment is directly impacted by many of our corporate activities today. This may be

PRIMARY ⟶ The impact of processes

SECONDARY ⟶ The impact of products

	The primary impact is regulated by environmental legislation, which has been prolific in recent years. The secondary impact is governed partly by legislation and partly by consumer opinion.
Society	Society, from the point of view of the company, is made up of consumers or potential consumers. As recognised above, consumers increasingly have opinions about 'green', environmentally friendly products and will direct their purchasing accordingly Society will also, through lobby groups, often speak out on behalf of the environment as it cannot speak out itself.
Employees	Employees have a relationship with the company in their own right, in terms of their livelihood and also their personal safety when they are at work. However, from the company's perspective, they are also a small portion of society at large, as they may purchase the products of the company or influence others to do so.

1.5 In some ways it is easier to see why the company is important to these stakeholders than why they are important to the company.

Environment	The company can cause harm to natural resources in various ways, including: • Exhausting natural resources such as coal and gas • Emitting harmful toxins which destroy the atmosphere
Society	Is concerned with the harm to the natural resources as they and their children have to live on the planet and may suffer direct or indirect effects of pollution or waste.
Employees	Have all the concerns that society do and, more immediately, depend on the company for livelihood and safety when at work.

1.6 For a company however, there is one simple need. Companies desire above all else to keep making their product and to keep making sales.

1.7 Employees are needed to keep making the product, as are natural resources, and consumers' (that is, society's) goodwill is required to keep selling it.

1.8 Obviously, loss of employees and consumers is going to make it impossible for companies to stay in business. Therefore it is important for companies to have policies in order to appease these stakeholders and to communicate the policies to them.

1.9 Companies are also constrained by prolific legislation regulating their behaviour towards the environment. Many countries have produced environmental legislation in recent years. Some UK examples are:

UK Environmental statutes

The Environment Protection Act 1990

Water Industry Act 1991

Water Resources Act 1991

Clean Air Act 1993

Exam focus point

The statues listed here are to illustrate the point only, you do not need to know details of legislation.

2 IMPLICATIONS FOR MANAGEMENT

2.1 The increasing importance of good corporate governance has been discussed in Chapter 5.

2.2 The Turnbull guidance states that management are responsible for internal controls which must comprise a sound system to mitigate against risks to the business. For many companies, environmental and social issues might be a significant risk.

2.3 The overriding business risk is the risk that the business might fail. Some of the risks arising from social and environmental issues have been discussed above.

Question 1

(a) What are the key environmental and social risks that a business might face?

(b) Why might they result in the failure of the business?

Answer

(a) The diagram below shows the risks that the business faces.

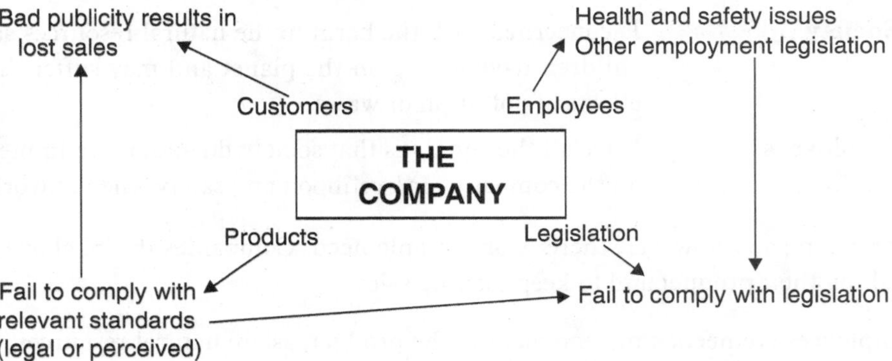

(b) Any of these issues could be at a level serious enough to cause significant business interruption or even business failure, for the reasons given below.

(i) **Bad publicity**. This could lead to customers choosing other products, boycotts and loss of market share significant enough to prevent the business from continuing in operation.

(ii) **Legislation**. The company could be discovered not to be complying (through whistleblowing by employees or auditors, or investigation by a regulatory body). This could have the following effects:

- **Fines/compensation**. These could be significant enough to prevent the continuance of the business.
- **Disqualification of directors**. If the staff involved are key members of the organisation, this could threaten the ability of the company to continue.
- **Bad publicity**. See points made above.

Management controls

2.4 The specific controls that management will put into place in line with their duties under the corporate governance codes will vary according to the needs of the business.

2.5 They are likely to involve specific measure designed to ensure that environmental legislation is complied with, for example they may relate to protective clothing, disposal of waste etc. The human resources department is likely to design policies to ensure that employment legislation is complied with.

2.6 The directors may also seek to incorporate social and environmental values into the corporate culture of the company, so that all employees are aware of the risks arising in these areas, and are focused on avoiding them.

2.7 This can be achieved by implementing a corporate code, or by setting targets of social and environmental performance.

2.8 One such target might be to obtain the British Standards Institute's ISO 14001, relating to Environmental Management Systems. This will involve having an assessment by the BSI, and may involve updating management systems to comply with the standard (ISO 14001).

2.9 ISO 14001 is often a formal condition for entry into supply chains and certain markets. It does not require the company to produce an environmental report however. The European equivalent, the Eco-Management and Audit Scheme (EMAS), does.

3 MEASURING SOCIAL AND ENVIRONMENTAL PERFORMANCE

3.1 As discussed in Chapter 5, a key part of risk management is monitoring and evaluating results.

3.2 Social and environmental performance is not such an easy thing to measure as financial performance. It is less easy to produce ratios and there is unlikely to be an obvious profit appearing from social and environmental activities.

3.3 One way to measure social performance is to set targets and sustainability indicators and then appraise whether the targets have been met and the indicators exist.

Targets and indicators

3.4 Again, these targets will vary from business to business, depending on what the issues are. To illustrate the point, a case study of Shell is given below.

Case Study: Measuring Social Performance

Shell is a large multi-national company that deals in oil, gas and chemicals. There are various issues which make social and environmental issues important to this company:

- It deals in the earth's natural resources
- The business is heavily environmentally legislated
- It employs a significant number of people
- Some employees work in risky environments
- It operates in areas of the world where Human Rights issues are not given sufficient priority

Targets

In response to the social and environmental issues raised above, the company have set targets of social and environmental performance which they evaluate and report on to shareholders on an annual basis.

The following are examples of targets which the company has set:

Environmental

- Reduce emissions of carbon dioxide from refinery activity
- Continue to develop cleaner fuels
- Reduce emissions of nitrogen oxides from burning fuel in our operations
- Eliminate spills of crude oil, oil and chemicals

Social

- Zero employee fatalities in work-related incidents
- Not exploit children in any country where child labour exists, by
    - Employing children under the legal age of employment
    - Dealing with other companies who employ children illegally
- Pursue equal opportunities for men and women in all countries that this is legally possible

Sustainability principles

The company has also set general sustainability principles which all staff should apply in daily business:

- Respect and safeguard people
- Engage and work with stakeholders
- Minimise impact on the environment
- Use resources efficiently
- Maximise profitability
- Maximise benefits to the community

Reporting

The company reports on all these issues to its shareholders, and where-ever possible, the facts included within this report are verified by independent verifiers.

3.5 The case study shows a number of targets and sustainability indicators. Some can be measured in mathematical terms, for example:

- Emissions
- Spills
- Elimination of work-related fatalities
- Employment of children

3.6 However, some of the targets are not specific enough to be able to measure in that way. For example, it is more difficult to identify whether the company is in relation to achieving a target of developing cleaner fuels until the cleaner fuel appears. Such a development target cannot have a prescribed timescale.

3.7 Equally, it is difficult to measure the effect of the general principles which the company has included within the culture of the company.

Social audits

3.8 The process of checking whether a company has achieved set targets may fall within a social audit that a company carries out. Social audits are discussed briefly in 3.3, *Performance Measurement*.

3.9 **Social audits** can be carried out. These will involve:

- Establishing whether the firm has a rationale for engaging in socially responsible activity
- Identifying that all current environment programmes are congruent with the mission of the company
- Assessing of objectives and priorities related to these programmes
- Evaluating company involvement in such programmes past, present and future

3.10 Whether or not a social audit is used depends on the degree to which social responsibility is part of the **corporate philosophy**. A cultural awareness must be achieved within an organisation in order to implement environmental policy, which requires Board and staff support.

3.11 In the USA, social audits on environmental issues have increased since the Exxon Valdez catastrophe in which millions of gallons of crude oil were released into Alaskan waters.

The Valdez principles were drafted by the Coalition for Environmentally Responsible Economics to focus attention on environmental concerns and corporate responsibility.

- Eliminate pollutants and hazardous waste
- Conserve non-renewable resources
- Market environmentally safe products and services
- Prepare for accidents and restore damaged environments
- Provide protection for employees who report environmental hazards
- Appoint an environmentalist to their board of directors, name an executive for environmental affairs, and develop an environmental audit of their global operations, which is to be made publicly available

Environmental audits

KEY TERM

Environmental audits seek to assess how well the organisation performs in safeguarding the environment in which it operates, and whether the company complies with its environmental policies.

3.12 An environmental audit might be undertaken as part of obtaining or maintaining the BSI's ISO 14001 standard.

3.13 The auditor will carry out the following steps:

- Obtain a copy of the company's environmental policy
- Assess whether the policy is likely to achieve objectives:
  - Meet legal requirements
  - Meet British Standards
  - Satisfy key customers/suppliers' criteria

- Test implementation and adherence to the policy by:
  - Discussion
  - Observation
  - 'Walk-though tests' where possible

Exam focus point

Social and environmental reporting is the topic of a series of articles in *Student Accountant* starting in May 2001, which you should ensure that you read.

4 IMPLICATIONS FOR THE STATUTORY AUDIT **Pilot Paper**

4.1 We now turn from the importance of social and environmental issues to the company and look at why they are important to the auditor in the context of the statutory audit.

4.2 The key reason that the issues are important to the statutory audit is that they are important to the company and therefore **can potentially impact on the financial statements.**

4.3 In the introduction, the impact of the issues on an audit was divided into three specific areas, which were:

- Planning the audit
- Undertaking substantive procedures
- Audit reviews

4.4 Another important point to note is the duties of the auditor arising under SAS 120 *Consideration of law and regulations*. We shall also consider this below.

Planning the audit

4.5 Social and environmental issues impact in two ways:

- Knowledge of the business (SAS 210)
- Inherent risk assessment (SAS 300)

4.6 You should be aware of the principles involved in these two issues, so there is no need to go into a lot of further detail at this stage.

4.7 As part of his knowledge of the business, the auditor should have an awareness of any environmental regulations the business is subject to, and any key social issues arising in the course of the business.

4.8 The auditor may be able to obtain knowledge of this aspect of the business by reading the firms procedures or reviewing any quality control documentation they have relating to standards. The auditor may be able to review the results of any environmental audits undertaken by the company.

4.9 This will then form part of his assessment of inherent risk.

Exam focus point

Remember that a question does not have to be specifically on social and environmental issues for them to be relevant. Be aware of any implications they might have in a standard question on planning or risks.

Substantive procedures

4.10 Social and environmental issues, although particularly environmental issues, may impact on the financial statements in a number of ways. Some examples are given in the box below.

Examples of the impact of social and environmental matters on financial statements

- Provisions (for example, for site restoration, fines/compensation payments)
- Contingent liabilities (for example, in relation to pending legal action)
- Asset values (issues may impact on impairment or purchased goodwill/products)
- Capital/revenue expenditure (costs of clean up or meeting legal standards)
- Development costs (new products)
- Going concern issues (considered below under reviews)

Exam focus point

When approaching an question about auditing specific items in financial statements, or issuing an audit opinion in regard to them, you should bear in consider whether there is an environmental/social issue which will impact on valuation or disclosure. Use your common sense, however, do not make up such issues where no obvious indicators are given in the question.

4.11 The auditor will have to bear in mind the effects of social or environmental issues on the financial statements when designing audit procedures. We will now look at some potential audit procedures that would be relevant in three of the key areas above.

Substantive procedures: asset valuation

4.12 The key risk that arises with regard to valuation is that assets might be **impaired**. FRS 11 requires an impairment review to be undertaken with regard to fixed assets if certain indicators of impairment exist. We have discussed the audit of impairments in Chapter 11, but shall consider the points specific to environmental and social issues here.

Knowledge from paper 2.5, *Financial Reporting*

FRS 11 gives a list of indicators that an impairment review is required. The indicators relevant here are:

(a) There is a **current period operating loss** or **net cash outflow** from operating activities, combined with **either** of:

(i) **Past** operating losses or net cash outflows from operating activities

(ii) An expectation of **continuing** operating losses or net cash outflows from operating activities.

> (d) There is a **significant adverse change** in of the following.
>
> (ii) The statutory or other regulatory environment in which the business operates.

4.13 The indicator in (a) could be caused by environmental and social issue risks as discussed in the answer to question 1.

4.14 The indicator in (d) is more specifically relevant to social and environmental issues. It is possible that a significant adverse change could have taken place in the regulatory environment.

4.15 The auditor should be aware of the regulatory environment of the client as part of its knowledge of the business (as discussed above), but the following **general procedures** could be undertaken as part of the fixed asset testing to **establish whether an impairment review is required**.

> - Review the board minutes for indications that the environmental regulatory environment has changed.
> - Review relevant trade magazines or newspapers to assess whether any significant adverse change has taken place.
> - Discuss the issue with management, particularly those nominated to have responsibility for environmental issues, if such a position exists.

4.16 If a significant adverse change has taken place, the directors may or may not have conducted an impairment review. If the directors have not, the auditors should discuss the matter with them. If the directors refuse to conduct an impairment review, the auditors should consider the result of that on their audit report.

4.17 If an impairment review has been undertaken, and the valuation of the asset has been adjusted accordingly, the auditor should **audit the impairment review**. This was discussed in Chapter 11.

Substantive procedures: provisions

4.18 Guidance on accounting for provisions is given in FRS 12. The audit of provisions has been discussed previously in Chapter 12. We shall consider the points specific to environmental and social issues here.

> **Knowledge from paper 2.5, *Financial Reporting***
>
> FRS 12 defines a **provision as a liability of uncertain timing or amount**. A provision should be recognised when:
>
> - An entity has a **present obligation** (legal or constructive) as a result of a past event
> - It is probable that a **transfer of economic benefits** will be required to settle the obligation
> - A **reliable estimate** can be made of the obligation
>
> The FRS gives some examples of provisions in the appendices. Some are relevant to environmental issues, for example, one deals with contaminated land and another deals with the issue of implementing new legislation requiring smoke filters.

4.19 As mentioned in the box, the FRS provides some helpful examples of environmental issues that result in provisions being required. The auditor needs to be aware of any circumstances that might give rise to a provision being required, and then apply the recognition criteria to it.

4.20 The **general substantive procedures** for **establishing if a provision is required** are the **same as** they were for identifying whether an **impairment review** was required.

4.21 If the directors have included provisions in the accounts relating to environmental issues, the **audit procedures** will be the same as were discussed in Chapter 12. Specifically, the auditor may be able to **review correspondence** from any regulatory watchdog, or obtain a copy of the **relevant legislation** to review its requirements.

Substantive procedures: contingent liabilities

4.22 Accounting for contingent liabilities is also governed by FRS 12.

Knowledge from paper 2.5, *Financial Reporting*

FRS 12 defines a contingent liability as either

(a) A possible obligation arising from past events whose existence will be confirmed only by the occurrence of one or more uncertain future events not wholly within the entity's control; or

(b) A present obligation that arises from past events but is not recognised because it is not probable that a transfer of economic benefits will be required to settle the obligation or because the amount of the obligation cannot be measured with sufficient reliability.

4.23 Social and environmental issues may also impact here. In fact, a contingent liability is likely to arise through items being identified in a provision review, when the items highlighted do not meet the recognition criteria for a provision.

4.24 This was discussed in Chapter 12. Given their relationship with provisions, the **general audit procedures to establish if contingent liabilities exist** are the **same as** the ones for **provisions**, given above.

4.25 If the directors have made **disclosures relating to contingent liabilities** in respect of environmental and social issues, the **procedures** to test them are set out in Chapter 12. **Specific evidence** would be on similar lines to as for provisions in respect of social and environmental issues: **correspondence with a regulator or relevant legislation.**

Audit reviews

4.26 As discussed in Section 2, environmental and social issues can impact on the ability of the company to continue as a going concern.

4.27 The auditor will need to aware of such issues when undertaking his going concern review. The procedures involved in going concern reviews were discussed in Chapter 9.

Auditor responsibility in the event of non-compliance with law and regulations

4.28 The auditors' responsibility with regard to law and regulations is set out in SAS 120 *Consideration of law and regulations*. This was discussed in Chapter 5, so you should refer back to this to remind yourself of the actions the auditor should take in the event of his discovering non-compliance.

4.29 Environmental obligations would be core in some businesses (for example, our oil and chemical company given in the case study above), in others they would not. SAS 120 talks of laws that are 'central' to the entity's ability to carry on business.

4.30 Clearly, in the case of a company who stands to lose his operating license to carry on business in the event of non-compliance, environmental legislation is central to the business.

4.31 In the case of social legislation, this will be a matter of judgement for the auditor. It might involve matters of employment legislation, health and safety regulation, human rights law and such matters which may not seem core to the objects of the company, but permeate the business due to the need of employees.

4.32 The auditor is not expected to be a specialist in environmental law. However, as part of his professional duty, he must ensure that he has enough knowledge to undertake the assignment, or that he engages the use of an expert if necessary.

5 IMPLICATIONS FOR ASSURANCE SERVICES

5.1 Auditors can provide a variety of services in respect of environmental and social issues. Most of these services are familiar to us, so there is no need to speak again about them in length. Remember that most of the services we have discussed could be applied in a environmental and social context:

- Internal audit services (reviewing controls)
- Review of internal controls and procedures
- Management letter concerning controls as a by-product of statutory audit
- Assurance services (see below)

5.2 As discussed in the introduction, **management increasingly report to members on social and environmental issues**, and there is a growing public perception that this is an important area.

5.3 This means that it is an issue that can give rise to **assurance services**.

REMEMBER

The **definition** of an **assurance engagement:**

One where the accountant evaluates a subject matter that is the responsibility of another party against suitable criteria and expresses an opinion, designed to provide the intended user with a level of assurance about that subject matter.

5.4 Assurance engagements give rise to assurance reports, which we outlined in Chapter 15. We shall consider the issue of specific verification reports in relation to social and environmental issues here.

5.5 If the directors issue an environmental and social report, it may contain figures and statements that are verifiable. Using the example of Shell (above), the directors could make the following assertions:

- Carbon dioxide emissions were Xmillion tonnes in 2001, which represents a 2% decrease from 2000.
- We have implemented a strategy aimed at ensuring that in 5 years time, no one we deal with will have an involvement in child labour.

5.6 These assertions can be reviewed and assurance given about them. For instance, in the first case, the level of emission could be traced to records of emission from the refineries, and the percentage calculation could be checked.

5.7 In the second instance, the accountants could obtain details of the strategy and ascertain how fully it has been implemented by making enquiries of the staff who should be implementing the strategy. They could also appraise the strategy and give an opinion of the chances of it achieving the objective within the given time frame.

Contents of an assurance report on environmental issues

5.8 There is no guidance in issue as to the contents of such a report. The box below shows some items that should be included as a minimum.

- Note of the objectives of the review
- Opinions
- Basis on which those opinions have been reached
- Work performed
- Limitations to the work performed
- Limitations to the opinion given

Chapter roundup

- There are various stakeholders in companies, which include:
  - Environment
  - Society
  - Employees
- Social and environmental issues might present a risk to the company, and by implication, the shareholders' investment.
- The directors are required to mitigate against and monitor risks as part of their corporate governance.
- However, measuring social and environmental performance can be a difficult area. Auditors can provide assurance services in this area – giving opinions as to whether directors' assertions about performance are fair.
- Social and environmental issues can affect the statutory audit
  - At the planning stage (risk)
  - While undertaking substantive procedures (impairment/provisions)
  - During audit reviews (going concern)
- The auditor must also bear in mind this responsibilities under SAS 120, *Consideration of Law and Regulations.*

Quick quiz

1 Draw a mindmap showing the major stakeholders in a company.

2 Management have a duty to monitor risks arising from social and environmental issues as part of their corporate governance.

True ☐

False ☐

3 Name three areas of a statutory audit where social and environmental issues are relevant.

(1) ____________________

(2) ____________________

(3) ____________________

4 Give an example of why social and environmental issues might impact on all of the following financial statement areas:

- Provisions
- Contingent liabilities
- Asset values
- Capital/revenue expenditure
- Development costs
- Going concern

5 List six items which should be covered on an assurance report relating to environmental issues

(1) ____________________ (4) ____________________

(2) ____________________ (5) ____________________

(3) ____________________ (6) ____________________

Answers to quick quiz

1

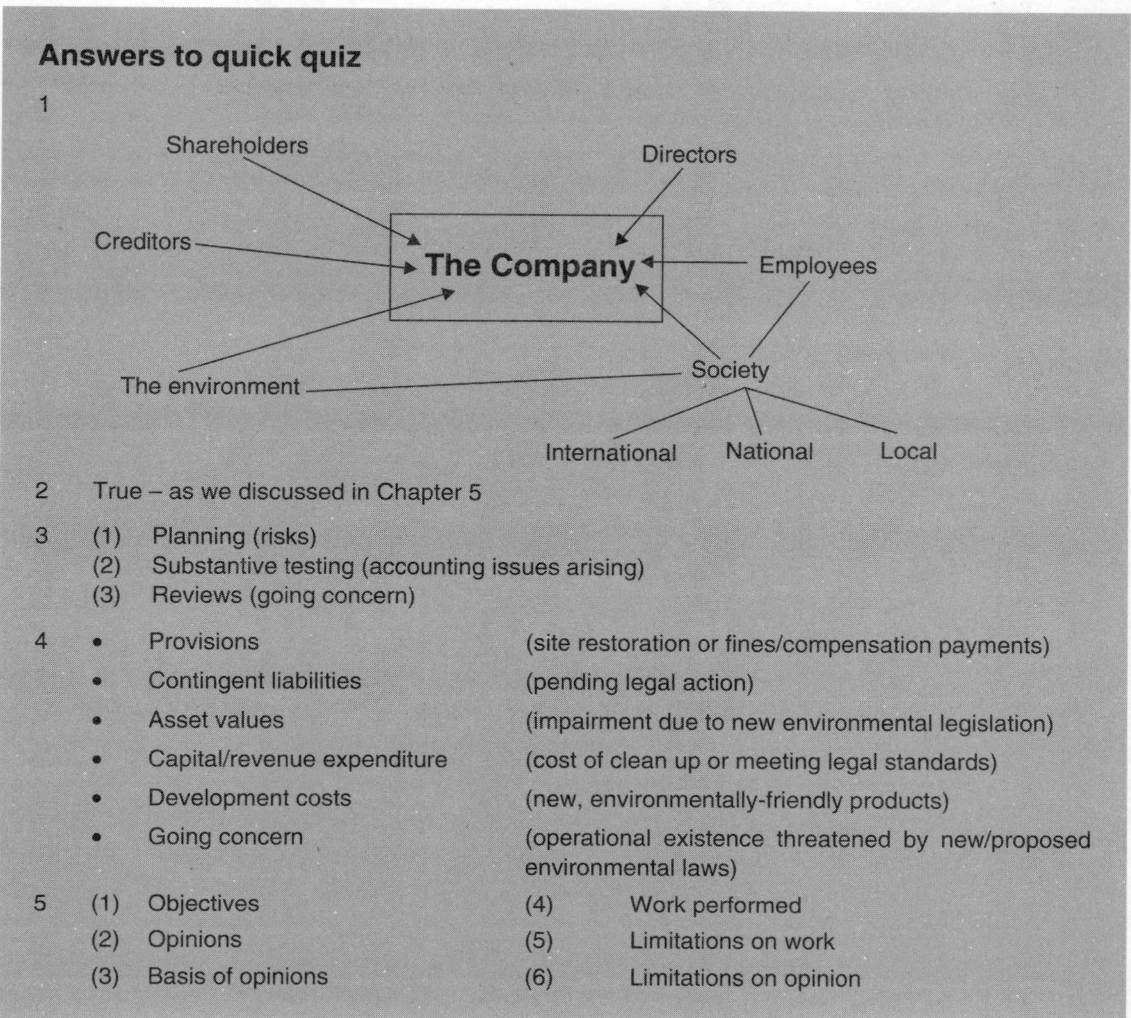

2 True – as we discussed in Chapter 5

3 (1) Planning (risks)
(2) Substantive testing (accounting issues arising)
(3) Reviews (going concern)

4
- Provisions (site restoration or fines/compensation payments)
- Contingent liabilities (pending legal action)
- Asset values (impairment due to new environmental legislation)
- Capital/revenue expenditure (cost of clean up or meeting legal standards)
- Development costs (new, environmentally-friendly products)
- Going concern (operational existence threatened by new/proposed environmental laws)

5 (1) Objectives
(2) Opinions
(3) Basis of opinions
(4) Work performed
(5) Limitations on work
(6) Limitations on opinion

Now try the question below from the Exam Question Bank

Number	Level	Marks	Time
18	Exam	15	27 mins

Part D
Reporting

Chapter 19

REPORTS

Topic list		Syllabus reference
1	The expectations gap	3(a)
2	Revision: true and fair	3(a)
3	The standard unqualified audit report	3(a)
4	Qualifications in audit reports	3(a)
5	Forming an audit opinion	3(a)
6	Special purpose audit reports	3(a)
7	Reporting to management and the audit committee	3(a)

Introduction

You should be familiar with the audit report from your previous auditing studies. You should already be able to:

- Explain the contents of audit reports
- Make judgements about audit evidence/form audit opinions, and appraise audit opinions
- Discuss a true and fair view

These things shall be revised in this chapter.

This chapter also seeks to provide a **critical evaluation of the audit report,** particularly in reference to the problem of the expectations gap. The standard audit report you have studied in the past is only a recent innovation, designed in response to criticisms about the information given to shareholders. It has not answered all those criticisms. You must be prepared to consider it dispassionately, and be aware of the issues surrounding it.

In Section 6, three types of **special purpose audit reports** are examined. These are additional reports required of the auditor by law in certain circumstances. You must be able to illustrate these special circumstances, and describe the relevant reports.

You should be familiar with the concept of reports to management, and in your studies for 2.6, *Audit and Internal Review* (old paper 6), you studied the issues you would include in such a report. That is revised here.

Also, in your studies for 3.1, you have looked at the importance of an **audit committee** in good corporate governance. The auditor might have the responsibility to **report to the audit committee** under the terms of his **contract with the company.** In Section 7, we also look at the **form and content of such a report.**

Study guide

Sections 24 and 25

- Explain and critically appraise the form and content of a standard unqualified auditors' report
- Describe the factors to be taken into account when forming an audit opinion
- Make judgements and form audit opinions which are consistent with the results of audit procedures relating to the sufficiency of audit evidence and/or the appropriateness of accounting treatments (including the going concern basis)

- Critically evaluate a proposed audit opinion
- Discuss 'a true and fair view'
- Describe and illustrate special purpose auditors' reports (eg on summarised financial statements)
- Identify and report systems weaknesses and their potential effects and make appropriate recommendations to management (eg accounting procedures and financial controls)
- Describe the criteria for evaluating the effectiveness of a management letter
- Outline the content of a report to an audit committee
- Explain the need for timely communication, clearance, feedback and follow up
- Discuss communications methods

Section 26

Information Technology

- Describe recent trends in IT and their current and potential impact on auditors (eg identify and discuss the audit implications of financial reporting on the Internet)

Exam guide

There was a question on the pilot paper concerning the impact of certain items on the audit report.

1 THE EXPECTATIONS GAP

1.1 A significant problem associated with auditing is that **people do not understand the role of the auditor,** and often believe that auditors perform a function that they, in fact, do not.

1.2 This lack of understanding is often referred to as the '**expectations gap**'. This is because there is literally a gap between what the auditors actually do, and what people believe that they do.

1.3 There is a key problem, and it was highlighted by the reports on corporate governance that we looked at in Chapter 5. The key problem is that people, specifically **investors** in this context, **believe that the audits give**

- **More assurance** than is actually the case
- **Assurance on different issues** to those which the auditor actually reports on

1.4 There are some **common misconceptions** in relation to the role of the auditors, even among 'financially aware' people, including the following examples.

- Many people think that the **auditors report to the directors** of a company, rather than the members.
- Some think that a **qualified audit report is more favourable than an unqualified audit report,** whereas the converse is true.
- There is a perception that it is the **auditors' duty to detect fraud,** when in fact the detection of fraud is the responsibility of the directors.

1.5 These misconceptions highlight the 'exceptions gap' between what auditors do and what people in general think that they do. Add the fact that many 'financially aware' people do not look at the report and accounts on a company they are considering investing in, and you have some sobering facts for the auditors to contemplate!

1.6 Some of the relatively recent large company collapses have emphasised the need not only to **improve corporate governance** and make directors more publicly accountable to the shareholders, but **also to reduce the expectations gap.**

1.7 Therefore reports such as the **Cadbury Report** on corporate governance both lay out a code of conduct for directors and make **suggestions for the content of company reports.**

1.8 For the auditor, the key document in reducing the expectations gap is the **audit report.** It is the document through which the auditors communicate with the shareholders of (investors in) a company.

1.9 In May 1993, subsequent to the Cadbury report, the APB issued SAS 600 *Auditor's reports on financial statements*. You should be familiar with the SAS and the types of audit report it contains from your previous studies.

1.10 We are going to revisit the SAS in this chapter. This will remind us of the format of the various reports and the judgements a auditor makes based on the evidence he has gained.

1.11 In our further study of the SAS, however, we shall also explore how, in SAS 600, the **APB sought to respond to** the points made about the expectations gap by the **Cadbury committee,** and how the **formal audit report now seeks to limit the expectations gap.**

2 REVISION: TRUE AND FAIR

2.1 You should not have got to this point in your studies and not have a thorough understanding of truth and fairness. If you struggle with question 1, you should return to your 2.6 text and revise this area.

Question 1

In an unqualified audit report, the auditor gives an opinion that the accounts give a true and fair view.

(a) What does this mean?

Another important concept underpins the concept of truth and fairness.

(b) Explain what the concept is and how it works.

Answer

(a) The auditor is reporting on the contents of the financial statements, that is,

- Balance sheet
- Profit and loss account
- Cash flow statements
- Notes to the accounts
- Comparatives

He is expressing an opinion as to whether the accounts are true and fair. These terms are not defined in law but the generally accepted meanings are as follows:

True: Information is factual and conforms with reality, not false. In addition the information conforms with required standards and law. The accounts have been correctly extracted from the books and records.

Fair: Information is free from discrimination and bias and in compliance with expected standards and rules. The accounts should reflect the commercial substance of the company's underlying transactions.

(b) An important concept which lies alongside the concept of true and fair is the concept of **materiality.**

Materiality is an expression of the relative significance or importance of a particular matter in the context of financial statements as a whole.

A matter is material if its omission or misstatement would reasonably influence the decisions of an addressee of the auditors' report.

Materiality may also be considered in the context of any individual primary statement within the financial statements or of individual items included in them.

Materiality is not capable of general mathematical definition as it has both qualitative and quantitative aspects.

Materiality is something that auditors must be aware of all the time they are gathering evidence to support their opinion. As noted in the definition above, some items are inherently material, but for others, the auditor will try to apply a value, based on values in the financial statements.

Question 2

A significant problem associated with audit is the existence of what is termed an 'expectations gap'.

Outline your understanding of the expectations gap, and give some examples of misconceptions that contribute to it.

Answer

The expectations gap is the gap between what auditors actually do and what people, or investors, think that they do.

Some common misconceptions that create an expectations gap are:

- Auditors report to directors, not members
- A qualified audit report is a positive thing
- Auditors have a statutory duty to detect and prevent fraud

---

3 THE STANDARD UNQUALIFIED AUDIT REPORT

3.1 The standard unqualified audit report outlined in SAS 600 is shown below. You should be familiar with it.

3.2 You should also be fully aware of the **two express opinions,** and particularly the **five implied opinions** given within it. If you cannot remember what these opinions are, go back to your textbook for 2.6, *Audit and Internal Review,* and revise them now.

3.3 The audit report below is split into a number of sections that you should be aware of. We will revise them now, bearing in mind the Cadbury report an the expectations gap.

3.4 First, however, we will look at an item which is not included in the audit report below.

3.5 It is a requirement of the voluntary corporate governance codes that the **directors make a statement of their responsibilities** in the report to the shareholders. The **auditor should only report on the responsibilities of directors if the directors fail to do it themselves.**

Example 1. Unqualified opinion: company incorporated in Great Britain

AUDITORS' REPORT TO THE SHAREHOLDERS OF XYZ PLC

We have audited the financial statements on pages ... to ... which have been prepared under the historical cost convention (as modified by the revaluation of certain fixed assets) and the accounting policies set out on page ....

Respective responsibilities of directors and auditors

As described on page ... the company's directors are responsible for the preparation of financial statements. It is our responsibility to form an independent opinion, based on our audit, on those statements and to report our opinion to you.

Basis of opinion

We conducted our audit in accordance with Auditing Standards issued by the Auditing Practices Board. An audit includes examination, on a test basis, of evidence relevant to the amounts and disclosures in the financial statements. It also includes an assessment of the significant estimates and judgements made by the directors in the preparation of the financial statements, and of whether the accounting policies are appropriate to the company's circumstances, consistently applied and adequately disclosed.

We planned and performed our audit so as to obtain all the information and explanations which we considered necessary in order to provide us with sufficient evidence to give reasonable assurance that the financial statements are free from material misstatement, whether caused by fraud or other irregularity or error. In forming our opinion we also evaluated the overall adequacy of the presentation of information in the financial statements.

Opinion

In our opinion the financial statements give a true and fair view of the state of the company's affairs as at 31 December 20.. and of its profit (loss) for the year then ended and have been properly prepared in accordance with the Companies Act 1985.

Registered auditors *Address*

Date

3.6 We shall now turn to each section of the audit report, considering how the APB have tried to ensure that auditors communicate their role more comprehensively.

Heading

Common misconception

Auditors report to the directors, not the shareholders.

3.7 The example auditor report in SAS 600 has a clear heading in capital letters 'Auditors' report to the shareholders of XYZ plc'. This heading seeks to dispel the belief that auditors report to the directors, by **spelling out clearly to whom the report is addressed.**

First paragraph

Common misconception

Auditors report on the business and its operations.

3.8 The first paragraph states categorically what the auditors are reporting on. It **states that the auditors have audited 'the financial statements'** and even lists the pages on which items that have been audited can be found.

Respective responsibilities of directors and auditors

> **Common misconception**
>
> The auditors are responsible for the financial statements and other management responsibilities, such as preventing and detecting fraud.

3.9 The audit report refers to the directors' report on their own duties (discussed above) and the **states** very simply the **duty of an auditor,** which is to form an independent opinion of the financial statements.

Basis of opinion

> **Common misconception**
>
> Auditors test everything relating to the financial statements before giving their opinion.
>
> The auditors' opinion gives complete assurance that there has been no fraud perpetrated on the business and that no mistakes have been made in putting the accounts together.

3.10 The two paragraphs which form the basis of opinion sections seek to **describe in simple terms what an audit comprises,** in other words the evidence gathering and evaluation which support the opinion in the following section.

3.11 In doing so, they set out arguments against some other misconceptions. For example, it states quite clearly that **evidence is gathered on a test basis.**

3.12 It also outlines the concept of **reasonable** assurance, stating that **material** misstatements have been looked for.

Opinion

> The common misconceptions outlined above all contribute to a **lack of understanding** of what the **auditors' opinion** actually means.

3.13 The opinion section of the audit report states what the auditors' opinion is. It covers a 'true and fair view' and the issue of proper preparation.

Criticisms of the standard unqualified audit report

3.14 Some people would argue that while the above points are all true, and the standard unqualified audit report given in SAS 600 has made steps to close the exceptions gap, the steps are **insufficient,** and the issue is still not clear to a 'non-financial' investor.

3.15 It could be argued that the report still includes a lot of **jargon** which people who are not auditors cannot be expected to understand. Examples include:

- Material misstatements
- True and fair view

3.16 As stated earlier, 'true and fair view' is not defined in legislation and the **technical audit meaning** ascribed to it is **not immediately obvious** to non-auditors. For example, if asked to define true, a person might very well say 'correct', which is not at all what it means in relation to the audit opinion.

3.17 **Materiality** is another difficult concept that is **not defined in the audit report.**

3.18 The unqualified audit report gives five **implied opinions.** You should know what these are, but for revision purposes, they are:

- **Proper accounting records** have been kept and proper returns adequate for the audit received from branches not visited.
- The **accounts agree** with the **accounting records** and **returns**.
- **All information and explanations** have been **received** as the auditors think necessary and they have had access at all times to the company's books, accounts and vouchers.
- **Details** of **directors' emoluments** and **other benefits** have been correctly **disclosed** in the financial statements.
- Particulars of **loans and other transactions** in favour of **directors** and others have been correctly disclosed in the financial statements.
- The **information** given in the **directors' report** is **consistent** with the **accounts.**

3.19 Readers who are not familiar with the concept of audit should not be expected to know what these implications are. They are not receiving a full understanding of the opinion by virtue of the **opinion not being completely expressed.**

3.20 It could also be argued that someone who has never considered the concept of audit before could be **misled by the descriptions of audit** given, despite the attempt at simplicity that has been made.

3.21 For example, a person could read the second paragraph of the basis of opinion section and assume that the auditors do investigate fraud, given the reference to fraud made in the paragraph, and that the **description of audit,** while fair, **might still be misleading to non-auditors.**

3.22 In fact, the criticism could be made of the standard audit report that the very **simplicity** that it uses to explain the concept makes it misleading and that more detail should be given. Opponents would argue that investors might find detail confusing.

3.23 The **issue of public confusion over the role of auditors still exists.** SAS 600 has clearly taken steps to reduce the expectations gap, but evidence exists for the view of the critics that **steps have been insufficient** and that **works still needs to be done** to give **clarity** to the auditors' communication.

Question 3

The following is a series of extracts from an unqualified audit report which has been signed by the auditors of Kiln Ltd:

'Auditor's report to the shareholders of Kiln Limited

We have audited the *financial statements on pages ... to ...* which have been prepared under the historical cost convention.

We have conducted out audit *in accordance with Auditing Standards* issued by the Auditing Practices Board. An audit includes examination on a test basis of evidence relevant to the amounts and disclosures in the financial statements.

In our opinion the financial statements give a true and fair view of the state of the company's affairs as at 31 December 20X3 and of its profits for the year then ended and have been properly prepared in accordance with the Companies Act 1985.'

Explain the meaning and purpose of the following phrases taken from the above extracts of an unqualified audit report:

(a) '... the financial statements on pages ... to ...'
(b) '... in accordance with Auditing Standards.'
(c) 'In our opinion ...'

Answer

(a) '... the financial statements on pages 8 to 20 ...'

Purpose

The purpose of this phrase is to make it clear to the reader of an audit report the part of a company's annual report upon which the auditor is reporting his opinion.

Meaning

An annual report may include documents such as a chairman's report, employee report, five year summary and other voluntary information. However, under the Companies Act, only the profit and loss account, balance sheet and associated notes are required to be audited in true and fair terms. FRS 1 requires a cash flow and FRS 3 requires a statement of total recognised gains and losses which, under auditing standards, is audited to true and fair terms. Thus the page references (for instance 8 to 20) cover only the profit and loss account, balance sheet, notes to the accounts, cash flow statement and statement of total recognised gains and losses. The directors' report, although examined and reported on by exception if it contains inconsistencies, is not included in these page references.

(b) '... in accordance with Auditing Standards...'

Purpose

This phrase is included in order to confirm to the reader that best practice, as laid down in Auditing Standards, has been adopted by the auditor in both carrying out his audit and in drafting his audit opinion. This means that the reader can be assured that the audit has been properly conducted, and that should he wish to discover what such standards are, or what certain key phrases mean, he can have recourse to Auditing Standards to explain such matters.

Meaning

Auditing Standards are those auditing standards prepared by the Auditing Practices Board.

There are a series of auditing standards on the **conduct** of an audit. They cover planning, obtaining evidence, assessing controls, using the work of others and issues such as law and regulations and fraud. There is also SAS 600 on the reporting requirements of the APB, which this report is in accordance with.

(c) 'In our opinion...'

Purpose

Under the Companies Act, an auditor is required to report on every balance sheet, profit and loss account or group accounts laid before members. In reporting, he is required to state his opinion on those accounts. Thus, the purpose of this phrase is to comply with the statutory requirement to report an opinion.

Meaning

An audit report is an expression of opinion by a suitably qualified auditor as to whether the financial statements give a true and fair view, and have been properly prepared in accordance with the Companies Act. *It is not a certificate;* rather it is a statement of whether or not, in the professional judgement of the auditor, the financial statements give a true and fair view.

4 QUALIFICATIONS IN AUDIT REPORTS

4.1 SAS 600 gives examples of reports containing the four standard qualifications of audit reports that you should be aware of. The reports are not reproduced in full here, because the content is extremely similar to the unqualified audit report. Instead, the relevant paragraphs are shown below.

4.2 The four standard qualifications are shown in the matrix given here for revision purposes.

QUALIFICATION MATRIX

Nature of circumstances	*Material but not fundamental*	*Fundamental*
Limitation in scope	Except for .. might	Disclaimer of opinion
Disagreement	Except for ...	Adverse opinion

Except for . . . might	Auditors disclaim an opinion on a particular aspect of the accounts which is not considered fundamental.
Disclaimer of opinion	Auditors state they are unable to form an opinion on truth and fairness.
Except for	Auditors express an adverse opinion on a particular aspect of the accounts which is not considered fundamental.
Adverse opinion	Auditors state the accounts do not give a true and fair view.

Common misconception

A qualified audit report is better than an unqualified one.

4.3 The reports in SAS 600 try to dispel this misconception by putting in clear headings about the qualifications and describing the issues that have led to the qualification and the problems that have been encountered.

Limitations in audit scope

Example 8. Qualified opinion: limitation on the auditors' work

(Basis of opinion: excerpt)

.... or error. However, the evidence available to us was limited because £... of the company's recorded turnover comprises cash sales, over which there was no system of control on which we could rely for the purposes of our audit. There were no other satisfactory audit procedures that we could adopt to confirm that cash sales were properly recorded.

In forming our opinion we also evaluated the overall adequacy of the presentation of information in the financial statements.

Qualified opinion arising from limitation in audit scope

Except for any adjustments that might have been found to be necessary had we been able to obtain sufficient evidence concerning cash sales, in our opinion the financial statements give a true and fair view of the state of the company's affairs as at 31 December 20.. and of its profit (loss) for the year then ended and have been properly prepared in accordance with the Companies Act 1985.

In respect alone of the limitation on our work relating to cash sales:

(a) we have not obtained all the information and explanations that we considered necessary for the purpose of our audit; and

(b) we were unable to determine whether proper accounting records had been maintained.

Example 9. Disclaimer of opinion

(Basis of opinion: excerpt)

.... or error. However, the evidence available to us was limited because we were appointed auditors on (date) and in consequence we were unable to carry out auditing procedures necessary to obtain adequate assurance regarding the quantities and condition of stock and work in progress, appearing in the balance sheet at £... . Any adjustment to this figure would have a consequential significant effect on the profit for the year.

In forming our opinion we also evaluated the overall adequacy of the presentation of information in the financial statements.

Opinion: disclaimer on view given by financial statements

Because of the possible effect of the limitation in evidence available to us, we are unable to form an opinion as to whether the financial statements give a true and fair view of the state of the company's affairs as at 31 December 20.. or of its profit (loss) for the year then ended. In all other respects, in our opinion the financial statements have been properly prepared in accordance with the Companies Act 1985.

In respect of the limitation on our work relating to stock and work-in-progress:

(a) we have not obtained all the information and explanations that we considered necessary for the purpose of our audit; and

(b) we were unable to determine whether proper accounting records had been maintained.

Disagreement

Example 7. Qualified opinion: disagreement

Qualified opinion arising from disagreement about accounting treatment

Included in the debtors shown on the balance sheet is an amount of £Y due from a company which has ceased trading. XYZ plc has no security for this debt. In our opinion the company is unlikely to receive any payment and full provision of £Y should have been made, reducing profit before tax and net assets by that amount.

Except for the absence of this provision, in our opinion the financial statements give a true and fair view of the state of the company's affairs as at 31 December 20.. and of its profit (loss) for the year then ended and have been properly prepared in accordance with the Companies Act 1985.

> **Example 10. Adverse opinion**
>
> *Adverse opinion*
>
> As more fully explained in note ... no provision has been made for losses expected to arise on certain long-term contracts currently in progress, as the directors consider that such losses should be off-set against amounts recoverable on other long-term contracts. In our opinion, provision should be made for foreseeable losses on individual contracts as required by Statement of Standard Accounting Practice 9. If losses had been so recognised the effect would have been to reduce the profit before and after tax for the year and the contract work in progress at 31 December 20.. by £.. .
>
> In view of the effect of the failure to provide for the losses referred to above, in our opinion the financial statements do not give a true and fair view of the state of the company's affairs as at 31 December 20.. and of its profit (loss) for the year then ended. In all other respects, in our opinion the financial statements have been properly prepared in accordance with the Companies Act 1985.

Criticisms of qualified reports

4.4 **Similar criticisms** can be made of qualified reports as were made of unqualified reports. They are necessarily dealing with **complex matters** and **'audit jargon'** and that does make them **difficult** for a non-auditor **to understand.**

Uncertainties

4.5 Uncertainties provide another particularly difficult area for non-auditors to understand. This is because they involve the concepts of materiality and truth and fairness that we have already discussed.

4.6 It is difficult to explain how a report can be unqualified despite there being things that the auditor knows he does not know, when a person does not understand the concepts of materiality and reasonable assurance.

> **Example 4. Unqualified opinion with explanatory paragraph describing a fundamental uncertainty**.
>
> *Fundamental uncertainty* (insert just before opinion paragraph)
>
> In forming our opinion, we have considered the adequacy of the disclosures made in the financial statements concerning the possible outcome to litigation against B Limited, a subsidiary undertaking of the company, for an alleged breach of environmental regulations. The future settlement of this litigation could result in additional liabilities and the closure of B Limited's business, whose net assets included in the consolidated balance sheet total £... and whose profit before tax for the year is £... . Details of the circumstances relating to this fundamental uncertainty are described in note .... . Our opinion is not qualified in this respect.

5 FORMING AN AUDIT OPINION — Pilot Paper

> **Exam focus point**
>
> There are two elements to your work on audit reports for this paper. Firstly, you must be able to **critically appraise** the standard unqualified audit report, and we have been studying the advantages and disadvantages of the audit report in the previous sections.
>
> Secondly, you must be able **to form an opinion on items in the financial statements,** as a partners does in practice at the end of an audit before issuing his audit report. This is a skill you learnt at 2.6 (old paper 6) and we shall only revise is briefly here. You know the theory behind forming audit judgements. It is **vital** for this exam that **you practice questions** which outline issues that have arisen in the course of an audit and ask you what the implications are for the report.

5.1 You have learnt the issues surrounding forming an audit opinion previously in your auditing studies. As you were working through Chapters 11-13, Audit of financial statements, you should have been thinking of the implications items could have had on the audit report.

5.2 Here is a brief revision of the topic from paper 2.6, *Audit and Internal Review* (old paper 6).

> The principal matters which auditors consider in forming an opinion may be expressed in three questions.
>
> - Have the **completed all procedures necessary** to meet auditing standards and to obtain all the information and explanations necessary for their audit?
> - Have the financial statements been **prepared in accordance** with the **applicable accounting requirement?**
> - Do the financial statements, as prepared by the directors, give **a true and fair view?**

5.3 SAS 600 gives a flowchart which illustrates the method of forming an audit opinion. You may find it useful to follow the steps it gives when forming opinions on matters given in exam questions on this topic, so it is reproduced below.

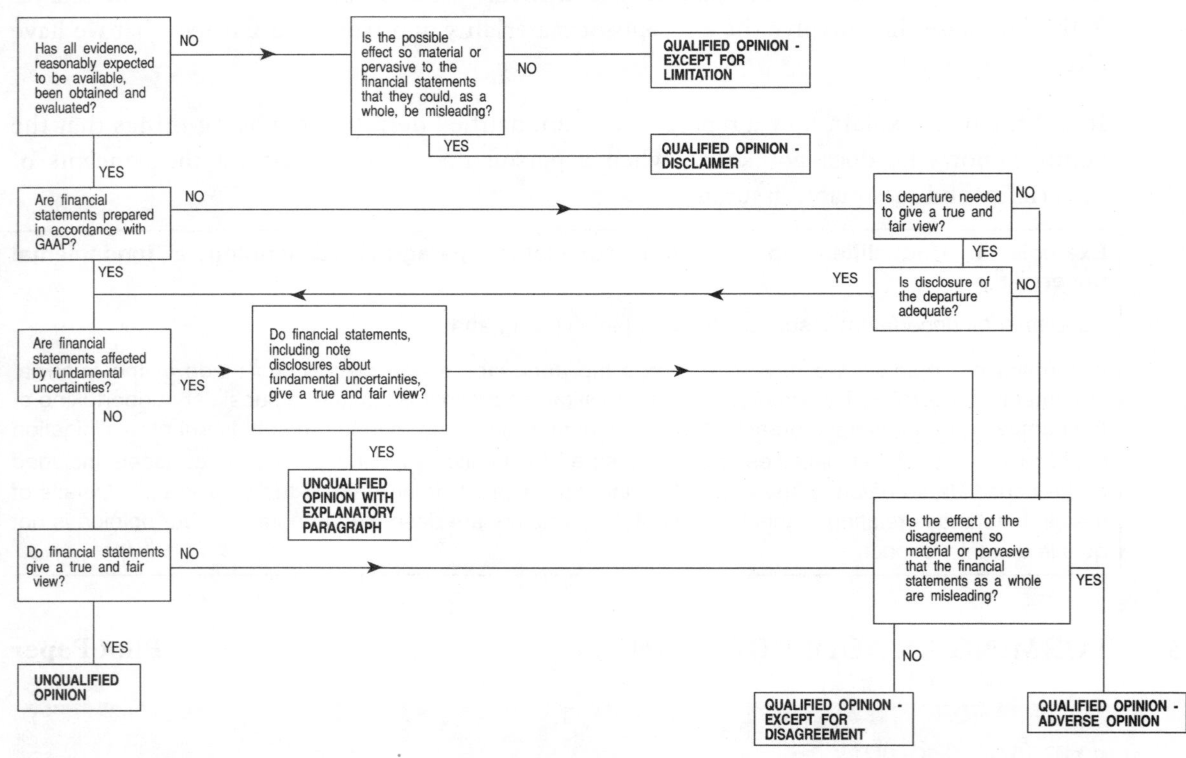

Question 4

Described below are situations that have arisen in three audits. The year end in each case is 31 March 20X1.

(1) Wulf commenced developments of a new type of cleaning process on 1 May 20X0. Expenditure on this project is expected to amount to £500,000 over five years. The outcome of the development work will not be certain until the end of the second year of the project. The directors have capitalised development costs of date of £100,000.

The pre-tax profits of Wulf plc for the year ended 31 March 20X1 were £500,000 and net assets on 31 March 20X1 amounted to £5 million.

(2) Sisters plc has four directors who have each borrowed £10,000 from the company. These loans, which total £40,000 have been included in the balance sheet as on 31 March 20X1 within the total trade debtors under the heading 'Debtors – due within one year'. No separate disclosure about the loans has been made in the directors' report or the financial statements. The audit senior has investigated this further and concluded that, whilst the loans are illegal, they are genuine collectible current assets of the company.

The pre-tax profits of Sisters plc for the year ended 31 March 20X1 were £278,000 and net assets on 31 March 20X1 amounts to £3 million.

(3) Mog plc manufactures light fittings. Certain of its finished stock lines are out of fashion and have a net realisable value which is £35,000 lower than their original cost. However, the directors have argued that, overall, the net realisable value of the entire stock exceeds original cost and that fashions may well change over the next few years such that the company can ultimately sell these lines above their current net realisable value.

The pre-tax profits of Mog plc for the year ended 31 March 20X1 were £900,000. Net assets and stock on 31 March 20X1 totalled £10 million and £4 million respectively.

(a) Explain what is meant by materiality, and list the factors that may be taken into account when deciding whether an amount is material.

(b) Discuss each of the situations outlined above, referring to materiality considerations and, where appropriate, Statements of Standard Accounting Practice, Financial Reporting Standards and the Companies Act 1985. For each situation indicate what kind of audit qualification (if any) would be appropriate, giving your reasons.

Answer

(a) Materiality is a concept close to an auditor's heart. It represents the point at which balances, transactions or adjustments become sensitive.

In general terms a matter should be judged material if **knowledge of the matter would be likely to influence the user of the financial statements.** Clearly application of the concept requires professional judgement as to whether or not any omission or misstatement would be likely to have influenced the judgement of the various possible users of financial statements. It should also be remembered that materiality refers both to the magnitude of an amount, and also its nature, and it should be judged in both relation to the financial statements as a whole, and in relation to individual areas of those statements.

In deciding whether or not a matter is material, the auditor must bear in mind the following factors:

(i) **Relative size** – this may be by the application of a simple 'rule of thumb', for instance a percentage of turnover, profit or net assets. It would be important to consider the amount as a percentage of the figure of which it is part, as well as in relation to main account areas such as turnover, profit etc.

(ii) **Critical changes** – in many circumstances it is likely that a user of financial statements would be influenced in his judgement by knowledge of an amount that changes, say, profit and loss, or net current assets to net current liabilities.

(iii) **Nature of item** – there are certain items within financial statements for which materiality considerations are irrelevant. For instance a loan to a director is to be disclosed regardless of its amount. Similarly, the nature of the two contrasting items 'Stocks and work-in-progress' and 'Bank and cash' are such that materiality measures may be different – bank balances are monetary items and as such one could not imagine concluding on such a figure at the same level of materiality as one would on a judgmental areas such as stock valuations.

(b) (1) **Wulf plc – deferred development expenditure**

(i) **Accounting treatment**

In principle the deferral of development expenditure is allowed by SSAP 13 provided stringent conditions are met. These are:

- The project must be clearly defined
- The expenditure must be separately identifiable

- The project must be technically feasible
- The project may be commercially viable
- The revenues must exceed the costs
- There must be adequate technical and financial resources available to complete the project

In the circumstances, there is insufficient information given in order to confirm all of the above requirements, but we do know that the 'outcome is uncertain'. This suggests that on the grounds of prudence, the expenditure should be written off to the profit and loss account as incurred, although once the uncertainty has been resolved, deferral can then take place (with no re-instatement of earlier amounts). The Companies Act 1985 states in the 4th Schedule that deferral is allowed providing 'special circumstance' apply. These are not defined but are thought to mean the deferral provisions of SSAP 13, thus it is doubtful whether the company had complied with either SSAP 13 or the Companies Act.

(ii) **Materiality**

In order to decide on the likely impact on the audit report, it is first necessary to consider the materiality of the amount involved. It represents 20% of pre tax profits and some 3% of net assets. In my opinion the amount is therefore material.

(iii) **Audit report**

Whilst material, the amount is not fundamental since it does not undermine the view given by the financial statements. Following the argument above, it would appear as if the circumstances are those of disagreement – non-compliance with SSAP 13 and the Companies Act. I would therefore issue a qualified audit report using the 'except for' wording for the opinion paragraph, and describe the circumstances and failure to comply with SSAP 13 and Schedule 4.

(2) **Sisters plc – Directors' loans**

(i) **Accounting treatment**

Regardless of the legality of such loans, they are required to be disclosed under s 330 and Schedule 6 of the Companies Act. The disclosures required are:

- The fact that the loans existed
- The names of the directors concerned
- The maximum amount outstanding during the period
- The amount outstanding at the beginning and end of the period
- Any interest due and not yet paid

Further, the amount should be included under the heading 'other debtors', and any amount due after more than one year separately shown.

(ii) **Materiality**

Concepts of materiality are relevant only to the extent of the amounts laid down in the Companies Act for legality/disclosability of such loans. Clearly the company is materially in non-compliance with the Act on both counts.

(iii) **Audit report**

The amounts are viewed as genuine collectable current assets of the company and as such it is unlikely that the audit report would be qualified on the grounds of the financial statements failing to give a true and fair view. However, the auditor is required to report by exception any failure to provide the disclosures required by the 6th Schedule, and to include those disclosures in the text of his audit report. The auditor should therefore include an additional paragraph giving the required disclosures and state that, except for the failure to comply with the requirements of the 6th Schedule, the financial statements have been properly prepared in accordance with the Companies Act 1985.

(3) **Mog plc – Stock valuation**

(i) **Accounting treatment**

This treatment is not in compliance with either SSAP 9 or the accounting rules embodied in the 4th Schedule of the Companies Act. Both SSAP 9 and the Companies

Act state that the valuation of items must be taken on an item-by-item (or groups of similar items) basis, rather than a gross comparison of cost and net realisable value. The argument about potential improvement in the market sometime in the future is irrelevant, since, provision should be made for all known losses even if the amount cannot be determined accurately.

Thus we must conclude that the treatment has led to an overstatement of both profits before tax and net assets of £35,000.

(ii) **Materiality**

The amount of the overstatement represents only 3.9% of pre-tax profit and, 0.9% of the stock figure and 0.35% of net assets. It is unlikely that an auditor would consider this amount to be material, unless it is indicative of other possible stock misstatement – only further investigation would confirm whether or not this was the case.

(iii) **Audit report**

In view of the fact that the amount involved is immaterial it is unlikely that any reference will be made to this matter in the audit report.

Overall comment on the three situations

On any occasion when an auditor qualifies his audit report, he must consider whether or not the qualification is material to the determination of the legality of any proposed dividends, and must report to members his opinion in this report. Clearly the qualifications in situations (1) and (2) require such a report, although situation (2) will not impact upon distributable profits.

---

6 SPECIAL PURPOSE AUDIT REPORTS

6.1 There are three special purpose audit reports that we are going to consider briefly here. They are reports on:

- Summary financial statements
- Revised accounts
- Distributions following an audit qualification

We will briefly consider the implications for auditors of reporting on the Internet.

Summary financial statements

6.2 S 251(1) of the Companies Act 1985 provides that a listed public company may issue only summary financial statements to its members instead of the full annual accounts and directors' report. Such statements must comply with Regulations laid down by the Secretary of State.

6.3 The summary financial statements must be accompanied by a statement from the company's auditors which states that:

(a) The **summary financial statements** are **consistent** with the **annual accounts** and the **directors' report.**

(b) The **summary financial statements comply** with s 251 Companies Act 1985 and the regulations made under that section (Companies (Summary Financial Statement) Regulations 1995 (SI 1995 2092).

6.4 Guidance for auditors is provided by the APB Bulletin 1999/6 *The Auditors' Statement on the Summary Financial Statement.* The terms of the engagement and the extent of the auditors' examination should be agreed in an engagement letter. The fact that auditors are reporting on **consistency** and **compliance** with **s 251,** and **not** on **truth** and **fairness,** will influence the work that they do.

6.5 Inconsistencies which auditors will seek include:

(a) **Information** which has been **inaccurately extracted** from the statutory accounts and the directors' report

(b) The **use of headings** in the summary financial statements which are **incompatible** with those used in the full accounts

(c) **Information** which has been **summarised** in a manner which is **inconsistent** with the statutory accounts and the directors' report

(d) **Omission** of **information** which is not required by the regulations but which is necessary to ensure consistency with the statutory accounts and the directors' report (for example information relating to an exceptional item)

6.6 If an inconsistency is found auditors should discuss with the directors how to eliminate the inconsistency, for example by including additional information. If the **inconsistency** is **not eliminated,** the auditors should **modify** their **statement.**

6.7 When checking for compliance with s 251, auditors should check whether the summary financial statement includes **information** that has **not** been **properly derived** from the full accounts and directors' report. Auditors will also consider whether a **qualified audit report** on the full accounts has been **accurately reproduced** in the summary statements, and any relevant extra information to enable the user to understand the qualification has been given.

6.8 The auditors should **read** prior to issue any **other information** which is contained in a document which also contains the summary financial statement. If there is an inconsistency between that other information and the summary financial statement, the auditors should take similar steps to those prescribed in SAS 160 for an inconsistency between the full accounts and other information.

6.9 An example unmodified auditors' statement on the summary financial statements is reproduced below.

Example unmodified statement on the summary financial statement

Auditors' statement to the shareholders of XYZ plc

We have examined the summary financial statements set out on pages … .

Respective responsibilities of directors and auditors

The directors are responsible for preparing the [summarised annual report]. Our responsibility is to report to you our opinion on the consistency of the summary financial statement within the [summarised annual report] with the full annual accounts and directors' report, and its compliance with the relevant requirements of s 251 of the Companies Act 1985 and the regulations made thereunder. We also read the other information contained in the [summarised annual report] and consider the implications for our report if we become aware of any apparent misstatements or material inconsistencies with the summary financial statement.

Basis of opinion

We conducted our work in accordance with Bulletin 1999/6 'The auditors' statement on the summary financial statement' issued by the Auditing Practices Board.

Opinion

In our opinion the summary financial statement above/overleaf is consistent with the full annual accounts and directors' report of XYZ plc for the year ended 20..... and complies with the applicable requirements of s 251 of the Companies Act 1985, and the regulations made thereunder.

Registered auditors *Address*

Date

Revised accounts

6.10 In May 1991 the APC published an exposure draft of an auditing guideline *Auditors' report on revised annual accounts and directors' reports*, which has not yet been replaced by APB guidance. The main provisions are discussed below.

6.11 The reason for the publication of a draft guideline is that CA 1989 introduced provisions dealing with the revision of annual accounts and directors' reports which have been found, after their laying or delivering, to be defective.

6.12 The revision may be voluntary or by court order, due to non-compliance with the Act. Voluntary revision of the accounts or the report under s 245 is not obligatory.

6.13 The revision of the accounts or directors' report may be undertaken by:

- **Revision by replacement**, replacing the original with a new version
- **Revision by supplementary note**

In both these cases, accounts or reports are to be prepared 'as if .... prepared and then approved by the directors as at the date of the original annual accounts', which means that the extent of any revision is limited to that resulting from the facts which were known or discoverable at the original date of approval.

6.14 The directors must include a statement in a prominent place in the revised accounts which gives full details of the revision.

6.15 The Regulations also state that the duties of the auditors set out in s 237 apply in respect of the report on revised accounts.

6.16 The guideline suggests factors to be taken into account when determining the extent of audit work to be performed in relation to the revised accounts.

- Whether the nature of the matter suggest that errors in the accounts may be **pervasive**
- Whether the facts discovered since the approval of the accounts **affect past assumptions** in areas of judgement
- The extent of any consequential **changes** to the form of accounts, which arise from the matter, for example, group accounts may be required for the first time
- The **steps taken by the directors** to investigate and correct the defect

6.17 The guideline also lists specific procedures which should be undertaken.

- **Review** the **original audit plans** in the light of the analysis of the matter leading to revision
- **Consider** the extent to which **additional audit evidence** is required
- **Reassess** the **various matters of judgement** involved in the preparation of the original accounts
- **Obtain evidence** that **relates to the adjustments made** to the original accounts
- **Carry out a review** of the **period after the date** on which the original accounts were approved
- **Perform a review** of the **revised accounts,** such as is sufficient, in conjunction with the conclusions drawn from the other audit evidence obtained, to give the auditors a reasonable basis for their opinion on the accounts
- **Consider** any **legal and regulatory consequences** of the revision

6.18 Examples of the auditors' report on revised accounts are given here, based on SAS 600.

(a) When revision is effected by replacement

Auditors' report to the members of XYZ Limited

We have audited the revised financial statements on pages ... to ... which have been prepared under the accounting policies set out on pages ... and ... . The revised financial statements replace the original financial statements approved by the directors on ... .

Respective responsibilities of directors and auditors

As described on page ... the directors are responsible for the preparation of financial statements. [*Note*]

It is our responsibility to form an independent opinion, based on our audit, on these revised financial statements and to report our opinion to you. We are also required to report whether in our opinion the original financial statements failed to comply with the requirements of the Companies Act 1985 in the respects identified by the directors.

Bases of opinion

We conducted our audit in accordance with Auditing Standards issued by the Auditing Practices Board. An audit includes examination, on a test basis, of evidence relevant to the amounts and disclosures in the financial statements. It also includes an assessment of the significant estimates and judgements made by the directors in the preparation of the financial statements, and of whether the accounting policies are appropriate to the company's circumstances, consistently applied and adequately disclosed. The audit of revised financial statements includes the performance of additional procedures to assess whether the revisions made by the directors are appropriate and have been properly made.

We planned and performed our audit so as to obtain all the information and explanations which we considered necessary in order to provide us with sufficient evidence to give reasonable assurance that the revised financial statements are free from material misstatement, whether caused by fraud or other irregularity or error. In forming our opinion, we also evaluated the overall adequacy of the presentation of information in the revised financial statements.

Opinions

In our opinion the revised financial statements give a true and fair view, seen as at the date the original financial statements were approved, of the state of the company's affairs as at ... and of its profit (loss) for the year then ended and have been properly prepared in accordance with the provisions of the Companies Act 1985 as they have effect under the Companies (Revision of Defective Accounts and Report) Regulations 1990.

In our opinion the original financial statements for the year ended ... failed to comply with the requirements of the Companies Act 1985 in the respects identified by the directors in the statement contained in note x to these financial statements.

Registered auditors *Address*

Date

Note. If the directors' responsibilities with respect to revised financial statements are not set out in a separate statement, the auditors will include a description in their report.

(b) When the revision is effected by issue of a supplementary note

> **Auditors' report to the members of XYZ Limited**
>
> We have audited the revised financial statements of XYZ Limited for the year ended ... The revised financial statements replace the original financial statements approved by the directors on ... and consist of the attached supplementary note together with the original financial statements which were circulated to members on ... .
>
> *Respective responsibilities of directors and auditors*
> As described on page ... the directors are responsible for the preparation of financial statements.
>
> It is our responsibility to form an independent opinion, based on our audit, on these revised financial statements and to report our opinion to you. We are also required to report whether in our opinion the original financial statements failed to comply with the requirements of the Companies Act 1985 in the respects identified by the directors.
>
> *Bases of opinion*
> We conducted our audit in accordance with Auditing Standards issued by the Auditing Practices Board. An audit includes examination, on a test basis, of evidence relevant to the amounts and disclosures in the financial statements. It also includes an assessment of the significant estimates and judgements made by the directors in the preparation of the financial statements, and of whether the accounting policies are appropriate to the company's circumstances, consistently applied and adequately disclosed. The audit of revised financial statements includes the performance of additional procedures to assess whether the revisions made by the directors are appropriate and have been properly made.
>
> We planned and performed our audit so as to obtain all the information and explanations which we considered necessary in order to provide us with sufficient evidence to give reasonable assurance that the revised financial statements are free from material mis-statement, whether caused by fraud or other irregularity or error. In forming our opinion, we also evaluated the overall adequacy of the presentation of information in the revised financial statements.
>
> *Opinions*
> In our opinion the revised financial statements give a true and fair view, seen as at the date the original financial statements were approved, of the state of the company's affairs as at ... and of its profit (loss) for the year then ended and have been properly prepared in accordance with the provisions of the Companies Act 1985 as they have effect under the Companies (Revision of Defective Accounts and Report) Regulations 1990.
>
> In our opinion the original financial statements for the year ended ... failed to comply with the requirements of the Companies Act 1985 in the respects identified by the directors in the supplementary note.
>
> *Registered auditors* *Address*
>
> *Date*

Distributions following an audit qualification

6.19 Under the Companies Act 1985, companies whose accounts have been qualified may only make a distribution (pay a dividend) only under certain circumstances.

6.20 The question whether a company has profits from which to pay a dividend is determined by reference to its '**relevant accounts**' which are generally the latest audited annual accounts: s 270. Relevant accounts must be properly prepared in accordance with the requirements of the Companies Acts.

6.21 If the auditors have qualified their report on the accounts they must also state in writing whether, in their opinion, the subject matter of their qualification (if it relates to statutory accounting requirements) is material in determining whether the dividend may be paid: s 271 CA 1985.

6.22 A copy of this statement must be laid before the company in general meeting. An example is given here.

> **Auditors' statement to the members of ABC Limited in accordance with Section 271(4) of the Companies Act 1985**
>
> We have audited the financial statements of ABC Limited for the year ended (date) in accordance with Auditing Standards issued by the Auditing Practices Board and have expressed a qualified opinion thereon.
>
> *Basis of opinion*
> We have carried out such procedures as we considered necessary to evaluate the effect of the qualified opinion in the context of determining profits available for distribution.
>
> *Opinion*
> In our opinion the subject of that qualification is not material for the purpose of determining, by reference to those financial statements, whether the distribution (interim dividend for the year ended ...) of £ ... proposed by the company is permitted under section 263 of the Companies Act 1985.
>
> *Registered auditor*

6.23 This statement (and the work of the auditors which precedes it) is very important, because a dividend paid **ultra vires** (that is, beyond the powers of the company) can be recovered by the company or the liquidator. This may leave the auditors open to a claim of negligence.

6.24 In order to issue a s 271(4) statement, the auditors must reassure themselves that the proposed distribution will be made out of profits available for that purpose (ie distributable profits). These will be **accumulated, realised profits**, so far as not previously utilised by distribution or capitalism, **less accumulated, realised losses**, so far as not previously written off.

6.25 S 264(3) defines **undistributable** profits as:

- The share premium account
- The capital redemption reserve
- Any excess of accumulated unrealised profits (not capitalised) over accumulated unrealised losses (not written off)
- Any other reserve which the company is prohibited from distributing by statute, memorandum or articles

Exam focus point

A question on this statement may be part of a question on the audit report.

Reporting on the Internet

6.26 The Companies Act 1985 (Electronic Communications) Order 2000 allows companies to publish their financial statements on the website and notify recipients of their availability rather than sending out copies, if shareholders agree.

6.27 The implication of this for auditors is that their audit report will be publicly available. There has been a recent trend to individuals to deal in shares independently over the internet.

6.28 The increasing convenience with which the public can access and use the reports of auditors on listed companies may impact on the rules of auditors liability you learnt about in Chapter 3.

Exam focus point

You should read the accountancy press to follow any developments in this area.

7 REPORTING TO MANAGEMENT AND THE AUDIT COMMITTEE

7.1 The concept of **reporting to management** was also covered in 2.6, *Audit and Internal Review* (old paper 6).

7.2 In this textbook we have highlighted the importance of the **audit committee** and the role that this committee has to play in ensuring good corporate governance. There will be occasions where the auditor reports to the audit committee instead of or as well as the finance director.

7.3 Ass we revise our knowledge of reports to management, we shall also consider relevant issues relating to **reporting to management in the form of an audit committee.**

7.4 Reporting to management is covered by SAS 610. It makes the following points:

> The main purpose of reports to directors or management are for auditors to communicate points that have come to their attention during the audit:
>
> - The **design** and **operation** of the **accounting and internal control systems** and to make suggestions for their improvement
> - **Other constructive advice,** for example comments on potential economics or improvements in efficiency
> - **Other matters,** for example comments on adjusted and unadjusted errors in the financial statements or on particular accounting policies and practices.

7.5 You know that the report to management is **not a substitute for the auditors' report** because the auditors' report is to members. The report to management is a **by-product of audit.**

7.6 If the auditors choose not to send a formal letter or report but consider it preferable to discuss any weaknesses with management, the discussion should be **minuted** or otherwise recorded in writing. Management should be provided with a copy of the note.

7.7 The auditors should explain in their report to management that it **only** includes those mattes which came to their attention as a result of the audit procedures, and that it should not be regarded as a comprehensive statement of all weaknesses that exist of all improvements that might be made.

7.8 The auditors should request a **reply** to all the points raised, indicating what action management intends to take as a result of the comments made in the report.

7.9 If **previous points** have **not been dealt with effectively** and they are still considered significant, the auditors should enquire why action has not been taken.

7.10 The report may contain matters of varying levels of significance and thus make it difficult for senior management to identify points of significance. The auditors can deal with this by giving the report a **'tiered' structure** so that major points are dealt with by the directors or the audit committee and minor points are considered by less senior personnel.

7.11 Other points to note about the management letter are as follows.

- The recommendations should take the form of **suggestions** backed up by **reason and logic.**
- The letter should be in **formal terms** unless the client requests otherwise.
- **Weaknesses** that **management** are aware of but **choose not to do anything about** should be **mentioned** to protect the auditors.
- If management or staff have **agreed to changes,** this should be mentioned in a letter.

Reports to audit committees

7.12 As implied above, the auditors may issue a general report to management which contains points they expect to be brought to the attention of the audit committee.

7.13 However, it may also be part of their audit agreement with the company that as a by-product of the statutory audit, the auditors issue a report to the audit committee themselves.

7.14 There are no formal requirements for the format this report should take, but the following general points can be made:

(a) The audit committee is comprised of non-executive directors. This has the following implications for a report by the auditors:

- They may have **limited time** to devote to the company
- They are **unlikely to have a personal relationship** with the auditor

(b) The audit committee is concerned with high level matters of policy, not 'nitty-gritty' details about the functions of specific controls.

7.15 The above points suggest that a report to the audit committee is likely to be more **formal** than a report to management. It is likely to be more concerned with **conceptual issues** or **total controls** rather than small specific issues. It should also be **focused** and presented with some form of an executive summary so that busy individuals can access it quickly.

7.16 It is likely that the auditor would also **meet** with the audit committee to discuss the findings in his report and to review any suggestions for improvements and plans for their implementation.

7.17 The audit committee might want to involve the auditor in implementing new control procedures, as they should advise the company on the auditors' other services to the company.

International guidance

7.18 You might find it helpful to look at the international guidance, which was released recently, on this issue. It can be found in ISA 260 *Communications of audit matters with those charged with governance*.

ISA 260.2

The auditor should communicate matters of governance interest arising from the audit of financial statements with those charged with governance of an entity.

7.19 The scope of the ISA is limited to matters that come to the auditors' attention as a result of the audit; the auditors are not required to design procedures to identify matters of governance interest.

ISA 260.5

The auditor should determine the relevant persons who are charged with governance and with whom audit matters of governance interest are communicated.

7.20 The auditors may communicate with the whole board, the supervisory board or the audit committee depending on the governance structure of the organisation. To avoid misunderstandings, the engagement letter should explain that auditors will only **communicate matters** that come to their attention as a **result** of the **performance** of the audit. It should state that the auditors are **not required** to **design procedures** for the purpose of identifying matters of governance interest.

7.21 The letter may also:

- **Describe** the **form** which any **communications** on governance matters will take
- **Identify** the **relevant persons** with whom such communications will be made
- **Identify** any **specific matters** of **governance** interest which it has agreed are to be communicated

ISA 260.11

The auditor should consider matters of governance interest that arise from the audit of the financial statements and communicate them with those charged with governance.

7.22 Matters would include:

- The **general approach** or overall scope of the audit, including limitations or additional requirements
- Selection of, or changes in, **significant accounting policies**

- The potential effect on the financial statements of any **significant risks** and **exposures**, for example pending litigation, that are required to be disclosed in the accounts
- Significant **audit adjustments**
- **Material uncertainties** affecting the organisation's ability to continue as a going concern
- **Significant disagreements** with management
- **Expected modifications** to the audit report
- Other **significant matters** such as material weaknesses in internal control, questions regarding management integrity, and fraud involving management
- Other **matters** mentioned in **terms** of **engagement**

ISA 260.9

The auditor should consider audit matters of governance interest on a timely basis.

7.23 Matters may be communicated orally or in writing, but they should be recorded in the audit working papers, however discussed. Auditors should make clear that the audit is not designed to identify all relevant matters connected with governance.

7.24 Auditors should have regard to local laws and regulations, and local guidance on confidentiality when communicating with management.

Effective management letters

7.25 You should be aware of the matters that make a management letter effective. Here is a checklist of matters to consider:

- Relevant
- Timely
- Focused
- Giving recommendations
- Explaining what problems are and why they have arisen

Chapter roundup

- A significant problem associated with auditing is the 'expectations gap'; the fact that people do not understand the role of the auditor.
- The APB have tried to combat the problem of the expectations gap by setting a standard for audit reports which gives explanations of what the auditors have done.
- Critics of the standard audit report issued in SAS 600 would say that:
  - The steps taken are insufficient
  - The report itself can add to confusion
- Before an audit report can be issued, the auditor needs to form an audit opinion based on the evidence has had gained during his audit. He should consider three matters:
  - Have all planned procedures been completed?
  - Have the financial statements been prepared in accordance with accounting standards?
  - Do the financial statements give a true and fair view?

- The procedure for forming an audit opinion can be expressed in a flowchart which you should learn.
- Auditors may issue special reports on:
  - Summary financial statements
  - Revised accounts
  - Distribution following an audit qualification
- As a by-product of audit, the auditors may report on the audit findings to:
  - The directors
  - The audit committee

Quick quiz

1 Name the common misconceptions about the work of auditors.

(1) ________________

(2) ________________

(3) ________________

2 Complete the definitions

(a) ____________: Information is free from ____________ and ____________ and in compliance with the expected standards and rules.

(b) ____________ is an expression of the relative ____________ or importance of a particular matter in the ____________ ____________ as a whole.

(c) ____________: Information is ____________ and conforms with ____________, not ____________. Information conforms with required standards and law.

3 List the main headings if the SAS 600, standard, unqualified report.

4 Complete the matrix.

Nature of circumstances	*Material but not fundamental*	*Fundamental*
Limitation in scope		
Disagreement		

5 Reproduce the 'forming an audit opinion' flowchart.

6 Define **distributable profits.**

7 Name three things which might be covered in a report to management/audit committee.

(1) ________________

(2) ________________

(3) ________________

Answers to quick quiz

1 (1) Auditors report to directors (as opposed to shareholders)
(2) Qualified audit report is more favourable
(3) Auditor's duty to detect fraud

2 (a) Fair, discrimination, bias
(b) Materiality, significance, financial statements
(c) True, factual, reality, false

3 Title, respective responsibilities of directors and auditors, basis of opinion, opinion.

4 QUALIFICATION MATRIX

Nature of circumstances	*Material but not fundamental*	*Fundamental*
Limitation in scope	Except for … might	Disclaimer of opinion
Disagreement	Except for …	Adverse opinion

5

FORMING AN OPINION ON FINANCIAL STATEMENTS

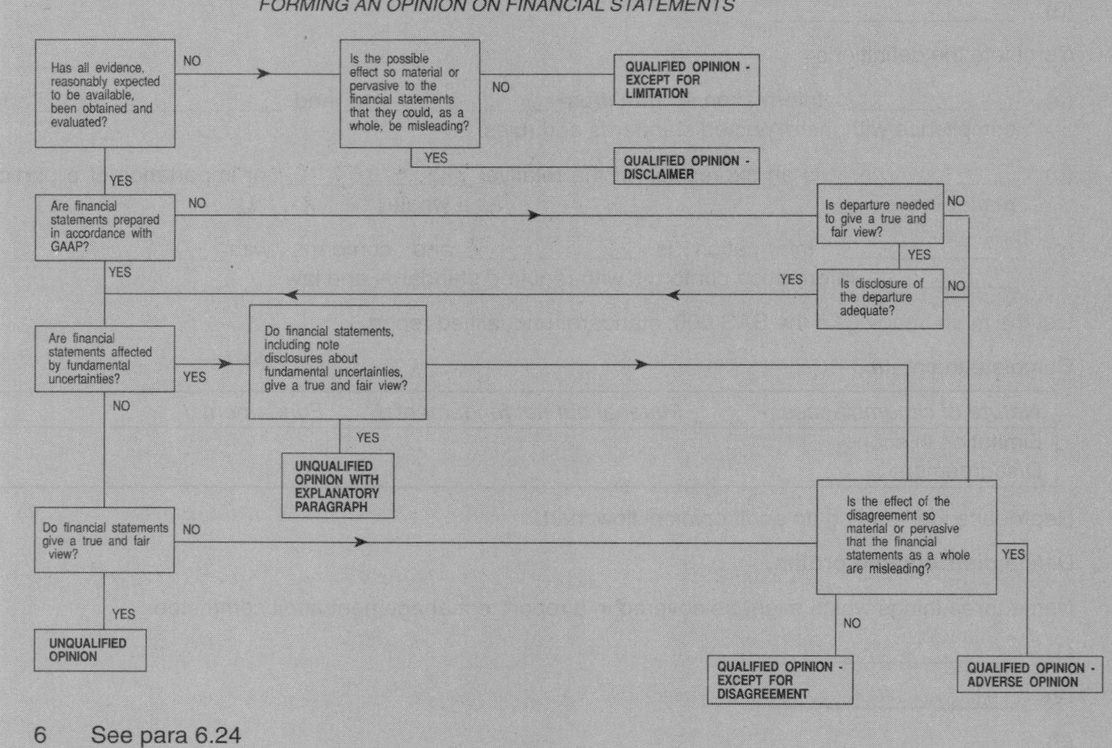

6 See para 6.24

7 (1) Design and operation of accounting and internal control system
(2) Other constructive advice
(3) Other matters (for example errors in the financial statements)

Now try the question below from the Exam Question Bank

Number	Level	Marks	Time
19	Exam	15	27 mins

Appendix

Client Acceptance Form - Audit clients Form A1.1

We perform our client acceptance procedures, and in particular the investigation procedures, as early in the proposal process as possible to avoid incurring significant time and effort on a prospective client that we might later decide not to accept.

Background Information

Prospective client________________ Accounting period ________

Address________________

Nature of business (eg industry, products or services, major customers, major suppliers)________

If the business was started within the past 5 years, indicate the year: 19 ___ Company reg. no. ________

Type of service(s) to be rendered________________

Does the prospective client meet the definition of a "Stock Exchange engagement"? Yes ______ No______

Is the prospective client considering "going public" in the next year? Yes ______ No______ N/A ______

Anticipated person in charge________________

Anticipated independent reviewer, if identified ________________

Total estimated fee (if available):

Year 1	£______	recurring	£______	non-recurring
Year 2	£______	recurring	£______	non-recurring

Billing and payment agreement and any special fee arrangements________________

Financial information (for last two years):

Year end	Total assets	Total debt	Shareholders' funds	Total turnover	Profit/(loss)

Has the prospectice client been investigated? Yes _____ No_____ If not, document in an attached memorandum the reasons for not requesting an investigation.

Was there any information in the investigative agency's (oral or attached written) report that indicates we should question whether to accept the prospective client? Yes _____ No_____ If yes, discuss in an attached memorandum along with any mitigating factors.

Key officers, directors, and major shareholders	Officer	Director	Own%	Other businesses/comments

Client Acceptance Form - Audit clients Form A1.2

List the principal solicitors, commercial bankers, and investment bankers with whom the prospective client has a relationship (indicate with an asterisk those individuals who are contacted as part of our client acceptance procedures) and other individuals contacted:

Individual	Firm or Bank
______________________	______________________________________
______________________	______________________________________
______________________	______________________________________
______________________	______________________________________
______________________	______________________________________

Did any matters arise in our contacts with the solicitors, commercial bankers, investment bankers, or others that need further consideration in deciding whether to accept the prospective client? Yes _____ No_____
If yes, describe the matters in an attached memorandum.

Predecessor Auditors/Accountants

Inquiries of prospective client regarding predecessor auditors/accountants:
Firm name and office ______________________________
Length of firm's relationship with the prospective client ______________________________
Services rendered to the prospective client ______________________________
____

Type of opinion issued last year ______________________________
Prospective client's reason(s) for changing auditors/accountants ______________________________
____

Were there any disagreements with the predecessor auditors/accountants over accounting principles, audit, review, or compilation procedures, or other significant matters during the entity's two most recent fiscal years and any other subsequent interim period? Yes _____ No _____ If yes, describe the disagreements in an attached memorandum.

Any reportable conditions/material weaknesses in the internal control structure? Yes_____ No _____
If yes, describe the conditions/weaknesses in an attached memorandum.

Enquiries of predecessor auditors/accountants:
Date of inquiries ______________________________
Names and titles of individuals who responded to our enquiries (should include the partner in charge) __________
____

Predecessor's understanding of the reason(s) for changing auditors/accountants ______________________________
____

Any facts that might bear on the integrity of management ______________________________
____
____

Have the predecessor's fees been paid in full? Yes _____ No _____ If not, indicate the reasons ______________
____

Were there any disparities between the prospective client's replies and the preceding auditor's replies?
Yes _____ No _____ If yes, describe the differences in an attached memorandum.

Client Acceptance Form - Audit clients Form A1.3

Other significant considerations (Explain answers with an asterisk in an attached memorandum)

	Question	Yes	No
1	Are there possible conflicts of interest with concerns of existing clients (eg conflicts with litigation services engagements)?	__*	__
2	Are there any independence issues, including family relationships, that need to be considered before we could accept the prospective client?	__*	__
3	Will the engagement require specialised (eg industry specific) knowledge and experience not now available in the local or area office?	__	__
	If yes describe in an attached memorandum the plan to obtain the neccessary expertise from other offices and/or to develop it within the office and obtain the concurrence of the national regional director of industry services.		
	Will the addition of the client adversely affect the ability of the office to staff any of its other engagements requiring similar expertise?	__*	__
4	Have any significant accounting or auditing issues been identified?	__*	__
5	Does the prospective client expect the firm to accept an accounting policy the predecessor auditors did not accept?	__*	__
6	Will we be auditing all entities under common control?	__	__
7	Are there significant related party transactions with consolidated or other entities that we will not be auditing?	__*	__
8	Does management have a proven track record in this or other businesses?	__	__
9	Does the prospective client have a high likelihood of (continued) business success?	__	__
10	Are there any conditions or events that indicate there could be substantial doubt about the prospective client's ability to continue as a going concern?	__*	__
11	For non-public entities, are there third parties (eg lenders or investors) whom we know would be receiving copies of our reports on the client's financial statements?	__*	__
12	Will the firm be assuming more than a low level of risk if this prospective client is accepted?	__*	__
13	Are there any other factors that should be considered in evaluating the prospective client?	__*	__

Other procedures

1 Seek information and advice from others in the firm who are likely to have significant information bearing on a decision to accept the prospective client, including other partners in the office, in other offices in the area, and where applicable, in other offices in cities where the entity has significant operations or where we have performed other services.

2 For a prospective client in a specialised industry, consult with the partner of industry services with regard to industry specific factors that should be addressed in considering the prospective client for acceptance.

3 For public and significant non-public prospective audit clients, contact the partner in charge of litigation services to determine if there are any conflicts or potential conflicts that need to be evaluated.

4 In the space below, list any head office personnel consulted when performing the client acceptance proceedures. If there are any unresolved issues remaining from those consultations, describe them in an attached memorandum.

Client Acceptance Form - Audit clients Form A1.4

Attachments (attach the following, where applicable, to this form)

- Memoranda, as required, to document considerations described elsewhere on this form
- Investigation report or memorandum documenting the reasons for not requesting an investigation

Accompanying information

- Public companies - the most recent annual shareholders' report, the form reporting the change in auditors and the predecessor auditors' letter. Any recent placing or other documents.
- Private companies - the most recent annual financial statements, and if available, the latest interim financial statements.

Conclusions

I have considered the professional, business, and economic factors regarding this engagement and recommend the acceptance of this prospective client.

Client will be ___ /will not be ___ designated for close-monitoring.

Evaluating Person ____________________ Date ____________

Approvals

I am satisfied that this recommendation is in compliance with our policy on client acceptance of this prospective client. Acceptance of this client does ___ /does not ___ require the concurrence of the National Managing Partner.

Office Managing Partner ____________________ Date ____________

I concur with the acceptance of this prospective client.

National Managing Partner ____________________ Date ____________

AN EXAMPLE OF AN ENGAGEMENT LETTER

To the directors of...

The purpose of this letter is to set out the basis on which we (are to) act as auditors of the company (and its subsidiaries) and the respective areas of responsibility of the directors and of ourselves.

Responsibility of directors and auditors

1 As directors of the above company, you are responsible for ensuring that the company maintains proper accounting records and for preparing financial statements which give a true and fair view and have been prepared in accordance with the Companies Act 1985. You are also responsible for making available to us, as and when required, all the company's accounting records and all other relevant records and related information, including minutes of all management and shareholders' meetings.

2 We have a statutory responsibility to report to the members whether in our opinion the financial statements give a true and fair view of the state of the company's affairs and of the profit or loss for the year and whether they have been properly prepared in accordance with the Companies Act 1985 (or other relevant legislation). In arriving at our opinion, we are required to consider the following matters, and to report on any in respect of which we are not satisfied:

(a) whether proper accounting records have been kept by the company and proper returns adequate for our audit have been received from branches not visited by us;

(b) whether the company's balance sheet and profit and loss account are in agreement with the accounting records and returns;

(c) whether we have obtained all the information and explanations which we think necessary for the purposes of our audit; and

(d) whether the information in the directors' report is consistent with the financial statements.

In addition, there are certain other matters which, according to the circumstances, may need to be dealt with in our report. For example, where the financial statements do not give full details of directors' remuneration or of their transactions with the company, the Companies Act requires us to disclose such matters in our report.

3 We have a professional responsibility to report if the financial statements do not comply in any material respect with applicable accounting standards, unless in our opinion the non-compliance is justified in the circumstances. In determining whether the departure is justified we consider:

(a) whether the departure is required in order for the financial statements to give a true and fair view; and

(b) whether adequate disclosure has been made concerning the departure

Our professional responsibilities also include:

(a) including in our report a description of the directors' responsibilities for the financial statements where the financial statements or accompanying information do not include such a description; and

(b) considering whether other information in documents containing audited financial statements is consistent with those financial statements.

4 Our audit will be conducted in accordance with the Auditing Standards issued by the Auditing Practices Board, and will include such tests of transactions and of the existence, ownership and valuation of assets and liabilities as we consider necessary. We shall obtain an understanding of the accounting and internal control systems in order to assess their adequacy as a basis for the preparation of the financial statements and to establish whether proper accounting records have been maintained by the company. We shall expect to obtain such appropriate evidence as we consider sufficient to enable us to draw reasonable conclusions therefrom

5 The nature and extent of our procedures will vary according to our assessment of the company's accounting system and, where we wish to place reliance on it, the internal control system, and may

cover any aspect of the business's operations. Our audit is not designed to identify all significant weaknesses in the company's systems but, if such weaknesses come to our notice during the course of our audit which we think should be brought to your attention, we shall report them to you. Any such report may not be provided to third parties without our prior written consent. Such consent will be granted only on the basis that such reports are not prepared with the interests of anyone other than the company in mind and that we accept no duty or responsibility to any other party as concerns the reports.

6 As part of our normal audit procedures, we may request you to provide written confirmation of oral representations which we have received from you during the course of the audit on matters having a material effect on the financial statements. In connection with representations and the supply of information to us generally, we draw your attention to section 389A of the Companies Act 1985 under which it is an offence for an officer of the company to mislead the auditors.

7 In order to assist us with the examination of your financial statements, we shall request sight of all documents or statements, including the chairman's statement, operating and financial review and the directors' report, which are due to be issued with the financial statements. We are also entitled to attend all general meetings of the company and to receive notice of all such meetings.

8 The responsibility for safeguarding the assets of the company and for the prevention and detection of fraud, error and non-compliance with law or regulations rests with yourselves. However, we shall endeavour to plan our audit so that we have a reasonable expectation of detecting material misstatements in the financial statements or accounting records (including those resulting from fraud, error or non-compliance with law or regulations), but our examination should not be relied upon to disclose all such material misstatements or frauds, errors or instances of non-compliance as may exist.

9 (Where appropriate). We shall not be treated as having notice, for the purposes of our audit responsibilities, of information provided to members of our firm other than those engaged on the audit (for example information provided in connection with accounting, taxation and other services).

10 Once we have issued our report we have no further direct responsibility in relation to the financial statements for that financial year. However, we expect that you will inform us of any material event occurring between the date of our report and that of the Annual General Meeting which may affect the financial statements.

Other services

11 You have requested that we provide other services in respect of ... . The terms under which we provide these other services are dealt with in a separate letter. We will also agree in a separate letter of engagement the provision of any services relating to investment business advice as defined by the Financial Services Act 1986.

Fees

12 Our fees are computed on the basis of the time spent on your affairs by the partners and our staff and on the levels of skill and responsibility involved. Unless otherwise agreed, our fees will be billed at appropriate intervals during the course of the year and will be due on presentation.

Applicable law

13 This (engagement letter) shall be governed by, and construed in accordance with, (English) law. The Courts of (England) shall have exclusive jurisdiction relation to any claim, dispute or difference concerning the (engagement letter) and any matter arising from it. Each party irrevocably waives any right it may have to object to an action being brought in those Courts, to claim that the action has been brought in an inconvenient forum, or to claim that those Courts do not have jurisdiction.

14 Once it has been agreed, this letter will remain effective, from one audit appointment to another, until it is replaced. We shall be grateful if you could confirm in writing your agreement to these terms by signing and returning the enclosed copy of this letter, or let us know if they are not in accordance with your understanding of our terms of engagement.

Yours faithfully

Certified Accountants

Exam question bank

1 BLAKE SEVEN (PILOT PAPER) *27 mins*

(a) Explain the importance of the role of confidentiality to the auditor-client relationship (5 marks)

(b) Your firm acts as auditor and adviser to Blake Seven Ltd and to its four directors. The company is owned 50% by Brad Capella, 25% by his wife Minerva and 10% by Janus Trebbiano. Brad is chief executive and Janus the finance director. Janus's sister, Rosella Trebbiano, has recently resigned from the executive board, following a disagreement with the Capellas. Rosella has now formed her own company, Blakes Heaven, in competition with Blake Seven.

Rosella is currently negotiating with her former co-executives the profit-related remuneration due to her and the sale of her 15% holding of shares in Blake Seven to one or all of them.

Rosella has contacted you to find out Brad's current remuneration package since he refuses to disclose this to her. She has also requested that your firm should continue to act as her personal adviser and become auditor and adviser to Blakes Heaven.

Required

Comment on the matters that you should consider in deciding whether or not your audit firm can comply with Rosella's requests. (10 marks)

(15 marks)

2 APPOINTMENT AND ENGAGEMENT *36 mins*

Your firm has been approached by the directors of Streethart Ltd who would like to engage your firm as the company's auditors for the next financial year, ending on 31 December 20X6. The directors feel that their current auditors do not give a value for money audit and they will be asked to resign.

Required

(a) What ethical and statutory matters would you consider and what investigations would you undertake before your firm could accept appointment and be appointed as auditors to Streethart? (11 marks)

(b) (i) State the main contents of the letter of engagement which you would send to Streethart's directors.

(ii) Discuss the reasons why auditors should send a letter of engagements to clients before they carry out an audit. (9 marks)

(20 marks)

3 PROFESSIONAL RESPONSIBILITIES *27 mins*

Consider the following quote.

> 'The auditors' professional responsibilities are clear. They should have a reasonable expectation of detecting material misstatements in financial statements. Serious fraud usually involves material misstatements; so, in general, auditors should have a reasonable expectation of finding it.
>
> Yet auditors do fail to detect fraud. In a recent survey of large companies, only a small proportion of all frauds were discovered by auditors.'

Required

Discuss, reaching a conclusion, what role auditors should have in the prevention and detection of fraud. **(15 marks)**

4 MERGER OF AUDIT FIRMS *36 mins*

The increase in the size of audit firms has been a source of concern to regulators and clients alike. Some audit firms feel that mergers between the largest firms of auditors are necessary in order to meet the global demand for their services. However their clients are concerned that such mergers will create a monopolistic market for audit services which will not be in their best interests.

Required

(a) Explain the reasons why the largest audit firms might wish to merge their practices. (10 marks)

(b) Discuss the potential problems created by mergers of the largest firms of auditors. (10 marks)

(20 marks)

5 DAXON *27 mins*

Daxon plc is a listed company that carries on business as a book wholesaler. In the financial year ended 31 October 20X5, the growth in sales turnover to £25m has continued to match the rate of inflation; costs have been contained by reducing staff from 96 to 90; the asset turnover rate has been maintained at five times.

The Daxon plc accountant has prepared draft accounts for the year ended 31 October 20X5, and included the following directors' responsibilities statement.

> 'The directors are required by UK company law to prepare financial statements for each financial period which give a true and fair view of the state of affairs of the group as at the end of the financial period and of the profit and loss for that period. In preparing the financial statements, suitable accounting policies have been used and applied consistently, and reasonable and prudent judgements and estimates have been made. Applicable accounting standards have been followed. The directors are also responsible for maintaining adequate accounting records, for safeguarding the assets of the group, and for preventing and detecting fraud and other irregularities.'

On receiving the statement, one of Daxon plc's directors commented that the statement included aspects that he had always assumed were the responsibility of the auditor and complained about the apparent proliferation of irrelevant new rules.

He requested that the accountant should prepare a memo for the board to explain certain of the items.

Required

Assuming that you are the accountant of Daxon plc, draft a memo to the board of directors explaining:

(a) The background to the inclusion in the annual report of a directors' responsibilities statement; (5 marks)

(b) What is meant by true and fair and how the board can determine whether the financial statements give a true and fair view; and (5 marks)

(c) What would constitute adequate steps for safeguarding the assets and preventing and detecting fraud. (5 marks)

(15 marks)

6 AUDIT ADVANTAGES AND RESPONSIBILITIES *36 mins*

For the last few years your firm has helped Colin, a sole trader, prepare his accounts for the Inland Revenue. Colin is about to incorporate his business and has asked your advice on a number of issues.

Required

Advise Colin on the following.

(a) The advantages to the company of having its accounts audited (you may assume that the company would be able to claim exemption from audit). (5 marks)

(b) The formalities involved in appointing your firm as the company's first auditor. (5 marks)

(c) The rights your firm will have as auditors. (5 marks)

(d) The responsibilities of Colin and other directors in relation to the company's accounting system. (5 marks)

(20 marks)

7 PLD ASSOCIATES *36 mins*

PLD Associates plc, a large quoted company, was founded and controlled by Mr J Scott. The principal business of the company was to develop derelict land in city centres into office accommodation. In 1993, the Inland Revenue became suspicious of the nature of the operations being carried out by the company and an investigation into its affairs commenced.

The resultant report stated that the organisation's internal controls were weak and non-existent in many cases. The investigators found payments to unknown persons, and fictitious consultancy firms. In addition, J Scott had maintained a secret expense account that was used to disburse funds to himself.

The board of directors of PLD Associates plc did not know of the existence of this account. The expense account was maintained by the partner of the firm of accountants responsible for the audit of the company. The auditors were heavily criticised in the report of the investigators.

The firm of auditors, Allcost & Co, had an aggressive marketing strategy and had increased its audit fees by 100% in two years. The audit firm had accepted the appointment in 1991 after the previous auditors had been dismissed. The audit report for the year ended 1990 had been heavily qualified by the previous auditors on the grounds of poor internal control and lack of audit evidence. J Scott had approached several firms of auditors in order to ascertain whether they would qualify the audit report given the present systems of control in PLD Associates plc. Allcost & Co had stated that it was unlikely that they would qualify their report. They realised that J Scott was 'opinion shopping' but were prepared to give an opinion in order to attract the client to their firm.

PLD Associates plc subsequently filed for insolvency and Allcost & Co were sued for negligence by the largest loan creditor, its bankers.

Required

(a) Describe the procedures which an audit firm should carry out before accepting a client with potentially high audit risk such as PLD Associates plc. (6 marks)

(b) Discuss the ethical problems raised by the maintenance of the secret expense account for Mr J Scott by the audit partner. (5 marks)

(c) Suggest measures that audit firms might introduce to try and minimise the practice of 'opinion shopping' by prospective audit clients. (5 marks)

(d) Explain how audit firms can reduce the risk of litigation and its effects upon the audit practice. (4 marks)

(20 marks)

8 TAURUS TRADERS (PILOT PAPER) *45 mins*

As manager responsible for prospective new clients you have visited Taurus Traders Ltd which supplies a range of specialist materials to the building industry. The chief executive and majority shareholder, Mr Aquila, has asked your firm to make a proposal for the company's audit and provision of financial advice.

During your initial meeting you have ascertained the following:

Turnover has grown from £4 million to £7 million in the last two years and the company is profitable. Further growth is anticipated as Mr Aquila has plans:

(1) To increase the company's customer base by making certain materials available to the public through builders merchants, and

(2) To expand the product base by setting up an overseas operation to manufacture silicon carbide components.

Mr Aquila negotiates prices directly with both suppliers and customers. A part-qualified accountant was recruited earlier this year to help with credit control and to set up more formal accounting systems and procedures. A desk-top computer provides basic sales, debtors, stock and payroll information. The software was written to Mr Aquila's requirements by his wife's brother. Most purchases require foreign currency translation and are recorded manually. Each month end there are varying, small and unreconciled differences on the debtors and creditors ledger control accounts.

The annual budget significantly understates actual revenue and expenses because of higher than expected growth. Management accounts are produced infrequently on an ad hoc basis.

For management accounting purposes, cost of sales is calculated as a percentage of sales value of different product categories. Historically, this method has proved reasonably reliable when compared to the year-end valuation of the annual stocktaking. However, margins on product lines have recently become much more varied.

Taurus is currently experiencing a high level of returns of faulty materials. These are returned to stock if they cannot be sold at a discount for cash.

Mr Aquila is negotiating a bank loan to finance the cost of planned new premises. Contracts with the builders have been signed and building work has commenced. The bank is waiting for a profit forecast before giving final approval to a £2 million loan.

Taurus Traders has increasingly tended to exceed its agreed overdraft facility. Mr Aquila has indicated that a large receipt from a major customer, expected at the end of next month, is to be used to clear tax payment arrears and repay his loan of £52,000.

Mr Aquila is recently married and has purchased a luxury apartment and a new car. He is dissatisfied with the firm of accountants which currently prepares and audits the annual financial statements. He attributes this to the firms failure to reconcile the ledgers. He also claims that the firm has been unable to suggest how his remuneration package can be increased to meet his personal needs.

Required

(a) Identify and describe the principal business risks relating to Taurus Traders (11 marks)

(b) Identify and comment on the factors that should influence the partner in deciding whether or not the firm should make a proposal for this engagement. (5 marks)

(c) Justify an appropriate audit strategy for the first audit of Taurus Traders. (6 marks)

(d) Suggest two procedures that Taurus Traders could implement immediately to improve its accounting procedures and financial controls. (3 marks)

(25 marks)

9 LAMBLEY PROPERTIES *36 mins*

A statement of auditing standards has been issued: SAS 440 *Management representations*. You are the manager in charge of the audit of Lambley Properties plc and you have been asked to prepare the letter of representation which will be signed by the company's directors.

You are aware that there are two material items in the accounts for the year ended 31 March 20X2 on which you want the company's directors to confirm that the treatment in the accounts is correct.

(a) One of the company's subsidiaries, Keyworth Builders Ltd, is experiencing going concern problems, and you want the directors' confirmation that they intend to support the company for the foreseeable future.

(b) Eastwood Manufacturing plc is in dispute with Lambley Properties over repairs required to a building they purchased from Lambley. Lambley Properties constructed the building for Eastwood, and three years after it was sold to Eastwood, the customer is claiming that repairs are required which will cost £3 million, and that Lambley is liable to pay for these repairs, as they are as a result of negligent construction of the building. In addition, Eastwood is claiming £2 million for the cost of disruption of the business due to the faults in the building and in the period when the repairs take place. Lambley Properties have obtained the advice of a lawyer and a surveyor, and the directors believe there are no grounds for the claim and any court action will find in their favour. However, Lambley Properties has included a note in its accounts concerning this contingency.

Required

(a) Prepare a letter of representation which the directors will sign and send to you, as auditors. In the letter, you should include the two items above and any other matters which you believe should be included. (8 marks)

(b) Discuss the reliability of a letter of representation as audit evidence and the extent to which the auditors can rely on this evidence. (4 marks)

(c) Describe the work you will perform to check whether a provision should be included in the accounts for the legal claim from Eastwood Manufacturing plc. (5 marks)

(d) Describe the matters you will consider and the further action you will take if the directors refuse to sign the letter of representation because of the legal claim from Eastwood Manufacturing plc. (3 marks)

(20 marks)

10 BESTWOOD ELECTRONICS *36 mins*

A statement of auditing standards has been issued: SAS 150 *Subsequent events*. Your firm is the auditor of Bestwood Electronics plc which assembles microcomputers and wholesales them and associated equipment to retailers. Many of the parts for the computers and the associated equipment are bought from the Far East. These computers are used by businesses for accounting, word processing and other computing tasks.

You have been asked by the partner in charge of the audit to consider your firm's audit responsibilities in relation to subsequent sheet events, and the audit work you will carry out on these matters.

Required

(a) Briefly describe the responsibilities of the auditors for detecting errors in the accounts during the following periods:

(i) From the period end to the date of the auditors' report

(ii) From the date of the auditors' report to the issue of the financial statements

(iii) From the date the financial statements are issued to the date they are laid before the members (5 marks)

(b) List and describe the audit work you will carry out in period (a)(i) above which involves consideration of subsequent events (or post balance sheet events). (11 marks)

(c) Briefly describe the work you will carry out in period (a)(ii) above to ensure no adjustments are required to the accounts. (4 marks)

(20 marks)

11 LOCKSLEY *45 mins*

The following is the draft balance sheet of Locksley Ltd for the year ended 31 January 20X3.

LOCKSLEY LIMITED
BALANCE SHEET AS AT 31 JANUARY 20X3

	20X3	*20X2*
	£	£
Fixed assets		
Development expenditure	59,810	-
Tangible assets	99,400	73,000
Investments	85,100	101,400
	244,310	174,400
Current assets		
Stock	58,190	63,010
Debtors	184,630	156,720
Cash at bank and in hand	9,970	62,620
	252,790	282,350
Creditors: amounts falling due within one year	276,510	215,900
Net current (liabilities)/assets	(23,720)	66,450
Total assets less current liabilities	220,590	240,850
Creditors: amounts falling due after more than one year		
Provisions for liabilities and charges	53,100	46,320
Deferred taxation	3,080	2,520
	164,410	192,010
Capital and reserves		
Share capital	89,700	89,700
Share premium account	11,300	11,300
Revaluation reserve	19,750	9,750
Profit and loss account	43,660	81,260
	164,410	192,010

Locksley Ltd produces garden furniture and has incurred expenditure during the year ended 31 January 20X3 on the development of mouldings for a new range of plastic garden furniture. The directors wish to carry forward the development expenditure indefinitely as they feel that the company will benefit from the new moulding for many years. The product range is being developed because profits have been declining over the last few years owing to the uncompetitiveness of the products made by the company. The company has sold many of its fixed assets during the year and purchased new machinery which will enable the company's productivity to increase. The directors decided not to fund the above expenditure using outside finance but to generate the necessary resources internally by taking extended credit from its suppliers and utilising its liquid funds held at the bank. The company also sold part of its investments, which are made up of stocks and shares of public limited companies.

One of the reasons for this method of financing the expenditure was that the company already has a loan of £45,000 outstanding which has been included in the figure for 'creditors: amounts falling due after more than one year'. This loan is secured on the fixed assets of the company and is repayable over ten years. The sale of fixed assets and investments did not yield as much as was expected and a small loss on sale of £1,200 has been included in the profit and loss account as part of the amounts shown for 'other expenses'.

The company had the fixed assets revalued by a professional valuer, at the year end. The gain on revaluation of fixed assets has been credited by the company to the revaluation reserve.

The directors felt that the shareholders should share in the gain on the revaluation of the fixed assets and increased the proposed dividend accordingly. Over 90% of the shares of the company are held by the directors.

Required

(a) List the audit tests the auditors would carry out to verify the value attributed to the development expenditure in the balance sheet of Locksley Ltd. (6 marks)

(b) List the audit procedures which should be carried out to verify the gain arising on the revaluation of fixed assets. (6 marks)

(c) Explain to the directors why development expenditure should not be carried forward indefinitely in the financial statements, and describe the circumstances in which the costs maybe deferred to the future. (8 marks)

(d) Describe the implications for the company and the auditors of the directors' decision to generate internally the funds required for the development of the business. (5 marks)

(25 marks)

12 PHOENIX (PILOT PAPER) *36 mins*

You are the manager responsible for the audit of Phoenix Ltd, a company which manufactures super alloys from imported zinc and aluminium. The company operates three similar foundries at different sites under the direction of Troy Pitz, the chief executive. The draft accounts for the year ended 31 March 2000 show profit before taxation of £1.7m (1999 - £1.5m).

The auditor senior has produced a schedule of 'Points for the Attention of the Audit Manager' as follows:

(a) A trade investment in 60,000 £1 ordinary shares of Pegasus Ltd, one of the company's major shipping contractors, is included in the balance sheet at a cost of £80,000. In May 2000, the published financial statements of Pegasus as at 30 September 1999 show only a small surplus of net assets. A recent press report now suggests that Pegasus is insolvent and has ceased to trade. Although dividends declared by Pegasus in respect of earlier years have not yet been paid, Phoenix has included £15,000 of dividends receivable in its draft accounts as at 31 March 2000. (6 marks)

(b) Current liabilities include a £500,000 provision for future maintenance. This represents the estimated cost of overhauling the blast furnaces and other foundry equipment. The overhaul is planned for August 2000 when all foundry workers take two weeks annual leave. (7 marks)

(c) All industrial waste from the furnaces ('clinker') is purchased by Cleanaway Ltd, a government – approved disposal company, under a five-year contract that is due for renewal later this year. A recent newspaper article states that 'substantial fines have been levied on Cleanaway for illegal dumping'. Troy Pitz is the majority shareholder of Cleanaway. (7 marks)

Required

For each of the above points:

(i) Comment on the matters that you would consider, and
(ii) State the audit evidence that you would expect to find,

in undertaking your review of the audit working papers and financial statements of Phoenix.

(20 marks)

13 RECOGNITION *27 mins*

Discuss the impact on the audit report of the proposed treatment of the following items in the financial statements.

(a) Beak plc sells land to a property investment company, Wings plc. The sale price is £20 million and the current market value is £30 million. Beak plc can buy the land back at any time in the next five years for the original selling price plus an annual commission of 1% above the current bank base rate. Wings plc cannot require Beak plc to buy the land back at any time.

The accountant of Beak plc proposes to treat this transaction as a sale in the financial statements. You may assume that the amounts involved are material. (6 marks)

(b) A car manufacturer, Gocar plc, supplies cars to a car dealer, Sparks Ltd, on the following terms.

Sparks Ltd has to pay a monthly fee of £100 per car for the privilege of displaying it in its showroom and is also responsible for insuring the cars. When a car is sold to a customer, Sparks Ltd has to pay Gocar plc the factory price of the car when it was first supplied. Sparks Ltd can only return cars to Gocar plc on the payment of a fixed penalty charge of 10% of the cost of the car. Sparks Ltd has to pay the factory price for the cars if they remain unsold within a four month period. Gocar plc cannot demand the return of the cars from Sparks Ltd.

The accountant of Sparks Ltd proposes to treat the cars unsold for less than four months as the property of Gocar plc and not show them as stock in the financial statements. At the year end the value of car stocks shown in the balance sheet was £150,720. The total assets on balance sheet are £1.3m. The cars unsold for less than four months have a factory cost of £22,500. (9 marks)

(15 marks)

14 BELLATRIX (PILOT PAPER) *45 mins*

Bellatrix Ltd is a carpet manufacturer and an audit client of your firm. Bellatrix has identified a company in the same business, Scorpio Ltd, as a target for acquisition in the current year.

As audit manager to Bellatrix and its subsidiaries for the year ended 31 December 2000, you have been asked to examine Scorpio's management accounts and budget forecasts. The chief executive of Bellatrix, Sirius Deneb, believes that despite its current cash flow difficulties, Scorpio's current trading performance is satisfactory and future prospects are good. The chief executive of Scorpio is Ursula Minor.

The findings of your examination are as follows:

Budget forecasts for Scorpio, for the current accounting year to 31 December 2000 and for the following year, reflect a rising profit trend.

Scorpio's results for the first half to 30 June 2000 reflect a £800,000 profit from the sale of a warehouse that had been carried in the books at historical cost. There are plans to sell two similar properties later in the year and outsourcing warehousing.

About 10% of Scorpio's sales are to Andromeda Ltd. Two members of the management board of Scorpio hold minority interests in Andromeda. Selling prices negotiated between Scorpio and Andromeda appears to be on an arm's length basis.

Scorpio's management accounts for six months to 30 June 2000 have been used to support an application to the bank for an additional loan facility to refurbish the executive and administration offices. These management accounts show stock and debtor's balances that exceed the figures in the accounting records by £150,000. This excess has also been reflected in the first half year's profit. Upon enquiry, you have established that provisions, to reduce stock and trade debtors to estimated realisable values, have been reduced to assist with the loan application.

Although there has been a recent downturn in trading, Ursula Minor has stated that she is very confident that the negotiations with the bank will be successful as Scorpio has met its budgeted profit for the first six months. Ursula believed that increased demand for carpets and rugs in the winter months will enable results to exceed budget.

Required

(a) Identify and comment on the implications of your findings for Bellatrix's plan to proceed with the acquisition of Scorpio. (10 marks)

(b) Explain what impact the acquisition will have on the conduct of your audit of Bellatrix and its subsidiaries for the year 31 December 2000. (15 marks)

(25 marks)

15 BUSINESS ASSURANCE *36 mins*

Audit practitioners have recently initiated substantive changes in the audit approach. It appears to be the strategy that audit firms are moving away from the audit of financial statements and more to the provision of assurances on financial data, systems and controls in those systems. Auditors are focusing on providing 'business assurance' and 'business risk' which gives clients wider assurance than the traditional audit has offered. Auditors are reviewing the business from a process standpoint utilising benchmarking, performance measurements and best control practices as the key criteria. It seems that the audit is moving more to the analysis of business risk and the alignment of the audit much more to the management perspective.

A wide range of risk assessment services is now part of the audit service which clients can subscribe to. The provision of internal audit services is becoming an increasingly larger part of the 'business assurance' service offered by auditors. It seems that the audit is becoming a management consultancy exercise with internal audit, external audit and consultancy assignments being seen as complementary services.

Required

(a) Discuss the implications of the external auditor providing an internal audit service to a client, explaining the current ethical guidance on the provision of other services to clients. (10 marks)

(b) Explain the principal effects of the external auditor providing wider assurance to the client. (6 marks)

(c) Critically evaluate the move by large auditing firms to providing 'business risk and assurance' services rather than the traditional audit assurance for investors and creditors. (4 marks)

(20 marks)

16 SIGHTHILL SUPERMARKETS *36 mins*

SAS 500 has been issued on 'Considering the work of internal audit'.

Your firm is the external auditor of Sighthill Supermarkets plc. The company has a head office, central warehouse and a large number of supermarkets which sell food to the general public. The company's financial director has suggested the audit fee could be reduced if your firm was prepared to place greater reliance on the work of the internal audit department.

The financial director has explained that the duties of the internal audit department include:

(a) Testing and reporting on the effectiveness of internal controls by maintaining up to date descriptions of the company's accounting systems and evaluating the effectiveness of controls in those systems. Recommendations are made of improvements in controls, and proposed changes in controls are assessed.

(b) Checking the operation and reliability of the computer systems. The department uses the computer assisted audit techniques of test data and computer audit programs (audit software). Particular attention is paid to controls over access to the computer and checking payment of suppliers and wages, and receipt of cash at supermarkets.

(c) Visiting the central warehouse to check operation of the systems and the effectiveness of controls. Stocktaking procedures are checked at the periodic stocktakes.

(d) Visits to supermarkets. All supermarkets are visited at least once a year with more frequent visits to larger supermarkets and those where serious weaknesses have been detected. At the supermarkets, the internal auditors check the effectiveness of controls and carry out cash counts and test counts of the stock. Visits are made to supermarkets to attend the periodic stocktakes and check procedures.

The financial director says the internal audit department would be willing to amend the timing of its work, so as to fit in with the external auditor's work. The results of the internal auditor's work can be reported directly to the external auditor.

In part (a) of the question, in considering the effectiveness of the internal audit department, you should consider factors which indicate the independence and competence of the internal audit staff, reporting arrangements and the extent to which their recommendations are implemented.

In part (b) of the question, you should consider the extent to which you can rely on the internal auditors' work and either reduce or eliminate certain aspects of the audit work carried out by your firm. The reduction in audit work will result in a reduction in the cost of carrying out the audit and thus allow a reduction in the audit fee.

Required

(a) Describe the matters you should consider at the planning stage to assess the effectiveness of the internal audit department. (6 marks)

(b) Consider the financial director's proposals, namely the extent to which you can rely on the work of the internal auditors and thus reduce your audit work in:

(i) Recording accounting systems and evaluating the effectiveness of the recorded controls
(ii) Performing tests of controls
(iii) Carrying out substantive procedures to verify assets and liabilities in the balance sheet
(iv) Auditing the computer systems, including using computer assisted audit techniques
(v) Visiting supermarkets (14 marks)

(20 marks)

17 BINGHAM ENGINEERING *45 mins*

You are auditing the accounts of Bingham Engineering Ltd for the year ended 31 March 20X7, which is experiencing going concern problems.

The company prepares monthly, as well as annual accounts and its accountant has supplied you with the following forecasts to enable you to assess whether the company will be a going concern. The forecasts have been prepared on a monthly basis for the year to 31 March 20X8, and are:

(a) Capital expenditure/disposal forecast
(b) Profit forecast
(c) Cash flow forecast

The capital expenditure/disposal forecast and profit forecast have been used to prepare the cash flow forecast.

Required

(a) Briefly describe what you understand by the term 'going concern' and state the minimum period you would expect the company to continue in business for it to be considered a going concern. (3 marks)

(b) List the factors which may indicate that a company is not a going concern. (9 marks)

(c) Describe the work you would perform to verify that the value of items in the following forecasts, prepared by the company's accountant, are reasonable:

(i) Capital expenditure/disposal forecast
(ii) Profit forecast
(iii) Cash flow forecast (10 marks)

(d) Briefly describe the further work, in addition to that described in (b) and (c) above, you would perform to enable you to determine whether the company is a going concern. (3 marks)

(25 marks)

18 ENVIRONMENTAL ISSUES (PILOT PAPER) *27 mins*

'The importance of the environment is increasingly recognised. Environmental issues often have implications for business and cannot be ignored by auditors. Auditors need a general awareness of the risk that environmental issues may have an impact on the financial statements'.

Required

Discuss. **(15 marks)**

19 REPORTING ISSUES (PILOT PAPER) *27 mins*

(a) Explain the importance of comparatives to the conduct of an audit. (5 marks)

(b) Libra & Leo, a small firm of certified accountants, has provided audit services to Delphinus Ltd for many years. The company, which makes hand-crafted beds, is undergoing expansion and has recently relocated its operations. Having completed the audit of the financial statements for the year ended 31 December 1999 and issued an unqualified opinion thereon, Libra & Leo have now indicated that they do not propose to offer themselves for re-election.

The chief executive of Delphinus, Mr Pleiades, has now approached your firm to audit the financial statements for the year ended 31 December 2000. However, before inviting you to accept the nomination he has asked for your views on the following extracts from an auditors' report.

> 'However, the evidence available to us was limited because we were not appointed auditors to the company until (date 2000) and in consequence we were not able to attend the stocktaking at 31 December 1999. There were no satisfactory alternative means that we could adopt to confirm the amount of stock and work-in-progress included in the preceding period's financial statements at £....
>
> In our opinion, the financial statements give a true and fair view of the state of the company's affairs as at 31 December 2000 and, except for any adjustments that might have been found to be necessary has we been able to obtain sufficient evidence concerning stock and work-in-progress as at 1 January 2000, of its profit[loss] for the year then ended ....
>
> In respect alone of the limitation on our work relating to stock and work-in-progress:
>
> - We have not obtained all the information and explanations that we considered necessary for the purpose of our audit; and
> - We were unable to determine whether proper accounting records had been maintained.'

Mr Pleiades has been led to understand that such a qualified opinion must be given on the financial statements of Delphinus for the year ended 31 December 2000, as a necessary consequence of the change in audit appointment. He is anxious to establish whether you would issue anything other than an unqualified opinion.

Required

Comment on the proposed auditors' report. Your answer should consider whether and how the chief executive's concerns can be overcome. (10 marks)

(15 marks)

Exam answer bank

1 BLAKE SEVEN

(a) Confidentiality

Confidentiality is an implied term of an auditor's contract with the client. It is also a requirement of the ACCA (the Rules of Professional Conduct) and IFAC (the Code of Ethics for Professional Accountants). Confidentiality is essential to the auditor-client relationship because in order to form an opinion, the auditor must work closely with those who have prepared the financial statements and have their trust. If this is lacking, the client will not be open with the auditor fearing that matters may be reported to competitors, other third parties or regulatory authorities.

The duty of confidentiality owed by the auditor is not absolute. There are circumstances in which auditors have a right or duty to disclose matters to third parties without the client's knowledge or consent. Duties are mainly legal duties to report matters such as any suspicions of money laundering, drug trafficking or terrorist offences. A right to report matters also exists in these circumstances but the duty to report is more important. An auditor may also disclose matters to defend himself in disciplinary proceedings.

It is not uncommon for regulatory authorities such as the tax authorities or the police to ask 'informally' for details of confidential matters. Only when the persons requesting the information have obtained the appropriate statutory or other authorities to demand such information should the request be granted.

Auditors are under no general duty to report illegal acts to the authorities, however, it is not appropriate for an auditor to continue a relationship with a client that engages in such activities, not least because the auditor may be implicated in the crime.

(b) Blake Seven

Auditors should avoid conflicts of interest where possible. One example of a conflict of interest is where two parties in dispute both request advice from the same firm. There is no absolute rule that says that a firm cannot act for both parties in these circumstances but there have to be stringent controls to ensure that the interest of one client do not adversely affect the interests of another, and of course permission of both parties is required, which may not be forthcoming. This is can be difficult with small firms because there are often insufficient staff to have two different 'teams' acting on behalf of the parties.

Request - remuneration package

Some information on directors' remuneration packages should be available by inspection of the financial statements filed with Companies House, although this information will be historical rather than current. There are also requirements for companies to make details of service contracts available for inspection by members of companies, such as Rosella, although these often constitute a very incomplete picture of the total remuneration package.

It is clear that as existing auditor and advisor to Blake Seven, it would be inappropriate to disclose any such information to Rosella, or even to help her find the information that is available on the public record, without the permission of Blake Seven which is unlikely to be forthcoming.

Personal advisor

It would only be possible to act as personal advisor to Rosella if the remaining directors of Blake Seven agreed (which seem unlikely) because the current 'negotiations' may well turn into a dispute over the valuation of the shareholding. The existing company might well wish to understate profits and assets in order to reduce the valuation, and Rosella may wish to see the amounts increased. It may be possible to act as personal tax advisor, although there are likely to be tax implications to the buy-out.

Auditor to Blakes Heaven

There are potentially serious problems associated with becoming auditor to the new company because it is both in competition with the existing client, and has a very similar name. Blake Seven may well have a legal case against Rosella and the new company for attempting to pass itself off as the existing company, and thereby damage the existing company's goodwill. The fact that Rosella has done this, together with her request for information, which she should know is confidential (in relation to remuneration), may cast doubt on her personal integrity which is a further reason not to act for her.

Alternatively, if the information presented in the question is incomplete, it may be possible to take the view that the firm would prefer to act as auditor and advisor to Rosella and the new company, rather than to the existing company, particularly if the terms of the engagement are attractive.

There is no specific 'rule' which prohibits this course of action, however, the requirement to behave with integrity in all professional and business relationships suggests that this would not be an appropriate course of action.

2 APPOINTMENT AND ENGAGEMENT

Tutorial note. You should try to mention a wide range of points in part (a) – do not restrict your answer to 'auditor independence' issues. You should not need to write out a letter of engagement in part (b).

(a) The matter which should be considered before accepting appointment are as follows.

(i) We must ensure that we are professionally qualified to act, not disqualified on any legal ground, that is, hold a valid practising certificate, sufficient indemnity insurance, registered auditors and members of an RSB.

(ii) We must ensure that the firm's existing resources are adequate to service the needs of the new client: this will raise questions of staff and time availability and the firm's technical expertise, that is, do we audit and other clients of this nature?

(iii) We should ensure that no partners (or audit staff) hold any shares in Streethart, or have any other relationship with Streethart or its directors which could affect our independence as auditors.

(iv) We should consider the integrity of Streethart's directors and determine whether we can establish a long-term beneficial relationship with them.

(v) We need to assess the risk associated with carrying out the audit of Streethart, in the sense of the danger to our firm's reputation. A low risk client is one which:

(1) Has a viable business with good long-range prospects (that is, no going concern problems)

(2) Is well financed with strong internal controls

(3) Applies conservative, prudent accounting principles, rather than those which are aggressive or dubious

(4) Has competent, honest management, particularly a good finance director, well qualified with a close relationship to the rest of the board

A great deal of this can be judged by examining the company's latest annual report: calculate ratios, look at the auditor's report, directors' report etc.

(vi) Further investigations might involve credit rating agencies, such as Dun and Bradstreet, or investigations at Companies House.

(vii) We should consider the level of fees to be charged, which will have a direct relationship to the perceived level of risk in carrying out the audit.

(viii) Conflict of interest problem should be considered; it will be important to establish that no existing clients will cause difficulties as competitors of the new client.

(ix) The likely fees from the audit of Streethart should not compromise out independence, that is, the fees should represent less than 15% of our total fee income.

(x) As well as considering all of the above, the firm should consider why the previous auditors are being replaced. It may be, as the directors of Streethart have stated, that the current auditors are not giving a good service and/or are charging too much, but there may have been some disagreement. This may be uncovered by communications with the current auditors (see below). The investigations in (v) above may reveal a qualified audit report, which could be the cause of disagreement (and would increase the perceived risk on accepting nomination as Streethart's auditors). Are the directors 'opinion shopping'? We should come to a conclusion on why this change is taking place.

There are other legal and ethical procedures to follow, both before and after accepting nomination.

Before nomination

(i) We should request the prospective client's permission to communicate with the auditors last appointed. If such permission is refused we should decline nomination.

(ii) On receipt of permission, we should request in writing of the auditors last appointed all information which ought to be made available to us to enable us to decide whether we are prepared to accept nomination. (*Note.* If no reply is received, a further letter may be sent which states that if no answer is received by a specific date, it will be assumed that there are no reasons not to accept nomination.)

(iii) If fees are owed to the previous auditors we may still accept nomination, although we may decide that Streethart will be slow to pay its bills and therefore decline nomination.

After nomination

(i) Ensure that the outgoing auditors' removal or resignation has been properly conducted in accordance with the Companies Act 1985. We should see a valid notice of the outgoing auditors' resignation (under s 392 CA 1985), or confirm that the outgoing auditors were properly removed (under s 391 CA 1985).

(ii) Ensure that our appointment is valid. We should obtain a copy of the resolution passed at the meeting appointing us as the company's auditors (special notice = 21 days, ordinary resolution = simple majority > 50%).

(iii) Set up and submit a letter or engagement to the directors of the company (see (b) below).

(b) (i) The main contents and form of the engagement letter to Streethart Ltd will be as follows.

(1) It will be addressed to the directors and on the audit firm's letterhead.

(2) It will lay out the responsibilities of the directors of the company.

- Maintaining proper accounting records
- Ensuring the accounts show a true and fair view
- Accounts are prepared in accordance with CA 1985
- Making all records/accounts available to the auditors

(3) It should also lay out the duties of the auditors, comprising mainly a statutory duty to report to the members our opinion in whether the accounts show a true and fair view and are prepared in accordance with CA 1985.

(4) The audit will be conducted according to auditing standards.

(5) The accounts should normally comply with accounting standards (SSAPs and FRSs) and the auditors will report if they do not.

(6) The letter should state that it is the directors' responsibility to detect fraud and error, but that audit procedures are designed so that there is a reasonable expectation of detecting material misstatements.

Other matters which might be covered include the following.

(1) Fees and billing arrangements.
(2) Procedures where the client has a complaint about the service.
(3) Arrangements to be made with the predecessor auditors, in case of an initial audit.
(4) A reference to any further agreements between the auditors and the client.
(5) A proposed timetable for the engagement.
(6) Any agreement about further services (tax, preparing accounts etc).

The letter should end by stating that it will remain effective from one audit appointment to another, until it is replaced. The directors should confirm acceptance in writing.

(ii) The main reasons why it is desirable for the auditors to send an engagement letter for each audit are as follows.

(1) It defines the extent of the audits' and directors' responsibilities and so minimises the possibility of any misunderstanding between the management of the enterprise and the auditor.

(2) It documents and confirms the auditors' acceptance of the appointment, the objective and scope of the audit, the extent of their responsibilities, and the form of their report(s).

In the auditors' case, it makes clear that their duties are statutory, ie governed by CA 1985, and cannot be changed at the directors' wish. Also, the auditors report to members, not the directors.

In the directors' case, it makes clear their responsibilities for proper preparation of the financial statements, for uncovering fraud and error and for ensuring a proper system of internal control.

The letter should also prevent arguments about fees as it lays out the basis on which fees are charged.

The agreement of these matters is very important, so an agreed revised letter must be drafted if the directors object to some matters. The directors must confirm acceptance in writing.

3 PROFESSIONAL RESPONSIBILITIES

The auditors set out to report on the truth and fairness of accounts prepared by the directors of a company. In doing so the auditors have a variety of responsibilities ranging from the consideration of going concern as an appropriate basis for the accounts, to consideration of the risks that financial statements contain material misstatements caused by fraud or error.

Material misstatement/fraud

Material misstatements caused by error, that is, an unintentional mistake causing the accounts not to reflect the true and fair position of the company, are likely to be discovered quite readily by the auditors throughout the normal cause of their testing. This is because a genuine error will not have been painstakingly concealed but may have occurred due to time pressure or misunderstanding by the preparer of accounts.

Hence the statement is in part true in saying that the auditors should have reasonable expectation of detecting material misstatements in financial statements. Material misstatements arising from fraud are generally not quite so straightforward. This is because the person or persons perpetrating the fraud will generally go to extreme lengths to avoid its discovery. There are may varieties of fraud too. Fraud may consist of the manipulation or alteration of accounting records, theft or other misappropriation of assets, intentional misapplication of accounting policies or recording of transactions without substance.

Fraud is a criminal word involving the proof of criminal intent to achieve personal gain or intentional loss to another party. For this reason auditors can only be considering a suspected fraud. Proven fraud will be determined by judge and jury.

Directors' and auditors' responsibilities

SAS 110 *Fraud and error* is quite specific that it is the responsibility of directors to prevent and detect fraud. In light of the many companies which have been devastated by alleged fraud in recent years, for example, Maxwell Communications Corporation, BBCI and Polly Peck, it is prudent for any company of reasonable size to have a board member specifically responsible for managing fraud risk internally. The management need to be aware if frauds which have occurred within similar businesses and construct appropriate internal control systems to aim to prevent fraud within their own organisation. The directors are appointed under company law to act as stewards of the assets of the company on behalf of the shareholders. The role of the auditor as stated earlier does not extend beyond a true and fair opinion on the financial statements.

It is the duty of management to design and implement internal controls. However, the auditors will test the relevance and reliability of such controls. They must also satisfy themselves that stated internal controls are being complied with. It is the duty of the auditors to report any weaknesses discovered in the internal controls as soon as it is practicable. The dramatic collapse of Baring Bank demonstrates the pressure under which individuals may be placed to perform well and emphasises the importance of internal controls which must not be relaxed even when results are temporarily favourable. The sudden collapse in this particular instance allowed no time for auditor intervention.

Planning stage

At the audit planning stage, the auditors will examine the principal areas of risk and tailor the audit accordingly. Risk warning areas which should be examined include the reliance upon the integrity and competence of management (for example, failure to correct weaknesses highlighted previously), usually pressure within an entity (for example, from the bank or shareholders) unusual transactions occurring especially near the year end of problems in obtaining sufficient audit evidence due to inadequate records, poor documentation or inability to extract required data from computer files.

Depending on the perceived risk the auditors must target particular areas. Areas most commonly open to manipulation are stock and WIP, debtor balances, consignment stock and contingent liabilities.

Other audit procedures

According to SAS 110, auditors are expected to design audit procedures which have a reasonable expectation of detecting misstatements arising from fraud or error. As stated previously, the principal responsibility for the prevention and detection of fraud rests with the directors who are in a position to ensure that internal controls are correctly implemented on a day to day basis. Careful planning of audits and recommendations of corrections to areas of weakness in internal control will assist auditors in preventing and detecting fraud. However, it must be remembered that although the auditors' responsibilities are far reaching, to extend them to cover the duties of directors, that is, safeguarding the assets of the company, is giving them responsibilities which, many argue, they are not in a position to discharge.

Normal audit procedures do not involve investigative techniques for the authentication of documents and signatures. Extending audit procedures in this way would increase the time spent on audits and therefore the cost, thereby penalising the majority to deter the minority.

Conclusion

I agree with the statement that the auditors have a responsibility to identify and report on material misstatements. A quality audit should achieve this. To give the auditors the responsibility of identifying criminal deception is overstepping the mark and could only serve to widen the expectation gap. Given that the Serious Fraud Office, with unlimited time, and it would appear, money, specialist staff and techniques has such problems proving 'fraud', what hope would the regular limited company auditors have?

4 MERGER OF AUDIT FIRMS

> **Tutorial note.** This is a topical question as these 'mega-mergers' have taken place relatively recently.

(a) The reasons behind a merger could include the following.

- The desire to operate on a **global scale** and increase market shares
- The wish to service **multinational clients** demanding an international presence
- Increased **expertise** and professional experience
- **Business expansion:** the competitive nature of auditing and consultancy services demands a larger firm to service clients globally
- **Increasing funds** available for investment. (Increasing investment in IT systems makes this necessary.)
- The need to **compete with banks** who are increasing management consultancy services
- To **resist liability claims**
- To reduce the ability of major clients to exert fee pressures and thus improve **financial independence**
- To increase the **range of opportunities** available to skilled staff
- To take advantage of **cost savings** achievable

(b) Possible problems could include the following.

- A reduction in **choice of clients**
- Possible **conflicts of interest** arising from mergers of firms providing services to competing clients
- A reduction in **auditors' independence**, particularly as a result of increasing provision of consultancy services
- The emergence of '**audit giants**' which weakens the arguments for limiting auditors' liability
- **Domination** of the profession by 'giant firms'
- Increase in the **influence of large firms** on the standard setting process

- **Redundancies** caused by elimination of overlapping departments
- **Scrutiny of the mergers** by outside agencies
- **Disputes** emerging between partners as to management styles leading to resignation of disaffected partners and loss of experience
- A **loss of the 'personal touch'** which is a feature of smaller firms

5 DAXON

MEMO

To: Board of Directors

From: An Accountant

Re: *Directors' responsibilities* Date: 3 February 20X6

This memorandum addresses some of the issues raised in the last board meeting arising from the draft accounts.

(a) **Statement of directors' responsibilities**

This statement is only one part of the response of the accountancy profession and regulatory authorities to the 'expectations gap'. This represents the difference between what the auditors and directors of a company are responsible for compared to the public perception of what these responsibilities and duties are.

The *Cadbury Report* on corporate governance recommended that the financial statements should contain statement(s) laying out the directors' and auditors' responsibilities. This requirement was included by the Auditing Practices Board in its Statement of Auditing Standards SAS 600 *Auditors' report on financial statements.*

The public concern about the responsibilities of both directors and auditors was brought to a head with the unexpected collapse of large groups of companies (Maxwell, Polly Peck etc) and even a bank (BCCI). When investors, shareholders and account holders looked for people to blame for these disasters, it became clear that very few people knew which of the auditors, directors and regulatory authorities was responsible for what in respect of a reporting entity.

(b) **'True and fair'**

The accounts of a limited company are required by s 226(2) of the Companies Act 1985 to show a true and fair view of the company's financial position as at the balance sheet date and of its profit or loss for the year ending on that date. The auditors are required to state in their report whether, in their opinion, the accounts satisfy that requirement.

Although the Companies Act 1985 contains many detailed requirements as to the form and content of company accounts, it does not attempt to define what is meant by the term 'true and fair view'. The meaning of 'true and fair' can best be understood by considering a written Counsel's Opinion prepared for the old ASC.

(i) The courts will treat compliance with accepted accounting principles as *prima facie* evidence that the accounts are true and fair. Equally, the deviation from accepted principles will be *prima facie* evidence that they are not.

(ii) 'True and fair view' is a legal concept and the question of whether company accounts comply with s 226(2) CA 1985 can be authoritatively decided only by a court.

(iii) The concept of true and fair is subjective in nature, in spite of the connection between accounting standards and 'true and fair' discussed above. CA 1989 has enhanced this relationship by enforcing full disclosure of departures from accounting standards.

As far as you are concerned, as directors of Daxon plc, in deciding whether the accounts show a true and fair view you should bring your business (and, where applicable, accounting) knowledge to bear. You will be aided by the finance director and other accounting staff. The first question must be whether accounting standards have been followed. If in some cases they have not, then you must consider whether this override was justified to show a true and fair view and that it is properly disclosed (according to UITF 7).

In making your decision, you should consider whether the accounting principles used are appropriate to Daxon's business, the qualitative characteristics of financial information reflected in the accounts and whether the accounts reflect the substance of transactions.

In summary, the directors should be satisfied that the financial statements reflect the true situation of the company and are not misleading in any way.

(c) **Detecting fraud and safeguarding assets**

The most important way in which the directors can try to prevent fraud and safeguard assets is to institute a strong system of internal controls. Although physical controls over tangible assets are important (for example, locking up cash, tagging computers etc), fraud is most often prevented by good *segregation of duties*. Controls of this nature mean that staff would need to collude with each other in order to steal.

A control with which the directors will be closely involved is *supervision* - in fact the directors are the ultimate supervisors within a company.

The *Cadbury Report* has suggested that the directors should make a report in the financial statements about whether an adequate system of control was in operations during the period. Although guidance has been produced on what the directors should consider when assessing the internal control system, it is still not possible to say exactly what a good control is. As the situation currently stands, the directors must state their responsibility for the system of internal control, but they do not have to comment on its effectiveness.

I hope this memorandum has cleared up these issues. Please contact me with any further queries or raise them at the next board meeting.

Signed: *An Accountant*

6 AUDIT ADVANTAGES AND RESPONSIBILITIES

(a) The advantages of having an audit include the following.

(i) **Shareholders** who are **not involved in management** gain **reassurance** from audited accounts about management's **stewardship** of the business.

(ii) Audited accounts are a reliable source for a **fair valuation of shares** in an unquoted company either for taxation or other purposes.

(iii) Some **banks** rely on accounts for the purposes of **making loans** and reviewing the value of security.

(iv) **Creditors and potential creditors** can use audited accounts to assess the potential strength of the company.

(v) The audit provides **management** with an **useful independent check** on the accuracy of the accounting systems; the auditors can recommend improvements in those systems.

(b) A company should **appoint** the **auditors** at each **general meeting** at which copies of the accounts for an accounting reference period are presented. The auditors will hold office from the conclusion of that meeting until the conclusion of the next such general meeting. The retiring auditors may be re-appointed at the general meeting, but this requires a positive resolution: re-appointment is not automatic.

The **first auditors** of a company may be appointed by the directors at any time before the first meeting at which accounts are laid before members. Auditors so appointed hold office until the end of the first such meeting. If the directors do not appoint the first auditors, the members are entitled to do so in general meeting.

A **casual vacancy** in the office of auditor may be filled by appointment by the directors or by the company in general meeting. Until such appointment is made, the continuing or surviving auditors may perform the role of auditor.

Where at any general meeting of the company at which accounts are laid before members no auditors are appointed or reappointed, the Secretary of State may appoint a person to fill the vacancy. The company must inform the Secretary of State within one week of his power becoming exercisable under this provision.

Sufficient notice should be given for certain resolutions at a general meeting relating to the appointment of auditors. The resolutions concerned are those:

(i) **Filling a casual vacancy** in the office of auditor, and

(ii) **Re-appointing as auditor** a retiring auditor who was appointed by the directors to fill a casual vacancy.

Copies of such resolutions must be sent by the company, immediately on receipt, to the person proposed to be re-appointed, or to the auditor who resigned, where a casual vacancy was caused by a resignation.

(c) The auditors will generally have the following rights.

(i) A **right of access** at all times to the books, accounts and vouchers of the company.

(ii) A **right to require** from officers of the company such **information** and **explanations** as they consider necessary for the performance of their duties.

(iii) A **right**, in the case of the auditors of a holding company, **to request information and explanations from subsidiaries** of the holding company and their auditors.

(iv) A **right to attend any general meetings** of the company and to receive all notices of and communications relating to such meetings which any member of the company is entitled to receive.

(v) A **right to be heard at any general meeting** on any part of the business of that meeting that concerns them as auditors.

(vi) A **right to make written representations** when the company proposes to appoint auditors other than themselves.

(vii) A **right to requisition an extraordinary general meeting** to consider any circumstances which members or creditors ought to know about in connection with their resignation (which may be effected at any time by giving written notice to the client setting out any such circumstances).

(viii) A **right to give notice in writing** requiring the holding of a general meeting for the purpose of laying the accounts and report before the members.

(d) The directors and the auditors of a company are both appointed by the members of the company but their duties are quite distinct.

Directors are appointed to fulfil the executive function of managing the company. In company law, company directors also have specific responsibilities in relation to the accounting function.

(i) **Directors** are expected to **safeguard the assets** of the company.

(ii) Directors are responsible for **preventing errors, irregularities and fraud**. This task should be addressed by setting up appropriate controls within the company. There should be appropriate measures in place to detect errors, irregularities and fraud which may occur. The auditors can only be expected to carry out their work so as to have a reasonable expectation of detecting material errors and fraud which may have occurred.

(iii) The company is expected to keep **accounting records** sufficient to enable the directors to ensure that the balance sheet and profit and loss account comply with legislation. In practice, the directors will, in all but the smallest companies, delegate much accounting work to employees of the company.

(iv) The directors must **prepare** for each financial year of the company a **balance sheet** as at the last day of the year, and a **profit and loss account**. The annual accounts are required to show a true and fair view of the state of affairs of the company at the balance sheet date and of its profit or loss for the accounting period then ended, and to be properly prepared in accordance with legislation.

(v) The directors are required to **lay a copy** of the annual accounts before the members in general meeting. A private company may be able to exempt itself from this requirement.

(vi) The directors must **file** a copy of the **accounts** with the Registrar.

7 PLD ASSOCIATES

> **Tutor's hint**. The assessment of audit risk is a fundamental part of each audit - it will *always* be necessary to carry out some kind of work to assess the overall risk at a client. You must relate your answer to the situation given in the question.

(a) PLD Associates plc is a high-risk client on two counts:

(i) The **nature of its business is property development**, a high-risk activity, and

(ii) The **weaknesses of the company's internal control system** and the lack of integrity of the founder Mr J Scott.

With such a potential client, the auditors must ensure that there are no independence or other ethical problems likely to cause conflict with the ethical code before accepting the appointment.

The procedures which an audit firm should carry out before accepting a potentially high audit risk client are as follows.

(i) **Request** the prospective clients' **permission to communicate** with the **previous auditors**. If such permission is refused the appointment should be declined.

(ii) On receipt of permission the prospective auditors should **request** in writing of the previous auditors all **information** which ought to be made available to them to enable them to decide whether they are prepared to accept nomination.

The information requested from the old auditors could go as far as asking about the integrity of the management of PLD Associates plc.

(iii) Ensure that the firm's **existing resources are adequate** to service the needs of the new client. This will raise questions of staff and time availability and the firm's technical expertise. This will be important in the case of PLD Associates plc as property development is a specialist area.

(iv) **Seek references** in respect of the new client company; it may be, as is often the case, that the directors of the company are already personally known to the firm; if not, independent enquiries should be made concerning the status of the company and its directors. Agencies such as Dun & Bradstreet might be of assistance together with a formal search at Companies House. The search at Companies House will uncover the qualified audit report if a copy of this has not already been obtained. It will be necessary to find out whether any regulatory authority has disciplined the company.

(v) A **preliminary assessment of audit risk** should be made. This will involve discussions with the management of the client and assessing the internal control structure (which in the case of the PLD Associates plc is obviously poor).

(vi) The **costs and benefits** of accepting the client should be estimated; this appointment may be considered too costly in terms of potential liability (or raised insurance premiums) and bad publicity.

(b) Ethical guidelines issued by the accountancy institutes require that the auditors are **independent and objective**. It is the integrity of the auditors which gives weight to the audit opinion. In this case the partner has shown a singular lack of integrity by maintaining this secret fund; his objectivity as an auditor has been impaired by his lack of independence. He has also contravened ethical guidelines by carrying out the **preparation** of **accounting records** for a **quoted company**.

The partner has, however, gone farther than this omission of fundamental ethical principles; he has in fact **colluded** with the **managing director** to conceal questionable transactions from fellow directors and shareholders. In the worst case this could be with a view to defrauding the company of which he is auditor. He has also concealed transactions which should have been disclosed to the Inland Revenue and the DTI. His position as auditor is untenable and his audit opinion, once knowledge of his involvement is known, is valueless.

(c) The measures that audit firms might introduce to try and minimise the practice of 'opinion shopping' by prospective audit clients are as follows.

(i) To **establish why the question is being asked**. Is the prospective client looking for auditors who will confirm his views on the treatment of a particular transaction? He may be trying to use this against his current auditors with whom he is in dispute.

(ii) No **opinion** should be **given** until the **present auditors** have been **informed**. This is not only a matter of courtesy but may reveal other aspects to the problem which had not been forthcoming from the prospective client.

(iii) If an audit firm decides to give an opinion it should do so **in writing** giving the facts of the problem as it has been presented to them. This will protect the audit firm against the situation where an incorrect opinion is given because the facts have been misrepresented by the prospective client to order to get the opinion which concurred with their own.

Current legislation exists to protect auditors, allowing them to present their case against removal to the members. Similarly, when the auditors resign they also have the right to make a **statement** regarding the resignation which must be sent to the **Registrar** and everyone who is entitled to receive the financial statements. Auditors often do not do so because of bad publicity etc.

In future the Review Panel might take a more active role in finding sets of accounts where an 'opinion shopper' has succeeded in obtaining an unqualified opinion which is unjustified.

(d) Audit firms can reduce the risk of litigation and its effects upon the audit practice by ensuring:

(i) **Auditing standards are applied** on all assignments

(ii) **Adequate quality control procedures** are in force

(iii) **Adequate review procedures** are in operation before a new client is accepted

(iv) **Adequate PI insurance** is obtained (this does not reduce the risk of litigation but limits the damage it causes)

8 TAURUS TRADERS

(a) **Business risks**

Environmental risks

The environmental risks facing the business relate to those external factors affecting the performance of business. These include:

(i) The nature of the business: suppliers to the building industry are subject to the same economic cycle as the building industry itself. Operators in the building industry need adequate reserves to see them through the inevitable downturns in the business.

(ii) The position of the business within the market: even in an economic upturn, a supplier may struggle if the market for building suppliers is saturated or highly competitive.

(iii) The stage of the business' development and the proposed future developments: Taurus Traders is experiencing a period of rapid growth, it requires additional funding and is moving into markets in which it may have little experience (builders merchants and the overseas operation). The owner-manager has very high expectations of returns that the business can provide and he does not appear to have an appropriate attitude to his professional advisors, financial controls, and compliance matters. All of these factors present additional risks that would not be present in an established business.

(iv) Overseas exposure: the business is already subject to fluctuations in exchange rates and the proposal to set up an overseas operation may increase those risks if they are not properly managed.

Financial risks

The company is experiencing rapid growth in turnover, it is seeking substantial loan finance which will need to be serviced, and it exceeds its overdraft facility which may also result in penalties. The business has clearly outgrown the company's financing structure. Financial controls in terms of the accounting system, the production of good management accounts, the employment of a competent accountant and the reconciliation of the ledgers are all inadequate. Debts are probably not being collected and suppliers may be left unpaid which may result in a loss of goodwill. Mr Aquila's intended repayment of his loan account in this context (instead of investing in the business) indicates a lack of understanding of the difficult financial position the company may be in. In extremes, this could amount to a going concern risk.

Operational risks

If the bank loan is not forthcoming, it may not be possible to continue with the new premises which have already been commenced. There maybe serious contractual implications with whoever has been contracted to construct the building if financing is delayed.

The business is experiencing a high level of returns which may indicate problems with the company's own suppliers, problems with the company's stock control systems or simply a deterioration in the market in which the company operates. If the trend continues, stock levels will rise and profit margins will fall. This in turn has implications for the profit forecast on which the application for the bank loan is based.

Compliance risks

The company appears to have very poor internal financial systems and controls. The basic system, written by a relative of Mr Aquila, is probably inadequate to cope with the volume of transactions now being put through it. The foreign currency transactions are not dealt with by the computer system at all and there are unreconciled differences on the ledgers. It is not therefore surprising that the annual budget and management accounts are of poor quality. This combined with Mr Aquila's poor relationship with his current auditors means that it is possible that the financial statements have been of poor quality, produced late, and possibly qualified or modified.

In the current year, these problems have serious implications because of the apparent intended reliance by the bank on the profit forecast – it is not clear who the forecast is to be provided by or when. If the loan is made, it is likely that the bank will require sight of the management accounts or similar, as well as the financial statements, and if systems are not improved, the company could encounter real difficulties in this respect.

(b) **Making a proposal**

The factors that should influence the partner in deciding whether the firm should make the proposal are as follows.

(i) The precise nature of the services to be provided - whether it will be the statutory audit and financial advice to the company only, or whether it will include financial advice to Mr Aquila personally, as seems likely, and whether any work on the profit forecast is required. Any sort of work on the profit forecast seems likely to present a risk to the firm, partly because it seems likely that provisions for stock and other adjustments may be required which will probably have the effect of reducing the profit forecast, which will not please Mr Aquila. The need for such adjustments and a thorough review of the information to be provided to the bank is even more important in the light of the fact that the bank will be taking account of the forecast as part of its lending decision;

(ii) The risk profile of the firm and its existing exposure to this type of business, any history of litigation between Taurus Traders and its professional advisors and an assessment of the overall integrity of Mr Aquila;

(iii) The experience of the firm in this sector, the independence of the firm and the availability of staff to complete the assignment(s) on time;

(iv) The likely level of fee income, and any expected difficulties in collecting the fees in the circumstances. Any positive response to the letter sent to the outgoing auditors asking if there are any professional reasons why the engagement should not be accepted should be carefully noted as should any statement made in the 'statement of circumstances' issued by the outgoing auditors.

(c) **Audit strategy**

A strategy for the first audit of Taurus Traders might be as follows:

(i) **Planning**

A thorough review of the prior year financial statements, accounting systems (such as they are) and the documentation available for the current year should be conducted as early as possible in order to establish whether the records are so bad as to possibly require a modified audit report (limitation in scope, lack of proper accounting records). Any such possibility must be communicated to Mr Aquila at the earliest possible stage because it is likely to affect his application for the bank loan.

The prior year financial statements, and any other information such as a reconciled trial balance should also give some indication of any problem areas that the firm is not already aware of.

Analytical procedures are unlikely to be as useful as they might be as a result of the growth in the business and the poor quality of the records.

Materiality levels should be set at a level to reflect the risks associated with this business.

(ii) **Systems testing**

On the assumption that there are sufficient very basic financial controls in place so as not to warrant a wholly substantive approach, at least initially, testing of systems in relation to sales, debtors, stock and payroll should be undertaken, although tolerable deviation rates, as with materiality, should be set at a level to reflect the control risks which are unlikely to be low. Assuming that systems can provide some comfort, substantive testing can be reduced.

(iii) **Specific account areas**

The specific areas that are likely to require attention are stock, the construction contract, the foreign currency transactions, debtors and creditors, and gross margins.

Detailed work on the provisions for the write-down or write-off of faulty stocks will be required and if the stock records are inadequate for these purposes, it may be necessary for the company, or the firm, to construct them. The year-end stock-take may help with this. Stock will be a material item in the balance sheet and it is unlikely that additional work can be avoided in this area in the current year.

Appropriate disclosures will need to be made for the construction contract in accordance with FRS 15 *Tangible fixed assets*, including any the capitalisation of interest costs. The likely outcome of the financing deal will affect the disclosures and if the possibility of difficulties arises, disclosure of any contingencies (such as penalties payable) will have to be made in accordance with FRS 12 *Provisions, contingent liabilities and contingent assets*, if they are material.

The foreign currency transactions and balances are recorded manually and computerised controls will not exist. The manual controls appear to be weak because of the unreconciled differences on the ledgers. It is likely that extensive substantive work in this area will be required because of the involvement of Mr Aquila in negotiating prices with both customers and suppliers. There is potential for significant manipulation of the records in relation to both transactions and balances because of the absence of, or weak, internal controls that can be overridden. Direct confirmation of balances with both customers and suppliers will be necessary.

(iv) **The going concern and overall review of financial statements**

It is important in the current year to aggregate errors and to review the financial statements as a whole and assess whether there is significant concern about the entity's ability to continue as a going concern. An independent review of the financial statements may be appropriate in accordance with SAS 240 *Quality Control* as the entity may be assessed as high risk. It is unlikely that the bank will make its decision before the financial statements and the profit forecast are signed and the firm will have to therefore take a view on this.

(d) **Two procedures to improve accounting procedures and financial controls**

Improved accounting procedures would be achieved if an integrated computer system were developed specifically for the company, properly tested and implemented. This would improve the efficiency of transactions processing and control (particularly foreign currency transactions), the quality of the management accounts and their usefulness for decision-making purposes (including stock control), and ultimately the quality of the financial statements.

Financial controls would be improved by the production of a well thought out annual budget that was compared to the management accounts and revised and rolled forward during the course of the year. This would provide the company and the bank with significant additional comfort on the control of the business generally.

9 LAMBLEY PROPERTIES

Tutorial note. You should not just assume that if the directors refuse to sign the letter of representation a qualification of the audit report is automatically required. There are other procedures to undertake first. Remember the circumstances (given in (b)) in which it is permissible to rely on a letter of representation.

(a)

Lambley Properties plc
Farmer Estate
Brickley

ABC & Co
7 The High Street
Brickley

30 April 20X2

Dear Sirs

We confirm to the best of our knowledge and belief, and having made appropriate enquiries of other directors and officials of the company, the following representations given to you in connection with your audit of the company's financial statements for the year ended 31 March 20X2.

General

We acknowledge as directors our responsibility under the Companies Act 1985 for preparing financial statements which give a true and fair view and for making accurate representations to you. All the accounting records have been made available to you for the purpose of your audit and all the transactions undertaken by the company have been properly reflected and recorded in the accounting records. All other records and related information, including minutes of all management and shareholders' meetings, have been made available to you.

Financial support

Keyworth Builders Ltd a subsidiary of the company, is experiencing going concern problems. We confirm that the company will continue to make financial support available to the subsidiary for the foreseeable future.

Claim

Eastwood Manufacturing plc has made a claim against the company for £5m arising from alleged negligent construction of a printing machine. The claim comprises £3m for repairs and £2m for the cost of disruption to Eastwood's business. Following discussions with the company's professional advisers we consider that Eastwood has no claim on the company and hence no provision for these costs is required in the accounts for the year ended 31 March 20X2. However the contingency is fully explained in a note.

Transactions with directors

The company has had at no time during the year any arrangement, transaction or agreement to provide credit facilities (including loans, quasi-loans or credit transactions) for directors nor to guarantee or provide security for such matters, except as disclosed in note X to the financial statements.

Post balance sheet events

There have been no events since the balance sheet date which necessitate revision of the figures included in the financial statements or inclusion of a note thereto. Should further material events occur, which may necessitate revision of the figures included in the financial statements or inclusion of a note thereto, we will advise you accordingly.

Yours faithfully

Signed on behalf of the Board of Directors

.... Director

(b) **Reliability of letter of representation**

The letter of representation is a written record of statements made by management to auditors during the audit. As it is a written record, it is stronger evidence than oral representations by themselves would be.

However representations do not come from an independent source. They should not therefore be relied on when other evidence is available or expected to be available.

Nevertheless representations may be the only available evidence when **knowledge of facts is confined to management**, or the matter is **one of judgement** or opinion. Independent confirmation will not be available in these circumstances.

In this context s 389A Companies Act 1985 provides that an officer of the company commits an offence if he knowingly or recklessly makes a statement (written or oral) to the company's auditors

which is misleading, false or deceptive concerning a material matter. (An officer in this context would include directors, company secretary and senior management.)

Reliance on letter

On receipt of a letter of representation the auditors will need to **ensure** that there is **no other evidence** that they have discovered during the course of their audit which conflicts with the written representation. They will then have to **review the representations** made and decide, given the results of the audit testing and their assessment of risk, whether they are able to rely on them to give an unqualified opinion on the accounts.

(c) Work to be performed to check whether a provision should be included in the accounts for the legal claim from Eastwood Manufacturing plc is as follows.

- **Obtain and review all correspondence** relating to the claim.
- **Review written advice** obtained from the company's lawyer and surveyor.
- **Review the original contract** between Eastwood and Lambley to assess the extent of Lambley's responsibility for repairs and any time period limitations.
- **Ascertain whether Lambley is covered by insurance** should the claim be payable.
- **Examine minutes** of meetings of the Board and management which deal with this matter.

These procedures will allow the probability of the company having to meet the claim to be assessed. Disclosure and/or provision to comply with FRS 12 *Provisions, Contingent Liabilities and Contingent Assets* will be required.

(d) In the circumstances where the directors refuse to sign the letter of representation because of the legal claim from Eastwood Manufacturing plc the following procedures could be considered.

(i) A **meeting** between the auditors and directors to discuss a revision of the wording of the letter, so allowing the directors to sign.

(ii) Failing this, a **letter of representation excluding the Eastwood claim** should be obtained.

(iii) The old APC auditing guideline recommended that where management refused to sign a letter of representation, the **auditors should prepare a statement** setting out their understanding of the principal representation and ask the management to confirm in writing that their understanding is correct. In this case this procedure could be carried out just for the Eastwood claim if a letter of representation excluding this matter had already been obtained.

Assuming that satisfactory representations are not obtained, either because the original letter is amended in such a way that the situation concerning the claim is not properly explained or that the directors refuse to confirm the auditors' statement, then the auditors will need to **consider the implications** of this scope limitation **for their report**.

Given that refusal by the management to give satisfactory representations concerning the claim indicates that they may be uncertain as to the eventual outcome, the auditors would probably decide to qualify their opinion on the grounds of uncertainty.

10 BESTWOOD ELECTRONICS

> **Tutorial note**. A knowledge of SSAP 17 is required here, as well as the practical knowledge of the audit procedures which must be carried out after the year end. Note that the SAS on this subject has produced a slightly different approach to the old guideline.

(a) (i) Auditors should perform procedures designed to obtain sufficient appropriate audit evidence that all **material subsequent events** up to the date of their report which require adjustment of, or disclosure in, the financial statements have been **identified and properly reflected** therein.

These procedures should be applied to any **matters** examined during the audit which may be **susceptible to change** after the year end. They are in addition to tests on specific transactions after the period end, eg cut-off tests.

Non-adjusting subsequent events should be disclosed in the notes to the accounts of the company, whereas all adjusting events should be incorporated in the accounts.

(ii) The financial statements are the **directors' responsibility** and they would therefore be expected to inform the auditors of any material subsequent events between the date of the auditors' report and the date the financial statements are issued. The auditors do *not* have any obligation to perform procedures, or make enquires regarding the financial statements *after* the date of their report.

When, **after** the date of their **report** but **before** the **financial statements** are **issued**, the **auditors** become **aware** of **subsequent events** which may materially affect the financial statements, they should:

- Establish whether the financial statements need amendment
- Discuss the matter with the directors
- Consider the implications for their report, taking additional action as appropriate

When the financial statements are amended, the auditors should extend the procedures discussed above to the date of their new report, carry out any other appropriate procedures and issue a new audit report dated the day it is signed.

The situation where the statements are not amended but the auditors feel that they should be is discussed below.

(iii) Auditors have no obligations to perform procedures or make enquiries regarding the financial statements **after** they have been issued.

When, after the financial statements have been issued, but before they have been laid before the members or equivalent, auditors become aware of subsequent events which, had they occurred and been known of at the date of their report, might have caused them to issue a different report, they should

- **Consider** whether the financial statements need **amendment**
- **Discuss** the matter with the directors
- **Consider the implications** for their **report**, taking additional action as appropriate

The SAS distinguishes between two cases:

(1) An event which **occurred before** the **date** of the **auditors' report**, but which the auditors became aware of thereafter, and

(2) An **event** which **occurred after** the **date** of the **auditors' report**.

Under (1), the auditors and directors should consider whether the financial statements should be revised (eg under ss 245 to 245(c) CA 1985). In situation (2) there is no statutory provision for revising financial statements; the auditors might take legal advice on withdrawing their report. In **both** cases, a statement by the directors or auditors at the AGM may be feasible, but in any event legal advice may be helpful.

Where the directors do **not** revise the financial statements but the auditors feel they should be revised, and where the statements have been issued but not yet laid before the members; or if the directors do not intend to make an appropriate statement at the AGM, then the auditors should consider steps to take, on a timely basis, to prevent reliance on their report eg a statement at the AGM. Remember that the auditors have no right to communicate to the members directly in writing.

(b) The audit work for post balance sheet events will normally be concerned with balance sheet values at and after the year end. The following procedures will be carried out.

(i) **Fixed assets**

(1) **Check for any sales** or proposed sales after the year end which may trigger a write down to net realisable value at the year end.

(2) **Consider obsolescence** of fixed assets, for example plant used to make a discontinue line, which might only become apparent after the year end.

(ii) **Stock**

(1) **Check post year-end selling price** of major items of stock and compare to value in year end accounts. Consider write downs to net realisable value.

(2) **Consider the possible existence of obsolete, damaged or slow moving stock** and the consequent value of any write down.

(3) **Perform a (limited) stock take** after the year end **if the existence of all stock is not known** for certain.

(iii) **Debtors**

(1) Review post year end receipts to determine recoverability.

(2) Take doubtful debts paid out of the provision and consider writing parts of the provision off for which no money has been received.

(3) Review trade press and correspondence and consult the sales manager about any major customers who have become insolvent recently.

(4) Check the issue of credit notes and return of goods after the year end to determine the provision for credit notes required in the accounts.

(iv) **Cash at bank**

(1) **Check that outstanding items** on the bank reconciliation have **cleared promptly after the year end** (to spot teeming and lading and late payment to creditors).

(2) **Write back any stale cheques** not cleared (over 6 months old).

(3) **Check all material payments and receipts around the year end** to check the completeness of both accruals and prepayments (including NI and PAYE sundry creditors).

(v) **Trade creditors**

(1) **Check reconciling items** on suppliers' statements have **cleared promptly** after the year end.

(2) If the creditors circularisation has been carried out then **examining post year end payments** will help to verify balances where there was no supplier's statement and no reply.

(vi) **Going concern problems and other matters**

The post balance sheet event review is important in terms of going concern investigations. The following procedures should be carried out as a matter of routine.

(1) **Check profit and cash flow forecasts**.

(2) **Review management accounts** and reports after the year end.

(3) **Review board minutes** after the year end.

(4) **Request any information** on post balance sheet events and going concern matters from the directors and check their information.

(5) The **directors should also state** they have given all such information in the letter of representation.

(vii) **Non-adjusting events**

Look for any matters which are non-adjusting but which should be disclosed in the accounts, for example, major sales of fixed assets, accidental losses and issues of shares and debentures.

(c) I will check whether there have been any material post balance sheet events in this period, particularly if there is a significant delay between the date of the auditors' report and the issue of their financial statements. I will not undertake such detailed enquiries as in (b) above, but I will perform the following procedures.

(i) **Ask the management or directors if any further material events have occurred** which might affect my opinion on the accounts.

(ii) **Review the latest board minutes, reports and management accounts** issued since the end of the audit.

(iii) Any **matters which were uncertain** at the end of the audit should be **reviewed** again to establish an outcome and any effect on the accounts. Examples would include doubtful debts, contingencies and stock obsolescence (perhaps due to new developments).

(iv) **Consider any matters** which have **arisen in the industry** or the economy which might affect the company.

11 LOCKSLEY

> **Tutorial note**. The audit of these assets is relatively straightforward, but it relies on your knowledge of the relevant accounting standards. You should cover every aspect of the audit of these items, perhaps by considering the balance sheet and then the P & L account effects.

(a) The relevant audit tests are as follows.

(i) The auditors should **obtain** from the client a **breakdown** of the figure for development expenditure which makes it possible to trace the amounts spent to the nominal ledger and the final accounts.

(ii) **Tests of controls** should be performed to ensure that a system exists for controlling the authorising and recording of development expenditure, and that the system is operating adequately. (This work may be covered where practicable by the audit tests performed on the company's purchases and payroll systems.)

(iii) Individual amounts should be **vouched** by reference to **supporting documentation**. The relevant documentation will vary according to the type of expenditure, but tests might include the following.

(1) Agree purchases to requisitions, orders, goods received notes, invoices, cash book and bank statement.

(2) Agree labour costs to the payroll and to supporting evidence, such as time sheets or job cards.

(3) If overheads have been included in the development figure, ensure that they have been calculated on a basis consistent with that used generally by the company.

The auditors will wish to set a materiality level for testing individual items; this will have to be established when the breakdown of the total figure is known. For instance, it may be possible to restrict testing considerably if one or two large invoices represent the bulk of the relevant expenditure.

(iv) The **arithmetical accuracy** of the schedule of expenditure should be **checked**.

(v) The auditors should **ensure** that there has been **no double-counting**, that is, that development items capitalised have not also been charged as an expense in the profit and loss account.

(vi) Finally, the auditors should carry out a **review of the development figure** in order to be satisfied that it is reasonable and consistent with what else is known about the company and its business.

(b) The following audit procedures may be performed to verify the revaluation gain arising on fixed assets.

(i) Ensure that the **valuer** appears to be **appropriately qualified** and **independent** of the company. If these conditions are not fulfilled, the auditors will need to consider their possible impact on the results of the valuation.

(ii) By reference to the instructions given to the valuer and the valuer's report, ensure that the **valuation** has been **performed on a basis reasonable and consistent** with previous valuations.

(iii) Check that **profits or losses on individual fixed assets** have been **correctly calculated** by reference to the fixed asset register and the detailed analysis of the revaluation.

(iv) **Check the arithmetical accuracy** of the compilation of the **revaluation schedule** and of the **calculation of asset profits and losses.**

(c) SSAP 13 lays down the basis on which development costs may be carried forward. They may be carried forward only if, and to the extent that, they represent an **asset** which is likely to generate income for the company in the future. It would contravene the prudence concept to carry forward expenditure which is not reasonably expected to generate future income.

According to SSAP 13, development expenditure should be written off in the year it is incurred, unless there is a **clearly defined project**, and the **related expenditure is separately identifiable**.

The outcome of a project must then be examined for:

(i) Its technical feasibility, and

(ii) Its ultimate commercial viability considered in the light of such factors as:

(1) Likely market conditions (including competing products or services)
(2) Public opinion
(3) Consumer and environmental legislation

A project will be of value:

(i) Only if **further development costs** to be incurred on the same project, together with related production, selling and administration costs, will be more than **covered by related revenues**, and

(ii) **Adequate resources exist**, or are reasonably expected to be available, to **enable the project to be completed** and to provide any consequential increases in working capital.

If, taking a prudent view of the available evidence, these conditions are met, development costs may be deferred and amortised over the period expected to benefit.

(d) The decision to finance development internally has resulted in a large increase in creditors and a decrease in cash and bank balances. This may lead to liquidity problems, especially since the company will still need funds to finance the new product. These funds will have to be generated either by the sale of further investments, the raising of a loan from the directors or an outside investor, or by the issue of shares. If **funding** is **not available**, the **development expenditure** should be **written off** on the basis that it will not be possible to complete the project. This would eliminate the profit and loss reserve and would create doubts about the company's status as a going concern.

The auditors should discuss with the directors their plans for obtaining **additional finance**, and request that they produce cash flow forecasts in support of these. If the auditors do not obtain satisfactory evidence of the company's ability to obtain finance, it may be necessary to qualify the audit report on the grounds of going concern problems which have not been fully disclosed.

12 PHOENIX

(a) **Trade investment**

(i) **Matters to consider**

At £80,000 the total investment is on the borderline of materiality to the profit and loss account for the current period at about 4.7%. However, if dividends receivable are added to this then the amount is more clearly material at nearly 6%. The total is unlikely to be material to the balance sheet. If the total amount has to be written off it seems likely that separate disclosure will be required but if not, a judgement will have to be made. SSAP 17 *Accounting for post balance sheet events* requires that as an adjusting event, the amount should be written off in the accounts. There may be amounts owing to Pegasus and there may possibly be a right of set-off against amounts receivable, although this seems unlikely.

The effect on the operations of Phoenix of the loss of the contractor also have to be considered. Alternative arrangements will have to be made for imported metals and this may, at least in the short term, result in increased costs if a suitable shipping contractor cannot be found quickly. Whilst this is not likely to affect the current year figures, disclosure maybe required as a non-adjusting post balance sheet event.

Disclosure of all matters will be required in the Directors' Report.

(ii) **Audit evidence**

Whether Pegasus is, or is likely to be, in receivership, administration or liquidation should be established. Copies of all press reports and any similar documentation should be obtained. If liquidators have been appointed, it may be possible to establish what level of pay-out is likely to shareholders (from the liquidator's report), whether shareholders have any priority in the liquidation (this is not normally the case), and whether a shareholders meeting has or is likely to be called in the near future.

Examination of the audit report on the most recent financial statements and any further press reports may provide persuasive evidence in this respect although it seems likely that a judgement will have to be made. If the matter is principally one of judgement and opinion, and there is little or no other evidence available, suitably worded management representations will have to be sought.

If there is serious doubt about Pegasus's ability to continue as a going concern it will be necessary to review management's plans (if any) for the replacement of the contractor and the need for disclosure of the operating and financial effects of the matter. If there is the intention to sell Pegasus as a going concern, it will be important for Phoenix to establish whether Pegasus will be continuing to honour its existing contracts.

The legal possibilities in relation to any right of set-off of dividends receivable and amounts payable should be reviewed with the assistance of the company's lawyers.

In Phoenix's financial statements, if the dividends or the investment are unlikely to be recovered, FRS 11 *Impairment of fixed assets and goodwill* requires that the impairment loss be recognised through the profit and loss account.

There is no indication that the company should be consolidated.

If appropriate adjustments are not made in the accounts, a qualified audit report may be necessary ('except for').

(b) **Provision for future maintenance**

(i) **Matters to consider**

£500,000 represents nearly 30% of profits and is therefore material. FRS 12 *Provisions, contingent liabilities and contingent assets* states that a provision should only be recognised when there is a present obligation (legal or constructive) as a result of a past event (in order to fulfil the criteria for a liability). The overhaul is planned for August. Unless a binding legal agreement for maintenance has been signed, or unless there is no real prospect that the company can avoid the obligation at the balance sheet date (this seems unlikely), the provision should not be recognised. Whilst there seems little uncertainty as to the timing of the expenditure, or as to the amount, there is no actual liability at the balance sheet date.

FRS 12 was designed to deal with the problem of over-provisioning for the purposes of profit smoothing. This seems a possibility in this case, even when taken together with the write off of the investment, above.

FRS 15 *Tangible fixed assets* requires that maintenance expenditure should be recognised when it is incurred, however, it could be argued that the lining is a separate asset and could be accounted for as a capital item, at the point at which the expense is incurred. This example is given in FRS 15.

Prior year accounting policies in relation to this matter are relevant and a disclosure of a change in accounting policy may be required.

(ii) **Audit evidence**

Past treatment of this expenditure, the rationale for it, the nature of the replacement (whether regular or *ad hoc*), and the intended current year treatment should be discussed with management – prior year working papers should also be reviewed.

Management representations should be sought on the appropriateness of the accounting policy.

Any documentation available regarding contractual arrangements and costings should be carefully examined.

(c) **Cleanaway Ltd**

(i) **Matters to consider**

Cleanaway Ltd. is highly likely to be a related party under FRS 8 *Related party disclosures* under which disclosure is required of the names of the related parties, the nature of the relationship, and a detailed description of the transactions entered into.

There are significant operational implications of the alleged illegal dumping. Firstly, there is the possibility that Cleanaway will not have its licence renewed which means that an alternative contractor must be found. Costs may be increased because the previous contract was negotiated five years ago. There may also be financial implications as Phoenix may be liable for actions of the contractors, for any associated clean-up costs, and may also be more likely to be subject to regulatory investigations.

The integrity of Troy Pitz is also called into question which has implications for the financial statements as a whole to the extent that he has a responsibility for them, and for the assessment of audit risk. There are also implications for the reputation of Phoenix which may affect customer and supplier goodwill, and any applications for renewed operating licences required by Phoenix itself.

(ii) **Audit evidence**

The proposed disclosure of all matters, including the required FRS 8 and FRS 12 disclosures in relation to related parties and contingent liabilities should be examined, as should the relevant disclosures in prior years.

The exact nature of the allegations should be investigated by discussions with management and any financial statements of Cleanaway, and regulatory notices placed on the public record, should be examined to determine the extent of the problem.

Management representations should be obtained on the likely effect of the matter on Phoenix from directors other than Troy Pitz. Any plans for dealing with the operational matters noted above and adverse publicity, including those in board minutes and minutes of shareholder meetings, should be reviewed and an assessment of whether there are any going concern implications for Phoenix should be made. This is particularly relevant when taken together with the loss of the shipping contractor.

Any correspondence with regulators and lawyers should be examined. The company may have taken legal advice on both the problems with Cleanaway, and with the implications for Troy Pitz's position as managing director.

The implications of all of the items above for other areas in the financial statements, the financial statements as a whole, and the audit report should be considered.

13 RECOGNITION

Tutorial note. This question focuses on some accounting treatments and materiality consideration. In the exam, questions on the topics in chapter 13 could also cover the following issues:

- Whether disclosure a presentation is fair
- Whether accounting treatments are reasonable or aggressive (in part a, the treatment of revenue is aggressive)
- Whether the issues raised are material or fundamental and therefore, pervasive to the financial statements

(a) **Accounting treatment**

Beak plc has sold the land to Wings plc at a price well under current market value for no discernible reason. It is able to repurchase that land at cost at any time in the next five years but cannot be forced to do so. Therefore unless the land value falls significantly it can be assumed that Beak plc will repurchase the land. Wings plc will not use the building or the land for redevelopment in that period otherwise on repurchase they would lose any investment they had made.

The **commercial effect** of this transaction, assuming land values do not fall significantly, is that of **a loan** to Beak plc secured on the land. The commission is in effect interest on the loan, payment being deferred until the repurchase takes place.

Hence Beak plc should not treat this transaction as a sale. The land should continue to be shown as an asset in the balance sheet and a loan of £20m should be recorded. The profit and loss account should be charged annually with the commission charge and the accrual shown as a deferral liability in the balance sheet.

As this is a material transaction, the auditors should qualify their report on the grounds of disagreement.

(b) **Accounting treatment**

The **substance** of this transaction appears to be that the **cars are part** of the **stock of Sparks Ltd** from the time they take delivery of them from Gocar plc. This is because Sparks Ltd bears the risks and rewards of ownership, ie it has to insure the cars, but only pays the wholesale price in force on the date the cars were first supplied, so avoiding subsequent price rises. The monthly rental is a form of interest charged by Gocar plc, varying with the length of time Sparks Ltd holds the stock.

This interpretation of the transaction is also supported by the fact that Gocar plc cannot demand the return of the cars from Sparks Ltd.

The cars unsold for less than four months should be treated as stock in the financial statements and the liability to Gocar plc for them recognised.

Materiality considerations

The auditors should make a judgement as to whether they feel the amounts are material. The value of the additional stock represents 15% of their stock already recognised on the balance sheet. It is 1.7% of the balance sheet total. Bearing in mind a general guideline for materiality of 1-2% of total assets, this is likely to be material.

Impact on audit report

If the matter is material to the profit and loss account (these details are not given in the question), or there are other errors in stock which would result in stock being increased in the balance sheet, they should qualify their report.

This would be on the grounds of disagreement, as before.

14 BELLATRIX

(a) **Implications of findings for acquisition of Scorpio**

Cash flow, profits and purchase price

The combination of poor cash flow and apparent rising profits is not a good combination as it implies poor quality profits. In this case, the main apparent reasons for the increased profit appear to be the profit on the sale of the warehouse and the reduction in the provision for stock and bad debts.

The basis on which the purchase price is negotiated should not include the non-recurring profit on the sale that has been made (or on the sales that are planned) and the reduction in provisions should be justifiable on the basis of previous experience of over-provisioning. If it is not, the provisions should be written back.

If the purchase price is also based on asset values, Bellatrix should consider the financial and operational implications of the disposals of the properties, as well as the efficiency of outsourcing warehousing. There may be economies of scale to be had by combining the warehousing capabilities of the two companies and given that there appears to be no contract of sale for the remaining properties, as yet, these plans may be altered as part of the purchase agreement.

Cash flow, as well as profits, has been improved by the sale of the properties and Bellatrix should consider the future funding needs of Scorpio and the possibility of consolidating bank borrowings. The cash flow issues in relation to the bank loan and refurbishment discussed below are relevant here.

Sale of warehouse, outsourcing warehousing, operational issues

Bellatrix should consider the operational issues arising from the sales of warehouses and the adequacy of detailed plans for outsourcing of warehousing, as noted above. Outsourcing is not necessarily the least expensive or the most efficient method of dealing with the issues and there may be some attempt to manipulate the management accounts by moving the costs of warehousing from the capital budget to the revenue budget. There are also implications for calculations of the return on assets.

Application for bank loan and refurbishment of offices

Given the cash flow difficulties, it seems, on the face of it, to be difficult to justify the refurbishment of offices, particularly if they are to be financed by a bank loan, because it is unlikely to generate significant additional revenues or profits at this point. It would be useful to establish the bank's likely position on this loan and it is very important to establish whether the reductions in the provisions for stock and bad debts have been properly disclosed to the bank in the management accounts provided to them. The bank may well want to take charges over the company's assets as security for the loan which may well have implications for the rights which Bellatrix has over the assets of Scorpio once it has been purchased.

Andromeda

It will be important to establish the effect of the purchase on the future relationship with Andromeda. If the relationship can continue as before, and if the sales are genuinely at arms length, there should be no problem but if this relationship is likely to change, there are implications for both cash flows and profits.

General

The reasons for the proposed purchase should be established, particularly given the poor cash flows, poor quality profits and the possible lack of integrity of the management of Scorpio if the reductions in provisions have not been disclosed to the bank or are not justified. The belief that profits (and presumably revenues) will increase because of the coming winter season should be investigated by Bellatrix with reference to the past performance of Scorpio.

(b) **Implications of the acquisition for the Bellatrix Audit**

Purchase of Scorpio

Assuming that the sale goes ahead in the current year, the purchase will need to be audited by reference to the purchase agreement, the associated legal documentation, any valuations performed as part of the purchase agreement, and the transfer of the purchase consideration whether this be in cash, shares, other assets or some combination of these.

The firm will also need to ensure that the appropriate company secretarial matters have been properly dealt with by the inspection of documentation sent to the Registrar of Companies and entries in the statutory books of both companies (changes in share ownership, changes in directors, etc.)

Accounting for the purchase

There is no indication in the question that the purchase is anything other than an acquisition. In the consolidated accounts, profits will therefore need to be split into the pre- and post-acquisition elements and accounted for either in the goodwill calculation or the profit and loss account. The assets to be incorporated on a line by line basis should be included at fair value and in this case, this is likely to involve reliance on the work of experts in accordance with SAS 520 *Using the work of an expert* because assets appear to be recorded in Scorpio's book at historical cost. Goodwill needs to be calculated as the excess of the fair value of the purchase consideration over the fair value of the assets acquired, and amortised in accordance with FRS 10 *Goodwill and intangible assets*. If the goodwill period exceeds 20 years, there must be a solid (and auditable) justification for this. The relationship with Andromeda and the transactions with it need to be disclosed (as well as details of the acquisition) in accordance with FRS 8 *Related party disclosures* in both the consolidated accounts and in Scorpio's individual accounts. If the year-ends to the two companies are not coterminous, further work may be required on Scorpio's accounts in order to perform the consolidation.

In the individual accounts of Bellatrix, it will be necessary to include the investment as an addition with the appropriate disclosure of the quantum and nature of the purchase consideration. Any charges over the assets of Scorpio need to be disclosed in the accounts of both Scorpio and in the consolidated accounts.

Group audit arrangements

On the assumption that Scorpio has other auditors for the current year, appropriate arrangements need to be made in order that the information needed by the firm for the audit of the consolidated accounts is provided on a timely basis in accordance with SAS 510 *The relationship between principal auditors and other auditors*. If the firm is already auditor to Scorpio, this problem will not arise, but if the firm is to be appointed in the current year, further work will be needed to audit the opening balances of Scorpio for the current year and the co-operation of the previous auditors may be sought. All of the normal first year work in terms of the assessment of risk and the documentation of accounting systems and internal controls will also need to be performed before the consolidation is signed off.

Audit administration

SAS 240 *Quality control* suggests that a second partner review is required in cases of high audit risk and in the public interest. The acquisition would appear to increase inherent risk and the review should therefore be built into the audit plan. Additional work is likely to be required for the consolidation (and for the audit of Scorpio if the firm is to be appointed for the first time) and the audit fee needs to be negotiated as early as possible on this basis.

Audit strategy

In the accounts of Scorpio, particular attention needs to be paid to several areas. These matters will be dealt with either by the firm, if appointed, or by Scorpio's auditors in the group audit instructions. The provisions for stock and bad debts will need to be examined carefully with reference to trading patterns and changes in them, the overall levels of stock and debtors, and the company's previous experience of accurate provisioning, for example. The valuation of fixed assets and the disclosure of profits on sales, probably as an exceptional item in accordance with FRS 3 *Reporting financial performance*, should be examined and if, as seems likely, they are material to the consolidated accounts they should be disclosed in the same way.

There may be group tax implications to consider in the accounts of both companies, and the consolidated accounts.

15 BUSINESS ASSURANCE

Tutorial note. This question could have been answered with basic auditing knowledge and did not need an in-depth knowledge of the services currently performed by auditors. However, you need to feel confident and familiar with the subject.

(a) Current ACCA guidance on the provision of other services to clients is very similar to IFAC guidance which applies in an international basis.

The view taken internationally by IFAC is that many companies would be restricted if they were unable to obtain the other services available from their auditors, provided these services do not interfere with the exercise of managerial functions and auditors' independence. It would seem that **IFAC guidance allows external auditors to act as internal auditors** of clients.

The view taken by the ACCA guidelines is as follows.

- The ACCA guidance states that **objectivity may be threatened** by the provision of non-audit services. Care must be taken not to give executive advice or to become part of the client's active management.
- Firms **should not provide accountancy services to plc clients.**
- If accounting records are prepared for a client, then the **client** must accept **responsibility for the records.**
- There is **no specific prohibition** from an external auditor undertaking the internal audit function.

Specific **problems** which could occur include the following.

- The **difficulty of reporting weaknesses** in internal controls in systems designed by employees of the auditor acting as internal auditors of the client.
- The **perceived difficulties in testing work** carried out by internal auditors who are colleagues of the external auditors.
- Internal audit programmes designed to **reduce the work** of external auditors.
- The danger of **breaching ACCA rules** of conduct if the internal audit department is deemed to be **part of the management** of the client.
- **Fee pressures** arising from the increase in fees for providing an internal audit service leading to breaching the fee guidelines.
- **Audit risk** assessed by the external auditor. The presumption is that control risk would reduce because of the involvement of the external auditor in the provision of internal audit services

(b) The **effects** would be as follows.

- Increased **risk of liability claims**
- **Additional costs** to the auditor incurred in employing suitable staff to provide wider assurance
- An impact upon **fees** charged to clients
- Possible **increased expectations** of audit clients
- The difficulty in formulating and wording an appropriate **audit report** which could require legislative changes

(c) The new approach could be seen as a '**repackaging**' of existing services where auditors concentrate upon providing services which add value to the audit fee in the eyes of the client. Basic audit work may be foregone as it is perceived as adding very little.

The difficulty with this approach is that auditors are increasingly faced with **litigation claims** and should therefore provide more basic assurance based lower materiality thresholds. It may be that external auditors came to view the roles of audit committees and internal audit departments as crucial in reducing control risk.

It is dangerous to assume that external audit is a consultancy exercise aimed at adding value because traditional audit assurance will be lost and overall levels of audit risk will rise.

16 SIGHTHILL SUPERMARKETS

Tutorial note. The approach to employ to part (b) is to consider the criteria external audit will use to decide how much assurance internal audit's work provides, and the extra work that external audit will have to do to ensure total assurance is sufficient. Your answer should demonstrate that you are thinking about how external audit's additional work can be minimised, since it does appear likely that quite substantial assurance could be placed on the work of internal audit.

(a) The factors that we should consider in assessing the effectiveness of the internal auditors would include:

(i) The **extent of their independence**, including their ability to communicate directly with the highest levels of management, and with external auditors. Their independence will be improved if the company has an audit committee, and the internal audit department can communicate directly with the audit committee.

(ii) The **scope and objectives** of internal audit, and the extent to which it covers areas relevant to statutory audit (systems review and testing of financial accounts).

(iii) The **quality of internal audit work**, and the extent to which it is properly controlled, recorded and reviewed.

(iv) The **technical competence** of the internal audit team, their **training**, **qualifications** and **experience**.

(v) The **quality of internal audit reports** issued, and the extent to which management acts upon them; internal auditors should perform follow-up procedures to confirm that weaknesses that they have identified have been remedied.

(vi) The **adequacy of resources** (staff, computer facilities and so on) available to them.

In order to make this assessment, we would draw upon discussions with internal auditors and management and make a detailed review of internal audit working papers and reports.

(b) (i) **Recording systems and evaluating the effectiveness of controls**

(1) We shall verify internal audit's recording of the system by carrying out **walk-through tests.** If the results of these are satisfactory, we can rely on internal audit's recording of the system.

(2) When reviewing internal audit's assessment of controls, we should check that the method they use appears to assess whether all **relevant control objectives** have been **achieved**, and **identifies** the **key controls.** We should confirm that the **conclusions** internal audit have drawn appear to be **reasonable**. We are more likely to place reliance on the assessment if the working papers clearly demonstrate it has been carried out systematically, using a **control questionnaire**, or a **control evaluation questionnaire**. It would reduce the time we spend if internal audit used similar assessment methods to our firm's.

(ii) **Performing tests of controls**

(1) As for (i) above, we should **review** the **work** internal audit has **done**, and **confirm** that the **relevant key controls** have been tested.

(2) Because internal audit is itself an internal control, we cannot accept internal audit's conclusions on controls without testing controls ourselves. We can either **re-perform** some of internal audit's work, or **carry out** our **own tests** of controls. We can rely on

internal audit's work and hence **reduce** our **substantive testing** if our tests do not uncover errors that internal audit has failed to find, or our error rate is not significantly higher than internal audit's. If problems do arise, we are unlikely to be able to rely on controls in the audit area being tested. We may also conclude that we cannot rely on internal audit's testing of controls in other areas.

(iii) **Carrying out substantive procedures**

(1) Various tests carried out by internal audit could provide substantive assurance in a number of areas, for example attending stocktakes, carrying out cash counts and inspecting fixed assets. How much assurance we gain from this work would depend on the **objectives** of the tests, the **extent** of the testing and whether the **conclusions** drawn were **reasonable**.

(2) We would have to carry out some substantive procedures ourselves in all material audit areas to confirm whether the work of **internal audit** is **reliable,** and because we cannot rely totally on internal audit. Nevertheless we can limit our substantive testing if internal audit's work appears to have been properly performed, and our own tests do not contradict internal audit's conclusions.

(iv) **Auditing the computer systems**

(1) We should **review** the **results** of internal audit's work, and confirm that all major aspects of the computer system's operations have been covered. In particular we should check that the **access controls** appear to be effective, and that internal audit has investigated and drawn the correct conclusions about any errors found. Internal audit should also have thoroughly tested any changes to the system that have occurred during the year.

(2) There are other aspects of the computer systems which would not be checked by computer assisted audit techniques. Aspects we should consider include **systems documentation**, the extent of **segregation of duties**, **virus checks** and controls to ensure the **continuity of operations** (storage of back-up programs, disaster prevention and recovery procedures).

(v) **Visiting supermarkets**

(1) Internal audit's work may provide assurance on controls (for example cash receipts and recording of hours worked) and substantive areas (stock-takes and cut-off). We should confirm that the **coverage** of supermarkets has been as the client has indicated (concentrated on largest/those with problems, but with every supermarket being visited once a year.) We should review the work done and **assess** the **response** to problems found. In particular if the same supermarkets are having to be visited frequently because the same problems continually occur, it will cast doubts on how effectively the recommendations of internal audit are implemented.

(2) We should carry out some supermarket visits ourselves during the year, concentrating on the largest sites, but also visiting a sample of smaller ones. We should **compare** our **results** with internal audit's work, and will be able to gain assurance if the results are similar. If we can rely on internal audit's work, we can gain substantive assurance at the **year-end** by having **internal audit visit supermarkets** which we do not visit.

17 BINGHAM ENGINEERING

(a) The 'going concern' concept assumes that the accounts are drawn up on the basis that the business will continue to exist as a viable commercial entity, without any need for any significant curtailment in its present level of activity for the 'foreseeable future'.

When forming his opinion at the conclusion of the post balance sheet period the auditor should have regard to the term 'foreseeable future' identified in SSAP 2 in the context of going concern. While the foreseeable future must be judged in relation to specific circumstances, the auditors should normally expect the directors to have considered information which relates to a minimum of 12 months following the date of approval of the financial statements.

(b) The most common factors indicating that a company may not be regarded as a going concern are as follows.

- Adverse financial figures or ratios:
  - Recurring operating losses
  - Financing to a considerable extent out of overdue suppliers and other creditors
  - Heavy dependence on short-term finance for long-term needs
  - Working capital deficiencies
  - Low liquidity rates
  - Over-gearing, in the form of high or increasing debt to equity ratios
  - Under capitalisation, particularly if there is a deficiency of share capital and reserves
- Borrowing in excess of limits imposed by debenture trust deeds
- Defaults on loans or similar agreements
- Dividends in arrears
- Restrictions placed on usual trade terms
- Excessive or obsolete stock
- Long overdue debtors
- Non-compliance with statutory capital requirements
- Deterioration of relationship with bankers
- Necessity of seeking new sources or methods of obtaining finance
- The continuing use of old fixed assets because there are not funds to replace them
- The size and content of the order book
- Potential losses on long-term contracts

Other factors, not necessarily suggesting inability to meet debts, may be internal or external matters.

(i) **Internal matters**

- Loss of key management or staff
- Significantly increasing stock levels
- Work stoppages or other labour difficulties
- Substantial dependence upon the success of a particular project or particular asset
- Excessive reliance on the success of a new product
- Uneconomic long-term commitments

(ii) **External matters**

- Legal proceedings or similar matters that may jeopardise a company's ability to continue in business
- Loss of a key franchise or patent
- Loss of a principal supplier or customer
- The undue influence of a market dominant competitor
- Political risks
- Technical developments which render a key product obsolete
- Frequent financial failures of enterprises in the same industry

The indications above vary in importance and some may only have significance as audit evidence when viewed in conjunction with others.

The significance of the indications above may diminish because they are matched by audit evidence indicating that there are mitigating factors. Indications that the business may be having to sell fixed assets to meet present cash demands may be mitigated by the possibility of obtaining new sources of finance or of renewing and expanding loan finance. Indications of problems that raise questions about the continuation of the business without suggesting inability to meet debts may be mitigated by factors relating to the enterprise's capacity to adopt alternative courses of action, for example, the likelihood of finding alternative sales markets where a principal customer is lost.

(c) (i) Under the present circumstances of the company, it is unlikely that the capital expenditure/disposal forecast will contain many items of capital expenditure because of the adverse effect that this would have on the company's cash flow. For such items as there are, the auditor should check that the quoted costs are reasonable, with any large value items being checked against price lists etc. Enquiries should be made of management as to whether there are any proposed items of capital expenditure not included in the forecast.

In relation to any intended disposals of fixed assets, the auditors should:

(1) Check whether the proceeds of sale appear to be reasonable with particular care being taken to see that any estimates are arrived at on a prudent basis.

(2) Consider whether the estimates of the timing of the receipt of sale proceeds appear to be reasonable and, once again, arrived at on a prudent basis.

(ii) The audit work required in relation to the profit forecast would be as follows.

(1) Check that the level of projected sales is reasonable, being similar to the previous year and consistent with current market conditions and the confirmed orders received from the company's customers.

(2) Consider whether the gross profit margin appears reasonable in the light of the company's recent experiences and there has been consistency in the recognition of those items affecting the calculation of this key ratio.

(3) Compare the level of profit and loss account items to the previous year, investigating carefully any areas of significant change. Any projected savings in expenditure must be justified and the auditor should take particular car to see that proper provision has been made for all bank charges and interest.

(4) All castings and extensions in the profit forecast should be checked and comparison made with common items dealt with in the other two forecasts.

(iii) The cash flow forecast which is based on the above two forecasts should be checked in the following way.

(1) The opening balance should be checked to the draft financial statements and the company's cash book. For the expired period of the forecast, the month end balance should also be checked to the cash book.

(2) All receipts and payments for the elapsed period of the forecast should be checked against supporting documentation.

(3) The reasonableness of the timing of future receipts and payments should be considered in the light of the normal period of credit taken by customers and extended by suppliers, due date for payment of PAYE, VAT etc.

(4) The consistency of items in the cash flow forecast with the other two forecasts should be considered, as well as consistency and accuracy of forecasts in previous years.

(5) All castings and extensions in the forecast should be checked.

(d) The reasonableness of the three forecasts referred to above and the willingness of the company's bankers and other creditors to supply the required funds will be the main factors to consider in assessing whether the company is a going concern.

If the work already carried out suggests that the forecasts are reasonable, then with the permission of the client, some direct confirmation of the future 'co-operation' of the bank and major suppliers should be sought. Such co-operation is more likely to be forthcoming if the company is forecast to make profits rather than losses and consideration should also be given to any security held by the various creditors and the chances of any single creditor precipitating a crisis by seeking to invoke his own security.

18 ENVIRONMENTAL ISSUES

Implications of environmental matters for business

Environmental matters affecting businesses are wide ranging. They have now extended beyond matters concerning pollution and emissions, to matters concerning sustainability and social responsibility. Pollutants and emissions are now controlled by most governments. Fines are imposed on those making illegal emissions of toxic waste for example, the level of emission of greenhouse gasses such as carbon dioxide is controlled, and industries which are heavy polluters such as the oil and extractive industries require licences to operate.

Many governments have signed up to agreements such as the Kyoto agreement, agreeing to reduce the level of emissions and companies are increasingly heavily regulated in these areas. The impact of such matters on the financial statements takes the form of the need to account for fines, penalties and clean-up costs (which are now recognised in accounting standards) and the need to consider the going concern status of companies that are in breach of their licences or have caused environmental disasters.

Reporting on sustainability and social matters is increasingly common for large companies. Matters reported on include the use of child labour and the use of sustainable resources. Companies increasingly look beyond their own direct activities to the activities of their suppliers in this respect. Whilst there is relatively little in the form of regulation on these matters, and there are rarely direct effects on the financial statements, reputational risk is important and pressure groups successfully lobby for the boycott of products and services produced by companies that are perceived as irresponsible in these matters. This may have a direct effect on performance.

There is little hard evidence as yet to suggest that the attitude of a company to such matters has a direct effect on the market valuation of a company, but this may well change. There are now indices tracking listed companies with good environmental credentials.

Many large companies have now implemented environmental management systems (EMS) and many now produce environmental and sustainability reports. Auditor verification statements often appear in these reports.

Impact on financial statements

The valuation of properties if often affected by environmental issues. Provisions for clean-up costs and associated liabilities may be material to a company's financial statements. UK accounting standards have increasingly clamped down on the use of over-provisioning for profit smoothing purposes, and as such, it is now harder to meet the criteria for including a liability than it once was. FRS 12 *Provisions, contingent liabilities and contingent assets* requires that for a liability to be recognised, there must be a present legal or constructive obligation as a result of a past event, that it is probable that a transfer of economic benefits will be required to settle the obligation, and that a reliable estimate can be made of the obligation. A constructive obligation might amount to a public commitment to environmental expenditure by a large company which, although not legally binding, the company has no realistic course of action but to honour, because of adverse publicity if it did not. The economic benefits usually amount to the expenditure of cash.

Even where no liability can be recognised, the disclosure of contingent liabilities is still required and extended notes on these matters often appear in financial statements.

Auditor awareness

If auditors are not aware of these issues they may overlook the need for relevant disclosures and provisions and issue unmodified auditor reports where modified reports are appropriate. The fact that these matters are significant, and that they are relevant to very large companies (as well as smaller ones) exposes auditors to additional risks.

SAS 120 *Consideration of laws and regulations* identifies three types of law and regulation of which auditors should be aware: those laws and regulations that relate directly to the preparation of financial statements (such as Companies Act disclosures), those that provide a legal framework in which entities operate (such as licensing laws), and other general laws that may affect the financial statements, such as health and safety laws. In the second category (laws and regulations relating to the legal framework in which the company operates), auditors should obtain a general understanding of the issues and the procedures adopted to ensure compliance. They should inspect correspondence with licensing or regulatory authorities, they should enquire of directors as to instances of non-compliance, and they should obtain written confirmation of full disclosure of all relevant matters from directors.

Conclusion

Companies and their auditors can no longer afford to ignore environmental matters because the implications of doing so are now very serious. Fortunately, a great deal of work is being put into raising awareness of such issues. There are a number of papers issued by bodies such as FEE and IFAC on the subject and there is considerably more guidance on the subject for both companies and their auditors than there was ten years ago.

19 REPORTING ISSUES

(a) **Comparatives**

Comparative figures and related disclosures are required in financial statements under the Companies Act 1985 and FRS 3 *Reporting financial performance*. Comparatives provide a context for the current year financial statements, without which the value of the current year figures for evaluation, prediction and decision making would be much reduced. Comparatives are required for both the primary statements and the notes to the accounts.

SAS 450 *Opening balances and comparatives* requires that auditors obtain evidence that amounts derived from the preceding financial statements are free from material misstatements and are appropriately incorporated in the financial statements for the current period. Opening balances must be properly brought forward and must not contain errors that affect the current year performance or position and accounting policies must be consistent (or disclosures made if policies are changed).

Despite the fact that auditors do not form an opinion on the comparatives *per se,* auditors do form an opinion on the financial statements that include the comparatives.

Problems can arise when the current auditors did not audit the prior period financial statements, where the prior period financial statements were not audited, and where the prior period financial statements had a modified audit report issued on them.

These problems are not necessarily insuperable, additional work in the current period can provide comfort on the comparatives, the work of any previous auditor can, in certain circumstances, be reviewed, and the work on current years figures can provide comfort on the accuracy of the opening position.

(b) **Audit report**

The audit report quoted is a fairly common report that is issued where there is a change of auditors. However, the qualification given is not always necessary and can be avoided. Stock is likely to be material in the financial statements of Delphinus.

The audit report is qualified - an 'except for' opinion is given on the grounds of a limitation of the scope of the work performed because the auditors were unable to obtain sufficient appropriate evidence in relation to opening stock. Opening stock affects both the comparative stock figure in the balance sheet and profit and loss account, and the profit figure for the current year. The Companies Act 1985 also requires that disclosure is made in the audit report where adequate information and explanations are not given, and where proper accounting records have not, or may not have been kept. Section 221 of the Companies Act requires stock records.

If the company wishes to avoid such a qualification, there are several possibilities. It is appropriate in any case for the firm to be appointed as early as possible and for the prior period financial statements and audit report to be examined for any qualifications or problems.

The firm should establish what stock records are kept and what stock control procedures are undertaken. If cyclical stock counting or regular periodic counts are undertaken, it may be possible to rely on the company's records provided that the records are kept up-to-date, that all stock is counted at least once a year, and provided that errors are investigated and promptly corrected. Work will need to be performed to ensure that these criteria have been met. Provided that records are adequate, analytical procedures on records of stock levels and on gross margins (which are likely to be stable) will also assist in providing comfort on the opening position.

It may also be possible, with the co-operation and permission of both the company and the outgoing auditors, for certain working papers or extracts from working papers to be examined in respect of the stock figure. The outgoing auditors are under no obligation to co-operate in this way however. If the relationship between the company and the outgoing auditors is not good, it is highly unlikely that they will co-operate.

Even if the outgoing auditors are not prepared to co-operate, and even if there are no regular stock counts, provided that adequate records have been kept, detailed substantive procedures on the opening figure may be possible by reference to purchases and sales records as well as analytical procedures.

If the firm is appointed early enough, and only a year-end stock count is performed, it may be possible to perform roll-back procedures to establish the opening position. Even if no year-end count was performed, it may be possible to perform and interim count, together with a roll-back, although if there was no year-end count and the records are not adequate, it is possible that a qualified audit report would have been issued in the prior year.

(b) Audit report

Index

Note: Key Terms and their references are given in **bold**

REVIEW FORM & FREE PRIZE DRAW

All original review forms from the entire BPP range, completed with genuine comments, will be entered into a draw on 31 January 2002 and 31 July 2002. The names on the first four forms picked out will be sent a cheque for £50.

Name: ______________________ **Address:** ______________________

____

How have you used this Text?
(Tick one box only)

- ☐ Home study (book only)
- ☐ On a course: college ______________
- ☐ With 'correspondence' package
- ☐ Other ______________

Why did you decide to purchase this Text?
(Tick one box only)

- ☐ Have used complementary Study Text
- ☐ Have used BPP Texts in the past
- ☐ Recommendation by friend/colleague
- ☐ Recommendation by a lecturer at college
- ☐ Saw advertising
- ☐ Other ______________

During the past six months do you recall seeing/receiving any of the following?
(Tick as many boxes as are relevant)

- ☐ Our advertisement in *ACCA Student Accountant*
- ☐ Our advertisement in *Pass*
- ☐ Our brochure with a letter through the post

Which (if any) aspects of our advertising do you find useful?
(Tick as many boxes as are relevant)

- ☐ Prices and publication dates of new editions
- ☐ Information on Text content
- ☐ Facility to order books off-the-page
- ☐ None of the above

Have you used the companion Kit/Passcard/Video/Tape * for this subject? ☐ Yes ☐ No
(* Please circle)

Your ratings, comments and suggestions would be appreciated on the following areas

	Very useful	*Useful*	*Not useful*
Introductory section (Key study steps, personal study)	☐	☐	☐
Chapter introductions	☐	☐	☐
Key terms	☐	☐	☐
Quality of explanations	☐	☐	☐
Case examples and other examples	☐	☐	☐
Questions and answers in each chapter	☐	☐	☐
Chapter roundups	☐	☐	☐
Quick quizzes	☐	☐	☐
Exam focus points	☐	☐	☐
Question bank	☐	☐	☐
Answer bank	☐	☐	☐
List of key terms and index	☐	☐	☐
Icons	☐	☐	☐
Mind maps	☐	☐	☐

	Excellent	*Good*	*Adequate*	*Poor*
Overall opinion of this Text	☐	☐	☐	☐

Do you intend to continue using BPP Products? ☐ Yes ☐ No

Please note any further comments and suggestions/errors on the reverse of this page. The BPP author of this edition can be e-mailed at: catherinewatton@bpp.com

Please return to: Katy Hibbert, ACCA Range Manager, BPP Publishing Ltd, FREEPOST, London, W12 8BR

REVIEW FORM & FREE PRIZE DRAW (continued)

Please note any further comments and suggestions/errors below

FREE PRIZE DRAW RULES

1. Closing date for 31 July 2002 draw is 30 June 2002. Closing date for 31 January 2002 draw is 31 December 2001.
2. No purchase necessary. Entry forms are available upon request from BPP Publishing. No more than one entry per title, per person. Draw restricted to persons aged 16 and over.
3. Winners will be notified by post and receive their cheques not later than 6 weeks after the draw date.
4. The decision of the promoter in all matters is final and binding. No correspondence will be entered into.

See overleaf for information on other BPP products and how to order

ACCA Order - New Syllabus

To BPP Publishing Ltd, Aldine Place, London W12 8AA
Tel: 020 8740 2211. Fax: 020 8740 1184
email: publishing@bpp.com online: www.bpp.com

Mr/Mrs/Ms (Full name)

Daytime delivery address

Postcode

Daytime Tel Date of exam (month/year)

PART 1	2/01 Texts	8/01 Kits	9/01 Passcards	MCQ cards	Tapes	Videos
1.1 Preparing Financial Statements	£19.95 ☐	£10.95 ☐	£5.95 ☐	£5.95 ☐	£12.95 ☐	£25.00 ☐
1.2 Financial Information for Management	£19.95 ☐	£10.95 ☐	£5.95 ☐	£5.95 ☐	£12.95 ☐	£25.00 ☐
1.3 Managing People	£19.95 ☐	£10.95 ☐	£5.95 ☐		£12.95 ☐	£25.00 ☐
PART 2						
2.1 Information Systems	£19.95 ☐	£10.95 ☐	£5.95 ☐		£12.95 ☐	£25.00 ☐
2.2 Corporate and Business Law (6/01)	£19.95 ☐	£10.95 ☐	£5.95 ☐		£12.95 ☐	£25.00 ☐
2.3 Business Taxation FA 2000 (for 12/01 exam)	£19.95 ☐	£10.95 ☐ (4/01)	£5.95 ☐ (4/01)		£12.95 ☐	£25.00 ☐
2.4 Financial Management and Control	£19.95 ☐	£10.95 ☐	£5.95 ☐		£12.95 ☐	£25.00 ☐
2.5 Financial Reporting (6/01)	£19.95 ☐	£10.95 ☐	£5.95 ☐		£12.95 ☐	£25.00 ☐
2.6 Audit and Internal Review (6/01)	£19.95 ☐	£10.95 ☐	£5.95 ☐		£12.95 ☐	£25.00 ☐
PART 3						
3.1 Audit and Assurance Services (6/01)	£20.95 ☐	£10.95 ☐	£5.95 ☐		£12.95 ☐	£25.00 ☐
3.2 Advanced Taxation FA 2000 (for 12/01 exam)	£20.95 ☐	£10.95 ☐ (4/01)	£5.95 ☐ (4/01)		£12.95 ☐	£25.00 ☐
3.3 Performance Management	£20.95 ☐	£10.95 ☐	£5.95 ☐		£12.95 ☐	£25.00 ☐
3.4 Business Information Management	£20.95 ☐	£10.95 ☐	£5.95 ☐		£12.95 ☐	£25.00 ☐
3.5 Strategic Business Planning and Development	£20.95 ☐	£10.95 ☐	£5.95 ☐		£12.95 ☐	£25.00 ☐
3.6 Advanced Corporate Reporting (6/01)	£20.95 ☐	£10.95 ☐	£5.95 ☐		£12.95 ☐	£25.00 ☐
3.7 Strategic Financial Management	£20.95 ☐	£10.95 ☐	£5.95 ☐		£12.95 ☐	£25.00 ☐
INTERNATIONAL STREAM						
1.1 Preparing Financial Statements	£19.95 ☐	£10.95 ☐	£5.95 ☐	£5.95 ☐		
2.5 Financial Reporting (6/01)	£19.95 ☐	£10.95 ☐	£5.95 ☐			
2.6 Audit and Internal Review (6/01)	£19.95 ☐	£10.95 ☐	£5.95 ☐			
3.1 Audit and Assurance services (6/01)	£20.95 ☐	£10.95 ☐	£5.95 ☐			
3.6 Advanced Corporate Reporting (6/01)	£20.95 ☐	£10.95 ☐	£5.95 ☐			
SUCCESS IN YOUR RESEARCH AND ANALYSIS PROJECT						
Tutorial Text (9/01)	£19.95 ☐					

SUBTOTAL £

POSTAGE & PACKING

Study Texts

	First	Each extra	
UK	£3.00	£2.00	£
Europe*	£5.00	£4.00	£
Rest of world	£20.00	£10.00	£

Kits/Passcards/Success Tapes/MCQ cards

	First	Each extra	
UK	£2.00	£1.00	£
Europe*	£2.50	£1.00	£
Rest of world	£15.00	£8.00	£

Breakthrough Videos

	First	Each extra	
UK	£2.00	£2.00	£
Europe*	£2.00	£2.00	£
Rest of world	£20.00	£10.00	£

Grand Total (Cheques to *BPP Publishing*) I enclose a cheque for (incl. Postage) £

Or charge to Access/Visa/Switch

Card Number

Expiry date Start Date

Issue Number (Switch Only)

Signature

We aim to deliver to all UK addresses inside 5 working days; a signature will be required. Orders to all EU addresses should be delivered within 6 working days. All other orders to overseas addresses should be delivered within 8 working days. * Europe includes the Republic of Ireland and the Channel Islands.